An Ghníomhaireacht um Chaomhnú Comhshaoil

Ireland's Environment

A MILLENNIUM REPORT

Editors
Larry Stapleton, Mícheál Lehane and Paul Toner

Environmental Protection Agency
PO Box 3000
Johnstown Castle Estate
Co. Wexford
Ireland

Telephone: +353 53 60600
Fax: +353 53 60699
Email: info@epa.ie
Website: www.epa.ie

April 2000

ISBN 1-84095-016-1

Published by

Environmental Protection Agency, Ireland

Typesetting, Layout and Design

Odile Le Bolloch, Annmarie Tuohy, Yvonne Doris

Design Concept and Print

Intacta Print Ltd.

Preparation of Maps

ERA-Maptec

FOREWORD

This second report by the Agency on the state of Ireland's environment comes at an opportune time. The turn of the millennium is clearly a time for taking stock, for reviewing the legacy from the past and for considering what the future may bring. This is as true in respect of the environment as it is for the economic, social and cultural spheres.

The timing of this report is opportune for a further reason, namely Ireland's current record rate of economic growth. It has long been accepted that most forms of development can give rise to pressures on the environment and that such pressures must be managed and controlled in order to minimise their impacts and to avoid serious environmental damage.

The focus internationally now, however, has turned to sustainable development, which takes full account of economic, social and environmental considerations. In respect of most of the strategic sectors the challenge of achieving sustainability in environmental terms tends to increase according as the sector expands. From now on, an important measure of success will be how well environmental considerations have been integrated, or taken on board, in all aspects of economic development. A yardstick for this will be whether the link has been broken between development and pressures placed on the environment.

In a number of important respects, the challenge has already intensified further and requires reducing emissions to the environment in absolute terms in a period of appreciable economic growth. The scale of this challenge, which applies in particular to the control of greenhouse gases and other emissions to air, should not be underestimated. Reductions are also necessary in the amounts of phosphorus entering inland waters, in road transport impacts on the urban environment, and in the amounts of waste consigned to landfills. Ireland's natural resources including its biodiversity must also be protected.

State of the Environment reports, complemented by environmental indicator reports, provide an important means of tracking progress in meeting these challenges. It is the Agency's intention to follow this report with a second report on key environmental indicators in two years time.

We always welcome your views on our reports and it would be appreciated if you can provide us with feedback; a response form is included at the back of the report.

Finally, a report of this nature would not be possible without the information provided through the dedication and expertise of the many people involved, across different organisations at local and national levels, in the monitoring, research and assessment of Ireland's environment. Also many outside organisations and individuals, in addition to Agency staff, actively participated in the preparation of this report, providing vital input. I should like to express my appreciation and thanks to all concerned.

L. M. McCumiskey
Director General

Wexford, April 2000

ACKNOWLEDGEMENTS

The Environmental Protection Agency (EPA) wishes to express its appreciation to the following organisations for their assistance in various ways towards the preparation of this report:

All County Councils and County Borough Councils; Department of Agriculture, Food and Rural Development; Department of Arts, Heritage, Gaeltacht and the Islands; Department of Enterprise, Trade and Employment; Department of the Environment and Local Government; Department of Finance; Department of Marine and Natural Resources (DMNR); Department of Public Enterprise; Department of Tourism, Sport and Recreation; Forest Service of DMNR.

An Bord Bia; An Bord Glas; An Bord Pleanála; Bord Fáilte; Bord Iascaigh Mhara; Central Fisheries Board; Central Statistics Office; Coillte Teoranta; Córas Iompair Éireann; Dúchas The Heritage Service; Economic and Social Research Institute; ENFO; Enterprise Ireland; Fisheries Research Centre of the Marine Institute; Geological Survey of Ireland; The Heritage Council; Iarnród Éireann; IDA Ireland; Irish Council for Science, Technology and Innovation; Irish Energy Centre; Marine Institute; Met Éireann; National Roads Authority; National Standards Authority of Ireland; Radiological Protection Institute of Ireland; Regional Fisheries Boards; Office of Public Works; Ordnance Survey Ireland; Teagasc.

Animal and Plant Health Association; An Taisce; Association of Consulting Engineers of Ireland; Association of Municipal Authorities of Ireland; City and County Engineers Association; Consumers Association of Ireland; Dublin Regional Authority; Environmental Resource Management; Environmental Sciences Association of Ireland; Industrial Waste Management Association; Irish Business Against Litter; Irish Business Employers Confederation; Irish Countrywomens Association; Irish Creamery Milk Suppliers Association; Irish Motor Vehicle Recyclers Association; Irish Refining Plc.; Irish Peatland Conservation Council; Irish Pharmaceutical and Chemical Manufacturers Federation; Irish Ramblers Association; Institution of Engineers of Ireland; Landscape Alliance Ireland; Mid East Regional Authority; Mountaineering Council of Ireland; Office of the Director of Consumer Affairs; REPAK; Royal Horticultural Society of Ireland; Royal Irish Academy; Rural Resettlement Ireland Ltd; Small Firms Association; West Regional Authority; Waste Management Association of Ireland.

The Agency also wishes to acknowledge the assistance of the members of the two Working Groups that were established to deal with specific aspects of the report. Organisations, other than the Environmental Protection Agency, that attended working group meetings were as follows:

Working Group 1, Economic Aspects:
Bord Fáilte (Mr. Noel Kavanagh); Bord Iascaigh Mhara (Mr. Tom Scanlon); Central Statistics Office (Mr. Pat Fanning, Mr. Adrian Redmond); City and County Engineers Association (Mr. Joe Beirne); Department of Agriculture, Food and Rural Development (Mr. Martin Farrell, Ms. Sinead McPhilips, Ms. Ruth Cosgrave); Department of Enterprise, Trade and Employment (Ms. Mary O'Donnell); Department of the Environment and Local Government (Mr. Michael Layde); Department of Finance (Dr. Liam Reamonn, Ms. Marie Smith); Department of Tourism, Sport and Recreation (Mr. Fionn Ó Gráda); Economic and Social Research Institute (Ms. Sue Scott); ENFO (Mr. John Kelleher and Mr. Gerry Smith); Irish Energy Centre (Mr. Brian Motherway).

Working Group 2, Natural Resources Aspects:
Central Fisheries Board (Mr. Trevor Champ); Department of Arts, Heritage, Gaeltacht and the Islands (Dr. Philip Buckley); Department of Marine and Natural Resources (Mr. Ben Dhonau); Dúchas, The Heritage Service (Mr. John Wilson); Forest Service (Ms. Bridie Cullinane, Mr. John Connolly, Mr. Gerhardt Gallagher); Geological Survey of Ireland (Dr. Bob Aldwell); The Heritage Council (Dr. Liam Lysaght) Marine Institute (Dr. Dan Minchin); Ordnance Survey Ireland (Mr. Malachy McVeigh); Teagasc (Dr. John Lee and Mr. Michael Ryan).

Special thanks are due to the following who provided additional material for the report or commented on specific aspects:

Ms. Carla Ward, An Taisce; Ms. Sylvia Reynolds, Botanical Society of the British Isles; Dr. Simon Berrow, British Antarctic Survey; Dr. Brigid O'Regan, Carlow Institute of Technology; Mr. John Tiernan, Cavan County Council; Dr. Paddy Fitzmaurice, Central Fisheries Board; Mr. Damien Malone, Central Statistics Office; Mr. Noel Duffy, Clean Technology Centre; Mr. John McLoughlin, Coillte Teoranta; Mr. Tony Reid, Mr. Sylvester Murphy and Mr. Frank Rath, Department Agriculture, Food and Rural Development; Ms. Yvonne Rowland, Mr. Niall Feeney, Mr. Noel Sheahan, Mr. John McDermott, Ms. Patricia Curran, Mr. Ken Mawhinney, Mr. Colum Keenan, Mr. John Sadlier and Mr. Eamon Markey, Mr. Gerry O'Donoghue, Mr. Oliver Fogarty, Mr. Owen Boyle, Mr. Pat Keane and Mr. Frank Gallagher, Department of the Environment and Local Government; Mr. Raphael Kelly, Ms. Loreto Farrell and Ms. Helen Condon, Department of Marine and Natural Resources; Mr. Brian McKeown, Dublin Corporation; Ms. Gill Weyman, Dublin Institute of Technology; Dr. David Nash, Dublin Naturalists' Field Club; Ms. Caitríona Douglas, Dr. Colman O'Críodáin, Dr. Mike Wyse Jackson, Dr. Tom Curtis, Dr. Alan Craig, Dr. Ciaran O'Keeffe, Mr. Michael Neff, Dr. John Cross, Dr. Niel

Lockhart, Dr. Ferdia Marnell, Mr. Jim Ryan, Dr. Martin Speight, Mr. Oscar Merne, Mr. Dave Norriss, Dr. Aideen O'Sullivan and Dr. Liz Sides, Dúchas, The Heritage Service; Mr. Liam Curran, Enterprise Ireland; Dr. Kevin Bradley, Environmental Resource Management; Mr. Karl Coggins, Forest Service; Mr. Matthew Parkes, Geological Survey of Ireland; Mr. Pat Doherty, IDA Ireland; Capt. Geoff Livingstone, Irish Marine Emergency Service; Dr. Catherine O'Connell, Irish Peatland Conservation Council; Mr. Peter Britton, Local Government Computer Services Board; Mr. Rick Boelens, Ms. Denise Maloney, Mr. Aengus Parsons and Dr. Andrew Walsh, Marine Institute Quality Status Report Project Team; Ms. Jacqueline Doyle, Dr. Martin Bloxham, Dr. Terry McMahon and Dr. Eugene Nixon, Marine Institute Fisheries Research Centre; Mr. Geoffrey O'Sullivan and Ms. Orla Ní Cheallachair, Marine Institute; Mr. Paraic Carrigan, Met Éireann; Mr. John Hussey, National Accreditation Board;

Mr. Sean Davitt, National Roads Authority; Mr. Patrick Hayes, National Standards Authority of Ireland; Dr. Ann McGarry and Dr. Veronica Smith, Radiological Protection Institute of Ireland; Ms. Fiona O'Regan, Renewable Energy Information Office; Ms. Heather Crick, SGS, England; Mr. Michael Walsh, Dr. Hubert Tunney, Mr. Eddie McDonald, Dr. Brian Coulter and Mr. David McGrath, Teagasc; Ms. Mary Waldron, The Royal Horticultural Society of Ireland; Prof. Fred Aalen, Prof. Graham Shaw and Prof. Adrian Phillips, Trinity College Dublin; Prof. Frank Convery, Mr. Conor Barry and Ms. Louise Dunne, UCD; Dr. Tom Hayden, Department of Zoology, UCD; Dr. Gavin Alexander, University of Glasgow.

Comment and advice on the structure and content of the report were provided by the Agency's Advisory Committee and Environmental Data Committee.

●●●

Several EPA staff were involved in the preparation of the report, as follows:

The report was edited by Mr. Larry Stapleton, Dr. Mícheál Lehane and Dr. Paul Toner with the assistance of Ms. Annmarie Tuohy, Ms. Yvonne Doris and Ms. Odile Le Bolloch.

The report was prepared under the direction of Dr. Padraic Larkin, Director, Environmental Monitoring & Laboratory Services Division. Advice and comment on the report were also received from the other Directors of the Agency: Mr. Liam McCumiskey, Director General, Mr. Declan Burns, Ms. Anne Butler and Mr. Iain Maclean.

The principal authors of individual chapters were as follows:

Chapter 1	Mr. Larry Stapleton
Chapter 2	Ms. Annmarie Tuohy and Mr Larry Stapleton
Chapter 3	Mr. Larry Stapleton, Ms. Annmarie Tuohy and Dr. Mícheál Lehane
Chapters 4 & 8	Mr. Michael McGettigan
Chapter 5	Mr. Peter Cunningham
Chapter 6	Dr. Matt Crowe, Mr. Andy Fanning, Ms. Kirsty Nolan and Mr. Gerry Carty
Chapter 7	Dr. Colman Concannon and Dr. Paul Toner
Chapter 9	Dr. Paul Toner, Dr. Jim Bowman and Mr. Kevin Clabby
Chapter 10	Mr. Peter Cunningham and Mr. John Lucey
Chapter 11	Dr. Mícheál Lehane and Ms. Odile Le Bolloch
Chapter 12	Mr. John Lucey and Ms. Yvonne Doris
Chapter 13	Dr. Paul Toner
Chapter 14	Dr. Mícheál Lehane
Chapter 15	Dr. Conor Clenaghan and Dr. Matt Crowe
Chapter 16	Mr. Larry Stapleton and Dr. Conor Clenaghan

The chapters prepared in consultation with the Working Groups are as follows:
Chapters 2, 3, 14 and 16   Working Group 1 - Economic Aspects;
Chapters 7, 10, 11 and 12 Working Group 2 - Natural Resources Aspects.

Co-ordination of layout and design: Annmarie Tuohy.
Co-ordination of the preparation of maps: Ms. Odile Le Bolloch.
Co-ordination of the preparation of figures: Ms. Yvonne Doris.

Assistance in relation to the production of the report was provided by Ms. Tracey Berney, Ms. Ann Bosley and Ms. Paula Crawford (MediaPro).

Input to specific aspects of the report was provided by Mr. Gerard O'Leary, Mr. Frank Clinton, Dr. Tom McLoughlin, Mr. Michael Neill, Ms. Maeve Quinn, Dr. Michael Flanagan, Mr. Paul Coleman, Ms. Loraine Fegan, Ms. Annette Cahalane, Ms. Jane Brogan, Mr. David Maguire, Mr. Donal Howley, Mr Paul Duffy, Dr. Vera Power, Mr. Martin McGarrigle, Mr. Eamonn Lacey, Dr. Jonathan Derham, Mr. Adrian Slattery, Ms. Josephine Coloe, Ms. Geraldine Ruane, Ms. Patrice Crawley, Mr. John Delaney and Mr. Mícheál MacCárthaigh.

Photographs used in this report were provided by the following: Mr. Felix Zaska, Mr. Eddie Dunne, Mr. Billy Clark, Mr. John Earley, Mr. Matthew Parkes (GSI), Dr. Simon Berrow (British Antarctic Survey), Mr. John Doheny (EPA), Mr. John Lucey (EPA), Dr. Tom McLoughlin (EPA), Mr. Brian Meaney (EPA) and Intacta Print.

CONTENTS

Chapter 7 Other Pressures

PART IV
ENVIRONMENTAL QUALITY

Chapter 8 Air Quality

Chapter 9 Inland Waters

PART V
ENVIRONMENTAL PROTECTION AND THE FUTURE

Chapter 13 Ireland's Environment: The Main Issues

Chapter 14 Environmental Economics

Chapter 15 Managing and Protecting the Environment

Chapter 16 Future Outlook

Abbreviations and Acronyms

Glossary

Comment Form

Summary

The Economic Boom

At present Ireland's record rate of economic development is causing an acceleration of pressures on the environment. This follows a period of several decades during which population growth, urbanisation and agricultural intensification have given rise to gradually increasing environmental pressures, for example on water quality.

Over the course of the 1990s, concomitant with the surge in the economy, a number of strong trends were notable. Even before the end of the decade:

- new housing completions had more than doubled and the number of households had increased substantially;
- personal consumption of goods and services had increased by one-third in a five-year period;
- the volume of industrial production had more than doubled;
- the total number of vehicles had increased by more than 50 per cent;
- the country's total primary energy requirement had increased by more than one-third;
- there was substantial expansion in forestry, tourism and trade.

Such rates of growth across strategic sectors are posing a major challenge for environmental protection. A majority of Irish citizens considers environmental pollution to be an immediate and urgent problem.

Pressures on the Environment

Concerning emissions to air, a major focus now, because of international commitments, is on emissions of greenhouse gases, mainly carbon dioxide, methane and nitrous oxide. These gases are implicated in the enhanced greenhouse effect giving rise to climate change. Ireland's international commitment is to limit greenhouse gas emissions in the period 2008-2012 to 13 per cent above 1990 levels. However, the percentage increase already exceeds this, and in a business as usual scenario, Ireland's emissions by that period would reach more than twice the limit. A process of major change must get underway urgently, if this country to fulfil its obligations.

At present, agriculture is the largest single source of greenhouse gases. Energy and transport are the next highest sources and it is in these sectors that the highest growth rate in greenhouse gas emissions is projected. In relation to other emissions to air, Ireland has failed to meet its international commitments on nitrogen oxides emissions and may not meet targets on sulphur dioxide. (Urban air quality issues related to transport are summarised later.)

In Ireland the main concern relating to substances entering inland waters from sources such as urban areas, industry and agriculture is the quantity of nutrients, in particular of phosphorus. Agriculture is by far the major source of phosphorus inputs. Urban waste water and industrial effluents, on an annual basis, give rise to much lower loads. While the timing and composition of agricultural discharges may lessen their potential impact, nevertheless surveys confirm that they remain the major cause of pollution of inland waters. Nitrogen is also of concern in certain areas, in relation to its impact on both surface waters and groundwater. In this case also the principal source is agriculture.

Quantities of non-agricultural solid waste are continuing to grow in Ireland, reaching over 15 million tonnes in 1998. The largest amounts of waste generated were in manufacturing (4.9 million tonnes), in mining and quarrying (3.5 million tonnes), in construction and demolition (2.7 million tonnes) and in the municipal sector (2.1 million tonnes). The amount of municipal waste has doubled since the mid-1980s and the amounts in other categories are also increasing. Landfill remains the predominant waste disposal practice in Ireland.

The most striking trend in waste recovery has been in the manufacturing sector, with reported recovery increasing from 31 per cent in 1995 to 51 per cent in 1998. The overall recovery rate for packaging waste was 14.8 per cent.

Other growing pressures on the environment include changes on the land surface resulting from road building, industrial development, housing, agriculture, afforestation, quarrying, mineral exploitation and recreational and tourism developments. Much of the water abstracted for supply is lost through leakages from the distribution systems and measures are being taken to address the problem. Noise and, in particular, odours are the major reasons for complaints in relation to activities licensed under the integrated pollution control (IPC)

system. Further pressures include impacts of fishing and aquaculture activities, accidental spillages and radioactive discharges from outside the State.

Environmental Quality

The smog problem associated with the burning of smoky coal, which was a feature of Dublin and some other cities and towns, has been eliminated, confirming the effectiveness of the Government's smoke-control regulations. The potential for damage to human health and the environment due to emissions of gases such as sulphur dioxide and nitrogen oxides from industry and power generation is also being reduced through fuel switching, IPC licensing and other measures. Following the phasing out of leaded petrol, concentrations of lead in air have reduced; they are well within existing and proposed limits.

Other emissions from road traffic, however, have now become the greatest threat to air quality in Ireland, especially in urban areas. The pollutants of concern from this source include nitrogen dioxide, fine particulate matter (measured as PM_{10}) and benzene. Little information has been available concerning benzene, but it is clear from the limited monitoring for nitrogen dioxide and PM_{10} that meeting future EU limits for these pollutants will present a difficult challenge.

Ireland, unlike many other European countries, does not have an environmental problem with ground level ozone. The deposition of acidifying compounds is low, the only concern being nitrogen deposition in sensitive ecosystems close to major agricultural sources of ammonia.

River water quality has continued to deteriorate with no halt in the trend, evident since the late 1970s, of a steadily increasing extent of slight and moderate pollution. This is caused by eutrophication (enrichment), which now affects about one-third of the river system.

Twenty-four of the 124 lakes covered in the most recent review of water quality were eutrophic to varying degrees. The condition of 17 of the lakes suggests either a strong or a very high level of nutrient pollution and a consequent likelihood of impairment of their beneficial uses.

While salmon and trout are still widespread in Irish inland waters, they have been adversely affected by factors including drainage and eutrophication. The charr has been lost from a number of lakes over the course of the twentieth century and appears to be particularly sensitive to eutrophication.

A national groundwater survey has shown that there is no widespread pollution of aquifers but that local contamination occurs, which is a major contributor to problems with drinking water quality in private group water supply schemes.

Only in a small number of estuaries is there any significant evidence of deoxygenation or nutrient enrichment. The quality of bathing waters is very good and shellfish water quality is generally satisfactory, albeit requiring purification of the shellfish from many areas prior to sale.

The discharges from the British Nuclear Fuels reprocessing plant at Sellafield continue to result in contamination of the Irish marine environment, but at levels that do not pose a significant health risk. The impacts of tributyltin (TBT) from anti-fouling paints used on vessels are evident on certain fauna in general port areas and particularly in fishing ports.

In general the seawaters around Ireland are clean and the main environmental issue relating to them is the impact of fishing activity on both target and non-target species. There is concern about the sustainability of some stocks of cod, hake, saithe, plaice and sole. There is serious concern about by-catch of harbour porpoises in the Celtic Sea hake fishery and more information on this is needed.

Litter and unauthorised dumping are continuing problems on the coast, as elsewhere. Various forms of coastal development, much of which is related to tourism and leisure, are increasing pressures on the coastal zone and particularly on its vulnerable habitats.

In the countryside, landscapes have been seriously affected by developments such as urban sprawl, inappropriate rural housing development, road construction and the growth of industry. Commercial forestry can impact adversely on landscapes and on the environment in other ways, but if properly implemented it can be an important sustainable resource.

Concerning soils, as a result of intensification of agriculture, there is now a considerable surplus of phosphorus applied to farmland over that removed in produce, with the content in many soils at levels that can give rise to significant losses, thereby causing eutrophication of waters. In upland areas and on western blanket bogs, overgrazing by sheep has caused serious damage.

In towns and cities, rising vehicle numbers and increased usage of cars are causing problems such as traffic congestion and noise, in addition to air pollution as noted earlier. While a beginning has been made to increasing the availability of alternative modes of transport, for example the provision of cycle lanes, there is major scope for improvement, particularly in the provision of good quality and efficient public transport.

Ireland has habitat types that are scarce or absent over much of Europe, including turloughs, shingle beaches, coastal lagoons, maërl beds, machair and a complete range of peatland types of international importance. The country has 30 per cent of the European lichen species - a relatively high proportion, which may be due partly to good air quality. Certain 'alien' species have become established, including problem species such as the giant hogweed.

Ireland's populations of certain faunal species, including the freshwater crayfish, lesser horseshoe bat and otter, are particularly important in the European context. Although conservation measures for the similarly important roseate tern and corncrake populations have achieved some success, these remain under threat along with several other bird species, one of which, the corn bunting, appears to have become extinct as a breeding bird in Ireland.

Environmental Challenges

Ireland's environment has come under pressure more recently than that of many other countries. Also, a number of favourable circumstances, including climatic and demographic factors, have tended to mitigate the potential impacts of the pressures that arose progressively over the latter half of the twentieth century. For these reasons, Ireland's environmental quality, overall, remains relatively good in comparison with that of most other European countries.

Nevertheless, a range of issues now arises in relation to the present state of the environment in Ireland, and five of these merit particular attention. They are as follows:

- eutrophication of inland waters;
- waste and litter;
- the urban environment and transport;
- climate change and greenhouse gases;
- protection of natural resources.

Eutrophication of inland waters is now widespread and the most recent water quality review noted a continuing deterioration. For these reasons it is perhaps Ireland's most serious environmental pollution problem. Dealing with it will require effective implementation of the 1998 Phosphorus Regulations, with significant reductions needed in the major sources of phosphorus noted above.

Much greater efforts will also be needed in relation to waste prevention, minimisation and recycling if Ireland is to meet EU targets and to curb the dramatic rise in waste volumes. A stronger emphasis on centralised composting is strongly recommended. It appears likely that, for larger urban areas, thermal treatment with energy recovery for municipal wastes will be introduced. The National Hazardous Waste Management Plan is due to be published by the EPA in 2000. The problem of litter must be tackled through a combination of education and strong penalties with effective enforcement.

With the numbers of vehicles projected to continue increasing, measures to restrict their use in urban areas are essential. The pace of development of sustainable transport systems for urban areas in Ireland has been much too slow. There is a need to integrate new housing development with public transport provision and to prevent significant environmental pressures resulting from urban sprawl and from the use of the private car for commuting long distances.

The Government's strategy for the abatement of greenhouse gases was in the course of preparation at the time of writing of this report. It is expected to have extremely far-reaching implications, requiring *inter alia* reductions in emissions at a time of continuing economic growth and consideration of the use of mechanisms such as emissions trading. The achievement of future more stringent international limits for emissions to air will be difficult and will have significant implications for all sectors.

There has long been major exploitation of certain natural resources, of forests in earlier centuries and of peatlands in more recent times. Present concerns include the following: overgrazing impacts on upland areas; damage to landscapes from insensitive development; loss of habitats and threats to certain species of flora and fauna; reduction of certain sea-fish stocks to critical levels; and impacts on the coastal zone.

There is considerable scope to reform the Irish fiscal system as part of overall approaches to addressing these key challenges facing Ireland. Potential economic instruments include the following:
- an excise tax on the sale of fertilisers to discourage overuse;
- waste charges and taxes;
- taxes and charges to discourage vehicle use in urban areas;
- greenhouse gas taxation;
- appropriate cost recovery for the provision of environmental services and avoidance of environmentally damaging subsidies.

An evaluation of whether Irish society is responding adequately to the pressures on the environment indicates that, while there have been significant advances in the development of policy and legislation, key deficiencies remain, for example in coastal zone management and in natural heritage legislation. These deficits are being addressed and merit high priority. There is a particular need to apply and enforce existing measures in an effective way to tackle the five major challenges outlined above.

General Outlook

There is the possibility of sustained growth in the global economy, and favourable economic projections have been made for Ireland. There is major continuing demand for new housing development. In many of the strategic sectors of the Irish economy there is significant potential for further growth and change, and unless properly managed, this poses a clear threat to the environment. Projected growth levels in transport, energy and forestry are highly significant, and sustainable development in these sectors will be a major challenge. Agriculture already features strongly as a source of pressure on the environment, for example in relation to greenhouse gas emissions and eutrophication. Environmental challenges for the marine resources sector include ensuring sustainable levels and methods of fishing and developing environmentally friendly aquaculture. Environmental issues will continue to come to the fore also in tourism and trade.

As with other sectors, industry will need to integrate environmental considerations fully into policy and decision-making. This can have a win-win outcome, conferring business advantages by ensuring that Irish products and services match the growing market sentiment internationally favouring products and services that are environmentally friendly.

Overall, de-linking economic growth from environmental damage (achieving eco-efficiency) is the major challenge facing all countries and facing Ireland in particular because of its exceptional economic growth. Ireland's economic surge is happening at a time when EU and other international environmental controls are becoming more rigorous. The combination of strong growth coupled with more stringent environmental targets greatly magnifies the challenge now facing public authorities and the strategic economic sectors in Ireland. At the same time, economic prosperity can provide the financial resources that are needed to make inroads into many of the problems.

This alone will not be enough, however. Present day environmental pressures derive from many sources, including modern lifestyles. A sustained long-term programme of environmental awareness raising and education is needed. Environmental awareness in Ireland must be raised significantly so that, in daily life, citizens are sufficiently informed and committed that they will take the environment into account in the way they manage their homes and their businesses, use transport and make consumer choices. Our present choices, both as a society and as individuals, determine the quality of the environment that we will hand on to future generations.

PART I

Introduction

BACKGROUND AND INTRODUCTION

The overall state of Ireland's environment is assessed for the third time. The assessment draws on many sources, including a recent national report on key environmental indicators and reports on the quality of air, water and the marine and coastal environment. Various strands of information - on salient social and economic factors affecting the environment, on the condition of the environment and on environmental protection measures - are brought together in this report in order to examine the causes and effects of environmental change and the trends and prospects for the future.

BACKGROUND

The timing of this assessment of Ireland's environment gives cause for some reflection. The environment has always been governed by natural cycles. This is especially evident along the coast, where natural processes of erosion and accretion have operated down the ages, with human influence apparent only in comparatively recent times. The influence of man is much more evident on the land, where, for example, the felling of trees over past centuries left just 1 per cent of the country covered by forests by the year 1900, and where human interaction has given rise to the distinctive field patterns and other cultural features of the Irish landscape. Down the years, predators such as the wolf and eagle were hunted to extinction in Ireland and some vulnerable species suffered a similar fate, including the great auk, a sea bird species which became extinct world wide. On the other hand, species now common, such as the rabbit and pike, were introduced by humans into Ireland.

In Ireland, as elsewhere, the growth of towns and cities over past centuries led to problems with poor sanitary conditions giving rise to disease. Serious inadequacies in this regard remained well into the twentieth century. In the latter part of the

century action was taken to curb a growing urban air pollution problem in Ireland from smoky coal. By that time, in the wider context, it had become understood that globally certain emissions to the atmosphere were leading to fundamental changes in its composition. It became apparent that these, in turn, would give rise to changes in the global climate, with impacts including sea

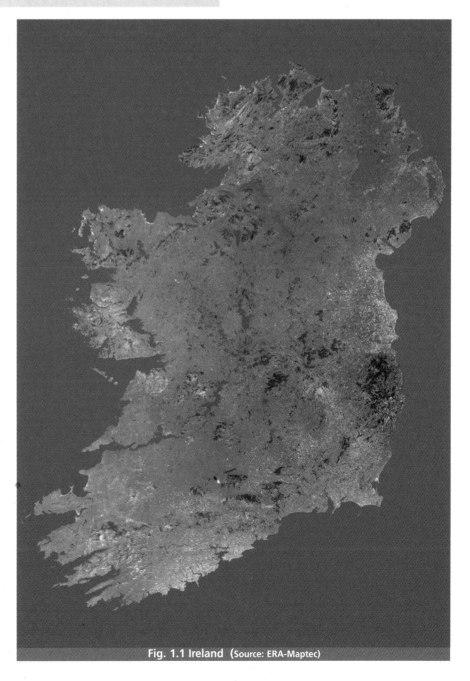

Fig. 1.1 Ireland (Source: ERA-Maptec)

level rise and more frequent storms and consequences such as inundation and erosion of vulnerable coasts.

These few brief examples illustrate some general features of the environment. Firstly, even under entirely natural conditions, it is not static. Secondly, human influence on the environment, at one time transitory and local, has grown and extended steadily, particularly over the course of the twentieth century. Because of this, assessments of the state of the environment must focus not just on the environment itself but also on society's influence. Thirdly, as impacts on the environment extend beyond local and national boundaries, making the environment increasingly an international issue, a report on Ireland's environment must take full account of the European and global contexts.

An overall assessment of Ireland's environment must of necessity reflect the many contrasting areas that make up the country, ranging from the rugged shores of the western seaboard across mountains, peatlands, forests and farmlands to the busy streets of Dublin. The aquatic environment too is diverse, including groundwaters, upland streams, rivers, lakes, estuaries and the surrounding seas. Land and water, and the margins where they meet, provide a great variety of habitats for flora and fauna. All are influenced by the air masses that cross the country, which

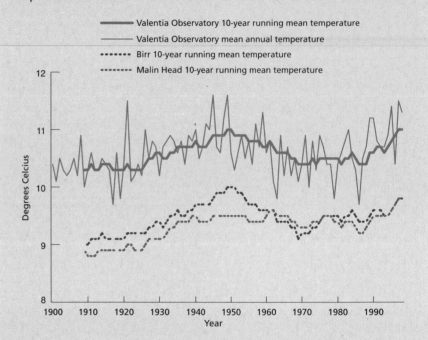

Box 1.1 Twentieth Century Temperatures in Ireland

One of the few aspects of the environment for which measurements exist over the course of the past century is climate. The figure shows the mean annual temperature and the 10-year running mean temperature at Valentia Observatory in the south west, and also the 10-year running mean temperature at both Birr in the midlands and Malin Head in the north.

— Valentia Observatory 10-year running mean temperature
— Valentia Observatory mean annual temperature
······ Birr 10-year running mean temperature
------ Malin Head 10-year running mean temperature

Note that while the data on which the figure is based have been verified, they have not been adjusted to take account of possible changes in instrumentation or exposure at the sites, and although the three series clearly follow a similar trend over the period, Met Eireann has not conducted any formal climate change analyses on them.

Source: Met Eireann

are usually, but not always, of Atlantic origin.

Protecting this varied environment is essential for human health and well-being, and to conserve an invaluable natural heritage that can be passed on, in turn, to future generations. A clean environment is a vital resource in terms of Ireland's green image, supporting, for example, tourism, agriculture and fisheries. A pleasant environment in which to work and live is a factor in attracting investment in services and high-technology industries. If, however, policies and actions to protect the environment are to be effective, then they must be supported by comprehensive and timely information, and hence the need for periodic reports on the overall state of the environment.

PHYSICAL CONTEXT

Salient features of the geography, geology and climate of Ireland were outlined in the last State of the Environment report (Stapleton, 1996). Ireland's climate is greatly influenced by the country's small size and its geographic location - an island bounded to the east by the Irish Sea and to the north, west and south by the Atlantic Ocean and hence under the influence of the warm North Atlantic drift. Thus there is a relatively narrow range of monthly mean temperatures, with comparatively high average rainfall and wind speeds. These climatic influences come to bear in various ways on the environment. Similarly, Ireland's geology - the underlying rocks and the soil cover - provide a further important part of the background influences on the environment.

INTERNATIONAL CONTEXT

In 1999 the world population reached six billion, with nearly half now living in cities. There are two overriding global developmental trends. Firstly, the global ecosystem is threatened by grave imbalances in productivity and in the distribution of goods and services, an unsustainable progression of extremes of wealth and poverty, which threatens the stability of society as a whole and with it the global environment. Secondly, the world is undergoing accelerating change, with environmental stewardship lagging behind economic and social development. Environmental gains from new technology are being overtaken by population growth and economic development. The industrial economies of North America, Europe and parts of East Asia consume immense quantities of energy and raw materials, and produce high volumes of wastes and polluting emissions, causing environmental damage on a global scale. In many parts of the developing world, poverty combined with rapid population growth is leading to widespread degradation of essential resources - primarily forests, soils and water (UNEP, 1999).

The European Environment Agency (EEA, 1999) has made an assessment of relevant economic, sectoral and environmental policies adopted by the European Union to date to

examine whether these would bring improvements in the environment or whether there were trends and developments that would cause environmental protection targets to be missed. An outlook on the future state of the environment in the EU was based on three factors: the current state of the environment, the projected socio-economic changes, and the implementation of existing and proposed EU policies that were in place or in the pipeline by August 1997. The report concluded that most of the existing major challenges will continue over the next decade. It stated that while environmental policy implementation has eased some problems, sectoral policies beyond the control of environmental policy have created new problems for the environment.

European governments accept that climate change is the gravest environmental threat to the world's sustainable development, public

health and future prosperity, and that it requires immediate counter-measures. At a 1998 conference in Aarhus, Denmark, organised by the United Nations Economic Commission for Europe (UNECE), the governments agreed that action is required also in the following fields: transport, agriculture, energy, chemicals, waters, soil degradation and biodiversity. They agreed a Convention on Access to Information, which covers three main areas: access to environmental information, public participation in environmental decision-making, and access to justice in environmental matters. The provisions of the Convention include that each party shall, at regular intervals not exceeding three or four years, publish and disseminate a national report on the state of the environment. It also requires that various types of environmental information, including reports on the state of the environment, progressively become

available in electronic databases that are easily accessible through public telecommunications networks.

NATIONAL CONTEXT

The Organisation for Economic Co-opeation and Development (OECD) 1999 economic survey of Ireland (OECD, 1999) states:

'The Irish economy has notched up five straight years of stunning economic performance. No other OECD Member country has been able to match its outstanding outcomes in a variety of dimensions. Output growth has averaged over 9 per cent per year on a GDP basis in the period 1994-98, bringing GDP per capita in purchasing power parity terms to a higher level than the European Union average.'

The OECD report notes also that Ireland faces a number of environmental challenges and lists three in particular: improving the treatment of waste water, the reduction of solid waste, and the restraint of greenhouse gas emissions.

The Government's Sustainable Development Strategy was published in 1997. It is designed to apply considerations of sustainability more systematically than heretofore to Irish economic policies. In terms of its overall vision the Strategy seeks:

To ensure that economy and society in Ireland can develop to their full potential within a well protected environment, without compromising the quality of that environment, and with responsibility towards present and future generations and the wider international community.

The Strategy document notes that a high quality environment has long been part of Ireland's national endowment, with the country's green image providing competitive advantage in a number of areas, food and tourism being notable examples. The symptoms of environmental stress, however, are becoming more apparent: increasing water pollution, depletion of natural resources, waste production, and damage to natural habitats and to landscapes. Although some improvements have been achieved, traditional policies and controls have not delivered all of the responses needed. The Strategy document states that several factors underlie these negative trends including:-

- conflicts between environment and development objectives;
- poor appreciation of the value of environmental resources and, as a result, inefficiency in their use;
- inadequate information.

The Strategy recognises the need for *integration*, which means bringing environment centre-stage in economic sectoral performance. This is the key to securing environmentally sustainable economic development. The Strategy contains a comprehensive assessment of major

---

Box 1.2 The National Development Plan 2000 - 2006

The National Development Plan for the period 2000 to 2006 is designed to provide the foundation for sustainable economic progress, improved competitiveness, balanced regional development and social inclusion.

The Plan will involve an investment of £40.588 billion, broken down as follows:

Economic and Social Infrastructure	£20.948 billion
Employment and Human Resources	£10.952 billion
Productive Sector	£8.588 billion
Peace Programme	£0.1 billion

The breakdown on a regional basis will be as follows:

Border, Midlands and Western	£13.313 billion (£13,793 per capita)
Southern and Eastern	£27.274 billion (£10,250 per capita)

The major portion of investment clearly is in economic and social infrastructure and it will be allocated to roads, public transport, water and waste water, coastal protection, energy, social and affordable housing and health capital.

A pilot-scale eco-audit is included in the Plan. This notes that the environmental dimension will be addressed through various measures, but that the possibility of the emergence of some unsustainable patterns of development within the framework of the Plan cannot be excluded - hence the critical importance to ensure the environmental dimension is fully integrated into the further stages of planning and implementation. The National Development Plan is considered further in Part V of this report.

sectoral interactions with the environment, and it defines an agenda to reinforce and deepen environmental integration.

In order to advance the national agenda for sustainable development through consultation and dialogue, the Government in 1999 established *Comhar*, the National Sustainable Development Partnership. Its terms of reference include evaluating progress, assisting in devising suitable mechanisms, advising on their implementation, and contributing to the formation of a national consensus.

Other national developments in recent years include new environmental legislation, in particular, the Waste Management Act, 1996, which requires that all significant waste disposal and recovery activities be licensed. The Environmental Protection Agency (EPA) has responsibility for the issuing and enforcement of licences for these activities. Another significant development has been the making of the 1998 regulations on water quality standards for phosphorus. These and other legislative developments are outlined elsewhere in this report.

The first set of key environmental indicators for Ireland was published in July 1999 by the Environmental Protection Agency. The indicators are intended to guide policy development by providing concise, scientifically credible information that is readily understandable and representative of key environmental concerns and trends. The complex relationship between economic growth and the environment was noted: emissions of pollutants can increase with economic activity but, alternatively, more efficient methods of production can reduce the use of natural resources and the burden on the environment. Such increases in 'eco-efficiency' can help to break the link between economic growth and environmental damage. The indicators are included in the relevant sections of this report.

The report on indicators focused in particular on statistics relating to the main issues identified in the last State of the Environment report, namely, emissions of greenhouse gases, eutrophication of freshwaters, waste management, and urban environmental problems including those deriving from the growth in transport. The general picture that emerged from the indicators report was that the environment was under increasing threat. While there had been improvements in some aspects, there had also been a marked deterioration in some significant areas (Lehane, 1999).

APPROACH AND FRAMEWORK

This is the third report on the state of the environment in Ireland and the second such report to be produced by the EPA. The previous report presented available information on the following:
- pressures on the environment,
- environmental quality and pollution, and
- management, control and economic aspects.

This report is based on the outcome of subsequent monitoring and research. Its objective is to inform environmental and sectoral policy makers and managers and the general public of the major environmental issues and prospects.

The report is structured in five parts. Following this Introduction, the next three parts follow the general causal chain: from developments in society and the economy, through the environmental pressures deriving from them, the consequences for the condition of the environment, and the impacts on human health and well-being and on biodiversity. The final part reviews economic aspects and the major environmental issues facing Ireland at present as well as responses designed to minimise environmental impacts and promote sustainable development. It concludes with a brief outlook to the future for Ireland's environment in the opening years of the new millennium. The report is thus organised along the lines the 'DPSIR framework' of driving forces, pressures, state, impact and responses, which was developed by the OECD and EEA.

The present volume is based on the work of many organisations and individuals engaged in environmental monitoring, research and related activities. It is only through their dedication and expertise that a report of this nature is possible. The report

draws also on the output from an environmental research programme which was undertaken over the five year period 1994-1999 with an overall budget of just over £5 million, of which 50 per cent was funded by the EU through the European Regional Development Fund. The research programme focused on environmentally sustainable resource management and on cleaner production. Some of the main gaps in information on Ireland's environment and its protection were filled over the course of the programme.

Several organisations made detailed submissions in relation to the content of this report. These and other organisations that provided information are listed in the Acknowledgements. The report draws also on many published sources, including national reports on air quality (McGettigan, 1997, 1998, 2000) and water quality (Lucey *et al.*, 1999) and an assessment of marine and coastal areas and adjacent seas (Boelens *et al.*, 1999).

REFERENCES

Boelens, R.G.V., Maloney, D.M., Parsons, A.P. and Walsh, A.R., 1999. *Ireland's Marine and Coastal Areas and Adjacent Seas. An Environmental Assessment.* Prepared by the Marine Institute on behalf of the Department of Environment & Local Government and the Department of Marine & Natural Resources. Marine Institute, Dublin.

EEA (European Environment Agency), 1998. *Europe's Environment: The Second Assessment.* European Environment Agency, Copenhagen.

EEA (European Environment Agency), 1999. *Environment in the European Union at the turn of the century.* European Environment Agency, Copenhagen.

Lehane, M. (ed.) 1999. *Environment in Focus - A Discussion Document on Key National Environmental Indicators.* Environmental Protection Agency, Wexford.

Lucey, J., Bowman, J.J., Clabby, K.J., Cunningham, P., Lehane, M., MacCarthaigh, M., McGarrigle, M.L. and Toner, P.F., 1999. *Water Quality in Ireland 1995-1997.* Environmental Protection Agency, Wexford.

McGettigan, M., 1997. *Air Quality Monitoring, Annual Report 1996.* Environmental Protection Agency, Wexford

McGettigan, M., 1998. *Air Quality Monitoring, Annual Report 1997.* Environmental Protection Agency, Wexford

McGettigan, M., 2000. *Air Quality Monitoring, Annual Report 1998.* Environmental Protection Agency, Wexford

OECD (Organisation for Economic Co-operation and Development), 1999. *OECD Economic Surveys 1999 - Ireland.* OECD, Paris.

Stapleton, L. (ed.), 1996. *State of the Environment in Ireland.* Environmental Protection Agency, Wexford.

UNEP (United Nations Environment Programme), 1999. *Overview GEO-2000. Global Environmental Outlook 2000.* UNEP, Nairobi.

PART II

Society and the Economy

SOCIETY AND THE ECONOMY

By 1996 Ireland's population had risen to 3.63 million, with 58 per cent living in urban areas. In those rural areas furthest from the major towns, however, a continuing population decline has been evident. Demographic factors have led to a substantial increase in the available work-force and a reduced ratio of economic dependency, with benefits for the economy. Ireland is now a world leader in a number of aspects of economic performance. Poverty levels have reduced, although some long-standing social problems remain. Consumption of goods and services has increased strongly, with implications for the amounts of wastes produced and for their impacts on the environment. Surveys indicate that, compared to other EU citizens, Irish citizens make less effort to become informed and take fewer environmentally friendly actions, but show a greater willingness to pay somewhat more for certain environmentally friendly products and services. A majority considers the environment to be an immediate and urgent problem.

INTRODUCTION

Clearly, the quality of the environment, the quality of life and economic progress are inter-linked and inter-dependent. This may be considered as a symbiotic relationship whereby the environment is on loan to society to sustain and develop its quality of life while in turn society is the caretaker of the environment for future generations. The balance

between the environment and society can be altered by economic progress, changing human settlement patterns and changing lifestyles.

Economic activities use two primary production factors: labour and nature. Nature is used in terms of raw materials, energy, water and air, and in terms of its capacity to assimilate residuals. Such uses of nature can put the environment under pressure. In recent years there is recognition that policies are required that focus in particular on the causes rather than symptoms of environmental degradation.

This chapter and the next consider the 'driving forces' - the recent trends and patterns in society that are of environmental significance. In this chapter, some general social and economic trends are outlined, including aspects of consumption patterns. In the following chapter, individual economic sectors - industry, agriculture and others - are considered. Later in the report, specific economic aspects pertaining to the environment, and the

implications of projections and plans for the future, are considered.

POPULATION

After a long period of decline caused by high emigration, Ireland's population reached the lowest census figure on record, 2.82 million, in 1961. By 1996, however, the population had risen by almost 29 per cent, reaching 3.63 million (Fig. 2.1). Continued population growth is expected (Chapter 16).

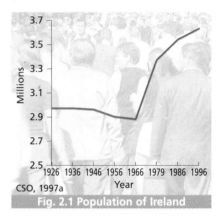

CSO, 1997a

Fig. 2.1 Population of Ireland

Some of the underlying demographic changes since 1971 are significant. The birth rate fell by over 40 per cent up to 1994, increasing somewhat thereafter (Fig. 2.2). The infant mortality rate fell by a factor of three,

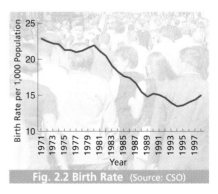

Fig. 2.2 Birth Rate (Source: CSO)

to 5.9 per thousand live births in 1998, amongst the lowest levels in Europe. Average life expectancy increased by approximately four years over the course of two decades. In recent years there have been major swings in overall net migration (Fig. 2.3), and there has been a trend of gradually increasing migration within the country.

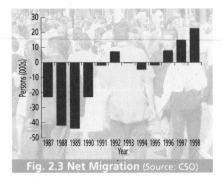

Fig. 2.3 Net Migration (Source: CSO)

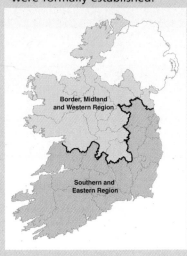

Table 2.1 Areas and Populations of Regions			
	Border, Midlands and Western	**Southern and Eastern**	**State**
Area (sq. km)	33,276 (47%)	36,997 (53%)	70,273
Population 1961	884,473 (31%)	1,933,868 (69%)	2,818,341
Population 1996	965,190 (27%)	2,660,897 (73%)	3,626,087
Population growth 1961-1996	+9%	+38%	+29%
Population density 1996 (persons/sq. km)	29	72	52
Cities and towns over 10,000 population (1996)	8 (29%)	20 (71%)	28
Towns of 1,500 to 9,999	32 (31%)	72 (69%)	104

Note: Based on NESC, 1997

Overall, the fertility and migration patterns mean that Ireland now has an unusual and changing demographic structure, particularly in relation to dependency (Fig. 2.4). From having the highest rate of economic dependency in the EU in the 1980s, it will have one of the lowest by 2005. Through releasing a large number of people into the paid labour force and through reducing the tax burden, this has a significant bearing on the economy (Duffy *et al.*, 1999).

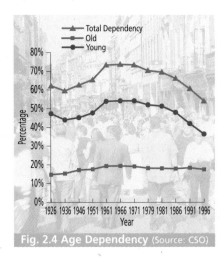

Fig. 2.4 Age Dependency (Source: CSO)

Table 2.1 shows some key statistics for the two new regions into which Ireland is divided. Although the regions are roughly similar in total area, there are significant differences in both total population and population density. Over the period

1961-1996, there was also a significant difference in population growth between the regions.

At the start of the twentieth century Ireland's population was approximately two-thirds rural and one-third urban; in 1961 the rural population remained in a slight majority; now, at the start of a new century, Ireland's population is mainly urban (Fig. 2.5).

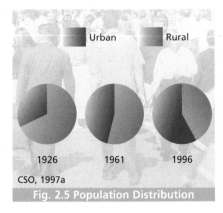

CSO, 1997a

Fig. 2.5 Population Distribution

Urbanisation is a major influence on population growth. The distributions of the national population in towns of different sizes in 1961 and 1996 are shown in Table 2.2.

Because most of the large towns are situated on estuaries or the coast, urbanisation has concentrated the majority of Ireland's population into coastal areas. All coastal counties, with the exception of some in the north-west, have shown an increase in population over the past decade. In all, the 15 coastal counties now account for some 80 per cent of the national population. The strip of land within 10 km of the coast accounts for just over half (52 per cent) of the national population (Boelens *et al.*, 1999).

Table 2.2 Percentage Distribution of Population		
	% 1961	% 1996
Greater Dublin Area	23.54	26.27
Cork, Limerick, Galway & Waterford*	7.78	9.94
Other towns 10,000 and over	4.32	10.49
Towns 1,500 - 9999	10.46	11.42
Towns 200 - 1499	7.44	7.33
Other areas	46.46	34.54

Note: based on NESC, 1997
* includes suburbs

Changes in the population size, structure and distribution significantly determine where, and by how much, pressures on the environment and on natural resources are altered. In particular, an expanding population, urbanisation and the trend towards smaller household sizes necessitate additional housing stock. New housing, particularly on green-field sites, in turn increases the requirement for roads, water and sewerage services, and for social infrastructure such as schools, public transport and amenities. Where such infrastructure is inadequate or inappropriate, then there are inevitable pressures on the environment in cities, towns

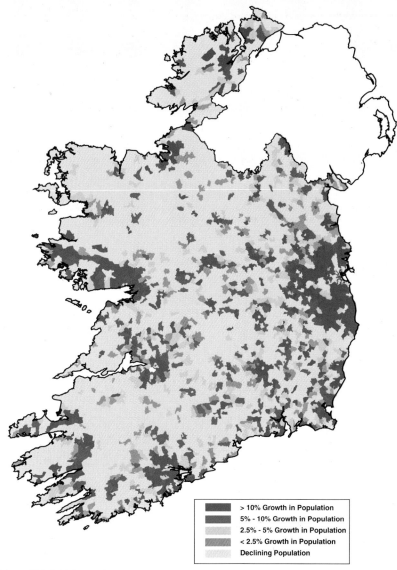

> 10% Growth in Population
5% - 10% Growth in Population
2.5% - 5% Growth in Population
< 2.5% Growth in Population
Declining Population

Fig. 2.6 Population Changes 1991 - 1996 (Source: CSO)

and their surroundings. While there are now further rural areas becoming influenced by Dublin or other major urban centres, certain counties and parts of counties are clearly outside their influence and continue to lose population (NESC, 1997). Such rural areas are affected by the imbalance of economic growth, with dereliction of buildings, and shortage of available finance to maintain and improve the physical and social infrastructure.

THE ECONOMY

Ireland has become a world leader in a number of aspects of economic performance, and in the period 1990 to 1998 was the fastest growing OECD economy (OECD, 1999a),

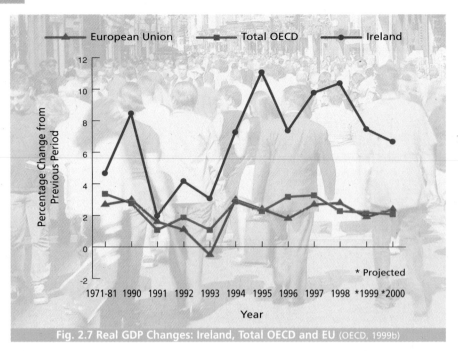

Fig. 2.7 Real GDP Changes: Ireland, Total OECD and EU (OECD, 1999b)

In 1993, the annual average unemployment rate in Ireland had reached a high of 15.6 per cent of the work force. Subsequently, the rising numbers employed during strong economic growth led to a substantial fall in unemployment (Fig. 2.9). The term 'long-term unemployed' refers to the number of persons out of work for more than one year. Between 1994 and 1998 long-term unemployment was halved.

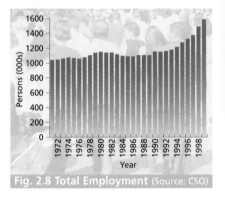

Fig. 2.8 Total Employment (Source: CSO)

with an average growth rate of 7 per cent per year (Fig. 2.7). By 1998 the per capita GDP had reached parity with the average for the 15 EU member countries. The challenge has shifted from how to make fuller use of under-utilised resources to one of how to manage congestion and shortages - and to do so in a manner that is in harmony with the environment.

The Economic and Social Research Institute (ESRI) notes that the strong growth in productivity has been driven both by changes in the composition of the Irish economy, from agriculture-based to industry-based, and by the switch within the manufacturing sector towards high-productivity, foreign-owned industries. The significance of foreign direct investment is such that, despite a shake-out of the indigenous manufacturing sector, the overall industrial sector has grown in importance. This gives the Irish economy a unique structure compared to our main trading partners (Duffy *et al.*, 1999). The rate of growth in Irish exports has far exceeded the OECD and EU averages. While net exports accounted for about 4 percentage points on average of the strong real GDP growth in 1997 and 1998, the

rest, about six percentage points, is attributable to domestic demand (OECD, 1999a). Industry, as a key sector of relevance to the environment, is considered further in Chapter 3.

There has been a particularly favourable combination of circumstances for labour force availability in the 1990s, in particular the demographic factors noted earlier. Ireland's recent performance in increasing employment has been dramatic (Fig. 2.8) and has been substantially better than either the EU or OECD averages.

The National Anti-Poverty Strategy (NAPS) has aimed at reducing poverty and social exclusion both generally and in a number of key policy areas, such as unemployment, income adequacy, educational disadvantage, urban disadvantage and rural poverty. The report for 1998/99 noted that the main targets set (for 2007) in the strategy have been substantially achieved and in some cases exceeded. Enhanced

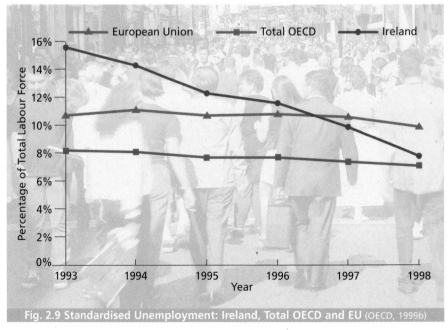

Fig. 2.9 Standardised Unemployment: Ireland, Total OECD and EU (OECD, 1999b)

prosperity, however, serves to highlight in a more marked way the existence, in certain areas, of long standing social problems such as homelessness, drug addiction and disaffection, particularly among young people (Inter-Departmental Policy Committee, 1999).

The Government, in the light of the latest data, set further social inclusion targets as follows:

- consistent poverty to be reduced to below 5 per cent by 2004;
- unemployment to be reduced to below 5 per cent by 2002;
- long-term unemployment to be reduced to 2.5 per cent by 2002.

Poverty, particularly in urban areas, is often accompanied by inadequacies in infrastructure and in amenities and by poor environmental quality. Clearly, while economic growth gives rise to diverse pressures on the environment, it also creates the capacity to deal effectively with many environmental problems, including those associated with poverty.

HOUSEHOLDS AND CONSUMPTION

Between 1991 and 1996 the number of private households increased by 94,154 or 9.1 per cent. The majority of new households comprised either one person, couples without children or lone parents with children. The number of multi-family households

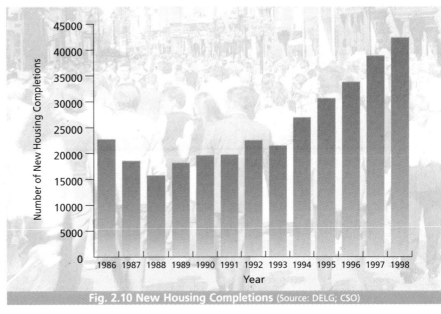

Fig. 2.10 New Housing Completions (Source: DELG; CSO)

on the other hand declined. The average size of private households accordingly fell, from 3.34 persons in 1991 to 3.14 in 1996, thus continuing a long-term decline (CSO, 1997a). This trend of an increasing number of households and smaller household size impacts on consumption patterns, including the demand for energy and household goods.

There has been a significant increase in the housing stock. Completions of new houses in Ireland in 1998 reached 42,349, an increase of 9 per cent over 1997 (Fig. 2.10). House building has doubled since 1993 to what is the highest rate in Europe relative to population. The number of dwellings per thousand population was 244 in 1971 and had risen to 318 by 1998. As noted earlier,

increased demand for housing gives rise to increased demand for development land and pressures on transport, water and sewerage facilities.

Overall consumer demand is determined by the population size, the economic situation, and also by factors including household sizes and individual preferences. During the last decade, consumption by households in the 15 EU countries accounted for around 60 percent of GDP (EEA, 1999). In Ireland, personal consumption of goods and services increased by over 32 per cent from 1993 to 1998 (Fig. 2.11). During the same period, central and local government net expenditure on goods and services increased by 22 per cent. The rate of increase of

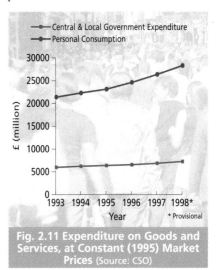

Fig. 2.11 Expenditure on Goods and Services, at Constant (1995) Market Prices (Source: CSO)

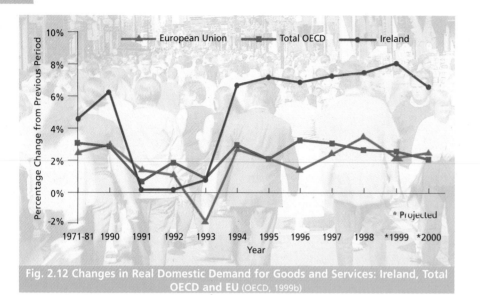

Fig. 2.12 Changes in Real Domestic Demand for Goods and Services: Ireland, Total OECD and EU (OECD, 1999b)

Box 2.2 Aspects of the Household Budget Survey 1994-95

Electrical Appliances

The Household Budget Survey 1994-95 showed significant increases in the incidence of certain household appliances since the 1987 survey. For example, the incidence of microwave ovens had increased from 6.3 per cent to 46.6 per cent, and dishwashers from 7.6 per cent to 18.7 per cent of households. The latter has implications for water use in addition to electricity use, which is rising with the general increase in electrical appliances.

Central Heating

In relation to central heating, the switch from solid fuel to oil and gas in urban areas is clearly evident from the diagram.

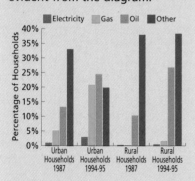

This is attributed to the increase in the availability of natural gas and the prohibition on the sale of smoke producing solid fuel in certain urban areas (CSO, 1997b).

consumption in Ireland has been well above the EU and OECD averages (Fig. 2.12).

Increased and altered consumption patterns are clearly important consequences of economic development, with implications for the use of energy and other natural resources and for the generation of waste and emissions affecting the environment.

ATTITUDES ON ENVIRONMENTAL ISSUES

A 'Eurobarometer' survey was carried out of citizens across the EU in the spring of 1999 to determine their perceptions of the environment and the extent of their knowledge and concerns. As noted in the summary report on the survey (EC, 1999a), the

mobilisation of citizens and, ultimately, their ability to act depends on their knowledge and awareness and the trust they place in the relevant authorities.

The results are presented in greater detail in a second report (EC, 1999b). The environment was considered to be an immediate and urgent problem by a clear majority (69.1 per cent) of those surveyed across the EU and by a majority also (55.6 per cent) of those surveyed in Ireland. It may be noted that in a

Box 2.3 Global, National and Local Issues: Levels of Concern in Ireland Relative to EU Average

In the EU survey citizens were asked about their degree of concern about nine specific environmental issues at a *global* level. The degree of concern in Ireland was greater than the EU average in relation to the following:
- nuclear power stations and radioactive waste processing;
- the use of GMOs in the food chain.

The degree of concern in Ireland was second lowest and lowest, respectively, of all EU countries in relation to the following:
- the disappearance of plants, animal species and habitats;
- the disappearance of tropical forests.

In relation to specific issues at the *national* level, the degree of concern in Ireland was again greater than average in respect of nuclear power and the development of biotechnology. The degree of concern was least of all EU countries in respect of the following:
- damage caused by tourism;
- motor sports in the natural environment.

In relation to the quality of life in their *local* areas, the degree of concern by Irish respondents was greater than the EU average in respect of traffic problems and the quality of food products and was relatively low in respect of noise and the organisation of civil defence in the face of disasters (EC 1999b).

---

separate survey in Ireland (RES, 1999) environmental pollution was seen as a problem by 87 per cent of those interviewed; for 63 per cent it was seen as an immediate and urgent problem and for 24 per cent it was seen as a problem for the future.

On environmental information, 42.8 per cent of respondents in Ireland (53.3 per cent in EU) believed that they knew enough about what they should do to contribute to the protection of the environment, while 50.9 per cent in Ireland (40.1 per cent in EU) felt that they did not know enough. Ireland was among the lowest-scoring countries in Europe for environmental knowledge (EC, 1999b). A low level in Ireland of environmentally sensitive consumer behaviours had been found in an earlier survey (Faughnan and McCabe, 1998). In the 1999 EU survey, 75.3 per cent of Irish respondents, more than in any other EU country, said that they made no particular effort to inform themselves on the environment.

In relation to a specific range of actions at a personal level to protect the environment, the overall aggregate level of engagement was least in Ireland of all the EU countries. At the European level the top five such actions were: save electricity; save water; sort domestic refuse; buy products with packaging that can be recycled, and travel by public transport.

Respondents were asked for which, if any, of a range of products and services would they be prepared to pay a little more than now, so that they are less harmful to the environment. The Irish were more willing than the other nationalities to pay more in this context for food products, household waste collection and petrol. While comparisons between surveys are not always valid, because of differences in methodologies, it may be noted that the earlier survey showed resistance to fiscal measures designed to tackle environmental problems (Faughnan and McCabe, 1998).

Concerning the actions of public authorities at the EU level, the Irish respondents were the most satisfied of all EU citizens about measures taken. In relation to the level at which

in the last ten years (32%) than said it had improved (26%). Ireland's rivers and lakes were thought by 43 per cent of respondents to be poorly or very poorly protected. Just 3 per cent thought that the rivers and lakes were excellently protected and 22 per cent said that they were satisfactorily protected (RES, 1999).

There is growing recognition of the importance of attitudes and behaviours in respect of the environment. Many of the pressures coming to bear on the environment are the direct result of lifestyle choices, in respect of housing, consumption, transport use and dealing with waste. Attitudes to fiscal measures for tackling environmental problems are equally important, and in particular the 'polluter pays' principle and its application.

This chapter has presented an overview of growth and change in Ireland, which includes an increasing and more urbanised population and an economy that has the strongest

authorities should get most involved in protecting the environment, support for the need for action to take place at global level ranged from just 11 per cent in Ireland to 37 per cent in Denmark (EC, 1999b).

In the separate study at national level (RES, 1999), the environmental problems most frequently placed highest on the list by respondents were as follows:

- litter (33%),
- the discharge of untreated sewage (17%),
- air emissions from cars and industries (13%),
- agricultural waste (11%),
- industrial waste (9%) and
- landfill sites (8%).

When asked about the quality of the environment (air, water etc.) in the area in which they live, more respondents said that it had declined

growth rate of developed countries. Ireland's surge in development, which has brought productivity levels to convergence with the EU average, has happened at a time when it is recognised internationally that development must be sustainable and in harmony with the environment. Some questions therefore arise. Since Ireland's rate of development exceeds those of other countries, does the country face a greater challenge than other countries in relation to sustainability? If so, then how well is Ireland succeeding in meeting this challenge? The first step in addressing these questions is to review developments in the more environmentally significant economic sectors, which is the subject of the next chapter.

REFERENCES

Boelens, R.G.V., Maloney, D.M., Parsons, A.P., and Walsh, A.R., 1999. *Ireland's Marine and Coastal Areas and Adjacent Seas - An Environmental Assessment.* Prepared by the Marine Institute on behalf of the Department of Environment & Local Government and the Department of Marine & Natural Resources. Marine Institute, Dublin.

CSO (Central Statistics Office), 1997a. *Census 96. Principal Demographic Results.* Stationery Office, Dublin.

CSO (Central Statistics Office), 1997b. *Household Budget Survey 1994 - 95 Volume 1 Detailed Results for all Households.* Stationery Office, Dublin.

Duffy, D., FitzGerald, J., Kearney, I. and Smyth, D., 1999. *Medium-Term Review 1999-2005.* Economic and Social Research Institute, Dublin.

EC (European Commission), 1999a. *What do Europeans think about the environment? The main results of the survey carried out in the context of Eurobarometer 51.1.* Office for Official Publications of the European Communities, Luxembourg.

EC (European Commission), 1999b. *Les Européens et l'Environnement en 1999. Enquête réalisée dans le cadre de l'Eurobaromètre 51.1.* European Commission, Brussels.

EEA (European Environment Agency), 1999. *Environment in the European Union at the Turn of the Century.* European Environment Agency, Copenhagen.

Faughnan, P. and McCabe, B., 1998. *Irish Citizens and the Environment. A Cross-national Study of Environmental Attitudes, Perceptions and Behaviours.* Environmental Protection Agency, Wexford.

Inter-Departmental Policy Committee, 1999. *1998/99 Annual Report of the Inter-Departmental Policy Committee - Social Inclusion Strategy.* Dublin.

NESC (National Economic and Social Council), 1997. *Report No. 102: Population Distribution and Economic Development; Trends and Policy Implications.* Dublin.

OECD (Organisation for Economic Co-operation and Development), 1999a. *OECD Economic Surveys 1998-1999 - Ireland.* OECD, Paris.

OECD (Organisation for Economic Co-operation and Development), 1999b. *OECD Economic Outlook 65, June 1999.* OECD, Paris.

RES (Research and Evaluation Services), 1999. *Environmental Issues. Public Attitudes to Local Authorities.* A report to the Environmental Protection Agency, Wexford.

CHAPTER 3

STRATEGIC SECTORS

Significant growth and change have occurred across the economic sectors. In agriculture, since the early 1980s, there have been substantial increases in livestock numbers, in silage production and in the use of nitrogen fertilisers. Forestry and fisheries expanded significantly in the decade up to 1995. Approximately 9 per cent of Ireland is now forested. The total tonnage of farmed fish, including shellfish, has increased three-fold since the mid 1980s. Between 1990 and 1998 the number of vehicles increased by more than 50 per cent, the country's total primary energy requirement increased by 35 per cent, and the volume of industrial production more than doubled. Exports in 1998 were 73 per cent of GDP, a high proportion by international standards. Tourist numbers have reached more than 1.5 times the resident population. Such rates of growth across the sectors pose a major challenge for preventing environmental damage.

INTRODUCTION

This chapter focuses on agriculture, forestry, marine resources, energy, industry, transport, tourism and trade, which are the key sectors addressed by the Government's Sustainable Development Strategy. To differing degrees, these sectors use natural resources and give rise to wastes and emissions. At the same time, agriculture and the food industry, along with tourism, forestry and marine resources, are dependent in various ways on good environmental quality. An outline is given of recent trends and patterns of activity that are driving forces for environmental change. The resulting pressures and their effects are dealt with in Parts III and IV of this report. Environmental management and protection measures in the sectors, along with anticipated future trends and impacts are discussed in Part V.

AGRICULTURE

In 1998 agriculture accounted for 5.2 per cent of gross domestic product (GDP), a percentage that is twice the EU average, and for 8.7 per cent of total employment. The agri-food sector taken as a whole, including agriculture, food, drinks and tobacco, accounted for 12.7 per cent of GDP and 11.8 per cent of total employment (Department of Agriculture and Food, 1999).

There are 146,300 farms in Ireland and the average size is about 30 ha. The total land area used for agriculture in 1998 is estimated at 4.4 million ha, with another 0.45 million ha in commonage. Grassland farming, including cattle raising and dairying, accounts for more than 90 per cent of farming activity. The main influence on livestock numbers in Ireland is the EU Common Agricultural Policy (CAP). Since 1980 there has been a significant increase in the numbers of sheep, pigs and poultry (Fig. 3.1).

Over recent decades the tillage area has reduced significantly. CAP reform in respect of grain in 1993 introduced 'set aside' and also put a limit on the total grain-growing area. The main crops grown are wheat, oats, barley, potatoes and sugar beet. Five field trials for genetically modified sugar beet took place during 1998 (Chapter 7). Horticulture in Ireland is distributed across the country in a range of different forms. The value of horticultural output is estimated at £240 million.

The quantities of artificial fertilisers used in Ireland increased significantly during the twenty years up to 1980. Since then, sales of nitrogen fertiliser have continued to increase, although in the last few years there has been some reduction in the use of phosphorus and potassium (Fig. 3.2).

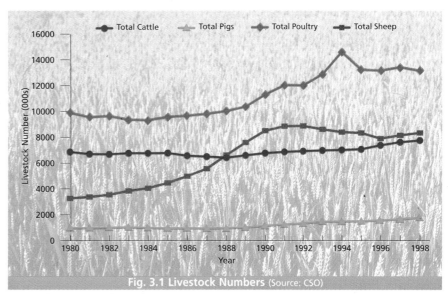

Fig. 3.1 Livestock Numbers (Source: CSO)

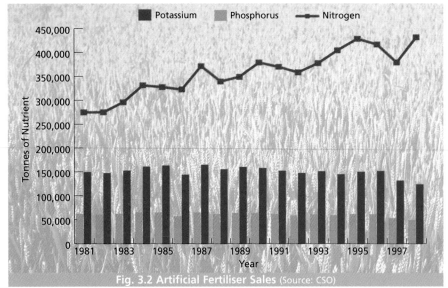

Fig. 3.2 Artificial Fertiliser Sales (Source: CSO)

Pesticides used in agriculture are mainly for cereals, field crops and horticultural crops, which account for only 9 per cent of total farmed area. The maximum quantity imported by companies in Ireland in the period 1994 to 1997 was 2325 tonnes per annum.

There have been changes from traditional farming practices. Fields have been enlarged to facilitate mechanisation. Increased use of over-winter livestock housing with slatted floors has given rise to increased amounts of slurry. Silage production became widespread in the decades between 1960 and 1990. The land area used for producing silage has continued to increase (by over 28 per cent) during the period 1991 to 1998 (Fig. 3.3). The introduction of baled silage has cut down on the risk of silage effluent leakage but has given rise to the problem of plastic waste.

Diversification continues into alternative areas, such as organic farming, forestry, agri-tourism, deer farming and cultivation of oilseed rape. Currently there are approximately 820 farmers registered as organic crop/livestock producers, farming approximately 23,600 ha, which represents a small proportion of the total area farmed. Organic farms are situated in all 26 counties but are mainly concentrated in counties Cork, Clare, Galway and Leitrim.

Increased specialisation and changes in farming practices can cause significant environmental impacts, as described in later chapters. Over-use of fertilisers adversely affects the quality of both surface and ground waters. Increased numbers of livestock lead to increases in slurries and to greater emissions of certain greenhouse gases and acidifying substances. Intensification and overgrazing are important issues, particularly in certain areas, affecting biodiversity (Chapter 12) which is also harmed by the drainage of land and by the loss of hedgerows.

FORESTRY

In past centuries much of Ireland was covered by forests but this was depleted to just 1 per cent by the beginning of the twentieth century. Currently almost 9 per cent (approximately 615,000 ha) of Ireland is under forest. This still leaves Ireland having one of the lowest percentages of forest cover among OECD countries (Fig. 3.4) and well below the OECD and EU averages of 33.5 per cent and 36.4 per cent respectively.

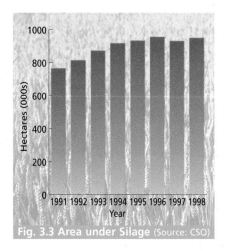

Fig. 3.3 Area under Silage (Source: CSO)

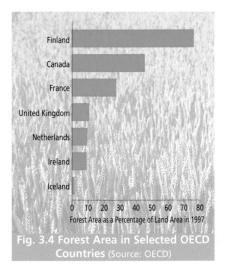

Fig. 3.4 Forest Area in Selected OECD Countries (Source: OECD)

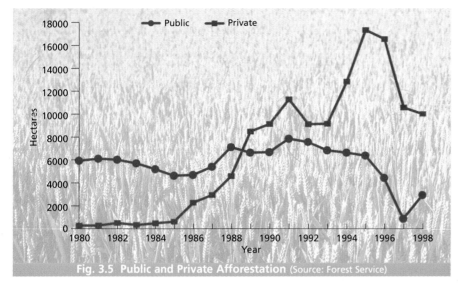

Fig. 3.5 Public and Private Afforestation (Source: Forest Service)

The most dramatic recent change in relation to commercial planting has been in the private sector which has increased from 300 hectares per annum in the early 1980s to 17,343 hectares in 1995 (Fig. 3.5). Tree planting per capita during this time was higher in Ireland than in many other developed countries. However, there has been a reduction in new planting since 1996 mainly due to increased incentives for agriculture and increased land prices. Current policy focuses on farm forestry, which is now the largest single component of the forestry programme. Farmers, full-time and part-time, accounted for 89 per cent of private afforestation in 1998.

The forestry industry and trade in wood products have significant economic value. It is estimated the sector employs up to 16,000 persons, of which 7,000 are directly employed in forestry (DoE, 1997).

Approximately 2.8 million cubic metres of wood is harvested annually in Ireland. Wood provides about 1 per cent of Ireland's total energy demand and as a fuel is used mainly in homes (see under 'Energy'). There is potential for wood to replace or complement coal and peat-fired power stations.

Forests constitute an important renewable resource and their environmental benefits include their role in providing amenity areas, in reducing soil erosion and in carbon sequestration. Adverse environmental impacts may include those deriving from land drainage, the high proportion of certain conifers planted, impacts on landscape and cultural heritage, isolation of rural dwellings, and acidification of waters.

MARINE RESOURCES

The marine resources sector includes marine food, tourism, shipping and energy production. The main focus here is the marine food sector, which embraces all economic activities deriving from the biologically productive capacity of the seas. The total employment in the industry is around 15,720 persons.

The sea fishing industry provides essential employment and economic activity in coastal and island areas. In 1997, the 1,400 Irish registered fishing vessels landed 300 kilotonnes (kt) of fish and shellfish, worth over £144 million (Fig. 3.6). The Irish fishing fleet currently accounts for approximately 30-35 per cent, of the total international landings of fish

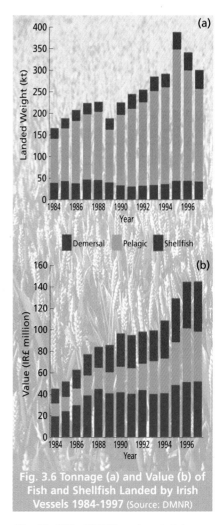

Fig. 3.6 Tonnage (a) and Value (b) of Fish and Shellfish Landed by Irish Vessels 1984-1997 (Source: DMNR)

(Note: The 1984 and 1985 figures do not include landings to foreign ports, which constitute approximately an additional 8 per cent of demersal and pelagic landings to Irish ports.)

and shellfish from the region that includes the seas around Ireland and off the west coast of Britain.

Pelagic (mid-water species) landings are the main factor in a doubling of total landings up to 1995 and also in the subsequent decline. Demersal (species at or near the sea bed) landings have remained relatively more stable. Shellfish landings increased by over two-thirds from 1984 to 1997.

Fish-farming in Irish marine waters began in the 1970s with the farming of rainbow trout in sea cages. This was followed by caged salmon production, which developed rapidly in the 1980s and has continued to do so (Table 3.1). The main fish farming areas are along the western seaboard (Fig. 3.7). In recent years research into new finfish species has led to their cultivation in small quantities.

Exports of fish and fish products in 1997 amounted to 255,000 tonnes, valued at £228 million. The value of aquaculture production is experiencing strong growth and has reached about £60 million. The fish processing sector is concentrated in counties Donegal, Galway, Kerry, Cork, Wexford and Dublin.

The Irish seaweed industry currently processes approximately 40,000 (wet) tonnes annually, for use in the alginate industry, for health and snack foods and body-care products. There is also harvesting of maërl (calcareous red algae) primarily for use in agriculture and horticulture.

Table 3.1 Mariculture Production (tonnes)

	1980	1985	1990	1995	1996	1997
Shellfish	5,214	10,675	19,221	14,138	19,025	20,100
Salmon	21	700	6,323	11,811	14,025	15,442
Rainbow trout (sea)	160	60	324	470	690	750
Turbot				15	30	
Total	5,395	11,435	25,868	26,434	33,770	36,292

Source: BIM

Environmental concerns relating to the marine resources sector include effects of modern fishing practices on target and non-target stocks, damage to the sea bed, and pollutants arising from fish farms and from the fish processing industry. The sector itself can be affected by marine environmental degradation from various sources.

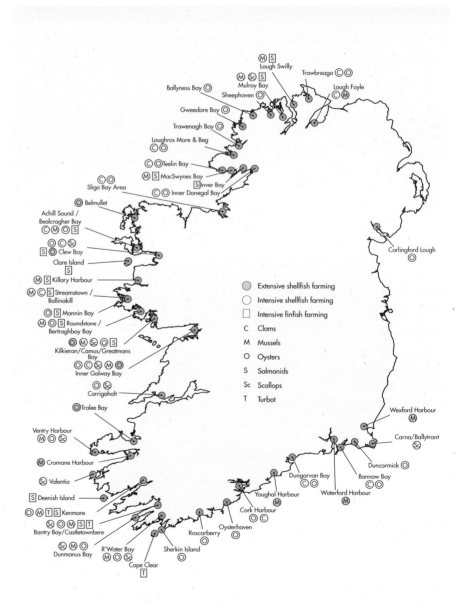

Source: BIM (Boelens *et al.*, 1999)

Fig. 3.7 Location of the Main Mariculture Areas and Species Cultivated

ENERGY

As Ireland's economy has grown, increases have occurred both in total and in per-capita energy consumption. The growth in energy consumption, however, has been less steep than the growth of the economy (Fig. 3.8). The real average price of energy for final consumers has been decreasing consistently since 1986 (Irish Energy Centre, 1999).

The total primary energy requirement (TPER) is a measure of all energy consumed. It includes energy consumed in transformation (for example, in electricity generation, oil refining and briquette manufacture) and in distribution. The TPER increased by 58 per cent between 1980 and 1998, including a 35 per cent rise since 1990 (Department of Public Enterprise, 1999).

Ireland's TPER is supplied by oil, natural gas, coal, peat and renewable energy sources (Fig. 3.9). Indigenous natural gas came on-stream in 1979 and its contribution grew significantly in the early 1980s. This, coupled with the coming on-stream of the coal-fired electricity generating station at Moneypoint in 1986, had the effect of reducing considerably Ireland's dependence on oil. During the 1990s, however, the oil share picked up again, due mainly to growth in transport demand (see below). The overall result is that energy supply remains heavily reliant on imported oil, which in 1998 accounted for 56 per cent of all supply.

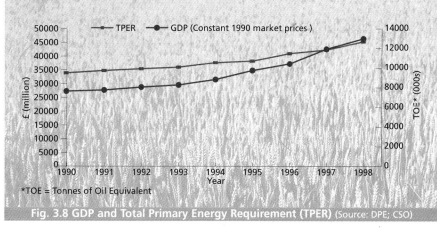

Fig. 3.8 GDP and Total Primary Energy Requirement (TPER) (Source: DPE; CSO)

*TOE = Tonnes of Oil Equivalent

The contribution of natural gas is continuing to grow and it is central to Ireland's strategy for reducing emissions of carbon dioxide and

sulphur dioxide. Almost 50 per cent of the gas supply is now being imported through the inter-connector pipeline between Ireland and the UK and this percentage is expected to increase. Consumption of energy from peat has been declining.

Until the early 1990s renewable energy in Ireland was largely confined to wood burning in open fires and hydro-electricity production by the Electricity Supply Board. More recently, independent hydro power

producers, wood processing plants and wind energy developers have increased the energy supply from renewable sources (Department of

Public Enterprise, 1999). Renewable energy comes mainly from industrial and traditional biomass (wood burning) and from large scale hydro power (Fig 3.10). Renewable energy provides 2 per cent of the total primary energy requirement in Ireland compared with 5 to 6 per cent in the EU overall (EEA, 1999).

Total final consumption is a measure of the amount used by consumers of final energy. It is essentially TPER less the energy consumed in

Fig. 3.9 Sources of Energy Supply (DPE, 1999)

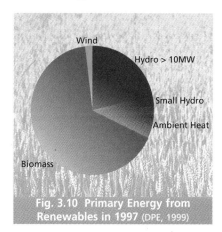

Fig. 3.10 Primary Energy from Renewables in 1997 (DPE, 1999)

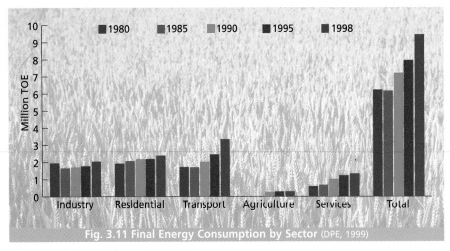

Fig. 3.11 Final Energy Consumption by Sector (DPE, 1999)

transformation and distribution. The changes in total final consumption over the period 1980-1998 are shown in Fig. 3.11 together with the consumption in five sectors; industry, residential, transport, agriculture and services (public plus private). Transport has become both the largest and the fastest growing user of energy in Ireland and accounts for more than one-third of total demand. Increased numbers of vehicles (see under 'Transport') and a trend towards larger vehicles are the main contributors (Irish Energy Centre, 1999).

Energy intensities are ratios between energy consumption and an indicator such as GDP, indicating the energy required to produce one unit of economic output. While reductions in energy intensity can be interpreted as showing improved efficiency or productivity, this simple view does not take account of other factors such as structural changes in the economy (Department of Public Enterprise, 1999). From Fig. 3.8 it may be deduced that although overall energy use has risen in Ireland, primary energy intensity (TPER relative to GDP) has fallen.

Considering individual sectors, the energy intensity of industry has fallen owing to both efficiency and structural changes. For example, in 1997 energy consumption in industry rose by 5.9 per cent whereas industrial output grew by 15.2 per cent. The energy intensity of

transport has remained relatively constant; advances in technical efficiency are being negated by the trend towards more powerful cars (Department of Public Enterprise, 1999).

Residential use of fuels for space and water heating per household has fallen somewhat since 1991 whereas electrical usage per household has risen steeply. A similar situation prevails in respect of the public and private services sector. The intensity of electricity use per employee increased by 65 per cent approximately between 1980 and 1997 due to the increased use of electrical equipment. Overall electricity demand in Ireland has grown in excess of 5 per cent per annum for the period 1988-1998, an extremely high rate by international standards, which is placing strains on existing electricity generation capacity.

Energy is recognised generally as a critical sector relating to the environment. Impacts on the environment arise at each operational phase of the energy system: production, transmission, transformation, distribution and consumption (EEA, 1999). The generation of emissions of greenhouse gases and acidifying compounds from the burning of fossil fuels is a major issue and is addressed in Chapter 4. Future energy policy must focus on these issues,

including the impacts of the fuel mix used in Ireland.

INDUSTRY

In the 1960s there was a significant restructuring of the Irish economy away from agriculture towards industry and services. The continued importance of industry is in contrast to the typical pattern of most modern economies where the service sector is dominant (ESRI, 1999). Industry accounts for 39 per cent of GDP, around 90 per cent of exports and 29 per cent of total employment. Industrial production in Ireland grew strongly over the 1990s (Fig. 3.12).

In June 1999 industrial production was up 9.8 per cent in volume compared with the same month in 1998. Overall industrial employment is now approximately 250,000, distributed as follows (CSO, 1999b):
- 40 per cent in metals and engineering (predominantly electrical engineering, instrument engineering and office machinery);

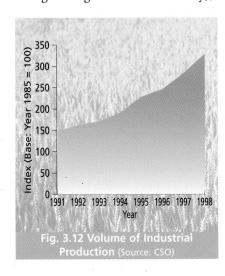

Fig. 3.12 Volume of Industrial Production (Source: CSO)

- 16 per cent in food;
- 9 per cent in chemicals (including man-made fibres);
- 7 per cent paper and printing;
- 22 per cent in a variety of other manufacturing industries;
- 4 per cent in electricity, gas and water;
- 2 per cent in mining, quarrying and peat.

Overseas-owned companies, employing about 108,000 persons, account for some 70 per cent of total manufactured exports. The highest growth rates in Irish industry over recent years have been in the high-tech sectors of manufacturing, particularly in engineering (notably computers). Output from the chemical and pharmaceutical sector has expanded considerably. There are 200 firms in this sector, with present employment at 16,000 and annual exports worth over £8.8 billion. Nine of the world's top ten pharmaceutical firms have manufacturing facilities in Ireland (ICSTI, 1999). Even in non high-tech industries, performance has been significant by comparison with other EU countries.

In 1997, the output from the food industry was valued at almost £10 billion, while exports amounted to about £5.2 billion. The sector accounts for two-thirds of total indigenous industry and comprises approximately 700 companies including some 600 that are medium or small. The main components of the industry, in terms of estimated 1997 output, are as follows:
- dairy products/ingredients £2.3 billion;
- beef £1.7 billion;
- other meats £1.13 billion;
- prepared consumer foods £1.3 billion;
- drinks £1.25 billion
(Food Industry Development Group, 1998).

Ireland is a leading producer of zinc ores and one of the world's largest

zinc/lead mines is located near Navan, Co Meath. Production of zinc concentrates is expected to double following the recent start up of major new mines.

Many industrial sectors are of significance in relation to the environment, for example chemical and pharmaceutical, food, mining and quarrying. Industry has the potential to create significant pressures on the environment through the use of dangerous substances, emissions to air and water, the generation of waste, the consumption of natural resources and energy, and the contamination of land.

TRANSPORT

Sea and air transport are essential for Ireland's economy, notably for tourism and trade as discussed later in this chapter. Transport within the country is heavily dependent on the

road network. Ireland has over 95,000 km of roads, equivalent to over 27 km per thousand persons - high by European standards. The national primary roads (3 per cent of the road network) carry 27 per cent of road traffic. National secondary roads (3 per cent of the network) carry 11 per cent of road traffic, and non-national roads (94 per cent of the network) carry 62 per cent of road traffic.

Ireland's growing economy is leading to increased car ownership. The total number of vehicles increased by 54 per cent during the 10-year period between 1988 and 1998. Private cars accounted for the major part of this increase (Fig. 3.13) but heavy goods vehicles increased by 58 per cent in the period.

In addition there have been changing travel patterns. Between 1986 and 1996, the number of persons travelling to work, college or school by private vehicles increased by 44 per cent while the number of persons

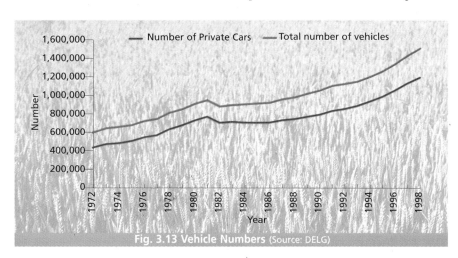

Fig. 3.13 Vehicle Numbers (Source: DELG)

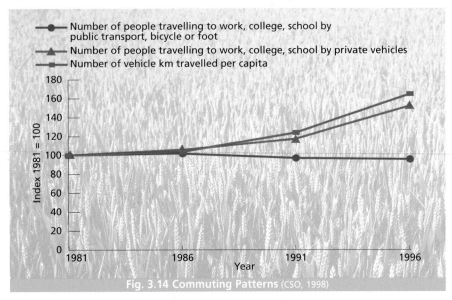

Fig. 3.14 Commuting Patterns (CSO, 1998)

city services (CSO, 1999c). The number of passenger journeys by bus increased by approximately 3 per cent between 1994 and 1998 (Fig. 3.15b).

The demands of modern economies and societies for mobility present a major environmental challenge. Rising vehicle numbers and increased usage of cars have caused significant traffic congestion and noise in urban areas and have contributed to local air pollution (Lehane, 1999). There is increased petrol and diesel consumption. Increased energy use in transport is a major emerging issue. The resultant emissions to air are considered in Chapter 4. Other issues include the environmental impact of road building on landscapes and habitats.

travelling by public transport, bicycle or foot decreased by nearly 6 per cent (Fig. 3.14).

Growth in traffic volume is reflected in vehicle km travelled. Per capita, this increased from 5,994 km in 1986 to 9,523 km in 1996, an increase of over 58 per cent. More than 20 per cent of vehicle km travelled is by goods vehicles.

Over recent decades the volume of freight carried by rail has reduced (Fig. 3.15a) while that carried by road has multiplied. The under-utilisation of rail for freight is likely to continue unless measures are taken to redress this. The amount of passengers using rail has increased, particularly on the Dublin Area

Rapid Transit (DART) and other Dublin suburban lines. Over 29 million passengers were carried by rail in 1997, of which 20.5 million were on DART and outer suburban services with the remainder on inter-

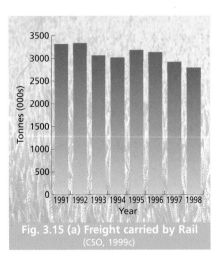

Fig. 3.15 (a) Freight carried by Rail (CSO, 1999c)

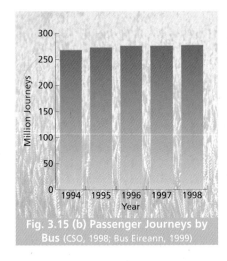

Fig. 3.15 (b) Passenger Journeys by Bus (CSO, 1998; Bus Eireann, 1999)

TOURISM

Tourism is one of Ireland's fastest growing sectors and is an important foreign currency earner. In 1998 it accounted for 6.4 per cent of gross national product (GNP) and 8.2 per cent of employment (Bord Fáilte, 1999). Many of the jobs provided by tourism are in rural communities. By 1998 the number of overseas tourists was over 1.5 times the resident population (Fig. 3.16). There were 5.53 million overseas visits to Ireland by non-residents, an increase of 10.5 per cent on the previous year. Dublin, the south-west and the west receive the highest numbers of tourists (Fig. 3.17). In 1998, 43 per cent of overseas tourists hired cars or brought their own cars while visiting Ireland.

In 1997 there were an estimated 10.3 million visits to 342 fee-charging attractions in Ireland, an increase of 25 per cent since 1995. Visitor numbers exceeded 100,000 at about 10 per cent of these attractions. The most popular were interpretative centres and museums, accounting for

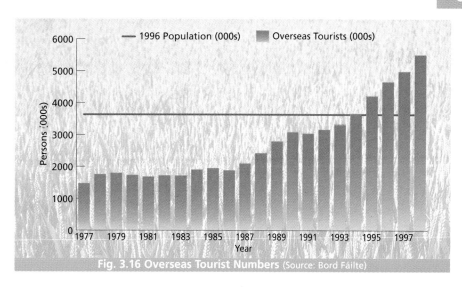

Fig. 3.16 Overseas Tourist Numbers (Source: Bord Fáilte)

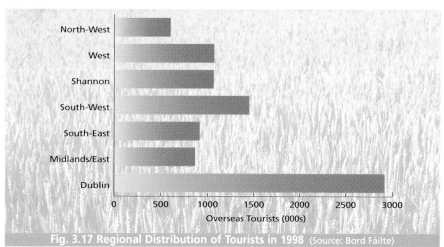

Fig. 3.17 Regional Distribution of Tourists in 1998 (Source: Bord Fáilte)

35 per cent of visits (Tourism Development International, 1998).

A total of 2.1 million trips abroad was taken by Irish residents in 1998 and total expenditure attributable to these trips was £1.1 billion.

Many of the visitors coming to Ireland do so to enjoy the country's environment. If not managed properly, growing tourist numbers can harm the very environment that attracts them. The major growth in the numbers of overseas tourists is adding to pressure on the physical infrastructure (roads, water and sewerage) and causing traffic congestion in major tourist areas. Furthermore, the increased concentration of tourists, both domestic and overseas, visiting the better-known tourist sites is placing pressures on the quality of the environment in these sensitive areas.

TRADE

Ireland's small open economy is strongly dependent on trade. Exports, almost three quarters of which are destined for the EU, represent over 73 per cent of GDP. In 1998 exports and imports amounted to £44.8 billion and £31.1 billion respectively (Fig. 3.18), giving a record trade surplus of almost £14 billion (CSO, 1999a). Some of the main growth areas of exports include chemicals, pharmaceuticals, and telecommunication and computer equipment.

Sea transport is the dominant route for trade, with the State's ports accounting for 76 per cent of trade in volume terms. Air transport accounts for less than 1 per cent of trade in volume terms, but 18 per cent in value terms. Most of the remaining trade is via ports in Northern Ireland.

The importation of non-coniferous timber (logs, sawn-wood, veneer and plywood) into Ireland has increased by over 61 per cent between 1994 and 1999. The importation of tropical timber is currently around 73,000 cubic metres per annum (Fig. 3.19). Trade in endangered species, as well as in derivatives and products from them, is controlled under an international Convention (CITES). The main provisions of the Convention have been implemented in Ireland.

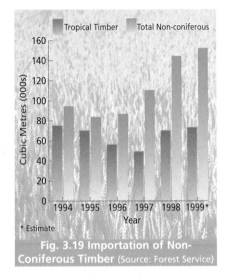

Fig. 3.19 Importation of Non-Coniferous Timber (Source: Forest Service)

The issue of trade and the environment is complex. Sustainable trade should support economic prosperity while protecting the global environment in all its diversity and should take account of the wider global impact of national policies regarding imports and

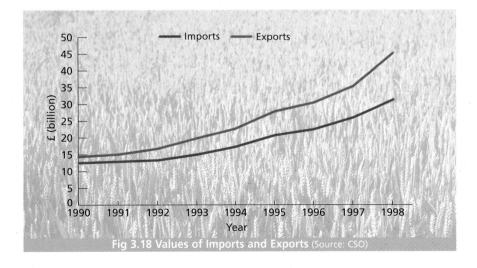

Fig 3.18 Values of Imports and Exports (Source: CSO)

exports (DoE, 1997). Because of increasing awareness of environmental issues by consumers world-wide, there is a need to demonstrate a high degree of environmental awareness and standards in relation to exports in order to develop and retain market shares in other economies.

Environmentally significant patterns and trends are apparent in all of the sectors considered. The pace of growth across the board is such as to raise doubts about any net environmental benefit from efficiencies or remedial measures introduced to date. The environmental consequences of these trends are therefore examined in greater detail in the main body of this report, starting in Chapter 4 with emissions to air. Many of the sectoral trends look set to continue. The overall issue of likely future developments and their consequences for the environment is considered in the final part of the report, including consideration of the proposals under the National Development Plan 2000-2006.

REFERENCES

Boelens, R.G.V., Maloney, D.M., Parsons, A.P., and Walsh, A.R., 1999. *Ireland's Marine and Coastal Areas and Adjacent Seas - An Environmental Assessment.* Prepared by the Marine Institute on behalf of the Department of Environment & Local Government and the Department of Marine & Natural Resources. Marine Institute, Dublin.

Bord Fáilte, 1999. *Tourism Facts 1998.* Bord Fáilte, Dublin.

Bus Éireann, 1999. *Annual Report and Financial Statements 1998.* Bus Éireann, Dublin.

CSO (Central Statistics Office), 1998. *Census 96 - Travel to Work, School and College.* Stationery Office, Dublin.

CSO (Central Statistics Office), 1999a. *External Trade. June 1999 (Details), July 1999 (First Estimate).* Central Statistics Office, Dublin.

CSO (Central Statistics Office), 1999b. *Industrial Employment. December 1998 (Final), March 1999 (Provisional).* Central Statistics Office, Dublin.

CSO (Central Statistics Office), 1999c. *Statistical Abstract 1998-1999.* Stationery Office, Dublin.

DAF (Department of Agriculture and Food), 1999. *Ensuring the Future - A Strategy for Rural Development in Ireland. A White Paper on Rural Development.* Department of Agriculture and Food, Dublin.

DoE (Department of Environment), 1997. *Sustainable Development: A Strategy for Ireland.* Stationery Office, Dublin.

DPE (Department of Public Enterprise), 1999. *Green Paper on Sustainable Energy.* Stationery Office, Dublin.

EEA (European Environment Agency), 1999. *Environment in the European Union at the turn of the century.* European Environment Agency, Copenhagen.

ESRI (Economic and Social Research Institute), 1999. *Medium Term Review 1999-2005.* Economic and Social Research Institute, Dublin.

Food Industry Development Group, 1998. *Report of the Food Industry Development Group.* Department of Agriculture and Food, Dublin.

ICSTI (Irish Council for Science, Technology and Innovation), 1999. *Technology Foresight Ireland. Report of the Chemical and Pharmaceutical Panel.* The Irish Council for Science, Technology and Innovation, Dublin.

Irish Energy Centre, 1999. *Energy Efficiency in Ireland.* Irish Energy Centre, Dublin.

Lehane, M. (ed.), 1999. *Environment in Focus - A Discussion Document on Key National Environmental Indicators.* Environmental Protection Agency, Wexford.

Tourism Development International, 1998. *1997 Visitor Attractions Survey, Presentation of Key Findings.* Dublin.

PART III

Pressures on the Environment

CHAPTER 4

EMISSIONS TO AIR

Over the past 15 years, progress in reducing the most important air pollutant emissions in Ireland has fallen well short of that required by international agreements. Having failed to stabilise nitrogen oxides emissions at 1987 levels by 1994, as required under the Sofia Protocol, it now appears that Ireland will not achieve the national target for sulphur dioxide emissions in 2000 required under the Oslo Protocol. Furthermore, an unprecedented rise in energy demand is set to increase greenhouse gas emissions, in a business as usual scenario, by more than twice that allowed under the Kyoto Protocol. Large livestock populations and nitrogen inputs to soil generate one-third of all greenhouse gases in Ireland and result in the highest ammonia, methane and nitrous oxide emissions per capita in the European Union.

The European Union's strategies on acidification and ground-level ozone have culminated in a proposed national emissions ceiling Directive, which sets limits on the total emissions of sulphur dioxide, nitrogen oxides, ammonia and volatile organic compounds in Member States to be achieved over the next ten years. Parallel strategies developed under the UN Convention on Long-range Transboundary Air Pollution have led to the Gothenburg Protocol, which also prescribes ceilings on these pollutants for all European countries. Fundamental changes are needed now in the energy, agriculture and transport sectors if Ireland is to achieve these new targets and simultaneously to curb the growing greenhouse gas emissions.

INTRODUCTION

The emission of pollutants into the atmosphere continues to be one of the greatest of all pressures on the global environment. Awareness of atmospheric pollution first developed some fifty years ago as a result of the local health effects of winter smog caused by coal burning, usually in urban or heavily industrialised areas. This was followed by an awareness of widespread environmental damage from acid rain caused by increased emissions of sulphur and nitrogen from industry, power generation and other activities. More recently, summer smog and increased levels of tropospheric (ground level) ozone, caused largely by emissions from road traffic, have become common occurrences in many parts of the developed world.

A separate issue, which has been widely publicised, is the depletion of stratospheric (upper atmosphere) ozone - the 'hole in the ozone layer'. Caused mainly by the effects of chlorofluorocarbons (CFC), the thinning of the ozone layer results in more ultraviolet-B (UV-B) radiation reaching the earth's surface, thereby posing a potential health threat.

However, the problem now causing most concern is the potential for the emissions of certain gases, originally considered harmless, to alter radically the global climate system. Several gases, notably carbon dioxide from the burning of fossil fuels and methane from agriculture, are accumulating in the upper atmosphere where they are acting to enhance the natural greenhouse effect of the atmosphere (see Box 4.1). Hence they are now collectively known as the 'greenhouse gases'.

Box 4.1 The Greenhouse Effect

The solar radiation absorbed by the earth's surface and atmosphere is balanced by outgoing infrared radiation (IPCC, 1994). Clouds and naturally occurring greenhouse gases (principally water vapour, carbon dioxide, methane, nitrous oxide and ozone) contribute to this balance by absorbing some of the infrared radiation emitted from the earth's surface. This keeps the lower part of the atmosphere warmer than it would otherwise be - the natural greenhouse effect.

Human activities such as the burning of fossil fuels and the intensification of agriculture are increasing the concentrations of the naturally occurring greenhouse gases and adding other gases, which act in the same way. By reducing the outgoing infrared radiation, this is giving rise to an enhanced greenhouse effect. The effects of increased greenhouse gas concentrations in the atmosphere may be offset to some extent by increases in the concentration of aerosols, also derived largely from human activities but also from natural sources such as volcanic eruptions, which increase the reflection and absorption of solar radiation.

GREENHOUSE GASES

The United Nations has adopted the Framework Convention on Climate Change (FCCC), with the ultimate objective of achieving stabilisation of greenhouse gas concentrations in the atmosphere at levels that would prevent dangerous interference with the earth's climate system (IUCC, 1993). All Parties to the Convention, which include Ireland, must publish and make available to the Conference of the Parties (COP), the Convention's implementation body, their national inventories of emissions and removals of all greenhouse gases not controlled by the Montreal Protocol. (While the Montreal Protocol, as outlined later, is aimed at reducing ozone-depleting substances, some of the gases responsible for ozone depletion also contribute to some extent to the greenhouse effect).

The three principal greenhouse gases are carbon dioxide (CO_2), methane (CH_4) and nitrous oxide (N_2O). The Convention also covers the two halogenated gas groups hydrofluorocarbons (HFC) and perfluorocarbons (PFC) as well as sulphur hexafluoride (SF_6).

Ozone is another greenhouse gas formed from several precursor pollutants including nitrogen oxides (NO_X), volatile organic compounds (VOC) and carbon monoxide (CO). Parties to the Convention must also submit data on the emissions of these gases.

Figure 4.1 shows the trend in emissions of the three main greenhouse gases in Ireland between 1990 and 1998, expressed in terms of

their Global Warming Potential (GWP) (see Box 4.2). The emission estimates (McGettigan and Duffy, 2000) have been compiled using the most recent guidelines from the Intergovernmental Panel on Climate Change (IPCC) for greenhouse gas inventories (IPCC, 1997) and they therefore show some revisions on previously published figures. The revised IPCC methodology gives methane emissions that are about 25 per cent lower than previously estimated and nitrous oxide emissions that are some 20 per cent higher than previously estimated.

Reliable emission inventories of HFC, PFC and SF_6 have not yet been developed due to the large range of substances involved and a lack of information on their use in Irish industry. However, tentative estimates suggest that their combined contribution would be less than one per cent of the estimated totals presented in Figure 4.1 for the three main greenhouse gases.

A comparison of the revised figures for 1990 and 1998 indicates that the overall total combined emissions of the three main greenhouse gases, carbon dioxide, methane and nitrous oxide, increased in the eight year period by approximately 19 per cent, to 64 million tonnes of CO_2 equivalent on a GWP basis (Box 4.2). The increase is driven by the CO_2 contribution, with the gross emissions

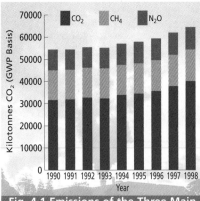

Fig. 4.1 Emissions of the Three Main Greenhouse Gases 1990 to 1998

of this gas (excluding carbon sequestration by forests) rising by one-quarter from almost 32 million tonnes in 1990 to 40 million tonnes in 1998. This results from an unprecedented increase of 35 per cent in total primary energy requirement (Chapter 3). The significance of the increase in greenhouse gas emissions in the context of Ireland's international commitments is discussed below following a brief overview of the principal sources of these emissions.

A comparison of the sectoral contributions of the three gases to the totals in 1990 and 1998 is given in Table 4.1. The transport and energy sectors account for most of the CO_2 increase, with increases amounting to approximately 77 per cent and 36 per cent, respectively. Some of the increase is offset by the carbon uptake in forests. The total forest area in

Box 4.2 Global Warming Potential

The various greenhouse gases are emitted in vastly differing amounts and have widely differing atmospheric lifetimes. The control options among them are also completely different. The concept of Global Warming Potential (GWP) was introduced to provide a means whereby scientists and policymakers could compare and combine the warming effects of the individual gases, in order to support policies and measures designed to mitigate climate change.

The GWP of a gas is a measure of the cumulative warming over a specified time period, e.g., 100 years, resulting from a unit mass of the gas emitted now, expressed relative to an absolute GWP of 1 for the reference gas carbon dioxide. Global Warming Potentials have been published for a wide range of greenhouse gases by the Intergovernmental Panel on Climate Change. For example, the GWP of methane, one of the more ubiquitous greenhouse gases, is 21 for a 100-year time horizon but the GWP is as high as 23,900 in the case of sulphur hexafluoride, the mass emission of which is comparatively very small. The mass emission of any gas multiplied by its GWP gives the equivalent emission of the gas as carbon dioxide - the CO_2 equivalent.

Table 4.1 Comparison of Sectoral and Total Greenhouse Gas Emissions in 1990 and 1998

IPCC Source Strategy	1990				1998			
	CO_2 kt	CH_4 kt	N_2O kt	Total as CO_2 kt	CO_2 kt	CH_4 kt	N_2O kt	Total as CO_2 kt
Energy and Transformation	11057		1.39	11488	15047		2.00	15667
Combustion In Industry	3833	0.15	0.38	3954	3917	0.12	0.40	4044
Combustion in Transport	4961	1.76	0.28	5085	8768	2.26	1.02	9132
Other Combustion	9726	4.27	1.05	10141	9974	2.83	1.09	10371
Fugitive Emissions from Fuels		6.05		127		4.03		85
Industrial Processes	1931		3.34	2966	2250		2.62	3062
Solvents	67			67	71			71
Agriculture		514.27	22.87	17890		563.93	25.34	19698
Land Use Change and Forestry	-5020			-5020	-6448			-6448
Waste		84.75		1780		75.90		1594
Gross Emissions	31575	611.25	29.31	53498	40027	649.07	32.47	63724
Net Emissions	26555	611.25	29.31	48478	33579	649.07	32.47	57276

*CO_2 sink in forests treated as a negative emission

Ireland absorbed an estimated 6.4 million tonnes of CO_2 in 1998 (shown as a negative emission in Table 4.1), an increase of 28 per cent on the 1990 value.

Agriculture is the dominant source of both methane and nitrous oxide emissions in Ireland. These emissions are unrelated to energy demand and show very modest increases compared to CO_2. At some 649,000 tonnes and 32,500 tonnes respectively in 1998, Irish methane and nitrous oxide emissions represent by far the highest per capita emissions of these gases in the EU (EEA, 1998). Together they account for about 40 per cent of Ireland's total greenhouse gas emissions as GWP. Agriculture generates approximately 87 per cent of methane emissions and 78 per cent of N_2O emissions, and for this reason agriculture is the source of one-third of all greenhouse gas emissions in Ireland.

Further details of the main sectoral activities giving rise to greenhouse gas emissions are given in Table 4.2. The table shows how just 12 major sources or activities account for almost three-quarters of all greenhouse gas emissions in Ireland. When compared on a CO_2 equivalent basis, the largest single source is enteric fermentation in cattle and other livestock (16.3 %), followed by nitrogen application to soils (11.2%) and electricity generation from coal (9.4%).

The increase of approximately 18 per cent in Ireland's net greenhouse gas emissions between 1990 and 1998 has serious implications for Ireland's commitment under the Kyoto Protocol to the Framework Convention on Climate Change (Box 4.3). The emission reduction commitment of the EU under the Kyoto Protocol is eight per cent on 1990 levels by 2010 to which Ireland's burden-sharing contribution is a growth limitation target of 13 per cent. This level of increase had in fact already accrued by the time the Kyoto Protocol was signed in 1997 and the growth rate is currently over four per cent annually (Figure 4.1),

---

Box 4.3 The Kyoto Protocol

In adopting the Framework Convention on Climate Change in 1992, the governments recognised that it would provide a basis for much stronger specific control measures in the future by developed countries. The first such commitment was realised with the adoption in December 1997 of the Kyoto Protocol under which industrialised countries will reduce their combined emissions of six greenhouse gases by 5.2 per cent on 1990 levels by the period 2008-2012 (the first commitment period).

Ireland's legally binding commitment under the Kyoto Protocol is a growth limitation target of 13 per cent. This was negotiated as Ireland's burden-sharing contribution to the European Union's reduction commitment of eight per cent.

Parties may apply a number of flexible mechanisms, viz., international emissions trading, joint implementation and the clean development mechanism in addition to their domestic measures in order to meet their targets. The Protocol requires that, by 2005, Parties must have made demonstrable progress towards achieving their commitments.

mainly due to carbon dioxide increases.

Based on the most recent forecasts for energy and agriculture, the net emissions of greenhouse gases in 2010 will have increased by approximately 30 per cent over 1990 levels. This is more than twice the growth limitation target, despite expected increases in the carbon sink capacity of forests. Given the nature of the activities which contribute to the bulk of emissions in Ireland (Table 4.2) along with continued growth in energy demand, it appears that radical changes are necessary to make any substantial impact on this upward trend in greenhouse gas emissions (see Part V).

OZONE-DEPLETING SUBSTANCES

Depletion of the stratospheric ozone layer has been taking place in certain parts of the globe for the past twenty

Table 4.2 Contribution of Twelve Main Sources to Greenhouse Gas Emissions in Ireland in 1998.

Source/ Sector	Activity	Fuel	Emissions (kt)			Total Equivalent CO_2 (kt)	Percent of Total	Cumulative Percent
			CO_2	CH_4	N_2O			
All Sectors			40027	649.07	32.47	63724		
Agriculture	Enteric Fermentation			493.56		10365	16.26	16.3
Agriculture	Nitrogen Applic. to Soils				22.98	7124	11.18	27.4
Energy	Electricity Generation	Coal	5680		0.90	5959	9.35	36.8
Transport	Road Traffic	Petrol	3667			3667	5.75	42.5
Transport	Road Traffic	Diesel	3529			3529	5.54	48.1
Energy	Electricity Generation	Oil	3519			3519	5.52	53.6
Energy	Electricity Generation	Gas	3066			3066	4.81	58.4
Energy	Electricity Generation	Peat	2465			2465	3.87	62.3
Agriculture	Manure Management			70.37	2.36	2209	3.47	65.8
Industry	Cement Manufacture	Coal	1624			1624	2.55	68.3
Landfill	Waste Disposal			75.90		1594	2.50	70.8
Industry	Ammonia Production	Gas	1564			1564	2.45	73.3

years due to build-up of chlorofluorocarbons (CFC), halons, carbon tetrachloride, methyl chloroform and other similar substances deriving from man-made emissions. The effect is to increase the amount of UV radiation reaching the earth, which can result in damage to human health and adverse impact on terrestrial and marine ecosystems.

The Montreal Protocol and subsequent amendments set out a programme for the phasing-out of the compounds with the greatest ozone-depleting potential, as well as some of their replacements, many of which are also greenhouse gases, by the mid to late 1990s. Current efforts are directed at tightening controls and speeding up the phasing out of methyl bromide and hydrochlorofluorocarbons (HCFC). Ireland has taken an active part in the global strategy to protect the ozone layer and pursues a policy of discontinuing the use of ozone depleting substances in line with targets, which have been agreed internationally.

ACIDIFYING GASES AND OZONE PRECURSORS

Deposition resulting from the emissions of sulphur dioxide (SO_2), nitrogen oxides (NO_X) and ammonia (NH_3) can lead to the acidification of soils and surface waters and may cause nitrogen saturation in terrestrial ecosystems. Increased ground-level ozone formation is caused by emissions of NO_X, VOC and CO

and all of these pollutants may have direct effects on human health and vegetation.

Estimates of the emissions of SO_2, NO_X, VOC and CO are presented in Figure 4.2 for the years 1990 through 1998, using a simple source-sector classification adopted for previous estimates. This time series has been recalculated to maintain consistency with the corresponding greenhouse gas emission estimates and to take into account better or recently acquired information for some sources and sectors (McGettigan and Duffy, 2000). The totals therefore show some changes on previously published estimates for the years concerned. A programme to retrofit a number of the largest power stations with NO_X control technology, resulting in some units being off-line for long periods, largely accounts for the year-to-year variations in SO_2 from this sector during the early 1990s. Some variations in other sectors and for other pollutants are due mainly to apparent inconsistencies or anomalies in national energy balances. The VOC emissions in the 'Other' category are highly uncertain due to the inclusion of emissions from solvent use, which are not well quantified.

Emissions of SO_2, NO_X, VOC, and CO, which emanate mainly from combustion sources, showed a general decrease from 1990 through 1995 but have since begun to rise again. This rise can be attributed to the

marked increase in the consumption of primary fuels since 1995 (Chapter 3).

The total for SO_2 is dominated by emissions from power stations (amounting to 60 per cent of the total) where the largest plants use coal and heavy fuel oil. Increased electricity demand means that these stations are now being used to almost full capacity. Consequently any reductions that had accrued from low sulphur coal and a shift to greater dependence on gas-fired plant in place of oil have been offset in latter

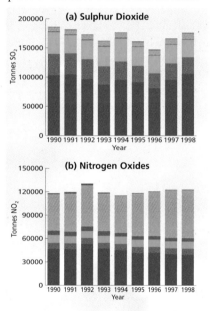

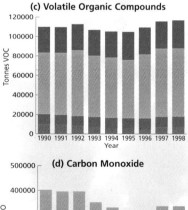

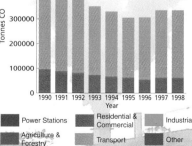

Fig. 4.2 Emissions of SO_2, NO_X, VOC and CO 1990-1998

years by the need to utilise fully the oil-fired plants. A general decrease in SO_2 emissions in other European countries has resulted in Ireland's position rising to third highest among EU Member States in 1995, marginally behind Greece and Spain, on the basis of emissions per capita (EEA, 1998).

In the case of NO_X, VOC and CO, the totals are heavily influenced by emissions from transport. The contribution of transport to the total 1998 emissions of these gases is as follows:
- NO_X 50 per cent.
- VOC 60 per cent.
- CO 81 per cent.

The benefits given by catalyst controls, which were beginning to appear after 1993, have already been offset by the huge increase in the use of transport fuels in recent years. Irish per capita emissions of NO_X and VOC remain close to the EU average.

The agriculture sector accounts for virtually all (99.5 per cent) of the ammonia emissions. These emissions show a clear upward trend, from 112,000 tonnes in 1990 to 126,000 tonnes in 1998, in line with increases in both livestock populations and inorganic fertiliser use. This current level of ammonia emissions in Ireland, generated by large amounts of animal manures (Chapter 6) and the application of some 400,000 tonnes of inorganic nitrogen annually, represent by far the highest per capita emissions in Europe.

In a manner similar to the use of global warming potential for greenhouse gases, *acid equivalents* are often applied to compare emissions of SO_2, NO_X and NH_3 in quantitative terms. The acid equivalents are used also to identify the contributions of various target sectors to the total emission of acidifying substances. The total such emission in Ireland in 1997 was 15,100 million equivalents (Meq) of acidity. The combined SO_2 and NO_X emissions from the energy, industry and transport sectors, traditionally regarded as the most important sources of acidifying substances, accounted for 6,713 Meq. However, the contribution from ammonia emissions emanating from animal manures and chemical fertilisers was larger at 7,213 Meq. This shows that, as in the case of greenhouse gases, the agriculture sector in Ireland is also a major source of acidifying emissions.

The Directive 88/609/EEC (CEC, 1988) on large combustion plants sets emission limits for SO_2 and NO_X. These limits apply to existing combustion plants (licensed for construction or operation before 1 July 1987) of greater than 50 MW thermal capacity in all Member States. The limits are to be achieved on a phased basis over a specified time frame. The limits for Ireland are 124,000 tonnes for SO_2 until 2003 and 50,000 tonnes for NO_X until 1998. Figure 4.3 shows how the emissions of the two pollutants from the plants covered by the Directive in Ireland compare to their respective

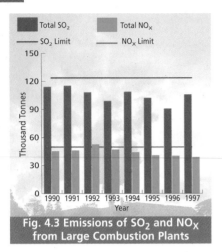

Total SO$_2$ Total NO$_X$
SO$_2$ Limit   NO$_X$ Limit

Fig. 4.3 Emissions of SO$_2$ and NO$_X$ from Large Combustion Plants

committed to stabilising NO$_X$ emissions at the 1987 level of some 105,000 tonnes by 1994. This target has not been met. A target SO$_2$ emission of 157,000 tonnes in 2000 (30 per cent reduction on 1980 levels) was adopted on Ireland's signing of the more recent Oslo Protocol (UN, 1994). SO$_2$ emissions in 1998 were about 176,000 tonnes, having been as low as 147,000 tonnes in 1996 (Fig. 4.2). There was therefore a clear need for substantial reductions to be made over two years for the 2000 target to be achieved.

The UN Gothenburg Protocol and the proposed EC Directive on national emissions ceilings (Box 4.4) both specify emissions ceilings for SO$_2$, NO$_X$, VOC and ammonia to be achieved by 2010 in order to meet a range of environmental quality objectives in Europe.

The proposed Directive on national emissions ceilings is particularly significant in that it sets limits on the total emissions of a number of

pollutants for the first time. Assuming that Ireland adopts the same targets under the Directive as those already agreed under the Protocol, the reductions needed range from about 10 per cent for ammonia to 50 per cent in the case of NO$_X$ and VOC and 75 per cent for SO$_2$.

CONCLUSIONS

There have been no substantial reductions in the emissions of important air pollutants, such as SO$_2$ and NO$_X$, or greenhouse gases in Ireland during the 1990s. Indeed emissions of greenhouse gases in particular have shown sustained growth in this period. Increases have also begun to show in the emissions of SO$_2$ and NO$_X$ in latter years following some earlier reductions or stabilisation. For many years, Ireland has generated the highest per capita emissions of ammonia, methane and nitrous oxide in the EU, due almost entirely to large livestock populations and large nitrogen inputs to soils from animal manures and inorganic fertilisers - and the emissions are still increasing.

ceilings. Large combustion plants currently account for approximately 60 per cent and 30 per cent of SO$_2$ and NO$_X$ emissions, respectively.

While compliance is being maintained with the ceilings in respect of the important subset of emission sources covered by the LCP Directive, as shown by Figure 4.3, it is proving to be more difficult to meet national objectives for total SO$_2$ and NO$_X$ emissions. Under the Sofia Protocol (UN, 1988), Ireland was

Box 4.4 The Gothenburg Protocol and the National Emission Ceilings Directive

Since 1985, a number of protocols have been adopted under the Geneva Convention on Long-range Transboundary Air Pollution aimed at reducing emissions of acidifying gases and ozone precursors. These protocols have covered SO$_2$ (UN, 1985; UN, 1994), NOx (UN, 1988) and VOC (UN, 1991). While these agreements have been very successful in reducing emissions of the substances concerned, in each case they were targeted at a single pollutant and one specific environmental problem.

Further development of the 'effects based' approach to emission control has shown that it would be more beneficial and more cost effective to devise an agreement that targeted all the major environmental concerns attributable to these gases simultaneously. This has led to the formulation of the *Gothenburg Protocol*, finalised at the end of 1999 (UN,1999). This so-called *multi-pollutant multi-effects* protocol sets out the reductions in the emissions of SO$_2$, NO$_X$, VOC and ammonia necessary in all countries to achieve specified environmental quality targets for acidification, eutrophication and the effects of ozone on both human health and vegetation. Attainment of the targets will entail very substantial reductions in the emissions of the four compounds in many countries and will result in considerable improvement for the environment and human health throughout Europe.

The *national emission ceilings Directive* is the culmination of the European Union's strategies on the control of acidification and tropospheric ozone formation. The EU environmental quality targets are largely coincident with those forming the basis of the Gothenburg Protocol, except that eutrophication is excluded. The Directive prescribes, for each Member State, the emissions ceilings for SO$_2$, NO$_X$, VOC and ammonia to be achieved by 2010 in order to meet the EU targets. Of the many Directives to date relating to air quality and emissions control this is the first to set limits on the total emissions of pollutants in each country.

Irish SO_2 emissions in 1998 were higher than in the mid-1980s while there has been a general decrease in most European countries in the past 15 years. Consequently, Ireland has become one of the three highest per capita SO_2 emitters in the EU, the rate being only marginally higher in Spain and Greece. One significant outcome of this trend is that Ireland is unlikely to meet the commitment to reduce SO_2 emissions to 157,000 tonnes, i.e. 30 per cent below 1980 levels, by 2000 under the Oslo Protocol.

The outlook in relation to greenhouse gases is of much more concern as emissions in 2010 will be at least 30 per cent higher than in 1990, on a business as usual scenario. The projected increase, largely due to that in CO_2 emissions, is more than twice that allowed by Ireland's legally-binding commitments under the Kyoto Protocol.

Very substantial reductions are required over the next ten years in SO_2, NO_X, VOC and NH_3 emissions to comply with the terms of the proposed national emissions ceilings Directive and the Gothenburg (multi-pollutant multi-effects) Protocol. The measures that would be necessary to achieve these reductions, together with those directed at simultaneous reductions in emissions of the main greenhouse gases, are likely to have far-reaching implications for the energy, electricity, transport and agricultural sectors. The difficulty of the challenge cannot be overstated, particularly in relation to the Kyoto target, given that the Irish economy is highly fossil fuel intensive and that the agricultural sector generates a substantially higher proportion of greenhouse gas emissions than in other countries.

Ireland's record in achieving emissions reductions as part of negotiated international agreement is not good compared with most European countries. As the number of compounds covered by this process now becomes larger than ever and their respective emission limits take a more legally-binding form, radical abatement measures must be implemented immediately if the targets are to be met and the control of emissions to air in Ireland is to catch up with Europe in general over the next 10 to 15 years.

REFERENCES

CEC (Council of the European Communities), 1988. Council Directive 88/609/EEC of 24 November 1988 on the limitation of emissions of certain pollutants into the air from large combustion plants. *O.J. L 336,* 7 December 1988.

EEA (European Environment Agency), 1998. *Europe's Environment: The Second Assessment.* European Environment Agency, Copenhagen.

IPCC (Intergovernmental Panel on Climate Change), 1994. *Radiative Forcing of Climate Change.* The 1994 Report of the Scientific Assessment Working Group of IPCC. UNEP, Geneva.

IPCC (Intergovernmental Panel on Climate Change), 1997. *Revised 1996 Guidelines for National Greenhouse Gas Inventories.* OECD, Paris.

IUCC (Information Unit on Climate Change), 1993. *United Nations Framework Convention on Climate Change.* UNEP, Geneva.

IUCC (Information Unit on Climate Change), 1998. *The Kyoto Protocol to the Convention on Climate Change.* UNEP, Geneva.

McGettigan, M. and Duffy, P., 2000. *Emissions to Air in Ireland 1990-1998.* Environmental Protection Agency, Wexford.

UN (United Nations), 1985. *Protocol to the 1979 Convention on Long-range Transboundary Air Pollution on the Reduction of Sulphur Emissions or their Transboundary Fluxes by at least 30 per cent.* ECE/EB.AIR/16, UNECE, Geneva.

UN (United Nations), 1988. *Protocol to the 1979 Convention on Long-range Transboundary Air Pollution concerning the control of emissions of Nitrogen Oxides or their Transboundary Fluxes.* ECE/EB.AIR/21, UNECE, Geneva.

UN (United Nations), 1991. *Protocol to the 1979 Convention on Long-range Transboundary Air Pollution concerning the control of emissions of Volatile Organic Compounds or their Transboundary Fluxes.* ECE/EB.AIR/R.56, UNECE, Geneva.

UN (United Nations), 1994. *Protocol to the 1979 Convention on Long-range Transboundary Air Pollution on Further Reduction of Sulphur Emissions.* ECE/EB.AIR/40, UNECE, Geneva.

UN (United Nations), 1999. *Draft Protocol to the 1979 Convention on Long-range Transboundary Air Pollution to Abate Acidification, Eutrophication and Ground Level Ozone.* ECE/EB.AIR/1999/1, UNECE, Geneva.

CHAPTER 5

DISCHARGES TO WATER

Towards the end of the 1990s, most of the main urban waste water discharges to freshwaters were subject to secondary treatment, while the majority of discharges to estuaries and coastal waters remained untreated. A major investment programme in sewerage capacity is currently underway, and all significant urban waste water discharges will receive at least secondary treatment within a few years. Septic tanks are the main form of waste water management in rural Ireland, though a significant number of these do not function properly owing to problems with location, construction and maintenance. By the end of 1998, most of the direct industrial discharges to estuaries and coastal waters were from industries subject to integrated pollution control (IPC) licensing, but non-IPC industries continued to make up the bulk of industrial discharges to rivers.

Definite relationships between the intensification of agricultural activity and nutrient levels in rivers and lakes have been found, and it is clear that agriculture is a major source of nutrients entering Irish waters. With the phasing out in 1999 of sewage sludge disposal at sea, the main type of material dumped in Irish marine waters is that produced by dredging activity.

INTRODUCTION

This chapter deals with the sources and amounts of materials discharged to rivers, lakes, groundwaters, estuaries and the sea. The polluting effects of these discharges depend on their volume, chemical composition, temperature and clarity in relation to those of the receiving waters. All natural waters, including those not affected by human activities, contain a variety of substances, such as organic matter, nutrients, metal ions and other suspended and dissolved materials. This natural enrichment supports the normal aquatic communities adapted to life in inland waters, estuaries and marine waters. However, if waters receive inputs in excessive quantities, the capacity of the water to assimilate the inputs is exceeded and the natural state becomes distorted.

Such distortion may include extremes of oxygen supersaturation and

depletion in the water, resulting respectively from excess daytime photosynthesis and night-time respiration by plants. This process is caused by overabundant supplies of nutrients and is known as *eutrophication*. In addition to oxygen depletion by the direct microbial

breakdown of organic matter, eutrophication is one of the most familiar forms of pollution in Irish waters.

Other forms of water pollution, such as contamination by metals, synthetic organic chemicals and hydrocarbons, can cause destruction of aquatic life directly by their toxic effects. In contrast to nutrient and organic enrichment, however, these forms of pollution are of minor significance in Ireland, reflecting the low level of heavy industry.

An estimate of the loads of organic matter and the nutrients nitrogen (N) and phosphorus (P) entering surface waters in 1998, from all of the major point and diffuse sources, was recently undertaken. The results of this work, which was carried out for the purposes of a submission to the OSPAR Convention (EPA, 1999), form the basis for much of the content of this chapter. The estimates were based largely on recent OSPAR guidelines for quantifying nutrient inputs (OSPAR Commission, 1999).

The quality of the estimates varies, depending on the source of the discharges, and is best for *point sources*, i.e., those such as sewage and industrial treatment plants for which the location of the discharge (the outfall) is fixed and identifiable, thereby facilitating monitoring and control. *Diffuse sources*, on the other hand, are those for which no individual discharge location can be identified. Diffuse emissions are consequently impossible or impracticable to measure directly. On a broad scale, these include effluents from septic tanks in rural areas, the runoff and leaching of fertiliser, slurries and other agricultural wastes, drainage waters from forestry developments and worked peatlands, and leachate from landfills, mines and quarries. Natural or *background* loss from the land is a further diffuse input, as is the deposition of substances from the atmosphere. The solid wastes from intensive agriculture, sewage treatment and certain industrial activities are typically treated by land-spreading and may also be regarded as diffuse inputs to the environment.

In this chapter, the main categories of point and diffuse sources are considered in turn, after which an overall national estimate of the loads of organic matter and nutrients entering waters is given. The occurrence of accidental and unauthorised discharges to water, and the dumping of solid waste materials to the marine environment, are then described.

URBAN WASTE WATER

Urban waste water is domestic waste water or its mixture with industrial waste water and/or runoff rainwater. In general the waste water from these sources is collected and transferred to treatment plants before discharge into rivers, lakes, estuaries or coastal waters. The level of treatment before discharge varies from none to advanced treatment (Box 5.1).

Box 5.1 Treatment of Urban Waste Water

There is a wide range of methods available for the treatment of sewage before discharge. The levels of treatment may be summarised as follows:

None: No treatment; or just coarse screening to remove larger objects. The full organic matter and nutrient load enters the receiving waters.

Primary: The first stage in waste water treatment. Sedimentation tanks are used to remove material that settles, resulting in the removal of a substantial amount of suspended matter but little or no dissolved matter. Organic matter, as BOD (Box 5.2), is typically reduced by about 20 per cent, but loads of nutrients and other dissolved substances are largely unchanged.

Secondary: Generally, a level of treatment that produces removal efficiencies of 85 per cent for BOD and suspended solids. Also called biological treatment, it involves mixing waste water with air and sludge to encourage the growth of bacteria that consume organic matter. Some nutrients may be removed in the final settled sludge, but the majority is released, often in a more readily available form for uptake by plants and microbes. The volumes of sludge produced are also increased relative to primary treatment.

Tertiary: Waste water treatment beyond the secondary stage, usually focused on the removal of nutrients such as phosphorus or nitrogen. This is typically achieved by a mixture of chemical treatments and additional biological processes.

Around two-thirds of the population now lives in urban areas (Chapter 2). Towns with populations greater than 200 persons total 641, of which almost half are in the smallest size category of 200 to 499 persons (NESC, 1997). The total number of Local Authority sewerage schemes in the country is 856; of these, 635 serve areas having population equivalents (see Box 5.2) greater than 200, an increase of 16 since 1996. The remaining 221 schemes are generally small sewer systems serving housing developments on the outskirts of towns.

Estimates of the loads of organic matter and nutrients generated in the collection areas of sewerage schemes

Box 5.2 Population Equivalents

To take account of the total amount of organic waste entering sewer systems, including that from industry and trade, the total organic load is expressed in terms of *population equivalents (p.e.)*. One population equivalent is defined in the urban waste water treatment Directive (CEC, 1991a) as the organic biodegradable load having a biochemical oxygen demand (BOD) of 0.06 kg of oxygen per day. This same figure may be applied also to an organic load discharging directly to water. It provides a convenient means of categorising sewerage schemes by size, in terms of the overall organic waste load entering the sewerage systems.

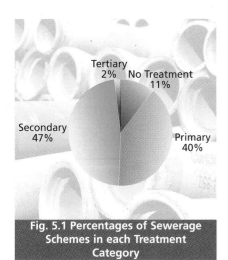

Fig. 5.1 Percentages of Sewerage Schemes in each Treatment Category

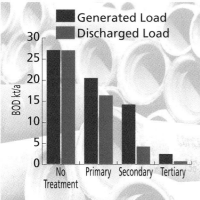

Fig. 5.2 Treatment Categories: Total BOD Loads (kt/annum) Generated and Discharged

were derived from population figures (CSO, 1997) and industrial licence limits (see *Industrial Waste Water* below). Discharged loads were estimated according to the level of treatment afforded before discharge. The percentages of schemes incorporating the various levels of treatment are shown in Figure 5.1, and the estimated waste loads generated and discharged in relation to each treatment category are shown in Figure 5.2. The *generated* BOD load is the overall load entering the sewerage schemes, whereas the proportion of this load *discharged* reflects the level of treatment. Nationally, the total annual generated BOD load is estimated to be 63.9 kt (thousand tonnes), whereas that discharged is 48.3 kt.

Figure 5.3 shows the percentages of sewerage schemes, and Figure 5.4 the proportion of the total BOD load,

discharging to rivers, lakes, estuaries and coastal waters. While 78 per cent of sewerage schemes discharge to fresh waters, these discharges make up only 15 per cent of the total discharged load.

Comparing the generated and discharged loads in Figure 5.4, it is clear that urban waste water discharging to inland waters receives

relatively advanced treatment, while the bulk of untreated and primary-treated waste water enters estuaries or coastal waters. This includes waste water from the major coastal cities and towns, including Dublin, Cork, Limerick, Galway, Waterford and Dundalk.

As mentioned above, urban waste water includes both domestic and

Fig. 5.3 Percentages of Sewer Systems Discharging to Rivers, Lakes, Estuaries and Coastal Waters

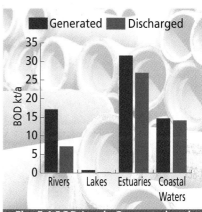

Fig. 5.4 BOD Loads Generated and Discharged to Rivers, Lakes, Estuaries and Coastal Waters

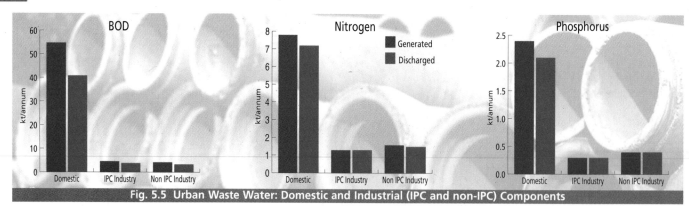

Fig. 5.5 Urban Waste Water: Domestic and Industrial (IPC and non-IPC) Components

industrial effluents. At a national level, the domestic contribution to the total urban waste water load is much larger than the industrial component (Figure 5.5).

Regulations made in 1994 transposing the EU Directive on urban waste water treatment (CEC, 1991a) into Irish law provide the framework for the construction and upgrading of collection (sewer) systems and treatment plants (O'Leary & Carty, 1998). The Regulations impose a schedule for the provision of collecting systems and treatment capacity based on the population equivalent of the urban area (the *agglomeration*) and the type of water body into which the treated waste water is discharged. Substantial investment is being made to meet these requirements (Chapter 14). The resulting increase in treatment capacity over the period 1994-2005 is shown in Figure 5.6.

INDUSTRIAL WASTE WATER

Up until 1993, licensing of industrial effluents was undertaken by the Local Authorities under the Water Pollution Act, 1977, and subsequent measures.

The Environmental Protection Agency Act, 1992, introduced the integrated pollution control (IPC) system, whereby the licensing function became a duty of the EPA for certain classes of industrial activity, while others remained within the remit of the local authorities. The IPC licence covers all emissions to air, water and sewer as well as solid waste. There were 311 IPC licences in force at the end of 1998, including 184 with consent to discharge to sewer and 83 with consent to discharge direct to waters. Local authority licences to discharge in force in 1998 numbered around 1020, of which two thirds were for discharges to sewer and the remainder for discharges to water.

The bulk of industrial waste waters produced in Ireland consists of readily biodegradable organic matter arising from food processing,

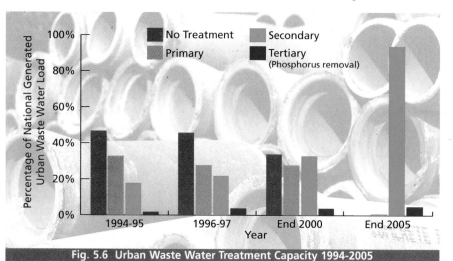

Fig. 5.6 Urban Waste Water Treatment Capacity 1994-2005

Percentage of national generated urban waste water load subject to each treatment level. Figures for 1994-95 from O'Leary *et al.*, 1997 and for 1996-97 from O'Leary and Carty, 1998. Figures for 2000 and 2005 are based on current p.e. loads and projected dates for completion of planned upgrading for the various waste water treatment plants (data supplied by the Department of Environment and Local Government and by the individual Local Authorities).

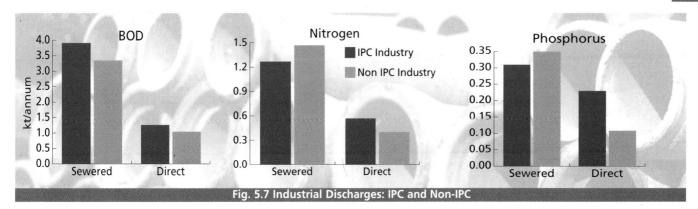

Fig. 5.7 Industrial Discharges: IPC and Non-IPC

brewing, textile manufacture and the pharmaceutical and fine chemicals sectors. Estimated annual loads of BOD and nutrients discharging to sewer and directly to waters, from IPC and non-IPC licensed industry, are shown in Figure 5.7. These estimates are based on the licensed emission limits for the individual companies (Box 5.3). The quantities of organic matter and nitrogen discharged to sewer are about three times the loads discharged directly to waters, both from IPC and non-IPC industries. The quantities of phosphorus discharged to sewer are also higher than those discharged directly, but the difference is not so great in the case of the IPC sector; this primarily reflects discharges to marine waters (Figure 5.8).

The direct industrial loads to fresh waters and to marine waters are approximately equal, around 1.15 kt BOD/annum. Two thirds of the direct industrial discharges to fresh waters originate from non-IPC licensed industries (Figure 5.8) while 75 per cent of the load discharged to estuarine and coastal waters originates from the IPC sector.

Box 5.3 Actual Emissions and Estimates based on Licence Limits

Continuous monitoring results for actual emissions are not available for all companies. Discharges were therefore estimated by assuming that, on average, a company's emissions amount to 25 per cent of the maximum load it is permitted to discharge under the terms of its license (OSPAR Commission, 1999). A recent compilation of monitoring data on actual emissions from 50 IPC companies has been examined to demonstrate whether this assumption is justified. The diagram below shows a comparison between the actual emissions and maximum licensed emissions of eight categories of material in the effluents from these companies.

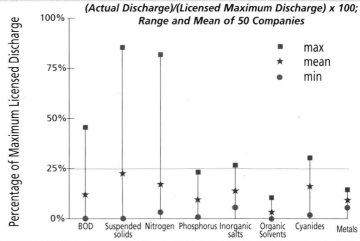

In all cases the average emission is less than 25 per cent of the licensed discharge, and for five of the eight substances nearly all companies discharged less than 25 per cent of their licensed limit. It is therefore apparent that load estimates made using the figure of 25 per cent of the maximum licensed emission provides a reasonable indication of actual loads discharged.

Other more persistent materials are also present in some industrial

effluents, though generally in much lower quantities. These include dissolved salts, inert particles, metals and synthetic organic substances such as solvents and chlorinated hydrocarbons.

Significant quantities of water are used for removing excess heat arising in power generation and in many industrial processes. The discharge of cooling water causes elevation of the ambient temperature of the receiving waters, and this must be limited in

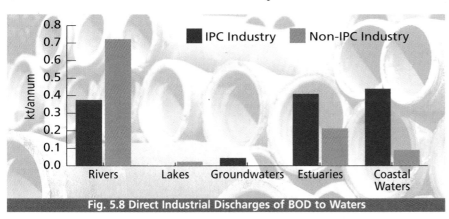

Fig. 5.8 Direct Industrial Discharges of BOD to Waters

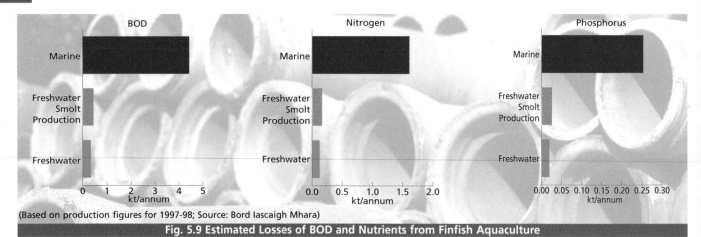

(Based on production figures for 1997-98; Source: Bord Iascaigh Mhara)

Fig. 5.9 Estimated Losses of BOD and Nutrients from Finfish Aquaculture

order to avoid harm to the resident biota or interference with the passage of migratory fish.

AQUACULTURE

The development of fin-fish aquaculture in Ireland was outlined in Chapter 3. Inputs to the aquatic environment associated with this industry include feedstuffs, chemotherapeutants and antifoulant agents. A certain portion of these materials is likely to be lost to the waters and sediments in the vicinity of the fish farm. Estimated annual loads of organic matter and nutrients entering freshwaters and marine waters from the fin-fish culture sector are shown in Figure 5.9. Licensed emissions of chemical treatments to freshwaters amount to less than 2 tonnes per annum, though the actual quantities used are known to be highly variable, and are likely to be significantly lower than permitted. Precise information on the usage of chemicals in the marine aquaculture sector is not currently available (Boelens *et al.*, 1999), though it is clear that fish farming represents a significant source of many substances in nearshore coastal waters.

RURAL DOMESTIC WASTEWATERS

In the absence of a connection to a sewer system, one of the most appropriate and cost-effective means

of treating rural domestic waste water involves the use of a properly located and constructed septic tank and percolation area. However, a recent study (Rodgers *et al.*, 1998) highlighted problems with some existing systems, which may potentially impact on the quality of local drinking water supplies (EPA, 1999). These include:
- ponding of percolation area;
- inadequate size of percolation area;
- lack of water tightness in construction;
- infrequent desludging of tank.

Guidelines for the proper siting, construction and maintenance of single house treatment systems will be published by the EPA in 2000. The implementation of these guidelines should lead to an improvement in the management of such waste waters over the next decade.

Because of the variable efficiency of septic tank performance, it is difficult to estimate accurately the quantities of organic matter and nutrients lost to waters from rural households. The figures given here are broad approximations for comparative purposes. The State's rural population in 1996 was 1.24 million persons. The organic waste load generated is estimated to be 28.6 kt BOD/annum; the actual load reaching waters is likely to be a small fraction of this figure, probably less than 5 per cent. Nitrogen and phosphorus loads to waters from this

source are estimated to be around 2.98 kt/annum N and 0.31 kt/annum P respectively.

AGRICULTURAL SOURCES

Agricultural inputs to surface waters include dirty water runoff from farmyards, slurry and silage leachate as well as washout of fertiliser and manures from the surface of the soil during heavy rain. Indirect inputs initially enter groundwaters via percolation through the soil and subsequently feed into rivers and lakes or directly to streams in overland flow. The most important indirect inputs to groundwaters are nitrates and microbes associated with organic matter.

Accidental spillages of silage effluent, manure liquors, milk and other fluids can have serious *acute* impacts on the receiving waters, often leading to fish kills and other damage. Major efforts are continuing to address the problems associated with the storage and management of these materials. *Chronic* impacts of agricultural activity on water quality relate to the continual inputs of nutrients originating in fertilisers and manures, leading to eutrophication of the receiving waters and increased levels of nitrate in groundwaters (see Chapter 9).

Fertiliser use in Ireland rose steadily in the twenty years up to 1980.

Since then, the usage of phosphorus (P) and potassium (K) has begun to level off or show a slight fall, though sales of nitrogen (N) have continued increasing (Chapter 3). Current annual application levels are 432 kt N (0.103 tonnes N/ha utilised land) and 50 kt P (0.014 tonnes P/ha), which are considered to be relatively low in relation to other European countries (Sherwood, 1998).

It is considered that appropriate fertiliser application in favourable weather conditions leads to minimal direct losses to water. However, nitrate leaches easily from soils into surface water and groundwaters. Phosphorus is rapidly immobilised by binding to soil particles, although recent work has indicated that higher soil P levels lead to greater losses to water, and that phosphorus applied to soils that are waterlogged or already close to full saturation with phosphorus is particularly susceptible to washout (Tunney *et al.*, 2000). Therefore, spreading of chemical fertilisers either in excessive quantities or in wet weather represents a major potential source of nutrients.

The main input from agriculture, however, is likely to be in the form of nutrients contained in animal manures and other by-products. The organic load and nutrient content generated in the form of animal manures and silage effluent in 1998 are shown in Table 5.1. Almost two-thirds of manures are excreted directly onto the ground by grazing livestock, and much of the nutrient content is probably taken up in plant growth, though there may be some loss to water. The remainder, equivalent to 725 kt of BOD, is largely produced by animals housed over the winter period, but includes all of the slurries produced in intensive pig and poultry production, which is coming increasingly under the IPC licensing system. This must be collected, stored and disposed of by landspreading in suitable weather conditions. Silage production is

Table 5.1 Organic Matter (BOD), Nitrogen and Phosphorus in Animal Waste and Silage (kt/annum)						
	BOD		Nitrogen		Phosphorus	
	Deposited	Managed	Deposited	Managed	Deposited	Managed
Cattle	1009	631	297	185	46	29
Sheep	132	6	79	3	12	1
Horses	6	6	2	2	0.3	0.3
Pigs	0	66	0	12	0	4
Poultry	0	16	0	12	0	3
Total Manures	1147	725	378	214	58	37
Silage Effluent	0	174	0	5	0	1
Total	1147	899	378	219	58	38

Note: Animal wastes include quantities deposited by grazing animals and by housed animals ("managed").

Source: EPA

currently of the order of 30 million tonnes per annum, and produces around 2.7 million tonnes of organically rich silage effluent, which also requires disposal by landspreading.

Manures and slurries represent an important recyclable resource but, because of the large volumes produced, it is difficult to manage these fluids without some loss to neighbouring watercourses. Runoff occurring as a consequence of landspreading of manures and silage effluent is thought to be the main potential pathway for aquatic enrichment associated with agriculture. It should be noted that sludges produced during the treatment of sewage and certain industrial effluents are also managed by landspreading, and similar concerns apply in relation to the management of these materials (Chapter 6).

A recent national approximation of agricultural nutrient loss, based on national figures for fertiliser usage and animal manures generated along with very approximate loss coefficients derived from various national and European sources, estimated that some 103 kt of nitrogen and 4.6 kt of phosphorus are lost by leaching and overland flow to surface and groundwaters annually (EPA, 1999). These figures represent around a quarter of the nitrogen and 8 per cent of the phosphorus applied as fertilisers at 1998 levels.

There is considerable uncertainty about the proportions of nutrients that leach into waters because of the numerous climatic and geographic influences controlling nutrient loss. These load estimates are therefore indicative only, and are subject to considerable error. Nevertheless, definitive relationships have been established between agriculture and nutrient levels in surface waters. For example, a direct relationship was found between river nitrate and the

percentage of land area ploughed in a river catchment (Neill, 1989). A continual increase in nitrate concentrations has been observed in the rivers of the south-east over the last two decades (Chapter 9).

FORESTRY AND PEATLAND

Although some runoff occurs naturally though seepage from natural forests and peatland, the worked lands are the most important sources, relative to the land area, of particulates, nutrients and other materials entering water. Fertilisers and pesticides applied to forestry may be leached to waters, and in upland areas forestry may constitute a major source of these substances. There is little precise information available on current loss rates, though a recent approximation (EPA, 1999) suggested that around 410 tonnes N and 25 tonnes P annually were lost to waters from plantation forestry.

Actively worked peatlands are also a source of suspended solids and nutrients. Peat milling operations in the Brosna River Catchment, part of the Shannon system, accounted for around 8 per cent of the total phosphorus load entering the river (Kirk McClure Morton, 1999).

Based on the area of land under the various types of forestry and the

distribution of worked and natural peatlands, along with indicative figures on nutrient leaching rates from these land types, annual inputs to water from these sources are broadly estimated to be around 2.61 kt N and 0.22 kt P.

ATMOSPHERIC INPUTS

Waters receive inputs of a range of airborne substances, directly and indirectly. These are mainly inert particles, but include sulphurous and nitrogenous compounds, which may contribute to the acidification of poorly buffered lakes (See Chapter 9). Certain metals, including mercury, cadmium, copper, arsenic, zinc and lead, as well as hydrocarbons and synthetic organic chemicals (PCBs and dioxins), may be deposited onto land and water.

Atmospheric nitrogen deposition to waters is the main external input into the open ocean and it may contribute up to 50 per cent of the total external supply into shelf waters (Paerl & Whitehall, 1999). It also contributes to the N load entering inland lakes, and may be the major input in upland areas. Recent modelling data from the European Monitoring and Evaluation Programme (EMEP/MSC-W, 1996) indicate net deposition of around 20 kt/annum

nitrogen onto the land surface of Ireland. Phosphorus in particulate form is also deposited from the atmosphere, at a rate estimated at around 1.5 kt/annum (Boelens *et al.*, 1999). However, due to the low intensity of these inputs it is likely that the portions lost to waters are extremely small.

NATURAL OR BACKGROUND LOSSES

Organic materials, nutrients, metals, salts and other substances are continually leached from the soil and dissolved out of rock, so that, as noted earlier, natural waters unaffected by human activities are nevertheless not chemically pure. Natural background levels of these substances in waters are determined largely by the geologic characteristics of the catchment as well as variations in rainfall and atmospheric deposition of organic materials.

Because low-level inputs of organic matter are rapidly degraded by microbial activity, an accurate assessment of natural levels of organic matter leaching is extremely difficult to achieve. Nutrients entering waters are more persistent, though they may be recycled through various inorganic and organic forms. A recent approximation of background nutrient loss to freshwaters (EPA, 1999) estimated N and P loads at 5.36 kt N/annum and 0.36 kt P/annum.

Levels of metals discharged by major rivers measured by the EPA during the period 1990-1996 were generally low, and were consistent with expected background loads resulting from physical weathering of soils. Higher loads were detected in several rivers whose catchments contain active or historical mining areas, notably the Avoca River (Lucey *et al.*, 1999).

A number of other chemicals can be found in waters remote from significant urbanisation and

industrialisation, including several synthetic organic chemicals. These cannot be naturally occurring, but instead reflect the global distribution of contaminants in the atmosphere, which has resulted from their widespread use over many decades. Although some, such as the chlorinated hydrocarbon pesticides (DDT and its analogues), are no longer in use in most parts of the world, they are extremely resistant to degradation, and will continue to persist in the environment indefinitely.

TOTAL DISCHARGES TO WATERS FROM POINT AND DIFFUSE SOURCES

Estimates of the annual loads of organic matter (BOD) and nutrients generated in each of the major quantifiable source categories have been detailed above. Based on these estimates, a breakdown of the loads discharged to waters from each source category is presented in Figure 5.10.

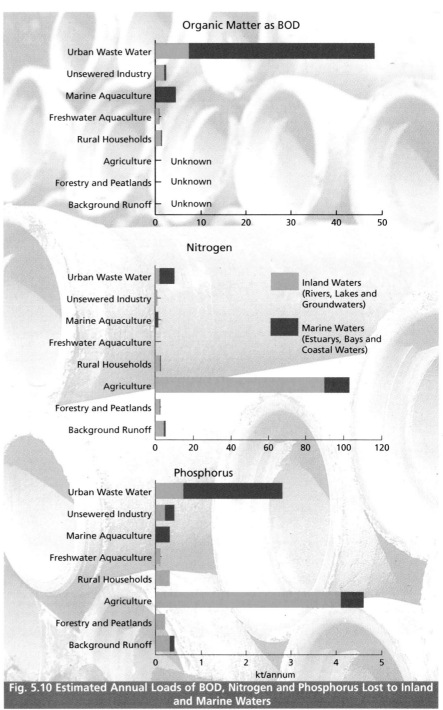

Fig. 5.10 Estimated Annual Loads of BOD, Nitrogen and Phosphorus Lost to Inland and Marine Waters

If it is assumed that the estimates are reasonable, then it is apparent that the loads of nitrogen entering waters from agricultural activities (82 per cent of the total) far outweigh all those from other sources, including urban waste water. Agriculture is also the main potential source of phosphorus, contributing three-quarters of the P load to rivers and lakes compared to just over 10 per cent arising from urban waste water.

Agricultural inputs probably comprise the largest source of organic matter also, but the organic matter load reaching waters from most diffuse sources is impossible to estimate directly, and no attempt to do so has been made. The main quantifiable source of organic matter is urban waste water, which is around twenty times as large as the directly discharged industrial load.

The marine aquaculture industry contributes 23 per cent of the quantifiable organic matter load discharging into open coastal waters (i.e., excluding export via rivers and estuaries), and almost 60 per cent of the load to the open coastal waters of the western seaboard, where this industry is largely concentrated.

RIVERINE NUTRIENT INPUTS TO ESTUARINE AND COASTAL WATERS

For the purpose of estimating the loads of nutrients, metals and other contaminants in rivers discharging into tidal waters, these substances have been monitored annually above the tidal limits of major rivers since 1990. Based on the results of this monitoring and records of river flows, the annual 'riverine input' loads are estimated and reported to the OSPAR Commission. Nineteen rivers, which drain approximately 60 per cent of the total land area, are included in this programme. The Shannon, Munster Blackwater and Suir carry the largest nutrient loads. When the catchment areas of the rivers are taken into

account, however, the highest export rates (i.e., load per unit area) of nitrogen are from the Bandon, Avoca and Slaney rivers. The highest phosphorus export rates are from the Maigue and Deel rivers in County Limerick. With the exception of the Avoca, in which the high nitrogen load primarily reflects an industrial emission, these high export rates are generally a consequence of intensive agricultural activity in the catchments.

The results of the riverine inputs study provide a broad indication of the quality and precision of the estimated loads described earlier in this chapter. Estimated and measured annual nutrient loads of nitrogen and phosphorus for the period 1995-1997 are shown in Figures 5.11 and 5.12. At a national level, the estimated nitrogen load from the major rivers is

72 per cent of the measured load, while the phosphorus estimate is closer to the measured figure (93 per cent). Figure 5.11 indicates that diffuse nitrogen loss rates are greater in the catchments of the eastern and south-eastern rivers than those occurring in other parts of the country. The phosphorus figures are reasonably close at a national level, though the phosphorus load from the Munster Blackwater in 1995-1997 was much higher than that predicted based on identifiable sources, reflecting the effect of flood events (Lucey et al., 1999). Excluding this river, the overall estimated and measured phosphorus loads were quite close to each other.

The loads discharged to tidal waters by the major rivers are affected by the differing geological composition, land

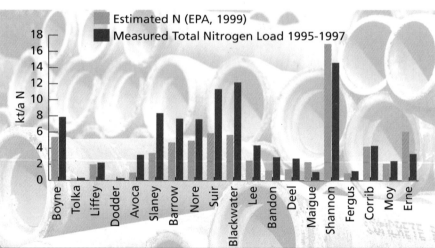

Fig. 5.11 Estimated and Measured Average Annual Loads of Nitrogen Exported by the Major Rivers

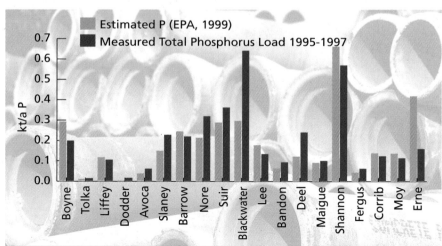

Fig. 5.12 Estimated and Measured Average Annual Loads of Phosphorus Exported by the Major Rivers

Department of Marine and Natural Resources under the Dumping at Sea Acts 1981 and 1996. Solid materials that have been dumped at sea include dredge spoil, inert geological material, sewage and chemical sludges, fish processing waste and man-made structures such as decommissioned vessels. However, in line with agreements reached under the OSPAR Convention, the dumping of industrial sludges ceased in 1994, and sewage sludge disposal at sea was discontinued in September 1999 under the terms of the EU urban waste water treatment Directive (CEC, 1991a).

The disposal of dredged material continues, subject to stringent controls on the quantities and composition of the material. Capital dredging (i.e., dredging for harbour development or other major engineering works) produces relatively large volumes of spoil, in essentially one-off events, whereas maintenance dredging produces smaller quantities of material, usually every few years. The latter, however, may contain significant amounts of contaminants resulting from harbour activity.

The quantities of materials dumped in Irish waters over the period 1987 to 1996 are presented in Table 5.2, and dumping sites are shown in

use and urbanisation in their catchments. There are also fluctuations from year to year, largely reflecting variations in rainfall and climate. Given the variability of the measured loads, there is a reasonable degree of correspondence between the estimated and measured loads at a national level. In turn, this suggests that the estimates provide a reasonable indication of the current magnitudes of discharges and the relative importance of the different sources of organic matter and nutrient inputs to Irish waters.

ACCIDENTAL AND UNAUTHORISED DISCHARGES

Accidental or unauthorised releases may occur from various sources and sectors, and range from uncontrolled farmyard runoff to major oil spillages. Structural failures or breaches of silage and slurry storage tanks are among the causes of fish kills in rivers, which are discussed in Chapter 9. Continual leaching from such tanks, due either to inadequate capacity or to poor construction, undoubtedly contributes to the slight and moderate pollution of rivers (Chapter 9). For instance, a recent study of selected regions of the River Shannon catchment found that up to

70 per cent of farms currently have inadequate slurry storage facilities (Kirk McClure Morton, 1999). Causes of accidental spillages from industry include breakdowns of control equipment, pumps and monitoring systems, ruptured pipelines and human error. Most accidental or unauthorised discharges tend to be minor, but serious pollution events occur from time to time (see Chapters 7 and 10).

MARINE DUMPING AND WASTE DISPOSAL

The dumping of waste material at sea is subject to licensing by the

Table 5.2 Quantities of Material Dumped in Irish Marine Waters 1987-1996 (wet tonnes)			
Year	Dredge material	Sewage sludge (3% solids)	Industrial sludge (5% solids)
1987	208,489	234,320	639,330
1988	425,639	243,000	533,703
1989	1,610,159	347,636	458,210
1990	1,103,565	288,200	4,740
1991	1,230,552	339,890	348,971
1992	493,927	380,397	111,692
1993	829,470	312,640	77,847
1994	937,905	336,346	0
1995	620,267	332,025	0
1996	1,388,734	391,933	0

(Boelens *et al.*, 1999)

presented in Chapters 9 and 10, which describe the quality of inland waters (rivers, lakes and groundwaters) and tidal waters respectively.

A number of important developments are currently taking place designed to address the potential for eutrophication and other forms of pollution in Irish waters caused by point and diffuse sources of discharge. These include the following:

- the implementation of national regulations for the control of phosphorus;
- the implementation of the EU urban waste water treatment and nitrates Directives;
- the incremental expansion of IPC licensing;
- the implementation of catchment monitoring and management systems;
- the establishment of nutrient management planning in agriculture.

These are considered further in Part V of this report. The proposed EU Framework Directive on water policy is expected to be a further significant development.

The EU Directive on dangerous substances (CEC, 1976) is aimed at the reduction and elimination of discharges of various potentially hazardous or toxic contaminants. A number of other directives, along with national legislation and international conventions, are in place which provide a framework within which the objectives of reducing and eliminating such discharges are being addressed.

Herbicides, pesticides and therapeutant agents enter the environment through their use in agriculture, aquaculture and in private gardening. There is an onus on the user to avoid excessive use, and on the regulatory authorities to monitor any effects of these compounds on aquatic biota.

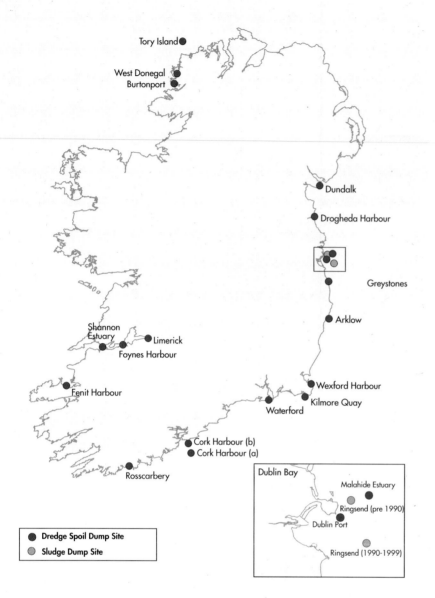

Fig. 5.13 Locations of solid waste disposal sites around the coast (Boelens et al., 1999)

Figure 5.13 (Boelens *et al.*, 1999). Nationally, the amounts of dredge spoil dumped in the period 1987-1996 range between 0.21 million and 1.61 million tonnes, while sewage sludge ranged between 0.23 million and 0.39 million tonnes. As indicated by analytical characterisation of materials dumped in 1996, dredge spoil discharged in Ireland is typically composed largely of inert material, with a total metals content of around 0.02 per cent. Monitoring of the effects of these discharges on the receiving waters and sediments is reviewed in Chapter 10.

CONCLUSIONS

This chapter has focused on the various sources of materials discharged to water. The quantities discharged have been estimated wherever possible; although the precision of the estimates varies, it is evident that the most important sources of organic matter and nutrients are agricultural runoff and urban waste water discharges. As noted earlier, such discharges are of concern primarily in relation to oxygen depletion and eutrophication in surface waters. Regular monitoring of waters is carried out to assess the impacts of discharges. The results of this monitoring are

Improved information systems are needed in order to achieve improved co-ordination and availability of information on discharges to waters. The Environmental Protection Agency has initiated work in this regard, which was ongoing at the time of the preparation of the present report.

REFERENCES

Boelens, R.G.V., Maloney, D.M., Parsons, A.P. and Walsh, A.R., 1999. *Ireland's Marine and Coastal Areas and Adjacent Seas: an Environmental Assessment.* Prepared by the Marine Institute on behalf of the Department of Environment & Local Government and the Department of Marine & Natural Resources. Marine Institute, Dublin.

CEC (Council of the European Communities), 1976. Council Directive of 4 May 1976 on pollution caused by certain dangerous substances discharged into the aquatic environment of the Community (76/464/EEC). *Official Journal of the European Communities* No L 129, Brussels.

CEC (Council of the European Communities), 1991a. Council Directive of 21 May 1991 concerning urban waste water treatment (91/271/EEC). *Official Journal of the European Communities* No L 135/40, Brussels.

CEC (Council of the European Communities), 1991b. Council Directive of 12 December 1991 concerning the protection of waters against pollution caused by nitrates from agricultural sources (91/676/EEC). *Official Journal of the European Communities* No L 375/1, Brussels.

CSO (Central Statistics Office), 1997. *Census 96 Volume 1: Population Classified by Area.* Stationery Office, Dublin.

EMEP/MSC-W, 1996. *Transboundary Air Pollution in Europe Part 2: Numerical Addendum.* Barrett, K., Berge, E., (eds), Det Norske Meteorologiske Institutt.

EPA (Environmental Protection Agency), 1999. *Screening Procedure for Irish Coastal Waters with regard to Eutrophication.* Final report to OSPAR on the outcome of the Screening Procedure, 8 September 1999. Dublin.

Lucey, J., Bowman, J.J., Clabby, K.J., Cunningham, P., Lehane, M., MacCarthaigh, M.L., McGarrigle, M.L. and Toner, P.F., 1999. *Water Quality in Ireland 1995-1997.* Environmental Protection Agency, Wexford.

Kirk McClure Morton, 1999. *Lough Ree and Lough Derg Catchment Monitoring and Management System: Management Proposals.* Shannon Lakes Project, July 1999.

MacCarthaigh, M., 1999. *Surface Waters in Ireland.* A paper presented to the Institution of Engineers of Ireland. Environmental Protection Agency, Dublin.

Neill, M., 1989. Nitrate concentrations in river waters in the south-east of Ireland and their relationships with agricultural practice. *Water Research* **23**, 1339 1355.

NESC (National Economic and Social Council), 1997. *Report No. 102: Population Distribution and Economic Development: Trends and Policy Implications.* Dublin.

North Sea Task Force, 1993. *North Sea Quality Status Report 1993.* Oslo and Paris Commissions, London. Olsen & Olsen, Fredensborg, Denmark.

O' Leary, G., Meaney, B. and Carty, G., 1997. *Urban Waste Water Discharges in Ireland. A report for the years 1994 and 1995.* Environmental Protection Agency, Wexford.

O' Leary, G. and Carty, G., 1998. *Urban Waste Water Discharges in Ireland. A report for the years 1996 and 1997.* Environmental Protection Agency, Wexford.

OSPAR Commission, 1999. *Harmonised Quantification and Reporting Procedures for Nutrients (HARP-NUT).* Presented by Norway to the October 1999 Meeting of the Working Group on Nutrients and Eutrophication (NEUT), Oslo and Paris Commission, London.

Paerl, H.W. and Whitehall, D.R., 1999. Anthropogenically-derived Atmospheric Nitrogen Deposition, Marine Eutrophication and Harmful Algal Bloom Expansion: Is There a Link? *Ambio,* **28**, No 4, June 1999.

Rodgers, M., Mulqueen, J., Gallagher, B., Faherty, G., Carty, G., O'Leary, G., Waldron, E. and Fehily, B., 1998. *Small Scale Wastewater Treatment Systems.* Synthesis Report, Environmental Protection Agency, Wexford.

Sherwood, M., 1998. *Impact of Agricultural Pollution on Water Systems: Ireland.* Paper Presented at Euraqua Technical Review Meeting, Oslo, 1998.

Tunney, H., Coulter, B., Daly, K., Kurz, I., Coxon, C., Jeffrey, D., Mills, P., Kiely, G. and Morgan, G., 2000. *Quantification of Phosphorus Loss from Soil to Water.* Report to the Environmental Protection Agency, Wexford.

CHAPTER 6

WASTE

Waste Management remains one of the most challenging areas of modern environmental management. The latest figures show clearly that waste quantities are continuing to grow in Ireland. Almost 80 million tonnes of waste were generated in 1998, of which over 64.5 million tonnes originated from agricultural sources, mainly animal manures. Over two million tonnes of municipal waste were generated in the same year. A comparison of waste collected by or on behalf of local authorities between 1984 and 1998 indicates an increase of over 100 per cent in 14 years. Between 1995 and 1998 there was a 47 per cent increase in the amount of industrial waste generated, from 6.2 million tonnes to 9.1 million tonnes. Hazardous waste also shows an increase of 13 per cent between 1996 and 1998. The amount of construction and demolition waste in 1998 was estimated at 2.7 million tonnes. Given the unprecedented level of construction activity in Ireland in the past five years and the likelihood that this activity will continue, amounts of this waste can be expected to continue to grow.

Landfill remains the principal waste disposal route in Ireland with 91 per cent of municipal waste generated in Ireland landfilled in 1998. The overall recovery rate for packaging waste in 1998 was 14.8 per cent and Ireland still has considerable progress to make if it is to meet the international targets set for 2001 and 2005. There has been improved recovery of industrial wastes from 12.4 per cent in 1995 to 26.6 per cent in 1998 and an increase in overall recovery within the manufacturing sector from 30 per cent in 1995 to 51.4 per cent in 1998.

INTRODUCTION

There have been major developments affecting the waste sector since the last State of the Environment report was published. These developments include the enactment of the Waste Management Act, 1996 and the publication of the following: the National Sustainable Development Strategy (DoE, 1997), a National Waste Policy Statement 'Changing Our Ways' (DELG, 1998), a proposed National Hazardous Waste Management Plan (EPA, 1999) and standards and guidance on many aspects of landfilling. Other developments include the development of the National Waste Database (EPA, 1996), the introduction of waste licensing, and the preparation of waste management strategies and plans for both hazardous and non-hazardous wastes.

Considerably more is known about waste management in Ireland now than was known in 1996. The scarcity of reliable, complete and up-to-date data on waste was identified as a key problem at that time. Two comprehensive surveys have since been conducted by the EPA, with national level information now available for 1995 and 1998. The waste information deficit has, therefore, largely been addressed. The challenge now is to maintain and improve the current system of data collection and reporting to facilitate better management of waste, at local, regional and national level and realistic planning for waste prevention and minimisation.

Recent Government policy on waste, as set out in *Changing Our Ways*, reaffirms the principle that waste management is firmly grounded in the waste hierarchy, with prevention and minimisation as the most favoured options and disposal as the least favoured option. It also recognises the distance to be travelled between the aspirations inherent in the waste hierarchy and the present-

day realities of increasing quantities of waste being generated and continued reliance on landfill. The Government has set clear targets for the future in relation to waste (see Box 6.1), aimed at stabilisation of waste generation, reduced dependency on landfill and increased recovery rates.

The policy emphasises the key role to be played by the local authorities in changing Irish waste management practice particularly in relation to wastes traditionally collected or accepted by them from households, commercial and industrial sources. Other key considerations are the implementation of the polluter pays principle and recognition of the importance of economies of scale when planning for waste infrastructure.

> **Box 6.1 Targets Set in *Changing Our Ways* (DELG, 1998)**
>
> - Diversion of 50 per cent of overall household waste away from landfill.
> - A minimum of 65 per cent reduction in biodegradable waste going to landfill.
> - The development of waste recovery facilities employing environmentally beneficial technologies.
> - Recycling of 35 per cent of municipal waste.
> - Recycling of at least 50 per cent of construction and demolition waste within a five year period, with a progressive increase to at least 85 per cent over 15 years.
> - Reduction in the number of landfills.
> - An 80 per cent reduction in methane emissions from landfill.

LEGISLATION

Ireland's waste legislation has undergone radical reform in the past five years, with the enactment of the Waste Management Act, 1996. A principal objective of the Act is to provide a legal framework to ensure that the holding, transportation,

recovery and disposal of waste do not cause environmental pollution. Producer responsibility is also at the heart of the legislation and the Act provides the Minister for the Environment and Local Government with significant powers in relation to the placing of responsibilities on waste producers.

Under the Waste Management Act local authorities can, where necessary, control how household and commercial waste is presented for collection. The Act also provides for comprehensive control of the collection and movement of waste both within the State and into and out of the State. Local authorities are responsible for regulating all aspects of collection and movement with the one exception of the importation of waste into Ireland, which is regulated by the EPA. All movements of hazardous waste within the State are regulated by local authorities, by means of a tracking system of documentation to be completed by the producer, transporter and receiver of the waste.

A permit system for waste collection has also been provided for and will require persons, other than local authorities, engaged in the business of collection of waste, to hold a waste collection permit granted by the local authority in whose area the waste is collected.

The final link in the waste chain is what happens to the waste at its final destination. The Act requires that all significant waste disposal and recovery activities be licensed by the EPA. This is discussed later in the chapter.

WASTE PLANNING

The Waste Management Act, 1996, also brought about radical changes to waste planning in Ireland. Waste planning is now focussed on waste prevention, minimisation, recovery, safe disposal of non-recoverable waste

without causing environmental pollution, making the polluter pay, and public consultation.

Local authorities are responsible for the preparation and implementation of waste management plans for all non-hazardous waste produced in their areas including agricultural waste and sludges. In general, local authorities are working together and the trend in the past two years has been to carry out regional waste management strategy studies. These studies provide information for the waste management plans, which, following public consultation, have to be adopted by each local authority. The making, review, variation or replacement of waste management plans is a reserved function. While waste management planning can provide the framework for improved waste management, the approach will only work if it is dynamic and targets and objectives set out in the plan are reviewed regularly.

In 1999, the EPA published a proposed National Hazardous Waste Management Plan (EPA, 1999). The plan will be published later this year. Local authorities must have regard to the recommendations made by the EPA and must take into account the requirements for managing hazardous waste in their waste management plans. Both sets of plans are to be reviewed every five years or earlier.

PRIORITY ISSUES

As Ireland moves into the new millennium, progress must be made in reversing the current trend of increasing quantities of waste, and to break the link between economic growth and waste production. The priority waste management issues are to establish adequate collection, recovery and disposal infrastructures, staffed by properly trained and competent staff, so that waste management is conducted in a responsible and environmentally sensitive manner.

OVERVIEW OF WASTE GENERATION

It is estimated that 80 million tonnes of waste were generated in Ireland in 1998. Of this over 64.5 million tonnes originated from agricultural sources, mainly animal manures. The municipal and industrial sectors are estimated to have produced over 15 million tonnes (Fig. 6.1 and Table 6.1). The increase in quantities of agricultural waste is partly a result of changes in the method of calculation. For example, dirty water washings from the dairy sector are included and it is assumed that cattle are kept indoors for a four-month period as opposed to a three-month period, which increases the amounts of cattle manure and slurry considerably. The increase in other waste types is due in

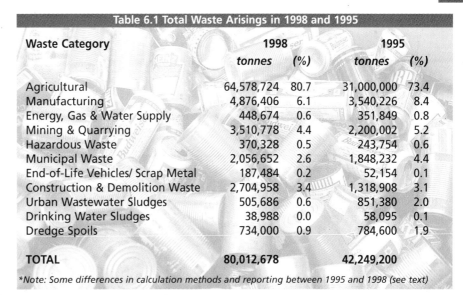

Waste Category	1998		1995	
	tonnes	*(%)*	*tonnes*	*(%)*
Agricultural	64,578,724	80.7	31,000,000	73.4
Manufacturing	4,876,406	6.1	3,540,226	8.4
Energy, Gas & Water Supply	448,674	0.6	351,849	0.8
Mining & Quarrying	3,510,778	4.4	2,200,002	5.2
Hazardous Waste	370,328	0.5	243,754	0.6
Municipal Waste	2,056,652	2.6	1,848,232	4.4
End-of-Life Vehicles/ Scrap Metal	187,484	0.2	52,154	0.1
Construction & Demolition Waste	2,704,958	3.4	1,318,908	3.1
Urban Wastewater Sludges	505,686	0.6	851,380	2.0
Drinking Water Sludges	38,988	0.0	58,095	0.1
Dredge Spoils	734,000	0.9	784,600	1.9
TOTAL	**80,012,678**		**42,249,200**	

Table 6.1 Total Waste Arisings in 1998 and 1995

Note: Some differences in calculation methods and reporting between 1995 and 1998 (see text)

part to improved reporting by local authorities and industry. However, based on specific waste streams, where historical data are considered to be reasonably reliable, waste quantities appear to be increasing more or less in line with economic growth.

MUNICIPAL WASTE

Amounts Arising and Trends

It is estimated that over two million tonnes of municipal waste were generated in Ireland in 1998. This consisted of approximately 1.22 million tonnes of household waste, 0.755 million tonnes of commercial waste and 81,000 tonnes of street cleansing waste. This is an increase of 11.3 per cent on the 1995 estimate of 1.85 million tonnes of municipal waste generated (1.32 million tonnes from households, 0.48 million tonnes from commercial sector and 47,000 tonnes of street cleansing wastes). Not all of the population is served by a waste collection service; a comparison of waste collected by or on behalf of local authorities between 1984 and 1998 indicates an increase of 100 per cent in 14 years (Fig. 6.2).

The composition of both household and commercial waste landfilled by local authorities for 1998 is illustrated in Figure 6.3. As can be seen, there is

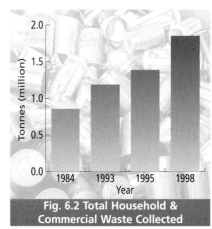

Fig. 6.2 Total Household & Commercial Waste Collected

a significant difference between the compositions of household waste and commercial waste, particularly in the paper and organic waste fractions.

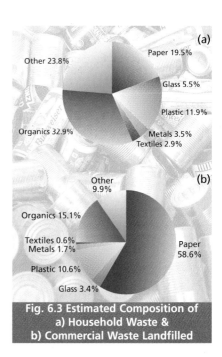

(a)
Other 23.8%
Paper 19.5%
Glass 5.5%
Plastic 11.9%
Metals 3.5%
Textiles 2.9%
Organics 32.9%

(b)
Other 9.9%
Organics 15.1%
Textiles 0.6%
Metals 1.7%
Plastic 10.6%
Glass 3.4%
Paper 58.6%

Fig. 6.3 Estimated Composition of a) Household Waste & b) Commercial Waste Landfilled

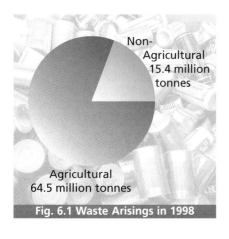

Non-Agricultural 15.4 million tonnes

Agricultural 64.5 million tonnes

Fig. 6.1 Waste Arisings in 1998

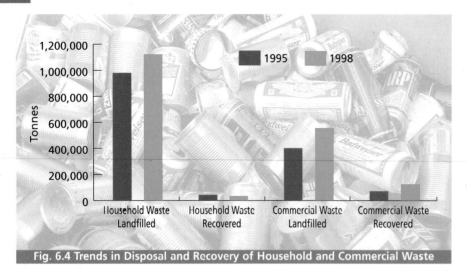

Fig. 6.4 Trends in Disposal and Recovery of Household and Commercial Waste

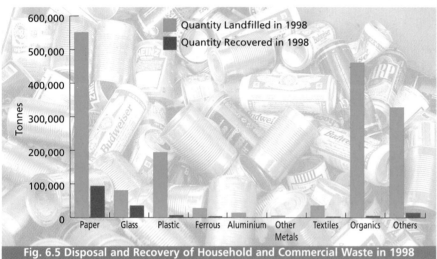

Fig. 6.5 Disposal and Recovery of Household and Commercial Waste in 1998

Note: 'Others Recovered' consists of wooden pallets and batteries

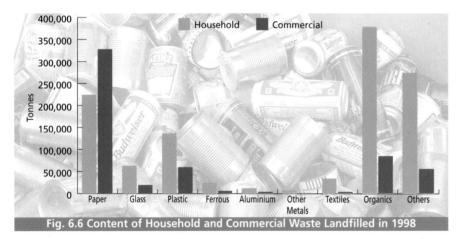

Fig. 6.6 Content of Household and Commercial Waste Landfilled in 1998

Note: 'Others' mainly consists of composites, fine elements such as ash, unclassified incombustibles and unclassified combustibles including wood waste

Disposal/Recovery Routes

The primary route for the disposal of household and commercial waste in Ireland is landfill. At present, Ireland, unlike the majority of its European neighbours, has no incineration capacity for such waste. In the absence of incineration, landfill will continue to be the primary disposal route for household and commercial waste, despite the fact that EU policy considers landfill to be the least desirable waste management practice.

Of the 1.85 million tonnes of household and commercial waste collected in Ireland in 1998, 91.0 per cent was consigned to landfill with 9.0 per cent recovered for recycling. Recent trends in the disposal and recovery of household and commercial waste are illustrated in Figure 6.4. A more detailed breakdown of the waste types landfilled and recovered in 1998 is given in Fig. 6.5 and 6.6.

The overall recovery rate for household and commercial waste increased from 7.8 per cent in 1995 to 9.0 per cent in 1998. However, the recovery rate for the household waste fraction decreased from 4.3 per cent to 3.2 per cent over that period. This is mainly due to a decrease in the collection of paper waste from households. In contrast, recovery of glass from households has improved considerably, from 7,900 tonnes in 1995 to 14,100 tonnes in 1998. There has also been increased recovery of batteries.

Considerable effort has been expended in providing infrastructure for improved waste recovery through the 1994-1999 Operational Programme for Environmental Services (DoE, 1994). However, material waste recycling is a volatile and uncertain business and is particularly sensitive to the ebb and flow of the market place.

PACKAGING WASTE

Amounts Arising and Trends

The Directive on packaging and packaging waste (94/62/EC) imposes targets for the recovery and recycling of packaging waste (glass bottles, tin cans, aluminium containers, paper, etc.) throughout the European Community. Targets are to be achieved through a mixture of recovery, including energy recovery, and recycling. However, 25 to 45 per cent of packaging waste has to be recycled, with a minimum of 15 per cent for each material. The target set for Ireland is 25 per cent recovery by 2001 and 50-65 per cent recovery by 2005. Owing to the absence of municipal waste incineration capacity in Ireland these targets have to be met by recycling alone. The Directive also establishes that Member States must take the necessary steps to set up return, collection and recovery systems so that the targets set by the Directive can be met. Total packaging waste arisings in Ireland for 1998 were estimated at more than 680,000 tonnes (Fig 6.7).

Disposal and Recovery

Figures 6.8 and 6.9 provide a summary of disposal and recovery rates for different packaging materials in the household and commercial waste stream and in the total waste stream in Ireland in 1998. In the household waste stream the recovery rate is estimated to be 5.6 per cent while in the commercial waste stream is it estimated to be 21.0 per cent. The principal disposal route is landfill while recovery routes tend to be material dependent. However, the recovery industry in Ireland consists of a relatively small number of players with the bulk of paper recovery and glass recovery, for example, handled by single companies.

Recovery rates achieved to date, together with the targets required by the Directive, are illustrated in Figure 6.10. The overall recovery rate for packaging waste in 1998 is 14.8 per cent which suggests that Ireland has considerable progress to make if it is to meet the targets set for 2001 and 2005.

The Packaging Regulations introduced in 1997 imposed producer responsibility obligations on all producers of packaging. While all

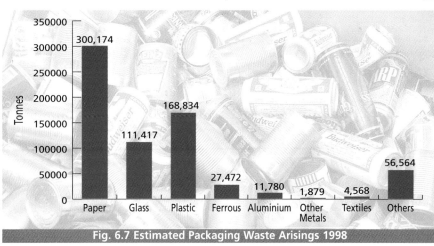
Fig. 6.7 Estimated Packaging Waste Arisings 1998

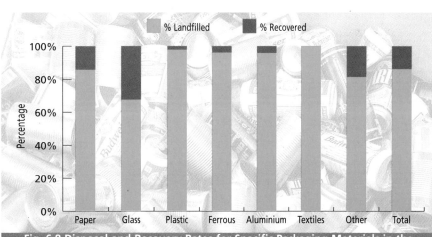
Fig. 6.8 Disposal and Recovery Rates for Specific Packaging Materials in the Household and Commercial Waste Stream

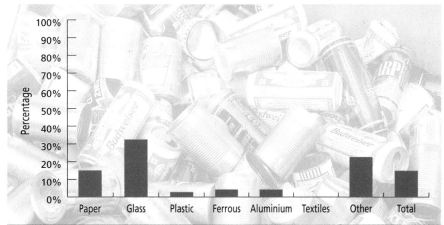
Fig. 6.9 Recovery Rates for Specific Packaging Materials in the Total Waste Stream

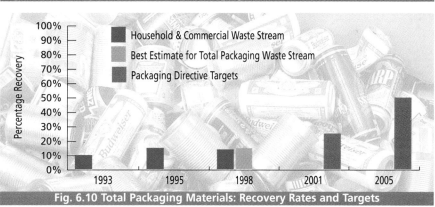
Fig. 6.10 Total Packaging Materials: Recovery Rates and Targets

producers are made responsible for the packaging they produce, more stringent obligations are placed on *major producers*, defined as producers that place more than 25 tonnes of packaging on the Irish market per annum and have an annual turnover of greater than £1 million. Major producers must either comply with specific obligations set out in the Regulations or participate in an approved waste recovery scheme. To date, one such scheme has been approved, REPAK, which was established as a result of an industry-led initiative to meet the targets set by the Packaging Directive on a voluntary basis.

INDUSTRIAL WASTE

Amounts Arising and Trends

Data on industrial waste generation in Ireland have improved considerably in the past five years with the creation of a National Waste Database and the continued implementation of integrated pollution control (IPC) licensing, which requires annual reporting on waste arisings and management by each licence holder. However, while historical data on industrial waste arisings are incomplete making it difficult to establish reliable trends, comparable surveys were conducted in 1995 and 1998. Although it is clear that the standard of reporting was considerably better in 1998, a direct comparison of estimated quantities suggests a growth in industrial waste in the period from 6.2 million tonnes in 1995 to 9.1 million tonnes in 1998, an increase of 47 per cent. Of this, it is estimated that 5.1 million tonnes were produced by the manufacturing sector, 3.5 million tonnes from mining activities and 0.5 million tonnes from the supply of electricity, gas and water.

A breakdown of the manufacturing sector industrial wastes is presented in Table 6.2 and the top ten (by quantity) industrial hazardous and non-hazardous wastes produced in Ireland are listed in Table 6.3.

Disposal and Recovery

In 1998, 73 per cent of industrial waste was disposed of through various routes, principally landfill, with 27 per cent recovered. This compares with 88 per cent disposed in 1995 and 12 per cent recovered (Fig 6.11). The main recovery routes were reuse, solvent reclamation and landspreading. A more detailed breakdown, by sector, is given in Table 6.4. The most striking trend is the increase in the recovery rate for the manufacturing sector, much of which is now controlled through the IPC licensing system. In this sector, reported recovery increased from 31 per cent in 1995 to 51 per cent in 1998.

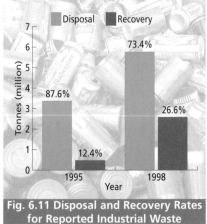

Fig. 6.11 Disposal and Recovery Rates for Reported Industrial Waste

HAZARDOUS WASTE

There have been major developments in information on hazardous waste in Ireland in the past five years, the most significant development being the publication of the proposed National Hazardous Waste Management Plan in 1999. Information contained in the proposed plan was based on 1996 data. Further surveys have since been conducted by the EPA with information now available for 1998.

Table 6.2 Estimated Manufacturing Sector Waste Arisings in 1998

Manufacturing Sector	Hazardous (tonnes)	Non-Hazardous (tonnes)	Total (tonnes)
Food Products; Beverages and Tobacco	2,343	2,356,418	2,358,761
Textiles and Textile Products	932	116,052	116,984
Leather and Leather Products	23	53,790	53,813
Wood and Wood Products	1,061	287,257	288,318
Pulp, Paper and Paper Products; Printing, Publishing	1,107	164,267	165,374
Coke and Refined Petroleum Products	6,690	22,584	29,274
Chemicals, Chemical Products and Man-Made Fibres	208,592	1,335,288	1,543,880
Rubber and Plastic Products	1,051	24,974	26,025
Other Non-Metallic Mineral Products (includes quarrying)	874	265,755	266,629
Basic Metals and Fabricated Metal Products	5,497	114,301	119,798
Machinery and Equipment (not elsewhere classified)	1,975	40,118	42,093
Electrical and Optical Equipment	4,385	48,401	52,786
Transport Equipment	2,183	32,228	34,411
Manufacturing (not elsewhere classified)	348	25,856	26,204
Total	**237,061**	**4,876,406**	**5,113,468**

Table 6.3 Top Ten Reported Non-Hazardous & Hazardous Industrial Wastes in 1998

Non-Hazardous Waste Description	Tonnes	Hazardous Waste Description	Tonnes
Mine tailings	2,112,302	Non-halogenated organic solvents, washing liquids and mother liquors from the MFSU* of pharmaceuticals	60,314
Waste from non-metaliferous mineral excavation	1,033,231	Non-halogenated organic solvents, washing liquids and mother liquors from the MFSU of fine chemicals and chemical products	50,133
Red mud from the alumina production	781,954	Aqueous washing liquids and mother liquors from the MFSU of pharmaceuticals	28,440
Sludges from on-site effluent treatment from the preparation and processing of meat, fish and other foods of animal origin	490,644	Waste salt and its solutions	28,111
Animal tissue waste from the preparation and processing of meat, fish and other foods of animal origin	378,505	Organic halogenated solvents, washing liquids and mother liquors from the MFSU of pharmaceuticals	6,790
Waste from mineral metaliferous excavation	350,000	Tank bottom sludges	6,003
Other mining wastes	266,130	Aqueous washing liquids and mother liquors from the MFSU of fine chemicals and chemical products	3,287
Coal fly ash	194,301	Other still bottoms and reaction residues from the MFSU of fine chemicals and chemical products	2,718
Waste gravel and crushed rocks	184,728	Calcium hydroxide	2,576
Mixed construction and demolition waste	149,917	Paint, inks, adhesives and resins	1,805
Total	**6,254,086**	**Total**	**190,177**

* Manufacture, Formulation, Supply and Use

Table 6.4 Disposal and Recovery Rates for Industrial Waste: 1995 & 1998

	Estimated arisings (tonnes)		Disposal (%)		Recovery (%)	
	1995	1998	1995	1998	1995	1998
Manufacturing	3,781,305	5,113,468	69.0	48.6	31.0	51.4
Mining	2,200,004	3,511,643	100.0	99.6	0.0	0.4
Energy & water	353,307	449,640	81.2	84.0	18.8	16.0
Total	**6,334,616**	**9,074,751**	**87.6**	**73.4**	**12.4**	**26.6**

Hazardous waste arisings in 1998 are estimated to be over 370,000 tonnes, compared with 328,000 tonnes in 1996, an increase of 13 per cent in two years (Table 6.5).

Disposal and Recovery

A comparison of the disposal and recovery routes for hazardous waste in 1996 and 1998 is presented in Fig. 6.12.

Overall, in 1998, 35.6 per cent of hazardous waste was disposed of or recovered on-site, 11.5 per cent recovered or disposed of off-site in Ireland while 26.9 per cent was exported. The remaining 26 per cent consisted of waste where the disposal or recovery methodology was not specified (6 per cent) and or where the waste was not reported (20 per cent). The total quantity reported to be disposed was over 120,000 tonnes with over 152,000 tonnes reported as

Table 6.5 Hazardous Waste Generation in 1998	
Hazardous Waste Type	**Quantity (tonnes)**
Organic halogenated solvents	6,997
Non halogenated organic solvents	111,520
Other organic solvents	1,213
Other pharmaceutical waste (mixed)	1,675
Oily sludges	19,063
Spent sheep dip	19,000
Waste oils	17,346
Saltcake/salts	28,121
Lead acid batteries	14,213
Filter cakes and metal containing sludges	3,129
Washing liquids and mother liquors	33,630
Household hazardous waste	6,831
Still bottoms and reaction residues	4,795
Clinical waste	3,659
Metal hydroxide sludges/ ion exchange resins	1,887
Small batteries	2,932
Oil filters	1,327
Paint/ink/varnish sludges	529
Acid/alkali waste	5,911
Paint/ink/varnish liquid waste	2,393
Photographic waste	1,609
General office waste	152
Dross from lead metallurgy	1,352
Veterinary medicine	483
Fluorescent tubes	554
Contaminated soil	45,486
Pesticides (agricultural)	340
Asbestos waste	1,335
Spent filters	56
Adhesive waste	318
Zinc oxide	245
Mercury containing wastes	536
PCB waste	190
Waxes/fats	255
Gold solutions	4
Waste catalysts	245
Paint and ink packaging	7,764
Hazardous thermal treatment residues	828
Other hazardous wastes	22,406
TOTALS	**370,328**

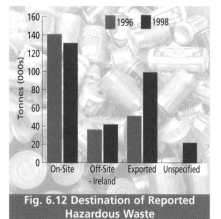

Fig. 6.12 Destination of Reported Hazardous Waste

recovered. This compares with 87,000 tonnes disposed and 139,000 tonnes recovered in 1996. The two main disposal routes were incineration and landfill which

accounted for 17.7 per cent and 9.2 per cent respectively. The main recovery route was solvent recovery, which accounted for 22.2 per cent of reported hazardous waste.

For hazardous waste that is known to arise but remains unreported, such as household hazardous waste, hazardous waste from the commercial sector and hazardous waste from the agricultural sector (e.g., sheep dip), accurate information on disposal/recovery routes is not available with some limited exceptions such as batteries and waste oils for which collection and treatment services exist. However, it can reasonably be assumed that much of this waste either is disposed of by the producer of the waste in an illegal manner or ends up in a landfill as part of mixed waste loads.

AGRICULTURAL WASTE

Amounts Arising and Trends

It is estimated that approximately 65 million tonnes of agricultural waste requiring manangement, arose in Ireland in 1998 (Fig 6.13). The bulk of this is animal manures, along with almost 20 million tonnes of dirty water from the dairy sector. The figures do not include other agricultural wastes such as farm plastics, waste oils, spent sheep dip and general farmyard waste, most of

which is accounted for elsewhere. The estimation of agricultural waste arisings is based on animal numbers, average waste production per animal and the length of time that animals are kept indoors. The manner in which this calculation is conducted is updated periodically, which makes it difficult to assess trends in waste production. The most reliable indicator for agricultural waste production is animal numbers. As described earlier in the report, in the 1990s there was growth in numbers of all animal types with the exception of sheep for which there was a drop in numbers of about 6 per cent; however, this followed a dramatic doubling in sheep numbers during the 1980s. Between 1991 and 1998, cattle, pigs and poultry numbers have increased by 13, 39 and 9 per cent, respectively.

Disposal and Recovery

Almost all organic agricultural waste arising in Ireland is spread on agricultural land. Whether landspreading of organic waste should be considered as disposal or recovery depends on a number of factors including the conditions under which the waste is spread, the timing of application, the soil type and general condition of the land and the nutrient requirements of grass, cereals or field crops to be grown.

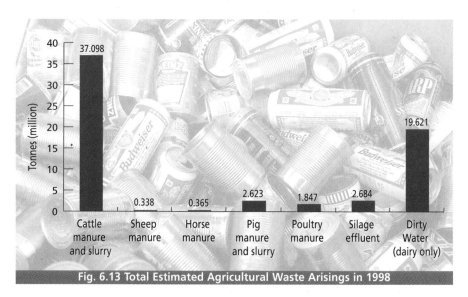

Fig. 6.13 Total Estimated Agricultural Waste Arisings in 1998

There is now a general consensus that run-off from the application to land of both artificial fertilisers and organic farm wastes is a major contributor to the steady decline in water quality observed in Ireland over the past twenty years or so. This issue is discussed further in Chapter 9.

URBAN WASTEWATER SLUDGES AND OTHER ORGANIC SLUDGES

Amounts Arising and Disposal/Recovery Routes

In 1998, the total urban wastewater sludge arisings for agglomerations with a population equivalent (see Chapter 5) greater than or equal to 1,000 was estimated to be 37,577 tonnes dry solids (TDS), which is equivalent in wet weight terms to approximately 493,000 tonnes. Of the 37,577 tonnes dry solids, 15.8 per cent was disposed/re-used in agriculture, 41.4 per cent was landfilled, 40.6 per cent was dumped at sea and the remaining 2.2 per cent treated by some other unspecified route (EPA, in prep.). In addition, there is also a significant quantity of sludge arising from small-scale wastewater treatment plants and septic tanks. It is estimated that in the region of 507 TDS of sludge arises from these sources per annum (Fehily, Timoney and Co., 1998). This is equivalent to approximately 12,675 tonnes wet weight, the bulk of which went to landfill, bringing the total estimated wet weight arisings for sewage sludges in 1998 to 505,686 tonnes.

Approximately 708,000 tonnes wet weight of other organic sludges, mainly from industrial sources, are estimated to have arisen in 1998 (EPA, 2000). The sector producing the greatest quantity of sludges was the food and beverage sector, which gave rise to 94 per cent of the total reported sludge arising. However, there are high recovery rates, in the region of 90 per cent. The primary recovery route is landspreading, with 583,000 tonnes of waste from the food and beverages sector alone reported to be landspread.

There is a considerable quantity of biological sludge produced in Ireland, both from the treatment of urban wastewater and from various industrial activities, mainly within the food and beverage sector. While only 15.8 per cent of urban wastewater sludges were put to agricultural or horticultural use in 1998, it is likely that this quantity will have risen significantly in 1999 and 2000 with the move away from sea disposal in Dublin. The most recent EPA report (EPA, 1998) indicates that the quantities of sewage sludge arisings will increase dramatically when secondary treatment facilities are in place in Dublin, Cork, Dundalk, Limerick and Galway. When these increases are considered together with the relatively large quantities of biological sludges from industrial sources, a precautionary approach is required in considering widespread application of these sludges to agricultural land.

CONSTRUCTION AND DEMOLITION WASTE

Amounts Arising and Disposal/Recovery Routes

The construction/demolition industry is one of the largest producers of waste in Ireland. In general, the operators dealing with this waste stream have not kept records of quantities or types arising. The most reliable information currently available on the waste stream is quantities reported to be landfilled. Given the high priority placed on construction and demolition waste in the policy statement, *Changing Our Ways*, particular attention needs to be paid to improving data on this waste stream.

The amount of construction and demolition waste reported to have been sent to landfill in 1998 is over 2.7 million tonnes. However, of this total it is estimated that 1.17 million tonnes (43 per cent) were recovered and put to beneficial use on the landfill sites either for the construction of roads and berms or as cover and capping material.

The amount of construction and demolition waste arising in 1998 is likely to be significantly higher than the 2.7 million tonnes reported. Given the unprecedented level of construction activity in Ireland in the past five years and the likelihood that this activity will continue, this waste stream can be expected to continue to grow.

OVERVIEW OF WASTE MANAGEMENT

As stated earlier in the chapter, the waste hierarchy is at the heart of waste policy in Ireland. This section

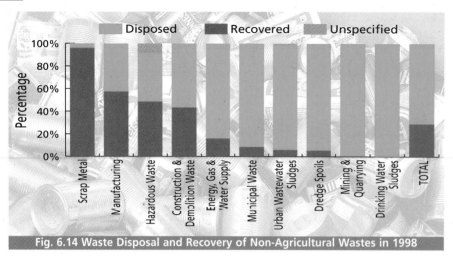

Fig. 6.14 Waste Disposal and Recovery of Non-Agricultural Wastes in 1998

provides a summary and review of the national situation as to where we are with the various steps on the hierarchy. Fig. 6.14 summarises the disposal and recovery rates for the various waste streams in Ireland for 1998. Overall, over 70 per cent of non-agricultural waste generated in Ireland in 1998 was disposed with less than 30 per cent recovered.

WASTE PREVENTION AND MINIMISATION

The preferred options in relation to waste are prevention and minimisation. They are also the most challenging options as their successful implementation requires a change in the attitudes of the waste producer. At product development and manufacturing level, each step in the chain has to be considered in relation to its waste production potential. At consumer level, the consumer needs to consider the waste implications of particular purchases. Planning for waste prevention and minimisation requires a knowledge of the sources of the waste, as realistic targets for individual sectors can only be set when it is known what quantities and types of waste are produced by each sector.

Waste prevention and minimisation strategies have a positive impact on the environment. In many cases, strategies are put in place either to replace or to modify existing processes leading to waste production

in order to reduce the volume and toxicity of waste produced. They also tend to lead to improved environmental performance and more efficient use of energy and natural resources as the life-cycle, or cradle to grave, approach is central to the success of such strategies. Waste prevention is an integral aspect of IPC licensing.

There have been a number of initiatives in the area of cleaner production and waste prevention/minimisation in the recent past. Of particular interest are the initiatives tied into the proposed National Hazardous Waste Management Plan and the Cleaner Production Pilot Demonstration Programme funded through the European Regional Development Fund, which are outlined below.

National Hazardous Waste Management Plan and Waste Prevention

The cornerstone of the proposed National Hazardous Waste Management Plan (EPA, 1999) is prevention. The plan sets out how hazardous waste prevention can benefit Irish industry and minimise hazardous waste costs. IPC licensing has to date resulted in the prevention of significant quantities of hazardous waste. The Plan recommends the adoption of an ambitious Prevention Programme with the following key elements:
- no increase in the quantity of

hazardous waste subject to disposal operations;
- the establishment of a core of expertise or 'prevention team' to prioritise and co-ordinate the implementation of the Prevention Programme;
- demonstration projects, information dissemination, assistance to industry, educational initiatives, research and support staff.

Under the Prevention Programme, significant amounts of financial and technical assistance would be invested in participating companies thereby increasing the net saving to industry - overall a 'win-win' situation for both industry and the environment.

The proposed Plan was published in September 1999 and, following the public consultation period which ran to December 1999, the EPA has been considering the various submissions received in order to make whatever revisions considered to be necessary. The Plan will be published later in the year 2000.

Cleaner Production Pilot Demonstration Programme

Under the Environmental Monitoring R&D Sub-programme of the Environmental Services Operational Programme 1994-1999, a cleaner production pilot demonstration programme was organised by the EPA. This programme sought to promote environmentally friendly production through the application and demonstration of cleaner systems, techniques and technology. The demonstration programme was aimed primarily at small and medium sized enterprises to help them operate in a more environmentally sustainable manner.

Trends

The promotion of cleaner production and waste prevention and minimisation is at the core of

environmental policy in Ireland. The Waste Management Act introduced a legal framework for waste prevention and minimisation by placing an obligation on any person who carries out any activity of an agricultural, commercial or industrial nature to have due regard, among other things, to the need to prevent or minimise the production of waste from that activity. In practice, this obligation will be enforced through the making of specific Regulations dealing with specific waste streams, the Packaging Regulations being the first to be made under the relevant section. It is expected that similar Regulations will be introduced for waste streams such as end of life vehicles, construction and demolition waste and waste from electrical and electronic equipment.

Waste prevention and minimisation strategies are to play a central part in waste planning in the future although it is too early to evaluate the relative success of measures contained in either local authority Waste Management Plans or the National Hazardous Waste Management Plan. The general trend towards the adoption of an environmental management systems approach to environmental protection should also lead to the adoption of realistic strategies for waste prevention and minimisation at company level.

RECOVERY

After waste prevention and minimisation, the next best environmental options in relation to waste management are re-use and recovery, which includes recycling and energy recovery. The main environmental advantage afforded by waste recovery is a saving on the use of natural resources or virgin material which might otherwise have been used had recovered material not been available. However, when considering the net environmental impact, this needs to be balanced against the overall cost to the environment in relation to energy usage and pollution that might arise as a result of the recovery process itself. Once a waste is produced its management is likely to result in negative environmental impacts whether the waste is recovered or disposed. This highlights the importance of waste prevention and minimisation and the integration of waste issues into the production/consumption cycle so that products are designed to have as little impact as possible on the environment when they become redundant.

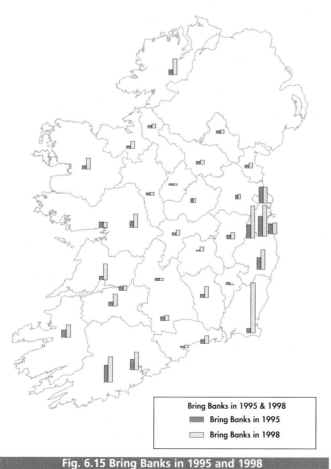

Bring Banks in 1995 & 1998
- Bring Banks in 1995
- Bring Banks in 1998

Fig. 6.15 Bring Banks in 1995 and 1998

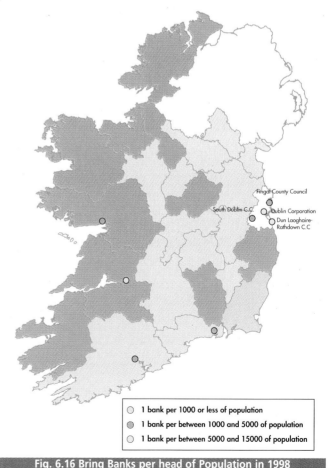

○ 1 bank per 1000 or less of population
◉ 1 bank per between 1000 and 5000 of population
○ 1 bank per between 5000 and 15000 of population

Fig. 6.16 Bring Banks per head of Population in 1998

The development of recycling and recovery infrastructure has also been encouraged through grants made available by the Department of the Environment and Local Government. During 1997 and 1998, 65 projects received funding, ranging from £1,500 to £400,000.

Trends

Trends in recovery between 1995 and 1998 show that glass recovery has increased from 28,500 tonnes to 36,000 tonnes and this trend is expected to continue. Similarly, paper recovery has also increased from a reported 84,000 tonnes in 1995 to a reported 94,302 tonnes in 1998. However, overall recovery rates for municipal waste are low and much work remains to be done to meet the specified targets. Figures 6.15 and 6.16 identify the geographical distribution and density of "bring banks" in Ireland with Figure 6.15 providing a comparison between numbers of "bring banks" in 1995 and 1998. Of the 837 bring banks reported for 1998, 649 have facilities for glass collection, 509 for cans, 380 for textiles, 34 for paper, 14 for waste oils, 7 for plastic containers and 6 for batteries. Clearly, while there is growing coverage for the collection of glass, cans (mainly aluminium) and textiles, there is very poor coverage for plastics, steel, paper and other materials.

Recovery of industrial wastes increased from 12.4 per cent in 1995 to 26.6 per cent in 1998. The recovery rate for the manufacturing sector was 51 per cent for 1998 compared to 31 per cent in 1995. This has been driven to a large extent by IPC licensing.

COMPOSTING

Composting of organic wastes, such as kitchen wastes and green wastes, provides a viable alternative to disposal of such wastes. A key component of the Government's waste strategy is a 65 per cent reduction in the quantity of biodegradable waste consigned to landfill and the development of biological treatment facilities, including composting, capable of treating up to 300,000 tonnes per annum. It is estimated that in excess of 1 million tonnes of biodegradable waste, consisting of paper and kitchen/garden wastes, were consigned to landfill in 1998.

Trends

The development of composting as an alternative to landfill has been slow in Ireland. A number of home composting schemes have been set up by local authorities, with eight such schemes receiving funding under the Operational Programme for Environmental Services, 1994-1999. Centralised composting of municipal waste is under development in South Dublin (green waste), Cork (green waste), Limerick (green waste and kitchen waste) and Kerry (green waste and kitchen waste). There will need to be considerable development in centralised composting in the short term if composting is to contribute significantly to the diversion of biodegradable waste away from landfill. Given that the decomposition of biodegradable waste is responsible for many of the environmental problems associated with landfills, such as leachate contamination, landfill gas and odour nuisance, a stronger emphasis on centralised composting as an alternative means of treating biodegradable wastes is strongly recommended.

THERMAL TREATMENT

There are, currently, no municipal waste incineration plants in Ireland, in marked contrast to other European countries. This is subject to some debate at present with many waste management strategies and plans considering incineration and other thermal treatments such as gasification and pyrolysis as key components of an integrated approach to waste management in their areas. In addition, three feasibility studies have been carried out which have examined the technical, environmental, financial and social advantages and disadvantages of thermal treatment in the greater Dublin area and in two regions, the North East and the Mid West.

Several regional strategies have recommended waste to energy recovery as a viable option for municipal waste management at regional level. It therefore appears likely that Ireland will see the introduction of thermal treatment with energy recovery for municipal wastes, particularly in larger urban areas.

Box 6.2 Home and Municipal Composting

Composting can be undertaken either in the home or at centralised municipal facilities, where biodegradable waste is collected separately from households and commercial enterprises and brought to a dedicated plant.
Biodegradable waste must be separated at source by the producer. This tends to be an impediment to the development of composting as it requires effort and commitment by individuals. Centralised schemes are more suited to urban areas, while home composting schemes suit rural areas with low density populations. A drawback to home composting is that the individual must both separate out biodegradable waste and compost the waste. Centralised composting, on the other hand, only requires separation of biodegradable waste and presenting it separately for collection. Significant commitment and support is therefore required to make home composting schemes successful. If composting is to play a serious part in the diversion of biodegradable waste away from landfill, it is clear that centralised composting with separate collection will be required.

In the industrial sector to date, six facilities have been licensed for the incineration of hazardous waste under the IPC licensing regime. In each case, incineration activities are limited to waste produced on the site.

LANDFILL

Current Status and Trends

Landfilling remains the predominant waste disposal practice in Ireland. In 1998, it is estimated that in excess of 8.8 million tonnes of waste were consigned to landfill, with 4.86 million tonnes disposed of in on-site private landfills and 3.94 million tonnes disposed of in landfills operated either by or on behalf of local authorities. A summary of waste accepted into landfills in 1998 is presented in Figure 6.17. Most of the industrial waste landfilled is mining waste and its possibilities for re-use are limited.

Figure 6.18 shows the geographical location and size of all operating landfills in Ireland in 1998, both

with 16 receiving greater than 40,000 tonnes per annum (Fig. 6.19). Since 1998, a further 26 of these landfills, mainly small rural ones, are thought to have closed, leaving a total of 50 local authority landfills in operation

at the time of going to press. The remaining lifespan of local authority landfills that are currently operational illustrates that 12 of them have an expected lifespan of more than ten years, 13 are expected to remain open

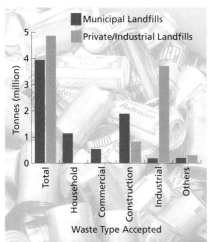

Fig. 6.17 Wastes Accepted by Municipal and Private/Industrial Landfills in 1998

public and private. Generally, there is a trend towards a decreasing number of local authority landfills with the relative size of landfills increasing. In 1995, there were 87 active local authority landfills compared with 76 in 1998. Of the 76 landfills reported to be receiving municipal waste, 30 were receiving less than 10,000 tonnes per annum

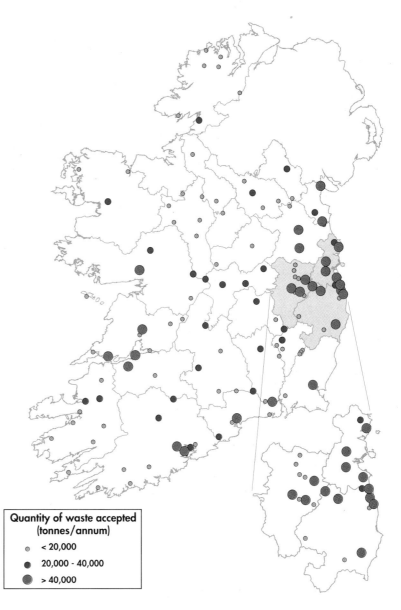

Quantity of waste accepted (tonnes/annum)

- < 20,000
- 20,000 - 40,000
- > 40,000

Fig. 6.18 Location and Size of Active Landfills in 1998

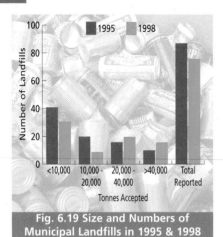

Fig. 6.19 Size and Numbers of Municipal Landfills in 1995 & 1998

growth in private landfills particularly in and around the Greater Dublin region. While private/industrial landfills received in the region of 4.9 million tonnes of waste in 1998, two sites, Aughinish Alumina in Limerick and Tara Mines in Meath, account for 3.2 million tonnes of this total. The remaining private/industrial landfills receive mainly construction and demolition type waste.

Figure 6.21 presents a comparison between landfill status in 1995 and 1998.

Recent developments affecting landfill activities include the introduction of a comprehensive licensing system under the Waste Management Act, 1996, and the publication of comprehensive guidance by the EPA on many aspects of landfilling, including site investigations, landfill design, environmental monitoring, operational practices and closure and aftercare. Prior to this, little

for between five and ten years, with the remainder expected to close within the next five years (Fig. 6.20). In addition, the EPA has received waste licence applications for six new landfills (in Wicklow, Limerick, Tipperary (2), Meath and Clare).

In relation to private/industrial landfills, the number reported in 1998 (50) was considerably higher than in 1995 (31). This is partly a function of better reporting by local authorities but also reflects the

attention was paid to the proper operation and management of landfills in Ireland. Standards were low and landfilling had a deservedly poor reputation.

These developments are leading to radical changes in landfilling in Ireland. The main change is probably the acceptance by most local authorities that landfilling must be conducted at a considerably higher

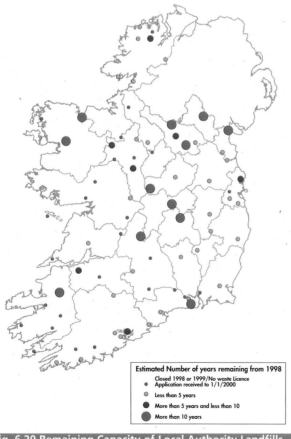

Fig. 6.20 Remaining Capacity of Local Authority Landfills

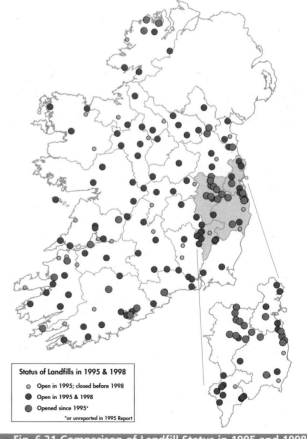

Fig. 6.21 Comparison of Landfill Status in 1995 and 1998

licences had been received (Table 6.6). The geographical location of these licence applications is shown in Figure 6.22.

A local authority permitting system has also been established for smaller activities including the recovery of scrap metal or other metal wastes, the dismantling or recovery of vehicles and the disposal of waste, other than landfill, at facilities where the annual intake does not exceed 5,000 tonnes per annum.

DISCUSSION AND FUTURE PERSPECTIVES

Information for 1998 shows clearly that waste quantities are continuing to grow in Ireland. Given the recent strong economic growth, this is not surprising as it mirrors the stubborn linkage between economic growth and waste production apparent in all developed countries. This continued growth is a clear reminder of the challenges that lie ahead.

Waste production, itself, can be viewed as an indicator of the sustainability or otherwise of our economy as it is directly related to the consumption and use of natural resources. While specific targets are

standard than heretofore and requires considerably greater investment. Landfill technology is well developed and the principal challenge is to ensure that high operating standards become the norm so that landfills are operated in a manner that will not result in environmental pollution and general nuisance to local communities.

LICENSED AND PERMITTED ACTIVITIES

The Waste Management Act, 1996 requires that the EPA license all significant waste disposal and recovery activities. Facilities requiring a licence include landfill sites, transfer stations, storage facilities, hazardous waste disposal and recovery facilities, large composting facilities and certain types of treatment facilities. A waste licence is designed to protect all environmental media including air, water and soil and to ensure that waste activities are operated in such a way that they do not cause environmental pollution. Waste licensing commenced in May, 1997 and for existing activities, the system is being introduced on a phased basis depending on the type and size of the facility. All new activities are required to obtain a licence prior to commencement. By the end of 1999, 136 applications for waste

Table 6.6 Summary of Waste Licence Applications Received and Licences Granted at End 1999						
Facility Type	Total	Local Authority applications	Private sector	Proposed decisions	Licences issued	Abandoned
Landfill	71	56	15	8	13	
Transfer Station	29	8	21	1	6	
Composting	7		7			
Hazardous Waste Treatment & Transfer	7		7		1	
Healthcare Risk Waste Treatment	6	2	4		3	2
Soil Remediation	4		4		1	
Hazardous Waste Transfer Station	3		3		2	
Integrated Waste Management Facilities	3	2	1		1	
Dredging	2	1	1		1	
Hazardous Waste Treatment	2		2			
Healthcare Risk Waste Treatment & Hazardous Waste Transfer Station	1		1		1	
Recovery	1	1				
TOTAL	136	70	66	9	30	2

EPA (Environmental Protection Agency), 1996. *National Waste Database Report 1995.* Environmental Protection Agency, Wexford.

EPA (Environmental Protection Agency), 1998. *Urban Wastewater Discharges in Ireland: A Report for Years 1996 and 1997.* Environmental Protection Agency, Wexford.

EPA (Environmental Protection Agency), 1999. *Proposed National Hazardous Waste Management Plan.* Environmental Protection Agency, Wexford.

EPA (Environmental Protection Agency), 2000. *National Waste Database Report 1998.* Environmental Protection Agency, Wexford.

Fehily, Timoney and Co., 1998. *Inventory of Non-Hazardous Sludges in Ireland.* Fehily, Timoney and Co., Cork.

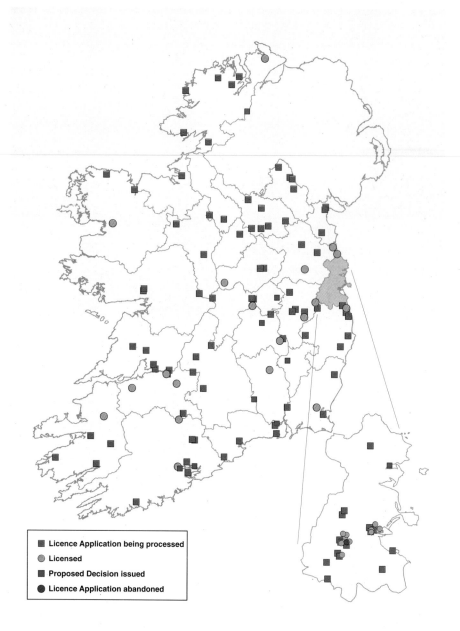

Legend:
- ■ Licence Application being processed
- ● Licensed
- ■ Proposed Decision issued
- ● Licence Application abandoned

Fig. 6.22 Location of Activities for which the EPA has received a Waste Licence Application in December 1999

necessary to plan for improvements in waste management, it is important to bear in mind that with waste, there will always be room for improvement. The only rational approach to 'sustainable waste management' is to improve the efficiency of the production/ consumption cycle so that resources are used more efficiently, less waste is produced and what is produced is either recovered or disposed of in an environmentally sensitive manner.

REFERENCES

DoE (Department of the Environment), 1994. *Operational Programme: Environmental Services 1994 – 1999.* Department of the Environment, Dublin.

DoE (Department of the Environment), 1997. *Sustainable Development. A Strategy for Ireland.* Department of the Environment, Dublin.

DELG (Department of the Environment and Local Government), 1998. *A Policy Statement. Waste Management, Changing Our Ways.* Department of the Environment and Local Government, Dublin.

CHAPTER 7

OTHER PRESSURES

Changes on the land surface can arise from road building, industrial development, housing, agriculture, afforestation, quarrying and mineral exploitation. Increasing housing development and road building in recent years have put greater pressure on land resources. Overall consumption of aggregates (sand, gravel and crushed rock) in Ireland is now estimated to be approaching 50 million tonnes per annum or approximately 14 tonnes per capita per annum. The extraction of minerals can have localised effects including air pollution, traffic generation, noise, and leachate from spoil heaps and tailings ponds.

Pressures on water resources arise through demands for water in densely populated areas and in many cases this is exacerbated by substantial loss through leakages from the distribution system. For example, an estimated 44 per cent of the water supply in the Dublin area is lost through leakages, mostly from the mains. An extensive leakage reduction and water conservation project is targeted at reducing the mains leakage figure to 22 per cent by the year 2000.

The dispersal of man-made chemicals in the environment may lead to directly toxic or other harmful effects on humans, animals and plants and interfere with natural processes in the atmosphere, e.g., reduction of ozone levels in the stratosphere. For many people, odours and excessive noise present the main experience of environmental deterioration, while genetically modified organisms represent a new risk to the environment that must be addressed. Finally, these effects should be contrasted with the equally hazardous but largely unavoidable effects of natural forces such as background radioactivity and flooding.

INTRODUCTION

The three preceding chapters deal with the main categories of pressure on environmental quality. There are further significant pressures, however, and this chapter is intended to provide a general overview of other sources of pressure, both natural and man-made, and to draw attention to the risks that they present.

As noted in Chapter 1, changes to the environment arise from both natural forces and human influences. The human transformation of matter and energy, when compared with natural processes, has been relatively insignificant for the greater part of history. However, since the industrial revolution, and particularly in the last fifty years, this situation has changed radically and human activities are now altering natural cycles at unprecedented rates.

It is evident that these activities adversely affect the environment and, consequently, the health and well-being of humans, flora and fauna. For example, smells, noise, air pollution and hazards from traffic can affect the built environment, where society spends a large portion of its time. The development of land for agriculture or forestry may lead to loss of habitat for certain animals and plants.

DEVELOPMENTS HAVING MAJOR IMPACTS ON LAND SURFACES

Mineral Exploitation

The exploitation of minerals has, since pre-historic times, been vital to man's economic progress. The mineral industry is a small but important sector of the national economy, Ireland being currently the sixth largest producer of lead and zinc in the world.

The extraction of minerals, unless properly controlled, can have localised effects through air pollution, traffic generation, noise, and leachate from spoil heaps and tailings ponds. Dewatering can affect the surrounding groundwater regime. Liquid effluent disposal can affect streams, water supplies and fisheries. Dust, depending on its composition, can affect people, agriculture and wildlife. Sediments in harbours can become contaminated during the loading and unloading of mineral ores. Mineral exploitation may be damaging to the landscape, especially if carried out in scenic areas. The impacts on wildlife and habitats also require consideration.

Most existing mining operations and all new mines are now required to apply for an integrated pollution control (IPC) licence, which will include conditions that will apply over the life of the mine and ongoing maintenance and monitoring of the on-site mine waste. Ireland's operational mines are shown in Fig. 7.1.

Source: DMNR

Fig. 7.1 Ireland's Operational Mines

Quarrying and Aggregate Removal

Large quantities of aggregates are needed each year by the construction industry. These can be defined as the granular material obtained by extracting, crushing and screening rock and gravels. The current national roads improvement programme along with the increased level of building construction has given rise to a considerable increase in quarrying activity.

Overall consumption of aggregates in Ireland is now estimated to be approaching 50 million tonnes per annum or approximately 14 tonnes per capita per annum. As an example of the quantities required for specific purposes, approximately 300 to 400 tonnes of aggregates are needed to build a typical house (Holmes, 1999). Approximately 35 million tonnes of aggregates are obtained from hard rock quarries by drilling and blasting, and around 15 million tonnes of sand and gravel are extracted by direct digging from pits. These extraction processes invariably involve the creation of unsightly areas in the landscape. More recent planning permissions for this activity therefore include conditions relating to visual amenity and other potential environmental impacts encompassing both the quarrying operations and subsequent restoration works.

Owing to an apparent scarcity of suitable inland sources in certain areas, there has been an increased interest in offshore extraction of sand and gravel. Some licence applications for aggregate extraction from the seabed are presently under consideration by the Department of Marine and Natural Resources.

The recycling of construction, renovation and demolition waste can mitigate the potential environmental damage from aggregate extraction. The composition of the waste is variable and depends on the type of activity from which it arises. The reported quantities arising, disposed and recovered are given in Chapter 6. Studies carried out by Fingal County Council, for example, suggest that such waste received by them can be recycled and the Council has now established a facility for this purpose.

Cork Corporation has also established a recycling facility to relieve pressures on landfill disposal. In addition to the local authority involvement there are also recycling centres operated by the private sector, mainly in the larger cities.

As long as stocks of natural aggregate remain high, the incentive to move towards recycled material will depend on the price differential. The increased use of recycled building materials will have the twin benefit of reducing both the environmental impact of quarrying and the material going to landfill.

Impact of Housing Development

Increasing housing development and road building in recent years have put increasing pressure on land resources. As noted in Chapter 2, the number of dwellings being built in the State has doubled since 1993 and is the highest in Europe per unit of population. Changes in demographic and social patterns related, in part, to economic factors are shaping the pattern of housing demand.

In view of this situation, planning guidelines recently issued by the government (DELG, 1999) promote the concept of increased residential density. The guidelines are intended to draw the attention of planning authorities, An Bord Pleanala, developers and the general public to the benefits of higher residential density in appropriate locations. They state that, subject to a number of specified safeguards, there should be, in principle, no upper limit set in the Development Plan on the number of dwellings that may be provided within any town or city centre site. More sustainable building types to optimise energy performance (thereby reducing carbon dioxide emissions) and to facilitate adaptation to changing uses are also encouraged. The Guidelines, if properly implemented, should deliver an increased supply of

housing from existing land and infrastructure, thereby improving the environment and reducing commuting distances. Local authorities are being asked to put the Guidelines into effect straight away and to review and vary their Development Plans to give full effect to the recommendations and policies.

Overgrazing

An unintended effect of the Common Agricultural Policy is the erosion of soil and peat from mountainous grazing areas, particularly commonages overstocked with sheep. The erosion is caused by severe cropping of the vegetative cover and by excessive treading. This has become a major problem, particularly prevalent on the hillside landscapes in the high-rainfall areas of the west of Ireland where vegetation and soil/peat are least resistant to erosion. In addition to loss of grazing land, the erosion leads to silting of streams with adverse implications in particular for the spawning grounds of salmon and trout.

Research shows that a controlled grazing intensity should help to maintain a stable and diverse plant cover (Walsh *et al.*, 1997). The Rural Environment Protection Scheme (REPS) has sought to address the problem of overgrazing by a system of payments to farmers to manage their land in an environmentally friendly manner including reducing stock numbers to sustainable levels (see Part V).

Afforestation

The development of forestry is considered to be of vital importance for Ireland because of the contribution it makes to economic development as a renewable resource and, in relation to the greenhouse gas issue, as a carbon sink (see also Chapter 4). Afforestation, however, can be a threat to the environment, for example through the drainage of

large tracts of marginal lands and the application of fertilisers. A further threat is the acidification of surface waters as a result of evergreen afforestation of poorly buffered acid-sensitive soils. This arises through the crowns of trees filtering pollutants, even at low levels, from the atmosphere which, along with the ion-exchange processes at the roots of these trees, gives rise to increased acidity and release of metals (which have been chemically bound in the soil) in the run-off waters from these soils. Habitats, particularly blanket bog, can also be threatened by afforestation while extensive plantations of evergreens may lessen the scenic value of the landscape. These issues are addressed further in Chapters 9, 11 and 12.

EXPLOITATION OF WATER RESOURCES

Background

A relatively low population density and high rainfall ensure that there is no overall problem of water availability in the State. Water supply infrastructure includes not only water treatment plants but also water mains and storage towers and reservoirs. It includes also the drainage system and wastewater treatment plants. All of these developments may have adverse effects on the aquatic environment, e.g., inundation of land to form

reservoirs, changes in the flow regime in rivers below dams and deterioration of water quality below the discharges from sewage treatment plants.

An additional pressure on water resources lies in the increased per capita use of water resources for drinking and industrial purposes brought about by economic prosperity. As a further consequence of economic prosperity there has been the reduction in the average occupancy per dwelling unit, which in turn has been shown to give rise to increasing per capita demand for water. For example, the use of water per person in a two person dwelling has been estimated to be one third greater than that in a four person dwelling. Some aspects of the water supply situation in the State are considered below. The impact of sewage discharges is dealt with in Chapter 9 and 10.

Leakages

Loss of water from the distribution network is a major problem affecting many water supply systems and leads to the abstraction of greater quantities of water than are strictly necessary to satisfy the demand from consumers. In Ireland this problem is typified by leakages due to the relatively poor condition of the older distribution mains in the inner Dublin area.

These leakages are caused by factors such as internal and external corrosion, frost damage, ageing of materials and heavy road traffic in the vicinity of installations. It has been estimated that 44 per cent of the water supply in the Dublin area is lost through leakages of which 39 per cent is due to mains leakage and the remaining 5 per cent due to domestic losses. An extensive leakage reduction and water conservation project assisted by national and EU Cohesion funding is now in place and is targeted at reducing the mains leakage figure to 22 per cent or less by the year 2000.

In relation to water conservation/leakage nationally, the Department of the Environment and Local Government commissioned consultants to carry out a comprehensive national water audit which has the objective, *inter alia*, of determining the extent of unaccounted for water in major public supply systems. This involves the collection and analysis of data on all public water supply schemes serving populations of over 5,000. It is now the policy of the Department before advancing funds for new or expanded works, to seek a water audit in order to confirm that no significant losses through leakages are taking place.

Paying for Water

Pressures on water resources may also arise from high demand for non-essential uses. Using the "polluter pays" principle, the draft EU framework Directive (EC, 1999) on water policy proposes that Member States shall take account of the principles of recovery of the costs of water services, including environmental and resource costs, having regard to an economic analysis conducted according to terms set out in an Annex to the Directive. Member States may in doing so have regard to the social, environmental

---

Box 7.1 The Dublin Water Supply

Considerable pressures on water resources exist in the main population centres and these pressures are most acutely felt in the Dublin region. In this area, which experiences a relatively low annual rainfall, around 75 per cent of the daily demand for water is supplied by the River Liffey through the treatment plants at Ballymore-Eustace and Leixlip. The abstractions at these points, along with the sewage treatment effluents from several towns along its course and the hydroelectric plants at Blessington and Leixlip, place significant pressure on the River Liffey as an environmental resource. The current rate of abstraction at Ballymore-Eustace is 240 megalitres per day and the agreement between the Electricity Supply Board and Dublin Corporation allows for a maximum daily abstraction of up to 318 megalitres, with further abstraction at Leixlip.

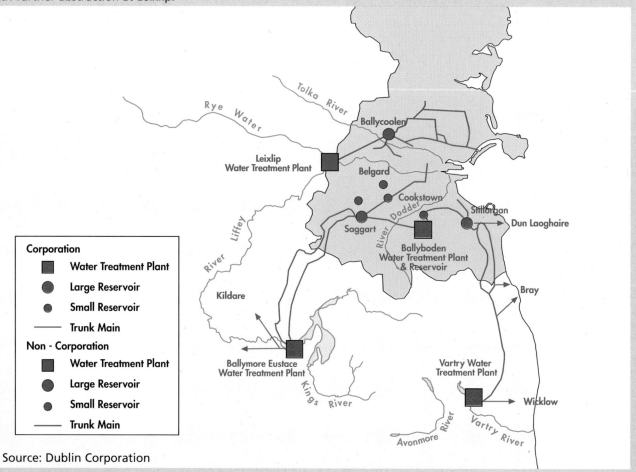

Source: Dublin Corporation

and economic effects of the recovery as well as the geographic and climatic conditions of the region or regions affected. It proposes that Member States shall report in river basin management plans on the practical steps and measures taken to apply this principle.

At present, only commercial users in Ireland are charged for water. This is usually achieved by metering of consumption, although for practical reasons some smaller users incur a fixed charge.

TOXIC AND DANGEROUS SUBSTANCES

Background

There are many thousands of natural and synthetic substances having some potential environmental impacts, whether used in pure forms or in formulations. Such impacts may occur through entry to any of the environmental compartments, water, air or soil, or through entry into food chains, and may take effect remotely in either time or space from the point of initial introduction into the environment. Little information is available on the toxicities of most of these substances (EEA, 1999). Furthermore, it is often difficult to obtain accurate information on the quantities of specific substances in use and thus the extent of the risk they present for environmental contamination.

Persistent Organic Pollutants

In recent years the use of specific chemicals in industry and as pesticides has increased dramatically. Many of these chemicals are important to modern society but they can also pose a serious threat to human health and the environment. In particular, a certain category of chemicals known as persistent organic pollutants (POPs) has for many years attracted international attention because of the tendency of these compounds to persist, bioaccumulate and pose a risk to human health and the environment. The persistence and toxicity of these substances are due to the presence of chlorine or certain carbon ring structures which allows them to resist the natural chemical or microbiological processes, which break down other pollutants rapidly into less harmful forms. Included in POPs are dioxins, furans and polyaromatic hydrocarbons (PAH), which arise as trace by-products of some chemical syntheses, waste incineration and other combustion activities.

Dioxins in the Irish Environment

Dioxins are chemical by-products, a number of which can be toxic to humans. They comprise a group of some 210 closely related compounds, the vast majority of which are considered to have little environmental significance at the levels normally encountered. However, 17 of these substances have been identified as demonstrating high toxicity, particularly in animal tests. Cows' milk is considered to be a particularly suitable matrix for assessing the presence of dioxins in the environment, because of the selective solubility of the compounds in fat. Cows tend to graze over relatively large areas, and these compounds will thereby, if present, concentrate in the fat content of the milk.

A national survey of dioxin levels in cows' milk was carried out in June 1995 (EPA, 1996a) when representative samples were taken from regional creameries throughout the country. Additional samples were taken from representative areas in the vicinity of waste incinerators and the chemical industry. The concentrations of dioxins found in the milk were uniformly low by comparison with those measured in other European countries; it is notable that the highest concentration found in the Irish survey was 38 times lower than the UK standard for dioxins in milk. Additionally, there was no evidence of higher levels in samples taken near areas of industrial activity. Nevertheless, the survey demonstrated the ubiquitous nature of these compounds and indicated their presence even in remote areas. It is intended to repeat the survey in 2000.

More recently, a number of surveys for dioxins in milk have been organised in particular localities adjacent to areas of industrial activity. The results of these surveys broadly reflect the outcome of the earlier national survey.

Endocrine Disrupters

For a number of years there has been mounting concern that some natural and synthetic substances can, through their release into the environment, cause the normal operation of the hormonal (endocrine) system to be disrupted. These chemicals have been shown to mimic or interfere with the binding action of natural endogenous hormones and thereby disrupt physiological processes that are under hormonal control. A wide range of abnormal effects has been attributed to such substances collectively known as *endocrine disrupters*. Examples of such suspect endocrine disrupters are organo-chlorine pesticides, polychlorinated biphenyls (PCBs), organotin compounds, alkylphenol ethoxylates (APEs), phthalates, phytoestrogens and phytosterols. To date, most attention has been focused on those substances that have a tendency to cause a feminising or *oestrogenic* effect.

Reproductive failures and associated population decline observed in a range of wildlife populations (birds, mammals, reptiles and fish) have all been associated with endocrine disruption. Most of the reported environmental impacts have occurred where the concentrations of the suspect chemicals were substantially higher than the background concentrations. Such occurrences in various countries have usually arisen from pollution incidents or from industrial discharges. A widely reported example is the case of reproductive abnormalities noted in alligators in Lake Apopka, Florida, following a major pesticide spillage into the lake with the active ingredient thought to be the degradation product p, p DDE (EA, 1998).

More recent investigations in the UK were initiated when oestrogenic effects were observed in roach (a cyprinid fish) from the settlement lagoons of a domestic sewage treatment plant. An assessment of oestrogenic substances in seven sewage treatment works effluents in the UK identified the natural oestrogens, oestrone and 17-ß-oestradiol, and the synthetic oestrogen ethinyl oestradiol in a biologically active form as the most oestrogenically active chemicals in the effluent (EA, 1996). It is not unlikely that similar concentrations of biologically active natural oestrogens are present in Irish sewage effluents.

In Ireland, a review study on endocrine disrupters commissioned by the EPA (Dempsey and Costello, 1998) was recently completed. The study noted that no adverse effects on the reproduction of wildlife populations have yet been observed in Ireland, with the exception of

imposex in marine molluscs attributable to the use of the pesticide tributyltin oxide (TBT) (see Chapter 10). Except in relation to the latter, however, there have been no surveys to monitor such effects. The report recommended that testing be carried out on the effluent from selected sewage treatment plants to establish any oestrogenic effects on freshwater organisms in Irish surface water systems. If such effects were to be found, the report recommends that fractionation of the effluents should be carried out to establish which chemicals were responsible. The main risk in Ireland from endocrine disrupters is likely to arise through dispersal from products, for example dispersal of pesticides or use of detergents, rather than their presence in industrial discharges.

Metals

Many metals are directly toxic to animals and plants and some, such as mercury and cadmium, have been associated with major pollution incidents affecting human health. Metals can have a wide variety of applications including metallurgy, paints, electronic components, batteries, catalysts, plastics and food additives. Again, indiscriminate consumer use or disposal arising from these activities can have a significant effect on the environment. These effects can be permanent, as metals, unlike organic substances, do not degrade. Pollution with metals may arise in surface and groundwaters due to industrial discharges and on land due to deposition originating from emissions to the atmosphere. Mining can be a major source of metal pollution, which, in the past, has had particular impact on the fish stocks of certain inland waters. The River Avoca in Co. Wicklow offers the most dramatic example of this sort of pollution in Ireland (see Chapter 9). The presence of lead in the emissions from vehicles constituted a major health risk, particularly for children, until control measures were

introduced in recent years (see also Chapter 8). In cases of serious contamination, metals may accumulate in animal and plant tissues in concentrations that present a risk to consumers.

Unlike the organic compounds discussed above, however, most metals occur naturally in the environment and may be present, for example, in soils in concentrations that are potentially toxic to grazing animals. Thus, when making an environmental assessment for metal contamination it is important to have knowledge of the background levels relevant to the local area.

ATMOSPHERIC POLLUTION

Stratospheric Ozone Depletion and UV-B Radiation

Solar UV-B (290-315 nm) radiation is the most energetic component of sunlight reaching the surface of the earth. Decreases in the quantity of total-column ozone, as now observed in many places, tend to cause increased penetration of UV-B radiation to the Earth's surface. These decreases in ozone levels are caused by the photochemical reaction of ozone with a variety of reactive substances released to the atmosphere from industrial and domestic sources. The increase in UV-B radiation associated with stratospheric ozone depletion is likely to have a substantial impact on human health. Potential risks include increases in the incidence and severity of eye defects, skin cancer, and infectious diseases. Quantitative estimates of risk are available for some effects (e.g., skin cancer), but others (e.g., infectious diseases) are associated with considerable uncertainty at the present time.

As noted in Chapter 4, the provisions of the Montreal Protocol and its amendments have brought about a marked decrease in production and use of ozone depleting chemicals.

Based on past emissions of ozone-depleting substances and a projection of the maximum allowances under the Montreal Protocol into the future, the maximum ozone depletion is expected to occur within the next two decades; thus, evidence for the recovery of the ozone layer will lie still further ahead.

Transboundary Pollution

It has long been established that the atmosphere is a dominant pathway for the transfer of pollutants to more remote marine and terrestrial regions. The defining attribute of atmospheric transfer of pollution is its relative speed compared with aqueous transport. Ireland's position at the western edge of the continent, together with prevailing winds which are predominantly from the west and south-west, ensures that its exposure to atmospheric transfer of pollution is generally low by comparison with other European countries. When winds come from the east, however, this exposure can increase considerably as was illustrated during the aftermath of the Chernobyl accident when substantial quantities of radionuclides were carried on easterly winds into Ireland.

Greenhouse Gases and Climate Change

Global warming ("the greenhouse effect") and the greenhouse gases have been discussed in Chapter 4. There is now convincing consensus that these man-made emissions of gases are enhancing the greenhouse effect and that this is leading to an increase in the mean temperature of the Earth's surface (EEA, 1999). On a world-wide scale, global warming is expected to affect sea levels, growth of forests, and the productivity of agricultural areas, with differing effects in tropical and high latitude regions. There is uncertainty concerning the likely impacts on Ireland of the enhanced greenhouse effect. The possible scenarios include

enhanced agricultural production, drying out of peatlands, more serious winter storms and flooding, lower summer flows in rivers and impacts from the rise in sea levels. There is the possibility of the vectors of tropical diseases spreading to northern European countries, including Ireland. In an alternative scenario, it is considered possible that the Gulf Stream would cease to flow towards north-western Europe and as a consequence there would be a dramatic cooling of the climate in the region.

NOISE AND ODOURS

For many people, the main experience of environmental degradation manifests itself as a nuisance that may not necessarily constitute a direct health hazard or carry any adverse implications for the ecosystem. However, such impacts may cause extreme irritation and adversely dispose those affected to the activities causing the problem. Chief among these nuisances are noise and odours.

Noise

Certain kinds of low-level sounds are regarded as desirable and enjoyable features of the environment. In contrast, continuous exposure to excessive noise can cause stress and even endanger health. The production of high noise levels is, therefore, a form of environmental pollution. Environmental noise, although unlikely to result in hearing impairment, can lead to annoyance and/or disturbance including disturbance of sleep. Annoyance is very difficult to quantify. It may be a result of the time of day and any one of a range of qualities of the offending sound such as the tone, the loudness or the frequency of occurrence of the noise events.

The causes of noise pollution include road and rail traffic, aviation, industry, construction and other economic activities. Road traffic noise can seriously affect living conditions in towns and working conditions in offices. The level of

---

Box 7.2 Monitoring Transboundary Pollution

The Convention on Long-range Transboundary Air Pollution was drafted under the auspices of the UNECE (United Nations Economic Commission for Europe) after scientists demonstrated the link between sulphur emissions in continental Europe and the acidification of Scandinavian lakes. The Convention relies on an extensive European monitoring network, EMEP (Co-operative Programme for Monitoring and Evaluation of the Long-range Transmission of Air Pollutants in Europe), measuring the chemical composition of the atmosphere and of rain and snow precipitation. The network is based on existing national monitoring activities. The objective is to assess the potential for acidification, eutrophication and photooxidants arising from long-range transport of pollutants.

There are four EMEP sampling sites in Ireland for measurement of air and precipitation quality, operated by Met Éireann at its Valentia observatory (Co. Kerry) and by the Electricity Supply Board (ESB) at the Burren, Co. Clare, Ridge of Capard, Co. Offaly and Turlough Hill, Co. Wicklow. Samples of air and rainfall are taken on a daily basis from these sites and are sent for analysis to the respective Met Éireann and ESB laboratories. The EPA fulfils a national quality assurance role. The monitoring data are applied by EMEP to validate and calibrate the mathematical models used to calculate quantities of atmospheric pollutants exchanged between countries.

A further international programme on the transport of pollutants in the atmosphere is carried out under the auspices of the OSPAR convention for the protection of the marine environment of the North East Atlantic and is concerned with the quantities of pollutants deposited on seawaters. In Ireland, measurements for the purposes of this convention are carried out at Turlough Hill and Valentia by the EPA in collaboration with Met Éireann and the ESB (See also Chapter 4.).

vehicle maintenance, the road surface, and the size and type of vehicle are factors that affect the extent of this type of noise. The noise from railways, which affects people living near them, is caused by passing trains, shunting, hooters, and engineering works.

Aircraft noise complaints come from areas overflown during take-off and landing, and those over which training and helicopter flights are made. Neighbourhood noise comes from a variety of sources such as factories, construction, roadworks, sports and entertainment facilities, car doors slamming, parties and other domestic activities, unattended burglar alarms and barking dogs. There is an increasing trend towards more noise at night and early morning due to factories working continuously and road users starting early to avoid traffic problems.

Local Authorities have a role under the provision of the EPA Act to control noise and to prevent and eliminate noise nuisance problems. The level of activity varies greatly from one local authority to another. The information available does not indicate any definite increase in the level of complaints being made, except perhaps in the Dublin urban area. Of the 535 recorded

complaints to the local authorities in 1998, three-quarters were made to Dublin Corporation.

The EPA is the responsible agency in the case of noise emanating from activities regulated by the IPC licensing system. Approximately 13 per cent of the total number (1,897 in 1998) of complaints received by the EPA in relation to such activities each year, are concerned with noise problems (EPA, 1999). The causes of these complaints are various. Some relate to sleep disturbance due to night-time noise from large industrial activities, some relate to nuisance caused by tonal or impulsive noises, and some relate to relatively low levels of noise causing problems in rural areas where the background noise levels are very low. A steady increase in the numbers of noise complaints received by the EPA in the period 1996 to 1998 in its regulation of larger industrial activities may be due to a combination of factors. On the one hand the number of companies being licensed under the IPC system was increasing each year, and therefore the number of companies about which the public might complain to the EPA was increasing. On the other, public awareness of the EPA's role in the control of the environmental practices and controls within industry

has also been increasing. It would also appear that the public is becoming generally less tolerant of noise nuisance.

Odours

Offensive and nuisance odours give rise to more public concern and complaints than any other aspect of air quality in Ireland. The high frequency of odour nuisance is explained by the fact that the human olfactory system has the capacity to detect a wide range of compounds at a fraction of the concentrations at which they might be injurious to health or at which they can be measured by the best available analytical methods. As in the case of noise and other nuisances, the degree of irritation caused by odours will vary from individual to individual depending on their everyday experiences and expectations.

The most offensive odours are usually associated with activities such as slurry spreading, the operation of wastewater treatment plants and rendering operations. Objectionable odours may also be generated by other farming operations, chemical and pharmaceutical industries, and some synthetic board manufacture. Odour control is exercised by Local Authorities under the 1987 Air Pollution Act, except in the case of IPC licensed activities where the responsibility rests with the EPA.

The numbers of complaints directed at IPC controlled activities in the period 1996-1998 are shown in Fig. 7.2. It is clear that odours were by far the most frequent cause of complaint, accounting for 78 per cent of the total in 1998. However, the bulk (67 per cent) of the complaints about odour referred to just three activities, two of which involve rendering operations and the third is a timber processing industry.

As indicated above, rendering plants were another common cause of odour

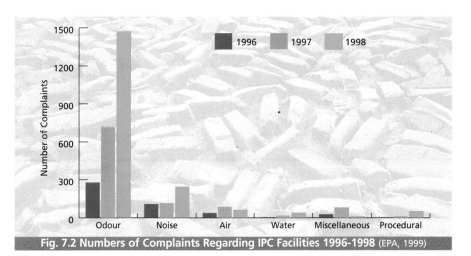

Fig. 7.2 Numbers of Complaints Regarding IPC Facilities 1996-1998 (EPA, 1999)

complaints. All rendering facilities are required to carry out an assessment of the odours generated at the site as a condition of the IPC licence. Once this assessment is carried out and is approved by the EPA, the facility is required to carry out whatever work is necessary to abate the odours. Improved negative air pressure and odour abatement equipment is being installed at some of these facilities. However, good management practices and proper operation of the abatement equipment are also of critical importance. These strategies have improved the situation in a number of facilities.

IMPACTS OF TOURISM AND RECREATION

Tourism in Ireland has experienced rapid growth in recent years (Chapter 3). The potential negative effects of a large influx of visitors into areas of high ecological and resource value cannot be ignored although there are frequently insufficient quantitative data by which to assess accurately the impact of tourism and recreation on these areas. It has been established, for instance, that sand dunes have been subjected to severe vegetative damage through the cumulative effect of vehicles, pedestrians and camping, picnicking and caravan use.

Recreational developments such as golf courses can result in damage to the dune habitat, particularly if they include artificial maintenance and fertilisation of grasslands. In some instances the development of golf courses has resulted in the restriction of public access to lands. However, golf development if handled sensitively can help to preserve the local environment, especially if excessive use of artificial chemicals is avoided.

The increased availability of funding for tourism-related infrastructural development has aided rapid expansion of facilities such as holiday homes, hotels, marinas, caravan parks and golf courses. The recent boost given to traditional resorts, which had been in decline, by the Resorts Renewal Scheme may have the unintended effect of putting severe strain on the local infrastructure, which can result in a complete breakdown in some instances.

There is a valid case for restriction of tourism numbers in certain sensitive areas where evidence of environmental damage due to excessive numbers of visitors has been established.

MAJOR POLLUTION INCIDENTS

The integrity of the environment and natural resources is always at risk from accidental or malicious damage. The explosion at the Chernobyl nuclear power plant in the Ukraine in 1986 and the *Sea Empress* oil tanker accident off Wales in 1998 are notable examples from recent years.

In Ireland, the contamination in 1996 of the Gortlandroe Well in Nenagh, Co Tipperary, which supplied a quarter of the water supply to the town of Nenagh, was one of the most serious incidents of pollution of a public water supply source in recent years. An investigation carried out by the EPA showed that the well was contaminated both by industrial and sewage effluents from the nearby Gortlandroe Industrial Estate (EPA 1996b).

In November 1997, an oil leak occurred in the heavy fuel oil pipeline at the jetty of the Irish Refining plc Whitegate Refinery in Cork Harbour. While minor in a European or world-wide context, the estimated spillage of 31 tonnes had a significant effect on local fauna particularly birds. The contingency plan for such an event was clearly inadequate, as the spillage

of this relatively small amount of oil should never have led to the environmental consequences observed. An investigation was undertaken by the EPA and recommendations were made to improve the regime of preventative maintenance and inspection of oil lines, and a review of the oil spillage contingency plan (EPA, 1998).

FISHING AND MARICULTURE

A review of the impacts of fisheries and mariculture was included in the recent assessment of the State's coastal and adjacent sea waters prepared by the Marine Institute (Boelens *et al.*, 1999). Commercial fishing has several direct impacts on the marine environment, the most obvious of these being the removal of target fish and shellfish and non-target species (as by-catch) from the ecosystem. The major part of the by-catch will consist of fish, and these discards, along with offal produced on-board, constitute a major food source for seabirds and other, mainly benthic, scavengers.

Towed gear in contact with the seabed, such as beam trawls and shellfish dredges, can cause injury or mortality of benthic organisms, an increase in the suspended sediment load, and the disturbance of spawning areas. Finally, passive gear (such as gill nets and driftnets) and mid-water trawls, may incidentally entangle non-target fish species, marine birds and mammals (see Chapter 10).

Many important fish species in Irish waters are heavily exploited. In addition

to taking a high proportion of the stocks of adult fish each year, catches often include many immature fish, which may be discarded or landed, depending on market forces. The intensity of fishing varies considerably between species and area. Juvenile sole, megrim, mackerel and herring have a different distribution to the adults and are usually not taken in the same fishery, whereas juvenile cod, haddock, and plaice tend to be mixed with adults outside the spawning season and are taken together in the respective fisheries.

The major environmental implications of finfish farming activities include the impacts of the loss of food and waste products (faeces and ammonia). These can represent a significant input of waste nutrients and organic material (Chapter 5), causing changes in the seabed community structure, similar to those found close to effluent outfalls and dump sites. The range of chemicals applied in finfish farming includes chemotherapeutants, such as antibiotics and pesticides, as well as antifoulants, which are applied to the cages and nets. Rearing of salmon in sea cages inevitably involves the risk of accidental escapes, and released fish have been shown capable of surviving and breeding with wild

populations and altering their genetic structure. Infectious disease and parasitism in farmed fish, although naturally-occurring and also found in wild stocks, can be severe due to the high densities at which the fish are held, and there is concern about the spread of parasites to wild populations.

GENETICALLY MODIFIED ORGANISMS

Genetically Modified Organisms (GMOs) are defined as bacteria, viruses, fungi, plant and animal cells, plants and animals capable of replication or of transferring genetic material in which the genetic material has been altered in a way that does not occur naturally by mating and/or by natural recombination.

In the last 25 years, the development and use of genetic engineering (GE) technology has brought many useful applications in healthcare, in the form of new pharmaceuticals, vaccines and new methods of diagnosing disease. This technology is also making a major impact in investigation of crime, in waste treatment, in environmental cleanup and in other areas.

While the above developments have been generally welcomed, the same cannot be said about the use of GE in crop production in Europe. In contrast, such crops are cultivated and widely accepted in the USA. Concerns in Europe about GM crops for food use include: inadequate labelling, meddling with the food chain, non-segregation from unmodified crops, use of antibiotic marker genes, ethical, moral and social concerns and the fact that GE foods were contemporaneous with the recognition of BSE in British cattle and the subsequent emergence of new-variant CJD in young people in 1996.

A number of environmental concerns have also been raised about GM crops in relation, particularly, to the use of 'input' traits such as herbicide and insect tolerance. The "pros" and "cons" of these particular developments are set out below.

In the case of the use of genetically modified (GM) herbicide tolerant (HT) crops the concerns raised include the following:

- the commercialisation of HT crops could lead to an increased and/or more widespread use of specific herbicides with associated environmental risks for biodiversity;
- the HT gene could be transferred to a related weed species or to a related crop species, or weeds could acquire multiple herbicide resistances thus causing a 'superweed' scenario which might be difficult to control;
- the possibility that seeds shed during or before harvesting could grow as weeds in future crops and might be difficult to control. The problem could be exacerbated if a subsequent crop was GM and was tolerant to the same herbicide;
- the treatment of a GM HT plant with the corresponding herbicide might produce new metabolites and residues;
- the use of HT plants could be a threat to sustainable agriculture - it could lead to the continuation and dependence on chemical weed control and provide fewer incentives for the development of non-chemical methods of weed control.

The potential advantages of using GM HT crops advanced include the following:

- it is established that some of the herbicides to which HT crops have been made tolerant are more biodegradable and less persistent than other commercially available herbicides, and this might have some environmental benefits;
- the use of such HT crops could result in lower residues due to a reduction in the use of herbicides;
- the farmer would not have to rely on cocktails of herbicides as is currently used to control different weed species;
- post emergence use of a herbicide will ensure that it is only used when necessary since farmers will be able to wait for weeds to emerge first before deciding if a herbicide use is necessary;
- research carried out in Denmark on the impact of HT sugar beets on future herbicide-use indicated that herbicide usage on GM sugar beet crop could be reduced by 50 per cent over a 20 year period; Dutch researchers reported that the possible introduction of GM sugar beet tolerant to glyphosate might reduce the environmental contamination caused by weed control in sugar beet cultivation in the Netherlands;
- Teagasc researchers reported greater than 60 per cent reduction in herbicide usage (active ingredient) in a GM sugar beet

field experiment carried out at Oakpark in Carlow during the 1997 growing season.

To date, ten field trials have been carried out with genetically modified herbicide tolerant sugar beet in Ireland regulated by the EPA under the Genetically Modified Organisms Regulations, 1994. More than 1500 GM crop field trials have been carried out in other EU Member States. In response to an increasing level of public interest and concern regarding the development of products containing or consisting of GMOs the Minister for the Environment and Local Government issued a consultation paper on the subject of GMOs and the environment in August 1998. The Department received over 200 responses to the consultation paper. In addition, the Department organised a two-day debate and invited representatives from industry, academia and non-governmental organisations. An independent Chairing Panel of four persons managed the debate.

Arising out of the Chairing Panel's Report, which was published in October 1999, the Government recognised the need for a programme of generic research on safety issues related to the deliberate release of GMOs to the environment. The EPA was requested by the Minister to identify a suitable programme of research in consultation with the

Box 7.3 Crops Genetically Modified for Insect Tolerance

A number of crops have been genetically modified for insect tolerance using the Bt genes. These genes code for the production of toxins and are derived from the soil bacterium, *Bacillus thuringiensis* (Bt). The toxins are effective against a variety of economically important crop pests.

Concerns raised in this case include the following:
- the possibility of resistance to the Bt toxins developing in insect species targeted by GM Bt crops thereby reducing the effectiveness of Bt biological pesticides; these Bt biological pesticides have been used in many countries including Ireland as alternatives to chemical pesticides for the last three decades;
- recent scientific reports claim that Bt expressed in corn pollen is toxic to the Monarch butterfly and to lacewing larvae;
- the spread of a gene conferring insect resistance to weeds could put at risk species of insects that depend solely on these for food.

Potential advantage of using such crops include the following:
- insect tolerant crops are intended to reduce or eliminate the need for treatment with chemical pesticides, which may result in low or lower residues of chemicals in the soil and this could result in more environmentally friendly farming practices;
- toxins from soil bacteria such as *Bacillus thuringiensis* are naturally occurring and have been used as biological pesticides in agriculture, including organic farming, for several decades; the long history of safe use as microbial pesticides, and the single-gene nature of the proteins are considered to be advantages for transferring these insecticidal proteins into plants;
- the presence of the Bt toxin inside the plant could provide a cost-effective strategy for the grower by the preclusion of the need for repeated spraying of a field with insecticides.

GMO Advisory Committee and other State agencies. At the time of writing, the Agency is in the process of identifying such a programme of generic research to be carried out under Irish climatic conditions in conjunction with relevant State agencies and the GMO Advisory Committee. The research results arising from the programme of generic research should provide an important input into an informed debate pertaining to the potential use of GM crops in Irish agriculture.

NATURAL ENVIRONMENTAL HAZARDS

Many of the most dramatic disruptions of the environment arise from natural phenomena. Earthquakes, volcanic eruptions and hurricanes are examples of the most destructive of such events, which not only affect the natural ecosystems but can also lead to large-scale loss of human life and of property and infrastructure. Ireland's position on the globe fortunately spares the country the worst of these events but significant risks are presented by flooding and natural radioactivity.

Flooding

Flooding can put lives at risk and can cause damage to and losses of property. It can also cause damage to various economic sectors such as agriculture and to transportation and other infrastructural facilities.

Specific pressures on the environment as a result of flooding include overflows from sewers, septic tanks, farmyards and slurry pits into streams and rivers. The effects of flooding on fauna can include death from drowning, loss of habitat and loss of feeding ground.

Flooding generally occurs where watercourses have not sufficient capacity to convey the water without overtopping the banks. Problems are most likely to occur where development has progressively encroached on the flood plains of rivers. In order to protect life and property in such areas, it has been necessary to build structures such as levees, embankments or walls to contain the floodwaters.

Various attempts to improve agricultural land through drainage and other reclamation works occurred in the eighteenth and nineteenth centuries under a series of Drainage Acts. However, it was not until the Arterial Drainage Act was enacted in 1945 that a comprehensive attempt was made to relieve the flooding problem and improve land drainage. The Arterial Drainage Act was amended in 1995 to allow local flood relief works to be carried out. Of particular concern are the karstic areas of the West where drainage is dependent on interconnected underground channels to carry away floodwaters. Drainage may have adverse impacts in respect of habitats and biodiversity.

Natural Radioactivity

Another example of a natural environmental hazard is the background radiation which arises from a number of sources and to which all living organisms are exposed. Prior to the first scientific experiments with naturally occurring radioisotopes and their medical use, no sources of radiation existed except these natural forms. Background radiation exposure arises from the following sources:
- cosmic radiation;
- terrestrial gamma radiation;
- radon inhalation;
- internal radiation.

Cosmic radiation reaches the earth from outer space and is a complex mixture of very high-energy radiation. On average humans receive an unavoidable annual dose of 0.3 milliSievert (mSv) from cosmic radiation at ground level. For comparison purposes, the radiation dose from a chest x-ray may be as low as 0.02 mSv. The atmosphere has a partially shielding effect so that the dose increases with altitude and as this radiation has sufficient energy to penetrate metal, frequent air travellers may be subject to significant doses. From the year 2000 onwards, national legislation will require that air crew are monitored to determine the radiation doses they receive due to cosmic radiation.

Terrestrial gamma radiation arises from certain radioactive elements (radionuclides) which were incorporated into the earth's crust when it was formed some 4500 million years ago. The most significant sources of terrestrial gamma radiation are the radionuclides uranium-238, thorium-232 and potassium-40, which are present in small quantities in all rocks and soils. The radionuclide potassium-40 also emits gamma rays as it decays. The gamma rays produced by these radionuclides are very penetrating. In Ireland, the average

Box 7.4 Survey of Radon Levels in Irish Houses

The Radiological Protection Institute of Ireland (RPII) has recently completed a survey of radon levels in Irish houses. Radon levels were measured in approximately 11,000 houses and the average radon concentration was 90 Bq/m³ (becquerel per cubic metre of air). In Ireland, the annual dose due to radon inhalation is estimated to be 2.25 mSv, on average. There are, however, significant variations in this value; in some houses the occupants have received doses which are ten to twenty times higher. The RPII has identified those areas in the country, called High Radon Areas, where homeowners are more likely to be exposed to high levels of radon. The map below shows radon levels found during the national survey carried out by the RPII.

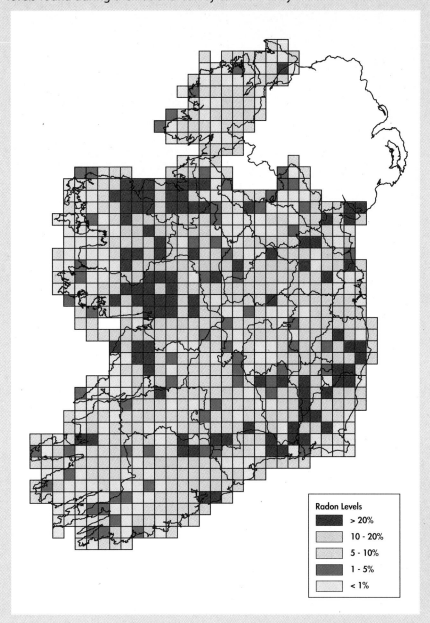

Radon Levels
- > 20%
- 10 - 20%
- 5 - 10%
- 1 - 5%
- < 1%

annual dose from terrestrial gamma radiation is approximately 0.3 mSv.

Radon gas inhalation is the most significant source of exposure to natural radiation in Ireland. The gas is a naturally occurring radioactive substance, which is part of the decay series of uranium. When radon is vented to the open air, it is quickly diluted to harmless concentrations, but when it enters an enclosed space, such as a house or other building, it can sometimes accumulate to unacceptably high concentrations. When inhaled into the lungs, radon and its radioactive decay products give a radiation dose that may damage cells in the lung and eventually lead to lung cancer.

In 1990, the Government adopted an annual average radon concentration of 200 Bq/m³ as the national Reference Level for radon in houses. Homeowners finding levels in excess of this value are advised to implement measures to reduce the radon level so as to reduce the risk of lung cancer. Such remedial actions could include measures to prevent gases from the ground entering the house or to improve ventilation through the house. In 1998, the building regulations were changed to ensure that all new houses have some protection against radon.

In addition to being exposed to radon in their homes, people can also be exposed to radon at work, or in the case of children, at school. In February 1998, the Minister for Education and Science announced the introduction of a survey of indoor radon levels in all primary and secondary schools in Ireland. The survey is being conducted over four years during which the radon levels will be measured in approximately 4,000 schools.

National legislation mentioned above in relation to exposure of air crew to cosmic radiation also has specific provisions relating to exposure to radon in the workplace. From 2000 onwards, the RPII will conduct surveys in various workplaces, beginning with those where high radon levels are most likely to be found. These include underground workplaces and workplaces which are located in High Radon Areas. If the exposure to radon is found to be significant, employers will be obliged to implement remedial measures or to introduce a system of radiological protection in the workplace.

Internal Radiation other than from radon may be caused by the radionuclides from the decay series of uranium and thorium, and by potassium-40, present in air, food and water. These radionuclides enter the human body when we breathe, eat and drink and so irradiate the body internally. It is estimated that we receive an average annual dose of 0.3 mSv from these internal sources.

How well the pressures on the environment are controlled by society can be determined by assessing and monitoring changes in biodiversity and in the quality of air, inland waters, marine and coastal waters, and soil, and by monitoring the uses made of the natural resource base. Such issues are addressed in Part IV of this report. Some emerging issues relating to pressures on the environment are addressed in Part V.

REFERENCES

Boelens, R.G.V., Walsh, A.R., Parsons, A.P. and Maloney, D.M., 1998. *Ireland's Marine and Coastal Areas and Adjacent Seas: An Environmental Assessment*. Prepared by the Marine Institute on behalf of the Department of Environment & Local Government and the Department of Marine & Natural Resources. Marine Institute, Dublin.

Dempsey, S. M. and Costello, M. J., 1998. *A Review of Oestrogen Mimicking Chemicals in Relation to Water Quality in Ireland*. EPA, Wexford.

DELG (Department of the Environment and Local Government), 1999. *Planning Guidelines on Residential Density*. DELG, Dublin.

EA (Environment Agency), 1996. *The Identification and Assessment of Oestrogenic Substances in Sewage Treatment Works Effluents*. EA, UK.

EA (Environment Agency), 1998. *Endocrine-Disrupting substances in Wildlife. A review of the scientific evidence and strategic response*. EA, UK.

EC (European Council), 1999. Common Position (EC) No. 41/1999 adopted by the Council on 22 October 1999 with a view to the adoption of a Directive 1999/.../EC of the European Parliament and of the Council establishing a framework for Community action in the field of water policy (1999/C 343/01). *O.J.* C 343/1. EC, Brussels.

EEA (European Environment Agency), 1999. *Environment in the European Union at the turn of the Century*. EEA, Copenhagen

EPA (Environmental Protection Agency), 1996a. *Dioxins in the Irish Environment, An Assessment based on levels in Cow's Milk, 1996*. EPA, Wexford.

EPA (Environmental Protection Agency), 1996b. *Report on the Contamination in 1996 of the Gortlandroe Water Supply Well, Nenagh, Co. Tipperary*. EPA, Wexford

EPA (Environmental Protection Agency), 1998. *Oil Spillage from Irish refining Plc., Whitegate, Co. Cork: 4th November 1997*. EPA, Wexford.

EPA (Environmental Protection Agency), 1999. *Report on IPC Licensing and Control 1998*. EPA, Wexford.

Holmes, J.S., 1999. *How Much Rock was Extracted to Build your House?* Institute of Quarrying, Northern Ireland Branch and Irish Mining and Quarrying Society, Extractive Industry Ireland, Main St. Publications, Portadown, N. Ireland.

Walsh, M., Collins, J.F. and Grennan, E.J., 1997. Vegetation and Soil Studies on a Western Hill Sheep Farm. *Irish Journal of Agricultural and Food Research*, Vol. 36, No. 1.

PART IV

Environmental Quality

CHAPTER 8

AIR QUALITY

Air quality monitoring and assessment in Ireland are undergoing a major change of focus. Smog associated with residential coal burning, which was a feature of Dublin and some other urban areas, has been eliminated, confirming the effectiveness of the Government's smoke-control regulations. The potential for damage to human health and the environment due to emissions of gases such as sulphur dioxide and nitrogen oxides from industry and power generation is also being reduced through fuel switching, integrated pollution control and other measures. Ambient levels of sulphur dioxide are within existing EU limits, and at most existing monitoring stations would also comply with proposed limits for 2005. Concentrations of lead in air are well within existing and proposed limits, following the phasing out of leaded petrol.

Other emissions from road traffic, however, have now become the greatest threat to air quality in Ireland, especially in urban areas. The pollutants of concern from this source include nitrogen dioxide, fine particulate matter and benzene. Information from the somewhat limited monitoring to date for nitrogen dioxide indicates that meeting future EU limits will present a difficult challenge. This is true also for fine particulate matter, measured as PM_{10}, which derives mainly from vehicles using diesel. The status in respect of benzene is not known, owing to very limited monitoring to date.

A detailed new programme for air quality monitoring has been drawn up in response to these changes and to meet the requirements of the new EU legislation, which sets stringent limit values for a wide variety of air pollutants to be met within 10 years and requires that adequate information on ambient air quality is made available to the public.

Ireland, unlike many other European countries, does not have an environmental problem with tropospheric (ground level) ozone. The deposition of acidifying compounds is low by virtue of Ireland's geographical position and the prevailing weather systems. The principal issue in this regard is nitrogen deposition in sensitive ecosystems contiguous to agricultural areas that are major sources of ammonia.

The state of air quality is assessed by undertaking monitoring to determine whether the levels of various pollutants comply with standards that are considered adequate for the protection of human health and the environment. Monitoring networks in Ireland were developed originally from a need to assess the impact of smoke and sulphur dioxide (SO_2) emissions on air quality and to implement a number of EU Directives introduced during the 1980s on these and other air pollutants. The air quality limit values prescribed by the Directives for smoke and SO_2, lead and nitrogen dioxide (NO_2) remain the only national air quality standards in Ireland. Since their adoption, the established monitoring networks have been applied to support these standards and to develop air pollution control policies and legislation under the Air Pollution Act, 1987.

During the 1990s, a national ozone monitoring network was established pursuant to the ozone Directive (CEC, 1992) and some authorities began to measure carbon monoxide, PM_{10} (small particles of less than 10

INTRODUCTION

Most air pollutants are principally of concern because of their effects on human health. Pollutants emitted into the atmosphere also give rise to acidification of soils and surface waters and increased levels of tropospheric ozone as well as damage to ecosystems and materials. Information on the concentrations of a variety of compounds in air is necessary to formulate strategies to control these problems and to monitor the effects of measures implemented. This chapter reviews the state of air quality and the level of acidifying deposition in Ireland.

Box 8.1 The Framework Directive on Air Quality Assessment and Management

Council Directive 96/62/EC (CEC, 1996) on ambient air quality assessment and management provides the framework for future legislation on air quality in Europe. The Directive embodies a substantially new approach to air quality monitoring, assessment and management with the following objectives:

- to define and establish objectives for ambient air quality in the European Community that will avoid, prevent and reduce harmful effects on human health and the environment;
- to assess ambient air quality in Member States on the basis of common methods and criteria;
- to obtain adequate information on ambient air quality and ensure that it is made available to the public by means of, inter alia, alert thresholds;
- to maintain ambient air quality where it is good and improve it in other cases.

The Directive lists sulphur dioxide, nitrogen oxides, particulate matter and lead as the priority pollutants to be covered first by the new approach. This will be followed by similar action on ozone, benzene, carbon monoxide, poly-aromatic hydrocarbons and some heavy metals. Each country will be divided into zones and the monitoring, assessment, management and reporting of air quality will be undertaken in relation to these zones and to *limit values*, *assessment thresholds* and *margins of tolerance* to be set for the listed pollutants. For some of the pollutants *alert thresholds* will also apply above which immediate action must be taken to inform the public of pollution incidences, thereby allowing persons at risk to take avoidance measures.

For each individual pollutant, the limit values will have to be met everywhere by a specified attainment date. The margin of tolerance, which decreases in equal annual increments to zero at the attainment date, will apply in the worst affected areas where concentrations are considerably in excess of the limit value. In such areas specific action plans will be needed to bring the concentrations below the limit value by the attainment date. Details of these action plans and their effects are part of the reporting obligations. Action plans are not required in the case of pollutants whose concentrations exceed the limit value by no more than the permitted margin of tolerance at any time. For this situation, it is assumed that the benefits accruing from existing general air pollution control measures in the period up to the attainment date will be sufficient to reduce the concentrations below the limit value by that date.

The extent of monitoring and assessment in any zone will be determined mainly by population size and the existing air quality status. Measurement is mandatory wherever concentrations are above the lower assessment threshold and the greatest monitoring effort applies if concentrations are above the upper assessment threshold, i.e., where they approach or exceed the limit value. Where concentrations are between the two thresholds, less intensive measurement combined with other assessment methods, such as air quality modelling, will suffice. Dispersion modelling, objective estimation and indicative measurement alone are sufficient for general assessment in zones with concentrations below the lower assessment threshold. However, the population size may still warrant that continuous measurement be undertaken for zones in this category in the case of pollutants for which alert thresholds have been set.

microns in diameter) and benzene in their local areas. While there are no national monitoring networks yet in operation for these compounds, monitoring will be required under the recently adopted EU Framework Directive on air quality assessment and management (Box 8.1).

AIR QUALITY STANDARDS

Air quality is assessed in relation to national and EU standards for a variety of pollutants. Air quality standards for smoke and SO_2, NO_2 and lead are set out in Table 8.1 (DoE, 1987). Smoke is one measure of particulates concentrations in air determined from the stain produced by passing the sampled air through an appropriate filter. The Irish standards correspond exactly to the limit values set by EU Directives for these

pollutants (CEC, 1980, 1982 and 1985). Guide values of 100 to 150 $\mu g/m^3$ for the maximum daily mean of both SO_2 and suspended particulates and 40 to 60 $\mu g/m^3$ for the annual mean are also given in the Directive on smoke and SO_2. In the case of NO_2, guide values of 135 $\mu g/m^3$ and 50 $\mu g/m^3$ are specified in respect of the median and 98-percentile, respectively.

The EU Directive 92/72/EEC on air pollution by ozone (CEC, 1992) established a harmonised procedure for monitoring, exchanging information, and informing and warning the public about air pollution by ozone. Unlike the other Directives on air pollutants, it sets no air quality limit values. Instead, it defines thresholds for ozone in air above which there may be effects on

human health and vegetation, in addition to thresholds for informing and warning the public in the event of ozone pollution episodes. The thresholds (Table 8.2) are broadly consistent with guide values promulgated by the World Health Organisation and are an appropriate reference for the assessment of ozone concentrations.

MONITORING NETWORKS

Table 8.3 summarises the extent of air quality monitoring in Ireland in terms of pollutants, networks and stations. The bulk of the air quality monitoring remains concentrated on smoke and SO_2 in urban areas where relatively simple and inexpensive measurement techniques are employed. These air pollutants arise predominantly from fossil fuel

Table 8.1 Air Quality Standards in Ireland

Pollutant	Air Quality Standard ($\mu g/m^3$)	Basis of Application
Smoke	80	Annual median of daily mean values
	130	Winter median of daily mean values
	250	98-percentile of daily mean values
	250	No more than three consecutive days
SO_2	80 if smoke > 40	Annual median of daily mean values
	120 if smoke = or < 40	
	130 if smoke > 60	Winter median of daily mean values
	180 if smoke = or < 60	
	250 if smoke > 150	98-percentile of daily mean values
	350 if smoke = or < 150	
	250 if smoke > 150	No more than three consecutive days
	350 if smoke = or < 150	
NO_2	200	98-percentile of hourly mean values
Lead	2	Annual mean

Table 8.2 EU Thresholds for Ozone

Purpose	Parameter	Threshold ($\mu g/m^3$)
Protection of Human Health	8-hour mean*	110
Protection of Vegetation	1-hour mean	200
	24-hour mean	65
Population Information	1-hour mean	180
Population Warning	1-hour mean	360

*the 8-hour mean is calculated four times per day from the eight hourly values in the four periods 01.00 through 08.00, 09.00 through 16.00, 17.00 through 24.00 and 13.00 through 20.00

Table 8.3 Air Quality Monitoring in 1998

Pollutant	Networks	Local Authority Sites Automated	Local Authority Sites Sampler	Other Sites Automated	Other Sites Sampler
Smoke	20		65		26
PM_{10}	1		5		
SO_2	20		65	2	26
NO_X	3	2	12	1	
Lead	1		6		
Ozone	2	1		6	
CO	2	2			
Benzene	2		12		

combustion and there has been some urban pollution associated with both smoke and SO_2 in the past in Ireland. The first monitoring networks were established over 30 years ago. Measurements are currently carried out at approximately 65 sites by a total of 17 Local Authorities. One-third of the sites is in the Dublin area and approximately two-thirds of all sites are designated for the implementation of Directive 80/779/EEC on SO_2 and suspended

particulates. The Electricity Supply Board and some large industries operate local SO_2 and smoke monitoring networks related to the emissions from their own plants. All sites employ the well-proven automatic eight-day active samplers incorporating air filtration and acidimetric bubblers. Daily average concentrations of black smoke particulates are based on the reflectance of the filter smoke stain, and SO_2 is determined from the total

acidity produced by passing the air sample through hydrogen peroxide solution.

The monitoring of air pollutants other than smoke and SO_2 remains very limited in Ireland. Continuous monitoring of nitrogen oxides has been undertaken at Rathmines and College Street in Dublin by the EPA and Dublin Corporation, respectively, for many years and serves to implement Directive 85/203/EEC on NO_2 (CEC, 1985). Cork Corporation commenced NO_X monitoring at a site in Cork City in 1997. Carbon monoxide is monitored at one station in Dublin and one station in Cork City. Passive sampling methods have recently been applied to undertake measurement campaigns for NO_2 and benzene. These involve the adsorption of the pollutant onto a chemical agent in a tube by diffusion over a period of weeks followed by subsequent analysis in the laboratory. The method gives the average concentration for the period of tube exposure.

STATE OF AIR QUALITY

Smoke and PM_{10}

The main concern in relation to particulates is their potential effect on human health, notably the functioning of the respiratory system. The success of smoke control legislation (DoE, 1990), introduced in the Greater Dublin area on 1 September 1990, in dealing with the problem of winter smog in Dublin was highlighted in the previous State of the Environment report. Summary smoke statistics for the Dublin Corporation network during the period 1985/86 to 1998/99, presented in Figure 8.1, show how smoke levels have stabilised at very acceptable values. The reduction in smoke concentrations since 1990 has been quite dramatic, obviously

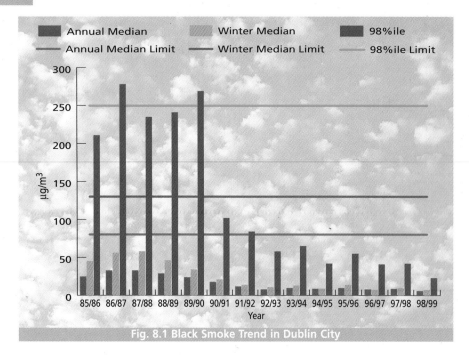

Fig. 8.1 Black Smoke Trend in Dublin City

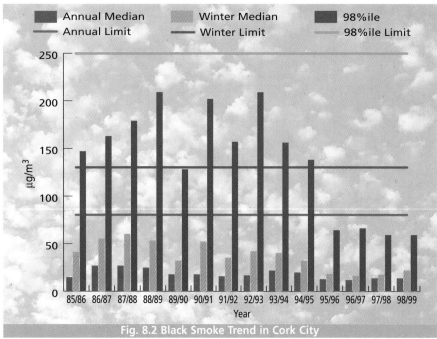

Fig. 8.2 Black Smoke Trend in Cork City

Table 8.4 98-Percentile Smoke Concentrations in Various Urban Areas									
Stations		1990/91	1991/92	1992/93	1993/94	1994/95	1995/96	1996/97	1997/98	1998/99
Dundalk	2	**	152	230	156	172	112	96	84	33
Drogheda	1	135	118	**	120	92	94	101	94	34
Bray	1	**	**	**	93	86	82	50	27	22
Arklow	1	**	**	**	162	130	99	79	88	47
Waterford	2	**	100	100	100	71	91	64	64	58
Wexford	1	157	144	171	139	106	137	141	169	**
Dungarvan	1	12	26	31	21	21	20	21	20	21
Limerick	3	81	126	124	112	101	107	99	104	47
Galway	2	60	64	45	65	47	33	38	58	40
Ennis	1	45	12	24	20	44	24	21	26	20

underlining the effectiveness of the smoke-control regulations. The 98-percentile values for the 15 stations in the network are typically in the range 60 to 75 $\mu g/m^3$ and the winter medians are usually less than 20 $\mu g/m^3$ which are very much in compliance with the standards.

Smoke control regulations came into force for Cork City in February 1995 (DoE, 1994) and they were extended to a number of other urban centres in 1998 (DELG, 1998). Smoke levels had approached the limits in some of these centres on occasion under unfavourable meteorological conditions, and the regulations have again brought about substantial reductions in smoke concentrations in the areas concerned. This is shown by Figure 8.2 which gives the trend in the levels in Cork City during the period 1985/86 to 1998/99 and by Table 8.4 which lists the 98-percentile values recorded for smoke in various other urban centres.

In recent years the emphasis with regard to particulate pollution has focused on PM_{10}, very small particles, which can penetrate deep into the respiratory tract, and therefore those that have the greatest potential for health effects. Road traffic, particularly diesel-engined vehicles, is the primary source of PM_{10}. Therefore, while Irish smoke control regulations have been instrumental in eradicating urban smog associated with coal burning, their effect on PM_{10} levels will have been relatively small.

Table 8.5 summarises the levels of PM_{10} measured at four monitoring stations in Dublin in 1996, 1997 and 1998 (Dublin Corporation, 1999). The results indicate that PM_{10} levels are very high along streets with large volumes of traffic and that substantial concentrations exist even in urban background areas. However, the College Street station is positioned on

Table 8.5 Daily Mean PM$_{10}$ Concentrations in Dublin

Station Name Station Type	College Street City Centre Kerbside			Merchants Quay City Centre Roadside			Rathmines Suburban Roadside			Phoenix Park Background		
	1996	1997	1998	1996	1997	1998	1996	1997	1998	1996	1997	1998
Mean (µg/m³)	44	43	49	40	41	38	23	21	19	16	17	14
Median (µg/m³)	38	40	43	34	37	31	18	18	16	12	15	12
98%ile (µg/m³)	110	102	127	101	92	99	65	55	62	51	50	47
Maximum (µg/m³)	163	151	173	149	149	143	90	79	83	96	99	97
Total daily values	275	250	300	100	281	309	277	277	267	244	287	302
Values > 50 µg/m³	86	73	116	20	74	66	19	9	12	6	6	5

a traffic island at an extremely busy city-centre road junction and the result is not representative of the typical exposure of the public to PM$_{10}$. The high values for Merchants Quay, however, are representative of an area where many people live and work and they are due mainly to large numbers of heavy goods vehicles travelling from Dublin Port. At this station, the number of days with average PM$_{10}$ greater than 50 µg/m³ is up to twice the number which will be allowed under new EU standards (Box 8.2) and the annual mean is around the EU Stage 1 limit of 40 µg/m³ to be achieved by 2005.

Sulphur Dioxide

Sulphur dioxide has effects on human health in that when inhaled it can constrict the bronchi and reduce the protective mechanism of the respiratory tract; it is also a major contributor to the acid rain phenomenon. The trends in concentrations over the past 15 years in Dublin and Cork (Figure 8.3 and Figure 8.4) indicate that ambient levels of SO$_2$ are not now a matter of concern. This situation is the result of several factors. These include increased consumption of natural gas in place of oil, coal and other solid fuel in several sectors, decreases in the sulphur content of oil and emission controls introduced by the IPC licensing system. The potential impact from electricity power stations has been reduced by the use of low

Box 8.2 New EU Limit Values for SO$_2$, NO$_2$ and NO$_X$, Particulate Matter and Lead

Council Directive 1999/30/EC (CEC, 1999), the first in a series of 'daughter' Directives to the Framework Directive on air quality assessment and management, specifies new and revised EU limits for sulphur dioxide, nitrogen dioxide and nitrogen oxides, particulate matter and lead. The primary class of particulate matter for which limit values are proposed is PM$_{10}$ but measurement and reporting of PM$_{2.5}$ is also required. It is generally accepted that measurements of these particle fractions are better indicators of the effects of suspended particulate matter in air on human health than those provided by the black smoke or total suspended particulates methods. The limit values are set out below.

Pollutant	Limit Value Objective	Averaging Period	Limit Value µg/m³	Basis of Application of the Limit Value	Limit Value Attainment Date
SO$_2$	Protection of human health	1-hour	350	Not to be exceeded more than 24 times in a calendar year	1/1/2005
SO$_2$	Protection of human health	24-hours	125	Not to be exceeded more than 3 times in a calendar year	1/1/2005
SO$_2$	Protection of vegetation	Calendar year	20	Annual mean	19/6/2001
SO$_2$	Protection of vegetation	1 Oct-31 Mar	20	Winter mean	19/6/2001
NO$_2$	Protection of human health	1-hour	200	Not to be exceeded more than 18 times in a calendar year	1/1/2010
NO$_2$	Protection of human health	Calendar year	40	Annual Mean	1/1/2010
NO + NO$_2$	Protection of vegetation	Calendar year	30	Annual Mean	19/6/2001
PM$_{10}$-Stage 1	Protection of human health	24-hours	50	Not to be exceeded more than 35 times in a calendar year	1/1/2005
PM$_{10}$-Stage 1	Protection of human health	Calendar year	40	Annual Mean	1/1/2005
PM$_{10}$-Stage 2	Protection of human health	24-hours	50	Not to be exceeded more than 7 times in a calendar year	1/1/2010
PM$_{10}$-Stage 2	Protection of human health	Calendar year	20	Annual Mean	1/1/2010
Lead	Protection of human health	Calendar year	0.5	Annual Mean	1/1/2005

Directive 1999/30/EC also specifies
- alert thresholds for SO$_2$ and NO$_2$ to be applied as the basis for informing the public in the event of pollution episodes ;
- temporary margins of tolerance which will apply in the case of some of the prescribed limits ;
- the upper and lower assessment thresholds in respect of the four pollutants concerned as required for the implementation of the Framework Directive ;
- criteria for determining the minimum number of fixed measurement stations for each pollutant ;
- data quality objectives ;
- the reference methods of measurement.

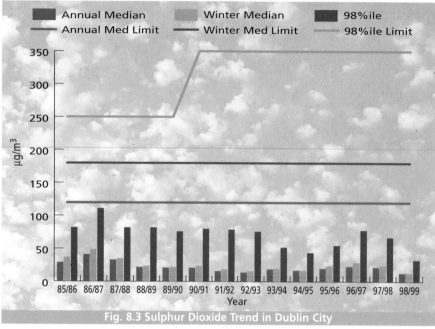

Fig. 8.3 Sulphur Dioxide Trend in Dublin City

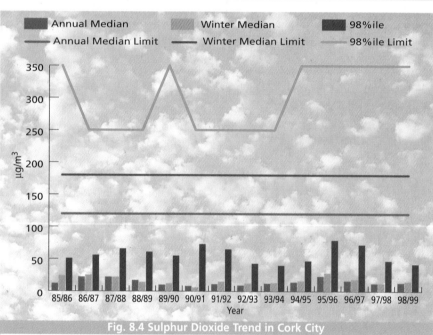

Fig. 8.4 Sulphur Dioxide Trend in Cork City

Street indicate high levels of NO_2 in a city-centre area subject to heavy traffic. However, as previously mentioned in relation to PM_{10} levels at this location, the results are not representative of typical population exposure to NO_2. The levels of NO_2 recorded at the Rathmines site are consistently lower than at College Street, reflecting lower NO_X emissions locally due to lower traffic density at this location. The significant reduction in NO_2 concentrations after 1994 is not fully understood but it probably reflects the relocation of the sampling intake to a somewhat higher position than previously used. The first year's data from the Cork City station give median and 98-percentile NO_2 values of 19 $\mu g/m^3$ and 96 $\mu g/m^3$, respectively which are intermediate between the corresponding values at the two Dublin stations.

Directive 1999/30/EC (CEC, 1999) sets an annual average limit of 40 $\mu g/m^3$, to be achieved by 2010, and no more than 18 hourly mean values should exceed 200 $\mu g/m^3$ (Box 8.2). As in the case of SO_2, these limits are considerably more stringent than current standards and the indications from various NO_2 measurement campaigns by diffusion tube (McGettigan, 2000) are that annual NO_2 levels are currently close to or slightly above 40 $\mu g/m^3$ in many areas affected by heavy traffic. Moreover, while the annual mean at the Cork City continuous monitoring station was well below 40 $\mu g/m^3$ in 1998, there were nevertheless 18 hourly mean values over 200 $\mu g/m^3$, the maximum number allowed by the new limits. Therefore, as for PM_{10}, the achievement of the new EU limits for NO_2 throughout urban areas in the future could present a difficult challenge.

A large proportion of total NO_X emissions emanate from electricity power stations (Chapter 4) but these

sulphur coal at the large Moneypoint plant and a switch from heavy fuel oil to natural gas at some other plants. It is worth noting also that because the current standards for SO_2 take into account the corresponding level of smoke (Table 8.1), reduced smoke concentrations allow a less stringent SO_2 standard to operate.

New EU limits for SO_2 after 2005 will allow no more than three daily mean values greater than 125 $\mu g/m^3$ per annum (Box 8.2), which is considerably more stringent than the current standards. Nevertheless, SO_2

concentrations at virtually all existing monitoring stations in Ireland would already comply with this limit.

Nitrogen Dioxide

Nitrogen oxides are harmful to the respiratory system; they contribute to the formation of acid rain and are involved in the formation of ground level ozone. Summary NO_2 results for the period 1988 through 1998 for the two Dublin sites are presented in Figure 8.5 and Figure 8.6 in relation to the limit and guide values of the NO_2 Directive. The data for College

emissions are efficiently dispersed on release from tall stacks.

Consequently, the emissions from these point sources have less impact on ambient concentrations of NO_2 than those arising from high-density diffuse sources at ground level, such as road traffic in urban areas. While the potential impact of SO_2 from power stations was reduced simply by changes in the fuels used, it has been necessary to retrofit NO_X-control technology at most of the larger power plants in order to achieve a similar level of control on NO_X emissions.

Lead

The presence of lead in air is a potential health hazard, particularly for growing children, in whom a high body burden of lead has been linked to retarded mental development. Petrol combustion is the primary source of lead emissions in Ireland and major reductions in emissions have occurred since the mid-1980s through progressive reduction in the lead content of leaded petrol and a very significant increase in the use of unleaded petrol. In this way the use of leaded petrol has been gradually phased out. The decrease in ambient lead levels resulting from these developments is readily apparent from the trend in annual mean concentrations of airborne lead at typical city centre and suburban roadside stations in Dublin over the period 1988 through 1998, as shown on Figure 8.7. Annual mean

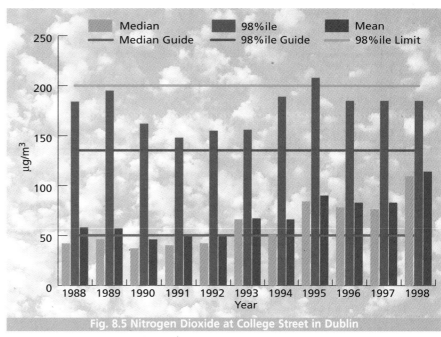

Fig. 8.5 Nitrogen Dioxide at College Street in Dublin

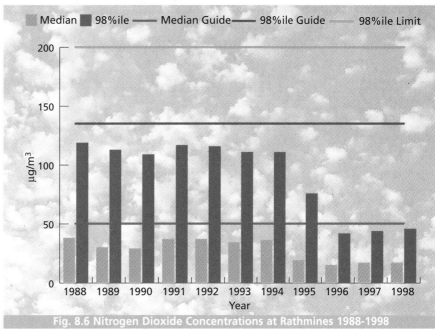

Fig. 8.6 Nitrogen Dioxide Concentrations at Rathmines 1988-1998

concentrations for most sites are currently less than 0.2 μg/m³, which is one-tenth of the current limit value. This means that the levels are also already well within the new lead limit of 0.5 μg/m³ prescribed by Directive 1999/30/EC.

Ozone

Higher concentrations of ozone in the troposphere have adverse implications for human health, and for crops and other vegetation. Ozone concentrations are currently monitored at six stations in Ireland for the purpose of implementing Directive 92/72/EC. Table 8.6 summarises the results for the years

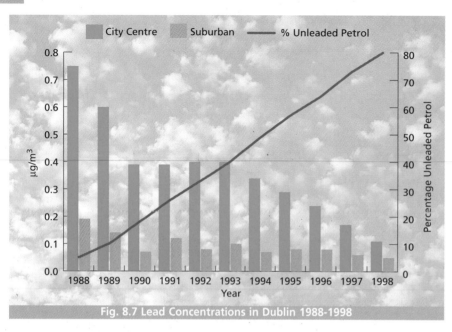

Fig. 8.7 Lead Concentrations in Dublin 1988-1998

Table 8.6 Summary Ozone Statistics

	1-hour Mean µg/m³			8-hour Mean µg/m³			Daily Mean µg/m³	
	Med	98%ile	Max	Med	98%ile	Max	Mean	Max
1995	48-72	100-125	160-233	47-71	94-120	145-190	46-71	106-159
1996	47-72	86-106	124-168	47-73	80-103	117-155	45-70	93-131
1997	40-66	82-106	114-173	39-66	79-104	110-162	39-66	82-133
1998	48-78	76-102	112-170	48-78	73-100	97-156	46-79	85-129

Table 8.7 Summary of EU Ozone Threshold Exceedances

	Population Information 1-hour 180 µg/m³		Protection of Human Health 8-hour 110 µg/m³		Protection of Vegetation 1-hour 200 µg/m³		24-hour 65 µg/m³
	Hours	Days*	8-hours	Days*	Hours	Days*	Days
1995	27	13	218	35	11	6	250
1996	0	0	57	14	0	0	251
1997	0	0	47	10	0	0	198
1998	0	0	17	10	0	0	301

Number of days on which the relevant threshold (1-hour or 8-hour) was exceeded

countries. For example, in summer 1998, hourly ozone levels reached 400 µg/m³ on some occasions in France, Greece and Italy and eight-hour mean values over 250 µg/m³ were common (de Leeuw and Camu, 1998). The 110 µg/m³ threshold was exceeded on as many as 50 days in many central and southern European countries.

since the monitoring network became fully operational. The levels recorded are normally very low and Ireland, quite unlike many European countries, does not have an environmental problem with tropospheric ozone. The low incidence of exceedance of the EU thresholds given in Table 8.2 for one-hour and eight-hour averaging periods as set out in Table 8.7 also reflects the low ozone levels. Exceedances of the 65 µg/m³ threshold for 24-hour values are

common but this is not surprising as this threshold is close to mean ozone concentrations in northern mid-latitudes. The 180 µg/m³ threshold for informing the public is usually not reached under normal summer conditions and with maximum one-hour concentrations typically around 150 µg/m³ there are relatively few exceedances of the eight-hour threshold of 110 µg/m³ above which there may be effects on human health. This contrasts sharply with the situation in many European

Ozone has a considerable potential for adverse impacts on forests, crops and other vegetation through the cumulative effect of successive episodes of elevated concentrations.

The critical levels concept is now being widely applied in an attempt to protect forests and crops from such exposure. Research has shown that there is a good correlation between the yield loss of crops and the dose accumulated from ozone concentrations above 40 ppb (Fuhrer and Acherman, 1994). The critical level is therefore defined as the cumulative exposure above 40 ppb (80 μg/m³), generally referred to as AOT_{40}, above which adverse effects could be expected. AOT_{40} is calculated as the sum of the differences between hourly ozone concentration and 40 ppb for each hour when the concentration exceeds 40 ppb during a relevant growing season. The critical level for crops is set at 3,000 ppb hours with respect to daylight hours in the May through July growing season. The AOT_{40} for forests is 10,000 ppb hours for daylight hours in the period April through September (Werner and

Spranger, 1996; Karenlampi and Skarby, 1996).

The critical levels concept has been developed within the workplan of the UNECE Convention on Long Range Transboundary Air Pollution and now also forms scientific support for the European Union's strategy to control tropospheric ozone. In this regard, specific targets for AOT_{40} are among the major environmental objectives, which underpin the Gothenburg Protocol and the national emissions ceilings Directive (Chapter 4). The draft revised ozone Directive, the third Daughter Directive to the Framework Directive on Air Quality Assessment and Management, also includes target and long-term objective AOT_{40} values for the protection of vegetation. Figure 8.8 shows AOT_{40} maps for crops for 1997, a typical year for ozone in Ireland, and for 1995 when the highest concentrations on record

occurred. The corresponding result for forests is given on Figure 8.9. When these are overlain with land cover maps, they indicate that approximately 15 per cent of total crop area exceeds the ozone critical level for crops in a typical year like 1997 but this could rise to 35 per cent in a hot summer like that of 1995. However, no exceedance of the critical level for forests is indicated even for the ozone levels that occurred in 1995.

Carbon Monoxide and Benzene

Carbon monoxide and benzene are substances that are of significance in relation to human health. The emissions from petrol combustion are the overwhelming source of carbon monoxide, while about 80 per cent of benzene in ambient air is due to the combustion and evaporation of petrol. The measurement of both compounds is relatively new in the

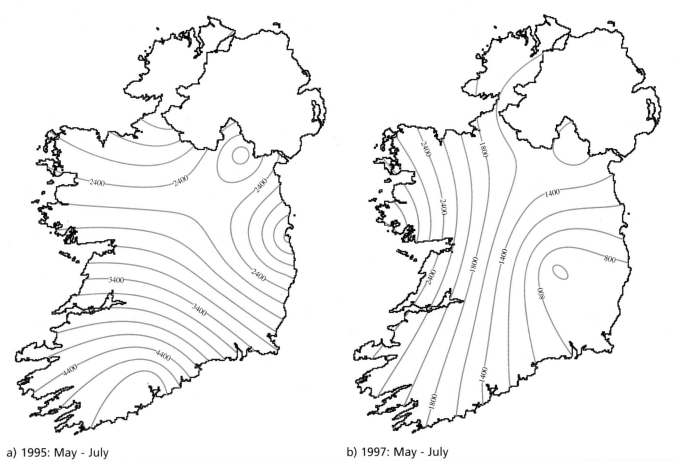

a) 1995: May - July

b) 1997: May - July

Fig. 8.8 Ozone: AOT_{40} for Crops: a) 1995: May - July and b) 1997: May - July (ppb hours)

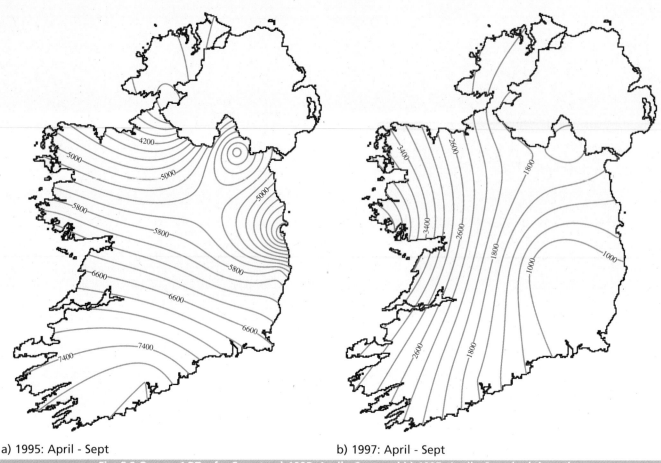

a) 1995: April - Sept

b) 1997: April - Sept

Fig. 8.9 Ozone: AOT_{40} for Forests: a) 1995: April - Sept and b) 1997: April - Sept (ppb hours)

context of air quality monitoring in Ireland and only very limited information is available. Limit values of 10 mg/m³ as an eight-hour rolling average and 5 µg/m³ as an annual average have been proposed for CO and benzene, respectively, by the European Commission in the second daughter directive to the Framework Directive on Air Quality Assessment and Management. The eight-hour average CO for city-centre areas based on measurement in Dublin and Cork is less than 2 mg/m³, which would be well within the proposed CO limit. However, mean benzene levels in Dublin during 1996, based on passive sampling campaigns, were up to 15 µg/m³ at some roadside stations subject to heavy traffic (Henderson *et al.*, 1997). Much more monitoring data, especially results based on continuous measurement, are required to establish more completely the

urban air quality status in respect of benzene.

ACID DEPOSITION

Many parts of Europe continue to suffer from the acidification of soils and surface waters, the eutrophication of terrestrial ecosystems and the deterioration of materials and cultural

monuments caused by the deposition of sulphate, nitrate and other compounds. Quantitative information on the deposition of these compounds is therefore necessary for the assessment of the impact of important emission sources. Furthermore, detailed spatial description of deposition patterns is a key requirement in the application of

Table 8.8 Typical Ion Concentrations in Rainfall 1990-1998

Station Name	Operating Body	Monitoring Period	Total Ion Concentrations (μeq/l)						Non-Marine Concentrations (μeq/l)			
			SO_4	NO_3	NH_4	Ca	Mg	K	SO_4	Ca	Mg	K
Brackloon	FERG	1991-1998	49.9	8.1	15.3	18.3	56.4	8.0	14.9	3.6	0.0	1.1
Cloosh	FERG	1991-1998	44.3	6.6	10.7	15.7	47.6	5.8	16.1	4.7	0.0	0.8
Roundwood	FERG	1991-1998	40.3	20.1	27.7	11.3	19.2	3.5	28.5	5.9	0.0	1.6
Ballyhooly	FERG	1989-1996	37.6	11.5	28.9	14.0	25.4	5.3	18.6	7.3	0.0	1.9
Valentia	MET	1991-1998	60.5	6.3	11.9	23.3	94.3	10.6	11.1	2.6	0.1	0.8
Turlough Hill	ESB	1991-1998	31.4	18.2	25.0	14.6	20.8	9.5	23.1	5.9	0.0	0.0
The Burren	ESB	1991-1998	55.7	11.4	20.9	21.0	66.6	2.6	20.3	7.9	0.2	0.0
Capard Ridge	ESB	1991-1998	29.9	13.4	33.8	10.1	18.9	1.5	20.0	6.3	0.3	0.1
Lough Navar	FSNI	1990-1994	35.5	11.4	13.9	27.1	44.7	3.6	16.7	20.2	2.1	0.3
Askeaton	EPA	1996-1998		9.0	20.5				23.5			

FERG: Forest Ecosystem Research Group   MET: Met Eireann
ESB: Electricity Supply Board   FSNI: Forest Service of Northern Ireland

the critical loads approach to emissions control where actual deposition loads are compared with threshold values above which there may be adverse effects.

For many years, Ireland has operated two deposition-measuring stations in the European Monitoring and Evaluation Programme (EMEP) network, which monitors the long-range transport of air pollutants in Europe. Deposition has also been measured at many other locations by various bodies and researchers (Figure 8.10). A summary of the annual average ion concentrations in rainfall recorded at the various sites in the period 1990 through 1998 is given in Table 8.8. The resultant deposition patterns of the most important components in rainfall are presented in Figure 8.11. Potential acidity (Figure 8.11d) takes account of both acidifying and neutralising agents and is included here as the best measure of the total acid load due to all inputs.

Annual non-marine sulphate deposition (i.e., deposition of sulphate originating from anthropogenic sources) varies from about 0.3 g SO_4-S/m^2 generally to about 0.7 g SO_4-S/m^2 in some areas. The highest annual deposition occurs where rainfall is very high e.g., parts of the West, or where long-range

Fig. 8.10 Deposition Monitoring Sites

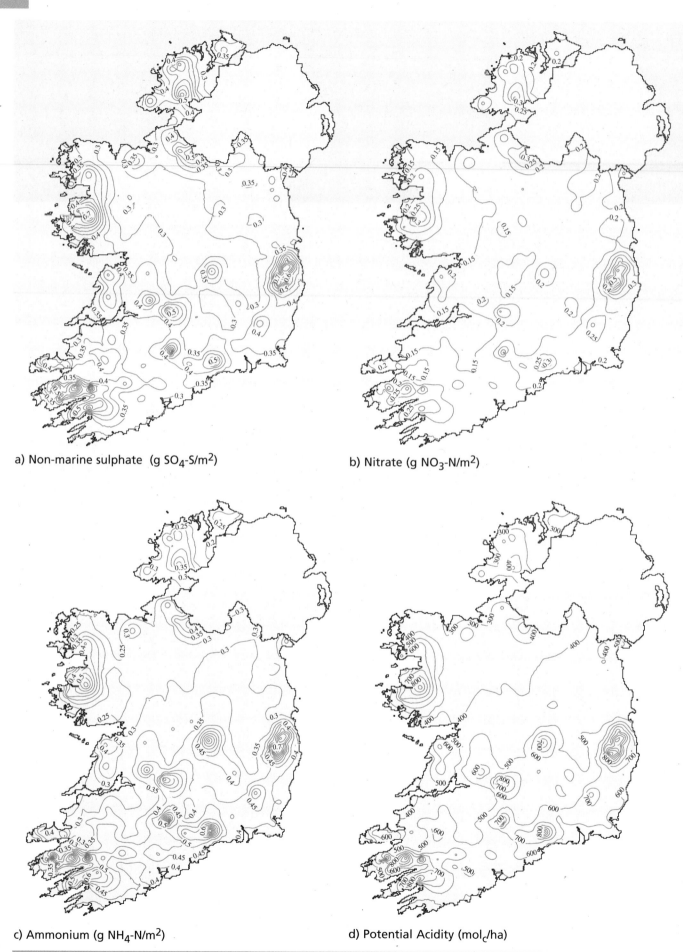

a) Non-marine sulphate (g SO$_4$-S/m^2)

b) Nitrate (g NO$_3$-N/m^2)

c) Ammonium (g NH$_4$-N/m^2)

d) Potential Acidity (mol$_c$/ha)

Fig. 8.11 Typical Deposition Patterns: a) Non-Marine Sulphate, b) Nitrate, c) Ammonium and d) Potential Acidity

transport from Europe gives sulphate concentrations in rainfall that are higher than the average, such as in the Wicklow mountains. Nitrate deposition has the highest values of up to 0.5 g NO_3-N/m^2 also occurring in the East. The low values in the West are close to background levels while the higher values in the East also indicate some influence from long-range pollutant transport from Europe. The ammonium deposition map shows a different pattern to that of sulphate and nitrate, reflecting the dominance of local ammonia sources and negligible import of ammonium. The annual deposition of ammonium ranges from about 0.3 g NH_4-N/m^2 in the

West to about 0.4 g NH_4-N/m^2 over much of the South and East. Overall, the representation of deposition given by Figure 8.11 has not changed over the past 20 years.

TRANSBOUNDARY AIR POLLUTION

Figure 8.12 shows the principal geographical areas of origin of the sulphur and nitrogen deposited in Ireland in 1997 and the main areas subject to deposition from pollutants emitted in Ireland due to transboundary transport (Tarrason and Schaug, 1999). These results have been obtained using complex EMEP transport and dispersion models, which provide the general relationships between sources and receptors of air pollutants in Europe. Approximately half of the sulphur deposition in Ireland is imported while only one-quarter of sulphur emitted in Ireland is deposited in the country. More than 80 per cent of oxidised nitrogen deposition in Ireland is imported and less than 20 per cent of Irish nitrogen oxide emissions are subsequently deposited in the country. In the case of ammonium, however, over 80 percent of total deposition is due to emissions in Ireland even though approximately half of all such emissions is exported.

CONCLUSIONS

Air pollution problems in Ireland associated with coal burning have been virtually eliminated and road traffic has replaced stationary combustion sources as the greatest threat to the quality of air. As a result of ever-increasing traffic, concern in urban areas has shifted to a number of pollutants for which this is the most important emission source. These include priority pollutants such as NO_2, PM_{10}, CO and benzene, which have not yet been subject to monitoring in a national sense.

The adoption of the EU Framework Directive on air quality assessment and management changes fundamentally the entire approach to air quality monitoring and assessment in Member States. The implementation of this and the associated series of daughter Directives, which prescribe new and revised limit values for a wide range of air pollutants, requires a radical restructuring and expansion of monitoring networks in Ireland. Greater emphasis will be placed on data dissemination and the need to keep the public fully informed on the state of air quality. These issues have been addressed in the first national air quality monitoring programme drawn up by the EPA (McGettigan *et al.*, 2000).

There is a general move, in the EU approaches, towards intensive monitoring over short averaging periods and the introduction of alert thresholds for some pollutants based on hourly concentrations. In the case of sulphur dioxide in particular, the eight-day bubbler method employed at existing stations will become redundant in this respect. Similarly, as the emphasis on particulates has shifted to the PM_{10} and smaller size fractions, measurement of black smoke becomes largely obsolete. New or extended monitoring networks are being established for NO_2, PM_{10}, CO and benzene, the main traffic-related pollutants. The information on most of these is still quite limited but the indications are that NO_2 and PM_{10} will present the greatest challenges in the context of meeting the new EU standards in urban areas in the future with associated implications for traffic management and transport policy. Ozone is not the threat to human health in Ireland that it is in many European countries and is probably only significant in relation to possible effects on crops.

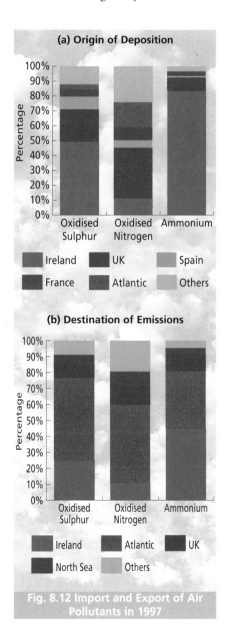

Fig. 8.12 Import and Export of Air Pollutants in 1997

The deposition of acidifying compounds is low and remains largely unchanged in Ireland over the past 20 years. This is due to several factors including small indigenous emissions of oxidised sulphur and nitrogen, the export of a large proportion of these emissions and relatively small input from emissions originating in other countries by virtue of Ireland's geographical position and prevailing weather systems. Given its relationship to other aspects of nitrogen input to terrestrial and aquatic ecosystems, it is the issue of local-scale ammonium deposition, which is probably the most important consideration relating to deposition now and in the near future.

REFERENCES

CEC (Council of the European Communities), 1980. Council Directive 80/779/EEC of 15 July 1980 on air quality limit values and guide values for sulphur dioxide and suspended particulates. *O.J.* L 229, 30 August 1980.

CEC (Council of the European Communities), 1982. Council Directive 82/884/EEC of 3 December 1982 on a Limit Value for Lead in the Air. *O.J.* L 378, 31 December 1982.

CEC (Council of the European Communities), 1985. Council Directive 85/203/EEC of 7 March 1985 on air quality standards for nitrogen dioxide. *O.J.* L 87, 27 March 1985.

CEC (Council of the European Communities), 1992. Council Directive 92/72/EEC of 21 September 1992 on air pollution by ozone. *O.J.* L 291, 13 October 1992.

CEC (Council of the European Communities), 1996. Council Directive 96/62/EEC of 27 September 1996 on ambient air quality assessment and management. *O.J.* L 296, 11 November 1997.

CEC (Council of the European Communities), 1999. Council Directive 1999/30/EEC of 22 April 1999 relating to limit values for sulphur dioxide, nitrogen dioxide and oxides of nitrogen, particulate matter and lead in ambient air. *O.J.* L 163, 29 June 1999.

De Leeuw, F. and Camu, A., 1998. *Exceedance of EC Ozone Threshold Values in Europe in 1998.* European Topic Centre on Air Quality, RIVM, Netherlands.

DoE (Department of the Environment), 1987. *The Air Pollution Act 1987 (Air Quality Standards) Regulations.* S.I. No 244 of 1987, Dublin.

DoE (Department of the Environment), 1990. *The Air Pollution Act 1987 (Marketing, Sale and Distribution of Fuels) Regulations.* S.I. No 123 of 1990, Dublin.

DoE (Department of the Environment), 1994. *The Air Pollution Act 1987 (Marketing, Sale and Distribution of Fuels - Cork) Regulations.* S.I. No 403 of 1994, Dublin.

DELG (Department of the Environment and Local Government), 1998. *The Air Pollution Act 1987 (Marketing, Sale and Distribution of Fuels) Regulations.* S.I. No 118 of 1998, Dublin.

Dublin Corporation, 1999. *Atmospheric Pollution and Noise Control Unit Annual Report 1998/99.* Environmental Health Section, Dublin Corporation, Civic Offices, Dublin.

Fuhrer, J. and Acherman, B. (eds.), 1994. *Critical Levels for Ozone*: A UNECE Workshop Report. Swiss Federal Research Station for Agricultural Chemistry and Environmental Hygiene CH-3097, Liebefeld-Bern, Switzerland.

Henderson, S., Jennings, S.G., Keary, J., Lee, M., McManus, B., O'Connor, T.C. and Shanahan, I. 1997. *A Baseline Study of the Concentrations of Volatile Organic Compounds and PM$_{10}$ in Dublin City.*

R&D Report Series No. 2. Environmental Protection Agency, Wexford.

Karenlampi, L. and Skarby, L. (eds.), 1996. *Critical Loads for Ozone in Europe : Testing and Finalising the Concepts.* A UNECE Workshop Report. Department of Ecology and Environmental Science, University of Kuopio, Finland.

McGettigan, M., 1996. *Ozone Monitoring Results and EU Threshold Exceedances for Ireland in 1995.* Environmental Protection Agency, Wexford.

McGettigan, M., 2000. *Air Quality Monitoring Annual Report 1998.* Environmental Protection Agency, Wexford.

McGettigan, M., O'Donnell, C. and Toner, P., 2000. *Draft National Air Quality Monitoring Programme.* Environmental Protection Agency, Wexford.

Tarrason, L. and Schaug, J. (eds.), 1999. *Transboundary Acid Deposition in Europe.* EMEP Summary Report 1999. Norwegian Meteorological Institute, Oslo.

Werner, B. and Spranger, T. (eds.), 1996. *Manual on methodologies and criteria for mapping critical levels/loads and geographical areas where they are exceeded.* Umweltbundesamt (Federal Environment Agency), Berlin, Germany.

CHAPTER 9

INLAND WATERS

The most recent overview of the state of the inland waters covers the period 1995-1997. This shows a continuation of a trend of increasing slight and moderate pollution of the river system, which has been recorded since the late 1970s and is attributed mainly to eutrophication. In that period, 32 per cent of the 13,000 km of channel surveyed was assessed as slightly or moderately polluted compared to 28 per cent in 1991-1994 and 22 per cent in 1987-1990. In a shorter length of channel, first assessed in 1971 to determine mainly the impact of waste discharges, the proportion of slightly or moderately polluted channel increased from 10 to 47 per cent over the 24 year period, while seriously polluted channel reduced from 6 to 2 per cent. Of the 120 lakes surveyed in 1995-1998, 19 per cent showed chlorophyll concentrations indicative of a lesser or greater intensity of eutrophication; these enriched lakes represented approximately 35 per cent of the total lake area surveyed. A national groundwater survey, which commenced in 1995, has shown that there is no widespread pollution of individual aquifers but that local contamination is not uncommon. Of greatest concern is the detection of faecal coliforms in over one-third of the groundwater samples tested, emphasising the need for improved protection of these waters.

Salmon and trout are still widespread in Irish inland waters but have been adversely affected by drainage and eutrophication over the last thirty years. The charr has been lost from a number of lakes since the beginning of the century and appears to be particularly sensitive to eutrophication. Coarse fish, which are non-native, now thrive in many rivers and lakes and roach, in particular, continues to expand its range.

The main issue to be addressed in the inland waters is eutrophication. This is particularly necessary if the indigenous salmonid fish are to be preserved. Recent measures intended to control phosphorus inputs are welcome in this regard but the risk presented by agricultural sources is likely to remain significant. In addition to counter-eutrophication measures, salmonid fish will also benefit from remedial works carried out on drained rivers and proposed measures to ameliorate the impacts of any future drainage operations.

INTRODUCTION

Relatively high rainfall and low population density ensure that Ireland is among the European countries with the highest availability of fresh water. This water constitutes one of the key economic resources of the State, the primary importance of which relates to the supply of drinking water and water for other domestic, industrial and agricultural purposes. In many areas of the country, rivers and lakes are attractive features of the landscape that help to promote tourism and increasingly provide outlets for recreational activities. More traditionally, they provide excellent game and coarse fish angling opportunities and the near ubiquitous occurrence of salmon and trout populations in Irish freshwater bodies is a situation that is presently unparalleled in many other European countries. Comprehensive reviews of Irish rivers and lakes were published recently to mark the holding in Dublin of the 1998 meeting of the international society for freshwater research (SIL) (Giller, 1998; Moriarty, 1998; Reynolds, 1998).

Rivers Draining in Excess of 2000 km²

Fig. 9.1 The Larger Rivers

There are some 400 separate drainage areas in the island but most of these are small coastal catchments. Only nine river systems lying wholly or partly in the State have drainage areas greater than 2,000 km² (Fig. 9.1). These nine rivers systems drain approximately 35,000 km² or 50 per cent of the land area of the State (a further 1,800 km² is located in the Northern Ireland part of the Erne catchment). The Shannon is by far the largest catchment, accounting for 32 per cent of the total area drained by the nine larger rivers and nearly 17 per cent of the State's area. From the pollution control point of view, it is the low flows in rivers that are of the greatest importance as they indicate the minimum dilution available for waste discharges. In general, the low flows in Irish rivers are less than 5 per cent and in some cases less than 1 per cent of the mean flows (McCumiskey, 1991) and create problems for water quality management at some locations, particularly in the upper reaches of rivers.

It is estimated that there are some 6,000 lakes in Ireland with surface areas greater than 1 ha. The great majority of these have surface areas less than 50 ha. Lakes are mainly situated in the midland, western and north-western parts of the country. With the exceptions of the reservoirs on the Liffey and Lee, the eastern and southern areas are practically devoid of sizeable bodies of standing water. There are 18 natural lakes with surface areas greater than 1,000 ha lying wholly in the State, of which seven are in the Shannon catchment or its sub-catchments (Table 9.1). One lake in this size category, Lough Melvin, lies partly in Northern Ireland. In addition Blessington (1,200 ha) and Inniscarra (2,850 ha, including subsidiary waters) reservoirs, situated, respectively, on the Liffey and Lee rivers, exceed 1,000 ha in area. Ireland has a relatively large number of lakes compared to most of the other EU Member States, apart from Sweden and Finland.

Ireland is well endowed with groundwaters and the total area of aquifers in the State is estimated to be of the order of 19,000 km². The potential recharge to the aquifers from rainfall has been estimated by taking account of factors such as topography and the permeability of the overburden. On this basis, a total groundwater flow of 3,370 Mm³/yr has been estimated. This is equivalent to 49 mm over the whole country with regional values ranging from 21 and 26 mm/yr, respectively, in the north-west and east to 65 and 67 mm/yr, respectively, in the mid-west and west.

This chapter presents an overview of the present quality status of the surface and groundwaters of the State as well as an assessment of fish stocks, the main biological resource likely to be affected by water quality. Data relating to water quality are based mainly on the most recent national report prepared by the EPA (Lucey et al., 1999). The report provided information for the three-year period 1995-1997 and this has been updated where possible.

Table 9.1 Lakes with Surface Areas Greater than 1,000 ha			
Lake	Water Resources Region	Surface Area ha	Maximum Recorded Depth m
Corrib	Western	16,900	50
Derg	Shannon	11,750	38
Ree	Shannon	10,500	38
Mask	Western	8,700	58
Conn	Western	5,000	40
Allen	Shannon	3,500	30
Leane	Southern	2,000	67
Sheelin	Shannon	1,880	20
Carra	Western	1,620	9
Gill	North Western	1,400	31
Oughter	North Western	1,300	10
Arrow	North Western	1,250	28
Gowna	North Western	1,240	12
Ennell	Shannon	1,180	30
Cullin	Western	1,140	3
Derravaragh	Shannon	1,100	23
Gara	Shannon	1,100	16
Currane	Southern	1,000	30
Lake not wholly in State:			
Melvin	Drowes	2,300	NA

Water quality data in the State arise mainly from the monitoring undertaken by the EPA and the local authorities, supplemented by the work of the fishery agencies in specific fishery waters. Most of the monitoring to date has been concentrated on the rivers, where over 13,000 km of channel is currently subject to regular chemical and/or biological sampling. Only a minor proportion of the estimated 6,000 lakes over 1 ha have been surveyed for water quality status to date, although this includes all of the larger water bodies. A national monitoring programme for groundwaters commenced in 1995, previous investigations having been of a local nature. Currently, national monitoring programmes for inland waters are being revised by the EPA.

RIVER AND STREAM WATER QUALITY

Scope of Current Surveys

The biological quality of the rivers and streams is currently assessed by the EPA at some 3,200 locations once every three years. These biological surveys have been in operation since 1971 and the resulting data probably constitute the largest and longest-term environmental quality database currently available in the State. The chemical sampling of the rivers is significantly less extensive, a total of some 2,100 locations being covered to a greater or lesser extent at present. This programme is operated directly by the local authorities or by the EPA on their behalf.

The National River Quality Classification System

The classification system is primarily biological and is based on a scheme of biotic indices, which codify the characteristic and well-documented changes induced in the flora and fauna of rivers and streams in the presence of pollution. The system has four quality classes as described below.

Class A waters (Unpolluted) include pristine waters of the highest ecological quality and also waters of a less high but acceptable standard, in which existing or potential beneficial uses are judged not to be at risk. These waters are suitable for game fisheries (salmon and trout), for abstraction for potable supply and for amenity and contact sport uses and they are, therefore, regarded as being in a 'satisfactory' condition.

Classes B, C and D reflect increasing levels of pollution and/or ecological impairment and they are consequently regarded as 'unsatisfactory' to lesser or greater degrees.

Class B (Slightly Polluted) and more notably Class C (Moderately Polluted) waters are mainly characterised by eutrophication, i.e., the artificial over-enrichment of waters by nitrogen and phosphorus leading to excessive growth of rooted plants and/or filamentous algae. The respiration of these plants may be sufficient to reduce dissolved oxygen concentrations to levels that put game-fish survival, in particular, at risk, especially at night-time when the photosynthetic production of oxygen has ceased. In some waters, the intense photosynthetic activity during the day may result in highly alkaline conditions due to the excessive uptake of carbon dioxide.

Class D (Seriously Polluted) stretches are characterised by the presence of high concentrations of biodegradable organic waste, the main potential impacts of which are deoxygenation and the growth of unsightly bacterial and fungal slimes ('sewage fungus'). In extreme cases these may blanket the substratum with malodorous anaerobic sludge. Only the most tolerant (e.g., sludge worms) of invertebrates are to be found in such conditions and virtually all beneficial uses are lost.

National River Quality: Present Status

The 13,100 km of channel currently covered by the biological surveys include all of the main rivers and their tributaries and many smaller streams (a total of 1,072 watercourses). The overall water quality situation in this baseline (Fig. 9.2) indicates that, while the bulk (67 per cent) of surveyed baseline channel

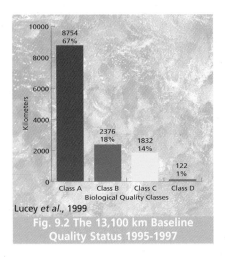

Lucey *et al.,* 1999

Fig. 9.2 The 13,100 km Baseline Quality Status 1995-1997

was in a satisfactory (Class A) quality condition, a considerable proportion was in an unsatisfactory condition in the 1995-1997 survey period: some 18 per cent (2,376 km) was assessed as slightly polluted (Class B), 14 per cent (1,832 km) as moderately polluted

(Class C) and 1 per cent (122 km) showed the characteristic symptoms of serious pollution (Class D).

River Quality: Regional Situation

A regional analysis of river quality is presented in Fig. 9.3 and the ranking of the regions in terms of the proportion (per cent) of channel in Class A is shown below.

1st	North-Western 'b' (Donegal-Sligo)	87
2nd	Southern	86
3rd	Western	79
4th	Mid-Western	62
5th	North-Western 'a' (Cavan-Monaghan)	60
6th	Shannon	59
7th	South-Eastern	53
8th	Eastern	45

The North-Western 'b' Region (Donegal-Sligo) has the highest proportion of unpolluted river channel while the Eastern Region has the least. The more intense levels of pollution are relatively most widespread in the Eastern Region where some 27 per cent of surveyed channel is classed as moderately polluted (Class C) and 3 per cent as seriously polluted (Class D). Elsewhere, the incidence of serious pollution is relatively low, mostly ranging from 0.5 to 1 per cent of

surveyed channel, and it was not recorded at all in the period in the Southern and the North-Western 'a' (Cavan-Monaghan) Regions. Moderate pollution is relatively widespread (22 per cent of channel) in both the Mid-Western and North-Western 'a' (Cavan-Monaghan) Regions. Slight pollution (mainly seen as eutrophication) is most widespread in the South-Eastern Region where some 29 per cent of channel is affected and it is also relatively widespread in the Eastern (25 per cent), and Shannon (23 per cent) regions. These contrasting regional situations largely reflect differences in population distribution and levels of agricultural activity.

Pollution Causes

In the period under review most (44 per cent) recorded instances of serious pollution were apparently due to sewage discharges, the remainder to agriculture or industry in roughly equal proportions (Fig. 9.4). In respect of the lesser levels (slight and moderate) of pollution, most instances can be attributed to agriculture and the bulk of the remainder to sewage. While the causes of the observed pollution have not been specifically proven, it is quite clear in most cases

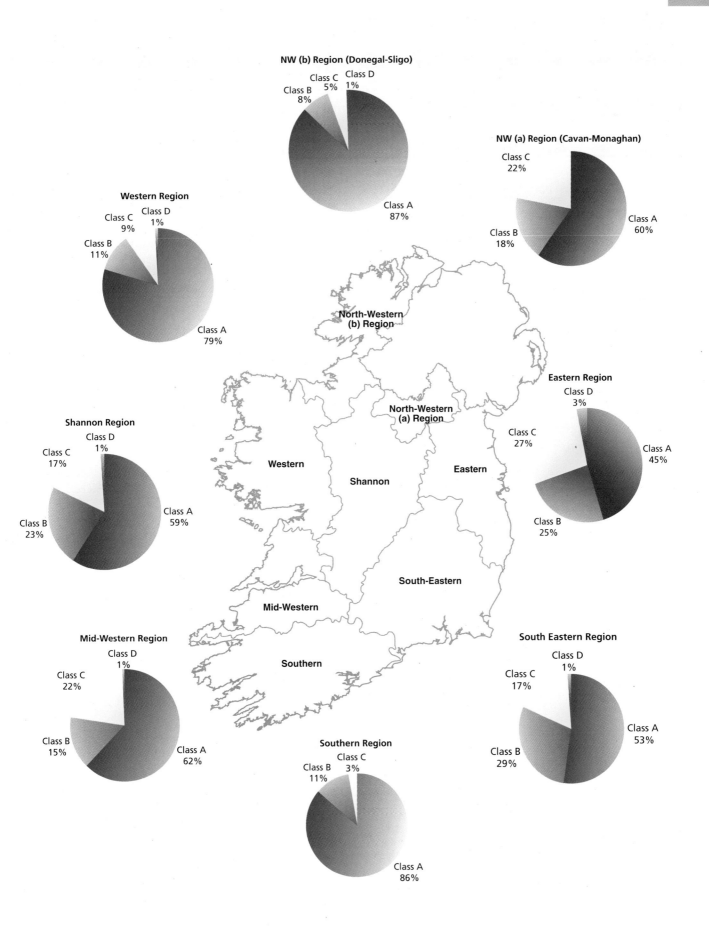

NW (b) Region (Donegal-Sligo)
Class C 5%
Class D 1%
Class B 8%
Class A 87%

NW (a) Region (Cavan-Monaghan)
Class C 22%
Class A 60%
Class B 18%

Western Region
Class C 9%
Class D 1%
Class B 11%
Class A 79%

Eastern Region
Class D 3%
Class C 27%
Class A 45%
Class B 25%

Shannon Region
Class D 1%
Class C 17%
Class B 23%
Class A 59%

North-Western (b) Region

North-Western (a) Region

Western

Shannon

Eastern

Mid-Western

South-Eastern

Southern

Mid-Western Region
Class D 1%
Class C 22%
Class B 15%
Class A 62%

Southern Region
Class C 3%
Class B 11%
Class A 86%

South Eastern Region
Class D 1%
Class C 17%
Class B 29%
Class A 53%

Fig. 9.3 River Quality in the Regions (Lucey *et al.*, 1999)

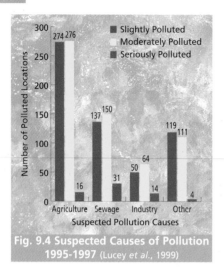

Fig. 9.4 Suspected Causes of Pollution 1995-1997 (Lucey *et al.*, 1999)

what they are likely to have been. However, the term 'suspected' is used in referring to such causes in order to indicate the circumstantial nature of the attribution.

Instances of Serious Pollution

Table 9.2 lists the 65 locations assessed as seriously polluted in the 1995-1997 period together with the likely or suspected causes of the pollution. Of these instances, 24 were already on record (five since 1971, five since the late 1970s/early 1980s, 12 since the late 1980s/early 1990s and two since the previous (1991-1994) period) but there were 40 'new' occurrences of serious pollution. A further 27 were at locations which previously had been moderately polluted, four were at formerly slightly polluted locations, four at previously unpolluted sites and a further five were at locations which had not been surveyed previously. Sewage discharges were the most frequently suspected cause of the instances of serious pollution in the period, including those not already on record from the previous period, with agriculture next in importance.

With the exceptions of the Avoca, Boyne, Dalgan, Feale, Liffey and Nore rivers, most of the serious pollution was recorded in smaller rivers and streams. The serious pollution of the Feale, Liffey and Nore rivers was confined respectively to short bankside stretches below Abbeyfeale, Straffan and Thomastown but the Boyne (below Edenderry) and Dalgan (below Ballyhaunis) were much more extensively affected. The most outstanding case of serious pollution is undoubtedly that in the Avoca river which has been grossly polluted by toxic mining wastes since the mid 1800s.

A partial recovery from serious pollution was recorded at 18 locations; these were assessed as moderately polluted in the 1995-1997 period. Most striking of these improvements were those in the Camlin below Longford and the Blackwater (Kells) above Bailieboro. In one instance, the Ballaghdoo (Kilcar, Co. Donegal) a complete recovery to satisfactory status was recorded.

Table 9.2 Seriously Polluted Rivers and Streams for the period 1995-1997 showing the Locations, Estimated Channel Lengths, Suspected Causes and the Year in which the Pollution was First Recorded (Lucey *et al.*, 1999)

River Name	EPA Code	Channel Length km	Location	On Record Since	Suspected Cause
Banoge	11B02	1.0	Bridge at E side of Gorey	1995	S
Boyne	07B04	2.0	Kinnafad Bridge	1997	S
Bredagh	40B02	0.5	Moville Bridge	1987	S
Bride (Lee)	19B04	*	Bridge at Crookstown (RHS)	1997	S
Broadmeadow	08B02	3.0	Bridge in Ratoath	1988	S
Broadmeadow	08B02	2.0	Milltown Bridge	1994	S
Camac	09C02	2.5	Bridge N of Brownsbarn	1988	S
Donagh	40D01	3.5	Two locations d/s Carndonagh	1980	S
Eyrecourt Stream	25E01	4.0	Bridge NNE of Fearmore	1996	S
Feale	23F01	*	0.2 km d/s Abbeyfeale Bridge	1996	S
Glory	15G01	1.0	Bridge N of Kilmaganny	1995	S
Hind	26H01	5.0	Three Locations d/s Roscommon	1986	S
Kilcolgan	29K01	5.0	Killilan Bridge	1997	S
Liffey	09L01	*	Straffan Turnings Lower (LHS)	1995	S
Lough Naminoo Stream	34L04	1.5	Bridge d/s Castlebar Rd Br, Balla	1995	S
Lyreen	09L02	0.5	u/s Rye Water confl	1971	S
Moate Stream	25M05	4.0	Two Locations d/s Moate	1996	S
Nore	15N01	0.5	Thomastown Bridge (LHS)	1987	S
Proules	06P01	1.0	Two Locations d/s Carrickmacross	1971	S
Rhine	26R04	1.5	Bridge N of Cartron	1996	S
Rock (Birr)	25R02	2.0	Aughnagann Ford	1996	S
Triogue	14T01	6.5	Two Locations d/s Portlaoise	1997	S
Yellow (Knock)	34Y02	1.0	120m d/s Bridge SW of Eden	1995	S
Total due to Suspected Sewage		**48.0 km**			
		39.2 %			

Table 9.2 cont.

River Name	EPA Code	Channel Length km	Location	On Record Since	Suspected Cause
Aighe	38A03	1.0	Two Locations in lower reaches	1997	I
Black (Westmeath)	26B05	2.0	Ballymahon Rd Bridge, Mostrim	1987	I
Camac	09C02	5.0	Two Locations in lower reaches	1981	I
Dalgan	30D01	4.5	2 km SW of Ballyhaunis	1979	I
Figile	14F01	8.5	Two Locations in upper reaches	1989	I
Greese	14G04	1.0	Bridge NW of Crosskeys	1997	I
Kill of the Grange Stream	10K02	0.5	Near Kill Lane National School	1990	I
Laurencetown Stream	26L07	3.0	Bridge E of Sycamorehill	1994	I
Santry	09S01	2.5	Clonshough Rd Bridge, Coolock	1988	I
Tully Stream	14T02	2.0	0.5 km d/s Bridge near Tully House	1997	I
Total due to Suspected Industry		**30.0 km**			
		24.5 %			
Ahavarraga Stream	24A02	1.5	Bridge W of Mundellihy	1996	A
Ballindine	30B03	3.0	Ballindine Bridge	1996	A
Ballyboghil	08B01	3.0	Bridge S of Trallie lodge	1996	A
Ballylongford	24B03	2.0	Bridge SW of Shrone	1996	A
Ballynagrenia Stream	25B16	1.5	Bridge S of Rosemount	1996	A
Broadmeadow	08B02	1.0	Cookstown Bridge	1996	A
Broadmeadow	08B02	3.0	u/s Ratoath	1981	A
Bunoke	24B06	1.5	Bridge S of Glenquin House	1996	A
Cappanacloghy	15C06	2.0	Bridge E of Clooncullen	1995	A
Clover	16C04	2.5	Bridge at Turnpike	1988	A
Dromore	36D02	*	Bridge NE of Corryloan (LHS)	1997	A
Lee (Tralee)	23L01	*	Ahnambraher Bridge (RHS)	1996	A
Pinkeen	09P02	0.5	Bridge SE of Powerstown House	1996	A
Roosky	40R01	1.5	1st Bridge u/s Lough Foyle	1987	A
Tolka	09T01	2.5	Bridge at Black Bull	1996	A
Wood	27W01	1.5	Bridge NE of Kilcarroll	1991	A
Total due to Suspected Agriculture		**27.0 km**			
		22.0 %			
Black (Westmeath)	26B05	1.0	Bridge nr Ballinlaghta d/s Mostrim	1982	S + I
Avoca	10A03	11.5	Two Locations in lower reaches	1850s	Avoca Mines
Tullaghobegley	38T01	0.5	Ford 1.5 km d/s L. Altan	1997	Fish Farm
Aughboy (Courtown)	11A02	2.0	Bridge NE of Middletown House	1995	O
Devlin's	07D02	1.5	Bridge S of Grange Crossroads	1997	O
Tolka	09T01	1.0	Rusk Bridge, Dunboyne	1971	O
Total due to Other Causes		**17.5 km**			
		14.3 %			
Total Length (km)		**122.5 km**			

Total : 54 Rivers / 64 locations / 122.5 km.
* = Less than 0.5 km
u/s = upstream; d/s = downstream; Br = Bridge; A = Agriculture; I = Industry; O = Other / Unknown
S = Sewage; LHS / RHS = Left / Right Hand Side.

Suspected Causes	km	Suspected Causes	%
Sewage	48.0	Sewage	39.2
Industry	30.0	Industry	24.5
Agriculture	27.0	Agriculture	22.0
Other/Unknown	17.5	Other/Unknown	14.3
	122.5		100.0

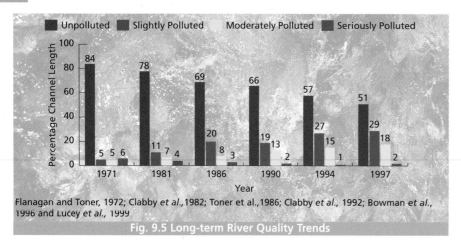

Flanagan and Toner, 1972; Clabby *et al.*,1982; Toner et al.,1986; Clabby *et al.*, 1992; Bowman *et al.*, 1996 and Lucey *et al.*, 1999

Fig. 9.5 Long-term River Quality Trends

Trends in River and Stream Quality

A baseline of 2,900 km of main river channel first surveyed in 1971 (Flanagan and Toner, 1972) has been re-examined at regular intervals since then (Fig. 9.5) and shows a major increase of the length of this channel affected by slight and moderate pollution, from 10 per cent in 1971 to 47 per cent in 1995-1997. However, there has been a continuing decrease since 1971 in the length of seriously polluted channel although this trend was reversed in the most recent period. Recent trends, based on the greatly expanded 13,100 km baseline fully established in the 1987-1990 period (Fig. 9.6), mirror the long-term trends, showing increases in Classes B and C, respectively, of 6

and 4 per cent over the ten year period. The proportion of channel showing serious pollution in 1995-1997 (0.9 per cent) was virtually unchanged from 1987-1990 despite an improvement to 0.6 per cent in 1991-1994.

On a regional basis, the most marked deterioration over the ten year period occurred in the South-Eastern and Shannon regions where there were losses of Class A channel, respectively, of 15 and 16 per cent; a smaller loss of Class A channel of 7 per cent was recorded in the Eastern region. In contrast, marked improvements were noted in the Mid-Western and in the Cavan-Monaghan part of the North-Western Region where the

proportions of unpolluted channel increased, respectively, by 12 and 22 per cent. An improvement was also recorded in the Southern region, raising the proportion of Class A channel from 81 per cent to 87 per cent, while the position did not change significantly in the Western and Donegal-Sligo part of the North-Western region. Almost all of the changes noted were due to increases or reductions in the lengths of channel classified as slightly or

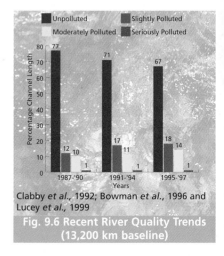

Clabby *et al.*, 1992; Bowman *et al.*, 1996 and Lucey *et al.*, 1999

Fig. 9.6 Recent River Quality Trends (13,200 km baseline)

moderately polluted. Of particular note over the 27 year period is the downgrading of a considerable proportion of the sites showing the highest biological diversity in the

earlier surveys. In the 1995-1997 period, the proportion of sampling locations rated as of high biological diversity was just over 25 per cent. While many of the formerly high quality sites are still classified as satisfactory, they are no longer in the near pristine state found when first examined. The downgrading is due to the loss or decreased abundance of the more pollution-sensitive invertebrate species reflecting, presumably, the influence of factors such as increased silting and growth of benthic algae.

Fish Kills

Fish kills are among the most dramatic and damaging of the impacts of pollution and in most cases arise from unauthorised or accidental discharges of high strength wastes such as silage liquors, manure slurries and sewage. The main effect of these wastes is to cause rapid deoxygenation and perhaps direct toxicity due to the presence of reduced compounds such as ammonia and hydrogen sulphide. Events of this type have been relatively frequent in the past and were attributed in many cases to farm wastes. More recently, programmes of education and advice undertaken by the local authorities and fishery agencies, allied with enforcement measures, have led to a reduction of such pollution but it continues to be a problem.

Records maintained by the Fisheries Research Centre of the Marine Institute show a marked upsurge in fish kills from just under 100 in the early 1970's to considerably more than twice that figure in the late 1980s-early 1990s (Fig 9.7). A very substantial reduction (to 116) in the 1992-1994 period was followed by a further, marked increase (to 173) in the 1995-1997 period. Table 9.3 indicates that the major upsurge in the late 1980s was primarily due to agriculture: kills attributed to this source increased over eight-fold while those attributed to industry increased only slightly and those due to sewage fell by approximately 80 per cent. The improvements noted in the early 1990s followed initiatives by central and local government and particularly by the Central and Regional Fisheries Boards in tackling the problem, especially pollution by the agricultural sector. Kills attributed to agriculture dropped by roughly one-third but the reductions of those due to industry and sewage were much more marked. While the most recent upsurge in the number of fish kills is contributed to by all of the sectors, it is notable that those attributed to sewage discharges show proportionally the largest increase.

Table. 9.3 Causes of Fish Kills						
Period		Agriculture	Industry	Sewage	Works*	Total
1971-'74	Number	19	47	32	0	98
	%	19	48	32		
1986-'88	Number	172	48	6	10	236
	%	73	20	3	4	
1989-'91	Number	117	65	22	19	223
	%	52	29	10	9	
1992-'94	Number	73	24	5	14	116
	%	63	21	4	12	
1995-'97	Number	97	37	24	15	173
	%	56	21	14	9	

* "Works" comprises the Marine Institute's categories "Civil Works" and "Waterworks". The Institute's categories "Enrichment", Deoxygenation" and "Unknown" have been here apportioned to the three main categories "Agriculture", "Sewage" and "Industry"

Lucey et al., *1999*

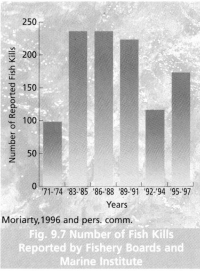

Moriarty,1996 and pers. comm.

Fig. 9.7 Number of Fish Kills Reported by Fishery Boards and Marine Institute

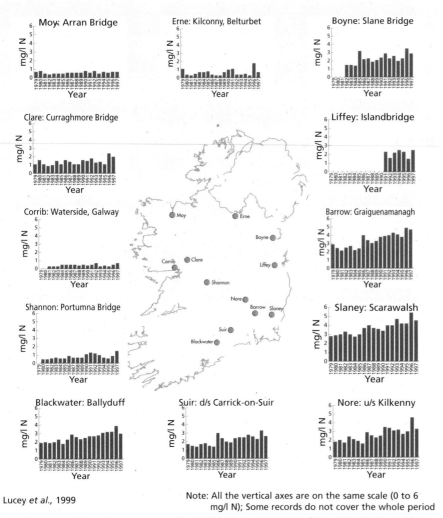

Lucey et al., 1999

Note: All the vertical axes are on the same scale (0 to 6 mg/l N); Some records do not cover the whole period

Fig. 9.8 Annual Median Nitrate (mg/l) Values at Selected River Locations

(CEC, 1991b) provides for the removal of nitrogen from such wastes in certain circumstances.

In general, the available data show that the level of nitrate enrichment in Irish surface waters is moderate and well within the limits set for abstraction and drinking waters. Annual median concentrations give an indication of the typical levels of nitrate and those for the larger rivers of the country are shown in Fig. 9.8. The data show that these concentrations are generally less than the EU guideline limit of 5.65 mg/l N. However, it is clear that the rivers in the west and north-west have significantly lower quantities of nitrate than those in the east, south-east and south of the country. This is likely to reflect differences between the two parts of the country in respect of population density and the intensity of farming activity, in particular the much greater extent of tillage land in the latter areas. It is also notable that nitrate levels appear to be increasing in the south-eastern rivers in contrast to the position in western rivers where levels show little sign of an upward trend (Fig. 9.9).

Nitrate and Phosphate in Rivers

Improved treatment for sewage and industrial wastes in recent years has greatly reduced the amounts of biodegradable organic matter discharged to rivers in European countries, including Ireland (EEA, 1998). While this has had a beneficial effect on the receiving waters, the level of treatment employed in most cases is not designed to remove the phosphate and nitrate released by the breakdown of the organic waste in the treatment plants and these substances continue to be released to the aquatic environment in the effluents. In addition, they may be discharged to surface waters from farmyards and agricultural land and from forested areas. For the protection of human health, the national Surface Water and Drinking

Water Regulations require that nitrate concentrations in raw water intended for human consumption and in drinking water must not exceed 50 mg/l NO_3 (or 11.3 mg/l expressed as nitrogen (N)). The corresponding EU directives (CEC, 1975, 1980) additionally recommend a guideline value of 25 mg/l NO_3 (5.65 mg/l N). Setting the same limits for both raw and treated water reflects the fact that conventional treatment processes do not remove nitrate. In 1991 the EU issued a directive (CEC, 1991a) requiring Member States to take specific measures to protect surface and groundwaters from nitrate contamination arising from agricultural activities. Direct waste discharges, such as sewage, also contribute significantly to such contamination and the EU Directive on urban waste water treatment

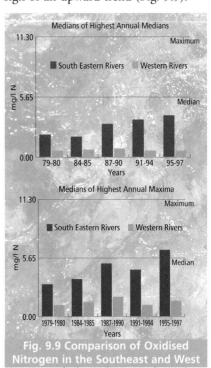

Fig. 9.9 Comparison of Oxidised Nitrogen in the Southeast and West

Note: Data are for the sampling stations showing the highest values for the annual medians and maxima in each river surveyed. The EU maximum and guideline limits for nitrate in abstractions are indicated.

The standard for phosphate in river waters set out in national Regulations (DELG, 1998) giving partial effect to the dangerous substances Directive (CEC, 1976) is derived from a comparison of the biological and chemical data at sampling stations where both methods of water quality assessment are used. This comparison has shown statistically significant correlations between the annual median phosphate concentrations and the values for the biotic index. In particular, this comparison has suggested that an annual median concentration of 30 µg/l P is the threshold above which the biological condition is likely to show the influence of eutrophication, i.e., it is the boundary value between Classes A and B in the scheme outlined earlier in the chapter.

Phosphate measurements were made at some 1,600 locations on rivers and streams in the 1995-1997 period. Assuming that the median values for that three-year period approximate to annual medians, it is estimated that the 30 µg/l P standard would have been exceeded at just over 50 per cent of the sampling locations. Table 9.4 shows the percentage of stations in a selection of the larger catchments at which the median concentration of phosphate exceeded this value in the period. As might be expected the highest rates of exceedance were in those catchments located in the eastern and south-eastern areas and the lowest in the west, reflecting again differences in population density and the intensity of farming activity. The Shannon sub-catchments, representing the midlands, show an intermediate rate of non-compliance. The Maigue and Deel catchments, south of the Shannon estuary, where none of the sampling locations were in compliance, are exceptions to this general pattern; however, this is in line with the biological assessments which show widespread eutrophication in the two catchments.

Table 9.4 Exceedance of the Standards for Phosphorus in Rivers 1995-1997		
Catchment	Total Number of Stations	Percentage with Median Phosphate Greater Than 30 µg/l
Boyne	117	93
Slaney	71	37
Barrow	66	74
Nore	121	73
Suir	174	60
Munster Blackwater	41	54
Lee	17	35
Bandon	21	29
Maigue/Deel	38	100
Lower Shannon	147	35
Upper Shannon	205	36
Corrib	74	18
Moy	79	15
Erne	51	82

Source: EPA

Other Contaminants in Freshwaters

Owing to the lack of traditional heavy industries and a largely grass-based agriculture, the potential for pollution of Irish inland waters by toxic substances has been assumed to be relatively limited. Thus the need for detailed monitoring for such substances has not been considered a priority to date, except in particular circumstances, and the available data are limited. Some localised metal pollution has arisen from mining

activity of which the most notable case is the Avoca River in Co. Wicklow. Also of note in this context is the Kilmastulla river in Co. Tipperary which has been affected by the Silvermines workings. Elsewhere, the results show that, in general, the metal levels in Irish rivers are near background and well within the limits set for fishery waters. Surveys carried out by the EPA in the mid 1990s in connection with the dangerous substances Directive (see below) showed that the levels of the two metals on List I (cadmium and mercury) were generally at background levels. Further work is now in hand to determine the position with other metals; measurements of metals being made currently by the Central Fisheries Board in relation to the typing of salmonid waters will add to the database available.

Measurements of the levels of synthetic organic compounds such as pesticides and PCBs in Irish rivers have been even more limited than those for metals. The EPA carried out sampling below the main inland towns in the mid 1990s to determine the position regarding the metals and organic compounds included in List I of the dangerous substances

Box 9.1 Water Quality in Canals

The first systematic water quality survey of the major Irish canals was undertaken in the 1990-1994 period by the Central Fisheries Board, on behalf of Dúchas, and some sampling was repeated in 1995 and 1997. These surveys were carried out as part of an overall fisheries development and aquatic weed management programme for Irish canals. In the more comprehensive 1990-1994 survey, water quality data were collected from 92 sites including feeder streams. The sampling locations were at approximately three-kilometre intervals along the canals and the frequency of sampling at each site was four to five times per year.

Overall the results of extensive nutrient sampling conducted between 1990 and 1994 indicated that water quality in the canals was good and that the canal systems may be categorised as between mesotrophic and eutrophic in trophic status. Four per cent of the sections examined exhibited signs of nutrient enrichment in that period, dropping to just two per cent in the follow-up survey in 1995. Nutrient concentrations in the feeder streams were generally low although some streams exhibited elevated levels. The water quality of the two summit feeders, which are the major sources of water supply for the canals, was good with low concentrations of nutrients throughout the period. The quality of many of the smaller supplementary feeders, however, was less good and these often contributed significantly to the nutrient budget of the canals. Phytoplankton production was generally low in the canals as indicated by consistently low chlorophyll levels suggesting that these communities did not utilise the bulk of the available phosphorus, possibly due to nitrogen limitation in the water.

The characteristics of the canals, i.e., relatively narrow and shallow watercourses with organically-rich mud substrata, favour the proliferation of an abundant and diverse aquatic flora although there was no evidence of elevated nutrient levels in most canal sections where high productivity of rooted plants was recorded. However, it was noteworthy that all instances of significant infestation with filamentous algae occurred downstream of, or adjacent to, nutrient-rich feeder streams. Given the abundance of weeds, slight supersaturation of oxygen, not surprisingly, was regularly recorded in some canal sections as well as in feeder streams; a degree of deoxygenation was also apparent in the latter at times. The dissolved oxygen values recorded would indicate that severe deoxygenation is not a feature of the canals although diurnal variation measurements were not made.

Since 1972 aquatic weeds in the canals have been controlled using chemical and mechanical methods with a shift more to the latter in the past decade. Cutting normally begins in June/July when plant biomass is close to maximum and the cut weeds are subsequently removed to prevent nutrient release and oxygen demand through decomposition. Where other methods have proved ineffective in controlling filamentous algae, the use of rotted barley straw has been effective in most situations.

Caffrey and Monahan, 1995; Caffrey and Allison, 1998; Caffrey and Johnston, 1998; Lucey et al., 1999

Directive. The results did not indicate any significant contamination with these substances (EPA unpublished data). A survey of drinking waters for pesticide residues in 1995 (O'Donnell, 1996) gave generally similar results. However, most of the compounds measured in these and other local surveys in recent years do not reflect the usage pattern in Ireland, the priority given to them being based mainly on a consideration of their potential toxicity. The EPA is presently undertaking further surveys, concentrating on substances imported to the State in the largest amounts and which, therefore, have the greatest potential to be lost to the environment in significant quantities. Most of these substances are herbicides.

LAKE WATER QUALITY

Eutrophication

The most extensive threat to the water quality of lakes in Ireland, as for the rivers, is eutrophication.

Increased nutrient loads, particularly of phosphorus, recorded in many rivers and streams in recent years, are affecting the trophic status of the lakes receiving these waters. Eutrophication commonly results in the excessive production of the

Table 9.5 Classification of Lake Water Quality

Lake Trophic Category		Annual Maximum chlorophyll mg/m3	Algal Growth	Degree of Deoxygenation in Hypolimnion	Level of Pollution	Impairment of use of lake
Oligotrophic	(O)	<8	Low	Low	Very Low	Probably none
Mesotrophic	(M)	8 - 25	Moderate	Moderate	Low	Very little
	Moderately (m-E)	25 - 35	Substantial	May be High	Significant	May be appreciable
Eutrophic	Strongly (s-E)	35 - 55	High	High	Strong	Appreciable
	Highly (h-E)	55 - 75	High	Probably Total	High	High
Hypertrophic	(H)	>75	Very High	Probably Total	Very High	High

suspended planktonic algae and Cyanobacteria ("blue-green algae") in the water column of the open waters of lakes. It may also lead to the growth of larger algae and of the rooted plants attached to the lake bottom in the shallow areas and at shorelines. These changes have an adverse impact on or prevent those uses of a lake that require a high standard of water quality such as abstractions for domestic and industrial supply, salmonid fisheries and water contact sports.

Assessment of Lake Water Quality for Eutrophication

The classification scheme currently used to classify Irish lakes (Table 9.5) is a modification of a scheme proposed by the OECD (1982) and considers only the annual maxima of the chlorophyll concentrations. The concentration of chlorophyll in lake waters is an indication of the biomass of algae present. The modification of the OECD scheme, which also incorporates phosphorus concentrations and water transparency, is necessary because the relevant data available are often limited to chlorophyll and measurements are not frequent enough to allow the calculation of the annual means used in the original scheme. Where data are available, these usually cover the summer and autumn months when the highest concentrations of chlorophyll are likely to occur. Thus, in many cases, the highest value measured in the latter periods is taken as a proxy for the annual maximum chlorophyll

concentration. In some lakes, higher concentrations may occur in the spring months during the peak of diatom growth. However, these growths are usually very short-lived and not likely to have the same impact as the large populations of Cyanobacteria which often affect polluted lakes in summer and autumn. A further modification of the basic OECD scheme is the sub-division of the very widely defined eutrophic category into three sub-categories in order to provide a more precise assessment of the trophic status.

Trophic Status of Lakes

The most recent assessments of lake water quality cover 124 waterbodies surveyed in the period 1995-1998 (Fig. 9.10) by the EPA, Central Fisheries Board and the local

authorities. Of these lakes (80%) were classified as oligotrophic or mesotrophic on the basis of their annual maximum chlorophyll concentrations and were, therefore, judged to be in a satisfactory condition. This group includes 18 of the 23 larger lakes and reservoirs (>750 ha) in the State, the exceptions

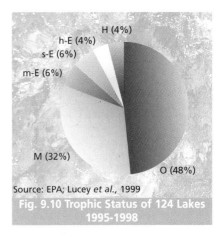

Source: EPA; Lucey et al., 1999

Fig. 9.10 Trophic Status of 124 Lakes 1995-1998

H (4%)
h-E (4%)
s-E (6%)
m-E (6%)
M (32%)
O (48%)

being Loughs Ramor and Oughter (hypertrophic), Loughs Sheelin and Leane (highly eutrophic) and Lough Ree (moderately eutrophic). Of the total 24 lakes remaining, seven (6%) were classified as moderately eutrophic and in these adverse effects on beneficial uses may not be of great significance. The concentrations of chlorophyll recorded in the other 17 lakes examined (14%) suggest a strong to very high level of nutrient pollution and a consequent likelihood of impairment of beneficial uses. These lakes have been classified as strongly eutrophic, highly eutrophic or hypertrophic. The combined areas of these unsatisfactory lake waters, which is mostly accounted for by the five large lakes identified above, amount to 190 km² or 21 per cent of the total area (892 km²) covered by the surveys in the period (Fig. 9.11). This is similar to the proportion of the numbers of lakes classified as unsatisfactory. The remaining 79 per cent (702 km²) were in a satisfactory position. It is estimated that the total

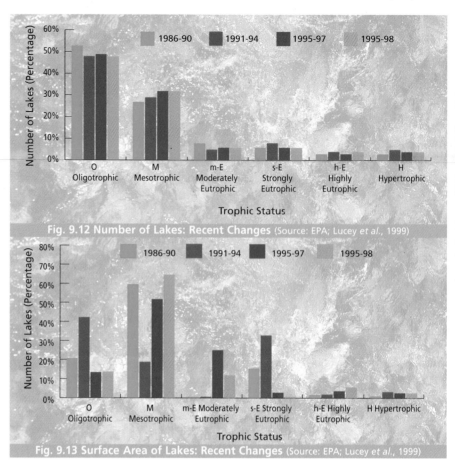

Fig. 9.12 Number of Lakes: Recent Changes (Source: EPA; Lucey *et al.*, 1999)

Fig. 9.13 Surface Area of Lakes: Recent Changes (Source: EPA; Lucey *et al.*, 1999)

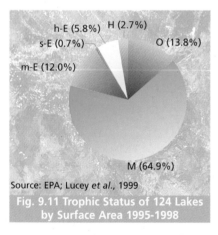

Source: EPA; Lucey *et al.*, 1999

Fig. 9.11 Trophic Status of 124 Lakes by Surface Area 1995-1998

area of lakes covered in the period is about 60 per cent of the national total for such waters.

Little change is apparent in the numbers of lakes allocated to each trophic category over the past decade (Fig. 9.12). However, when this comparison is made on the basis of the surface areas examined (Fig. 9.13), marked changes are apparent in recent years. A significant reduction of the surface area assigned to the oligotrophic category has occurred since the 1991-1994 period due to the change of the assessment of Loughs Corrib (170 km²) and Mask (80 km²) from that category to mesotrophic. The lake area in the latter category has also been added to by a progressive improvement in the water quality of Lough Derg (117 km²) from a strongly eutrophic status in 1991 to a mesotrophic status in 1998. It should be noted that Loughs Corrib and Mask both exhibited mesotrophic levels of algae and Cyanobacteria twenty years ago; due to the essentially arbitrary

divisions between the categories in the classification scheme, minor year-on-year variations in these lakes are likely to change the assessments of trophic status between oligotrophic and mesotrophic periodically without implying any significant overall change in their water quality.

The improvements in Lough Derg and in Lough Ree (the latter improving from strongly to moderately eutrophic) together with a further decline of Lough Sheelin in the 1995-1998 period to the highly eutrophic category has led to a striking reduction in the surface area classified as strongly eutrophic since 1991-1994. The classification of the latter lake as highly eutrophic accounts for the increase in this category in the 1995-1998 period. While recent upgrading of waste water treatment at several locations in its immediate vicinity is likely to have contributed to the improvements in Lough Derg, it is also probable that the marked reduction of algal growth observed there and perhaps in Lough

Ree too is due to the recent colonisation of both lakes by the zebra mussel (*Dreissena polymorpha*). The filtering mode of feeding of these bivalve molluscs has been shown to be very effective in removing algal cells from lake waters (Reeders *et al.*, 1989).

There has been a small reduction in the surface area classified as hypertrophic since 1991-94, attributable to improved conditions in Abisdealy Lake and Inniscarra Reservoir in Co. Cork. However, Loughs Egish, Oughter, Ramor and Sillan remain in the most polluted category.

Acidification

In Ireland, the potential for artificially acidic rainfall is mitigated by the State's geographical position at the western edge of Europe and the direction of the prevailing winds which have an oceanic origin to the west and south-west. However, there are many small lakes in areas of base-poor bedrock, especially in the west and north-west, that have very limited buffering capacity and which are, therefore, potentially at risk of acidification. Investigations were

undertaken in the 1980s to determine the position in these sensitive waters and to assess the quality of the rainfall in the catchments. The results (Bowman, 1986; 1991) indicated that acidification of surface waters due to atmospheric pollution was not a significant problem in the State, although rainfall associated with easterly winds showed greater levels of acidifying substances than that from other directions. Acidification was detected in some afforested catchments and was attributed to the ability of the crowns of the trees to filter pollutants, even at low levels, from the atmosphere and also ion exchange processes which occur at the roots of the trees.

Following these studies, several representative lakes and their feeder streams, viz., Lough Veagh in Co. Donegal, Lough Maumwee in Co. Galway and Upper Glendalough lake in Co. Wicklow, were selected as representative waters for long term monitoring and these have been examined on an annual basis since 1991. The assessments are based mainly on the composition of the invertebrate fauna, using a score system related to the sensitivities of

the individual species. The most recent surveys show that the lakes in Donegal and Galway retain the biological diversity expected in waters unaffected by acidification as first observed in the mid 1980s. However, Upper Glendalough Lake and one of its tributaries, the Lugduff river, continue to show biological features characteristic of acidified waters; this is attributed to the afforestation of the catchment of the tributary. It is notable that another tributary of the lake, the Glenealo River, which has no tree cover, has a good diversity of acid-sensitive species. Physico-chemical measurements made in the same period are generally in line with the biological findings (see also Chapters 8 and 11).

Quality of Bathing Waters

There are nine freshwater bathing areas designated under the national regulations giving effect to the EU bathing waters Directive and all are located on lakes. Data for the 1995-1998 show that all of these areas complied in that period with the mandatory limits set by the Directive and with the national standards. In 1997, Ireland was the only country in

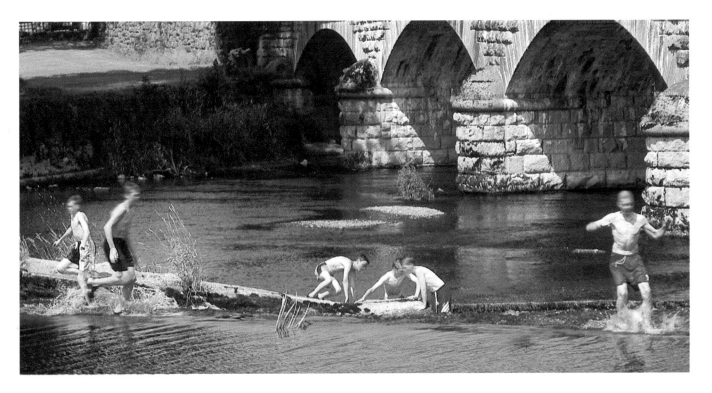

the EU to have all its freshwater areas complying with the EU mandatory standards. The locations and compliance status of the inland bathing areas sampled during 1998 and further information on the provisions of the bathing water Directive are given in Chapter 10.

QUALITY OF GROUNDWATERS

General Remarks

The main concern regarding the quality of groundwaters is their suitability as a source for drinking water supply and for use in food processing and related industrial operations. Special measures are needed to protect the quality of groundwaters in areas where large amounts of waste are stored or where wastes are applied to land. National guidelines have been issued recently on the development of protection schemes for groundwaters (DELG *et al.*, 1999).

Groundwater Surveys

A national monitoring programme for the systematic assessment of the quality of groundwaters was drafted by the EPA in 1995 as part of its mandate to draw up and publish monitoring programmes for the environment. This programme was implemented on a provisional basis in 1995 pending further discussion with interested parties and publication as a general discussion document. The purpose of the programme is to define the state of groundwater quality, to detect trends and to determine the causes of any changes in quality that are identified. The network consists of some 300 sampling locations but not all of these have been included in the monitoring that has been undertaken to date. Sampling is carried out biannually to correspond with periods when the highest and lowest groundwater levels are likely to occur.

Monitoring Results

The data arising from the monitoring surveys carried out in the 1995-1997 period have been documented in some detail by Lucey *et al.* (1999) and a digest only is presented here. Overall, the data indicate that there is no widespread contamination of individual aquifers and most samples taken were reflective of unpolluted conditions. Intermittent and localised pollution was recorded, however, in an appreciable number of instances.

Of particular concern was the fact that over one-third of the samples subjected to bacteriological examination tested positive for the presence of faecal coliforms (Fig 9.14). This is an indication of contamination with sewage or similar wastes and has serious implications for the use of the waters concerned as sources of drinking water. Annual reports on drinking water quality (e.g. EPA, 1999) draw attention to the relatively high incidence of faecal coliform contamination in samples from private water supply schemes. Since many of these schemes use groundwaters as a source, the results of the 1995-1997 monitoring suggest that some at least of this contamination may be due to the lack of or insufficient disinfection of the waters used in these schemes.

The public health significance of high nitrate concentrations in drinking waters has already been highlighted. Groundwaters are particularly vulnerable to nitrate contamination due to the high mobility of the substance in the soil and the consequent ease with which it can leach downward through the water table. Most at risk are those groundwaters located in agricultural areas where there are high rates of applications of artificial fertilisers or animal manures.

Results from the 1995-1997 national monitoring programme show that approximately 80 per cent of the sampling points had mean concentrations of nitrate equal to or less than the EU guideline value of 25 mg/l for drinking waters (Fig. 9.15). Mean concentrations greater than the EU mandatory value of 50 mg/l were recorded at five sampling points (2.6 per cent). However, 26 individual samples taken in the surveys had concentrations over this limit, most of these being at the stations with the highest mean concentrations. Overall the results show that nitrate contamination is localised and likely to be due to infiltration from nearby activities.

The monitoring programme does not include measurements of potentially toxic pollutants as part of the basic suite of parameters. As for surface waters, the assumption is that these pollutants are not a major risk. A number of surveys were carried during the 1990s to determine the level of contamination of certain groundwaters with pesticides and other synthetic organic compounds (e.g., Cullen and Co., 1994).

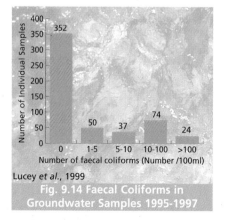

Lucey *et al.*, 1999

Fig. 9.14 Faecal Coliforms in Groundwater Samples 1995-1997

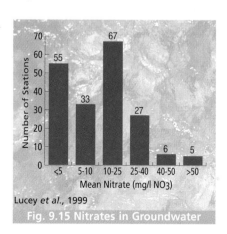

Lucey *et al.*, 1999

Fig. 9.15 Nitrates in Groundwater

Contamination with such compounds has been detected in groundwaters near to industrial sites, dumps and agricultural activities, most of the compounds identified being herbicides. In most samples taken in the period, such substances were undetectable or the levels found were below the limits set in the EU directives. However, as already remarked in the case of river waters, there is a need for a more systematic approach to the investigation of the occurrence of these potentially harmful substances in groundwaters.

FISH STOCKS

Introduction

The presence of thriving fish populations, particularly the salmonid species, is an excellent indicator of the good health of rivers and lakes; depleted stocks, on the other hand, usually reflect a significant deterioration of the aquatic ecosystem, in many cases involving pollution. In Ireland, as pointed out above, the ubiquitous presence of salmonid fish is a distinctive feature of the inland waters and attests to their still relatively good quality. This situation is mainly threatened by the growing extent of eutrophication but other factors such as drainage, acidification of headwaters and fishing pressure may have detrimental effects on

stocks. An overview of the current status of the main species of fish, provided by the Central Fisheries Board, is presented below, and is based on surveys and other investigations carried out by the Central and Regional Fisheries Boards.

Salmon *(Salmo salar)*

The downward trend in the combined commercial and sports salmon catch has continued with only 520 tonnes recorded in 1999 (Table 9.6). Catches in recent years are likely to have been influenced by restrictions on the commercial salmon fishery imposed by the Minister for the Marine in 1997. These restrictions included later opening dates for the drift and draft net

fisheries which have effectively eliminated commercial exploitation of spring salmon, one of the principal aims of the legislation. On average over the last five years drift nets accounted for 67 per cent of the total salmon catch, which represents a substantial decrease on the previous decade. Over this period the rod catch (35,000 – 40,000 fish per annum) has remained stable, accounting for about 19 per cent. In the latter half of the decade there has been an improvement in sea survival rates.

There has also been a downward trend in spring salmon stocks over the past three decades (O' Muircheartaigh, 1999). The initial decline was attributable to Ulcerative Dermal

Table 9.6 Total Salmon Catch 1994-99	
Year	Weight (tonnes)
1994	816
1995	790
1996	688
1997	570
1998	623
1999	520

Source: Central and Regional Fisheries Boards

Necrosis disease (UDN) and stocks have not recovered to pre-UDN levels. Prior to the introduction of the new legislation, measures to conserve spring salmon (i.e., two-sea winter fish) stocks in the River

Slaney, a noted spring salmon fishery, including curtailment of the draft net and rod fisheries, were introduced for a five-year period commencing in 1994. These measures are likely to have contributed to substantially increased rod catches in 1999. A gradual increase in the numbers of salmon redds (spawning areas) has also been observed up to 1999 although preliminary results for 1999/2000 (M. Kelly, pers. comm.) indicate a possible reduction in spawning in this latest winter. Increases in juvenile salmon densities, compared to earlier in the decade, in the extremities of the catchment where spring salmon tend to spawn, suggest an overall improvement in spring salmon production in this river system (Roche, 1998a).

Trout (Salmo trutta)

Brown trout: Recent surveys of two major tributaries of the Shannon, the Suck and the Brosna, showed that juvenile trout densities were generally low. Reduced habitat quality was a contributory factor. From a trout angling perspective it is accepted that both catchments have declined substantially since the 1970s although sections of tributaries, including the Bunowen and Shiven Rivers in the Suck catchment and the Gageborough and Clodiagh in the Brosna catchment, held good stocks of adult trout. Under the EU-funded Tourism Angling Measure (TAM), a major fishery survey of the middle and lower reaches of the R. Inny and of its tributaries was carried out in 1997 by Central Fisheries Board and Shannon Regional Fisheries Board. The survey examined the status of fish populations and habitat attributes in this arterially-drained catchment with a view to drawing up proposals to enhance the angling fishery. Instream uniformity was identified as a major limiting factor on juvenile trout production. Many channels had a base width or a wetted width that was excessive in low flow conditions and did not facilitate the

normal interaction between flowing water and bed/bank material, which creates instream diversity. These constraints are being mitigated in similar rivers elsewhere in the State (see Improvements to Salmonid Waters, below).

Trout stocks showed varied responses in lakes which have been or remain affected by eutrophication. Lough Ennell continues to contain a large population of large brown trout. The feeder streams to this lake have received substantial habitat restoration and protection of the riparian corridors. Increases in recruitment of brown trout to the lake fishery are evident as a consequence of this work. The North Western Regional Fisheries Board confirmed a substantial increase in rod caught trout for Lough Conn in 1999. Average weight of the fish captured remains high but anglers reported a big increase in smaller and undersized trout. Rehabilitation works commenced on the L. Conn feeder streams in 1994 and this has resulted in increased recruitment of young trout to the fishery. In contrast, a serious deterioration is apparent in the ecology of Lough Sheelin with a comprehensive die-back in charophyte (stonewort) cover, a marked expansion in roach stocks and a substantial reduction in trout

numbers. Many feeder steams to the west and north of the lake dried up in the drought year of 1995. This seriously impacted on trout recruitment while the high temperatures favoured better than average survival of the 1995 roach year class in the lake. The subsequent very wet years in 1997 and especially 1998 caused excessive phosphorus loadings which stimulated dense and prolonged algal blooms in 1998 and again in 1999.

Sea trout: Since 1994 sea trout stocks in Connemara have remained in a critical state and rod catches are low (Table 9.7). Some improvements have occurred in individual fisheries, largely as a result of improved lice management and fallowing of aquaculture sites (closure of rearing cages for periods of weeks in spring). Effective management of sea lice on salmon farms remains the key to the

Table 9.7 Annual Sea Trout Rod Catch in Connemara 1994-1998	
Year	**Numbers**
1994	1577
1995	1563
1996	2240
1997	1082
1998	1988

Source: Central and Regional Fisheries Boards

recovery of the Connemara sea trout stock. New strategies including single bay management and new technologies like offshore salmon rearing cages (which are being assessed currently) offer scope for better lice management and increased survival of sea trout at sea.

Charr (*Salvelinus alpinus*)

As noted in the previous State of the Environment report (Stapleton, 1996), the charr is sensitive to eutrophication and appears to have been lost from a number of waters this century, including, most recently, Lough Conn in Co. Mayo and Lough Corrib in Co. Galway. The status of this species in Ireland is described as 'vulnerable' (Whilde, 1993). Recent information suggests that charr populations are reasonably stable in lakes where water quality is adequate. However, the impacts of other processes such as acidification (e.g. Lough Dan) and water drawdown (Kindrum Lake, Co. Donegal) on charr populations in oligotrophic/mesotrophic waters needs to be ascertained. Charr appear to be extinct in Lough Dan (J. O'Brien, pers. comm.) and drawdown may have impacted on the juvenile stages of the fish in Kindrum Lake (Roche, 1998b), the most northerly site of their recorded distribution in Ireland (see also Chapter 12).

The Central Fisheries Board carried out a fish population survey on Lough Leane, Killarney, at the request of Kerry County Council in 1999. This was a repeat of an initial survey in 1991. Only a single charr was recorded during the 1999 survey and the species may currently be represented in Lough Leane by migrants from the middle and upper lakes. The original population native to the lake is thought to be extinct due to excessive enrichment, a factor thought to have contributed to the demise of charr in L. Conn (McGarrigle *et al.*, 1993; McGarrigle and Champ, 1999).

Twaite Shad (*Alosa fallax*)

Sampling for twaite shad in the R. Suir at Carrick-on-Suir during the traditional spawning season of late May-early June in 1999 yielded a solitary fish of this species. Combined with information provided by staff of the Southern Regional Fisheries Board, this finding points to a very tenuous status for this Annex 2-listed (Habitats Directive) species in this river system. In the survey of Lough Leane in 1999, the investigations indicated the presence of a substantial population of the Killarney shad (*Alosa fallax killarniensis*) although the species was not as numerous as in the earlier (1991) survey.

Improvements to Salmonid Waters

Beginning in 1994, a major programme of river restoration and rehabilitation was undertaken by the Central and Regional Fisheries Boards. This programme is funded under the Tourism Angling Measure with EU, exchequer and private funds. River areas negatively impacted by a variety of land uses are being restored to their natural conditions. The main emphasis of the programme is to regenerate salmonid (salmon, sea trout, brown trout) habitat damaged in the past by restoring the riparian vegetation, removing obstacles to fish migration, introducing instream physical complexity, and generally returning these channels to their "natural state". In doing so the requirements of all life stages of these salmonids are addressed. Over 400 km of channel have already been restored or made available to salmonids. On average, a four-fold increase in juvenile salmonid numbers has been measured in rehabilitated sections monitored by Fishery Board personnel. Improvements in other wildlife aspects have also been noted including increased brook lamprey (*Lampetra planeri*) numbers in some of the developed areas. The restored riparian corridors now provide refuge for a multitude of aquatic, semi-aquatic and terrestrial species.

Since 1990, the Drainage Division of the Office of Public Works (OPW) and the Central Fisheries Board have been engaged in a programme to examine both the environmental impacts of standard channel maintenance and the feasibility of alternative or experimental digging strategies. The latter are beneficial or at least less deleterious to the fish populations and the river corridor habitat while providing an adequate capacity for flood flows. Since 1996 the programme, initiated as a pilot study, has been expanded to cover all drained channels managed by OPW. Digging strategies that create an asymmetrical cross-section are of particular benefit in creating hydraulic diversity and suitable habitat for older trout (King, 1996a; King *et al.*, in press). Maintenance strategies also impact on the aquatic plants with some strategies being of benefit both to fisheries and to retention of a clear open channel (King, 1996b).

Cyprinids (Coarse Fish)

Between 1995 and 1999, coarse fish stock surveys were conducted on more than 200 lakes throughout Ireland. The objective of the work was to provide detailed information on the current status of coarse fish stocks in these lakes and to make recommendations regarding their development as angling waters. Data on the physical, physico-chemical and biological characteristics of the lakes were also collected. The surveys revealed the presence of healthy and diverse coarse fish populations in most lakes surveyed. Roach (*Rutilus rutilus*) were widespread throughout the country and high population densities were commonly recorded. New records for the species were established in the Moy catchment and in Lough Mask.

Recent years have seen a significant increase in the numbers of roach-bream (*Abramis brama*) hybrids in Irish coarse fisheries. These fish now form a large proportion of angler catches in fisheries such as the Royal and Grand Canals, the River Shannon and a large number of premier coarse fish lakes throughout the seven fishery regions. They provide excellent fishing and are keenly sought by competition anglers, in particular. Surveys conducted in the Barrow and Nore rivers have revealed large populations of dace (*Leuciscus leuciscus*), up to 0.5 kg in weight. Dace have also been recently reported from the River Shannon, downstream of Castleconnell. Populations of tench (*Tinca tinca*) have increased dramatically since the

last State of the Environment report was produced. While previously this species was localised in the Royal, Grand and Barrow Canals, it is now both widespread and numerous. There has been an appreciable increase in the demand for more carp (*Cyprinus carpio*) angling waters in Ireland in recent years. To accommodate this ever expanding specialist angling group, carp from the few existing fisheries have been selectively stocked, to suitable watercourses. The progress of the fish in these waters is being monitored and further introductions into suitable natural and man-made lakes is proposed.

DISCUSSION AND CONCLUSIONS

The observations set out in the previous State of the Environment report regarding the adverse effects of the increasing pressures on the aquatic environment are even more pertinent today. As a consequence of rapidly expanding urban populations many local authority waste treatment facilities are under severe pressure and, in many instances, are unable to cope with the increasing volumes of waste generated. In rural areas there is a continuing threat to the aquatic environment from the intensive livestock rearing and dairying sectors, which generate large quantities of

high-strength waste, the bulk of which is disposed of by spreading on land without pre-treatment.

It is not surprising, therefore, that the recent surveys of the fresh waters of the State show a continuing increase of the length of the river channel subject to slight and moderate pollution and highlight eutrophication as the main problem to be addressed by management measures. While this deterioration in the quality of the aquatic ecosystem is relatively minor in many cases, it signals a change from the near pristine conditions which obtained in many areas up to the 1970s. The main threat presented by these developments concerns the health of the game fish stocks which are not favoured by the more productive waters resulting from artificial enrichment. There are already signs that the populations of these fish are declining in some waters and that this appears to be linked to eutrophication.

The problem of eutrophication has now been fully recognised at Government level and is marked in particular by the publication of a catchment-based strategy to address the problem (DoE, 1997). This has led more recently to the adoption of the phosphorus standards for rivers and lakes and to the funding, with EU support, of studies of monitoring

and management systems in a number of catchments including those of Loughs Ree and Derg on the Shannon and Lough Leane in Killarney. These and other measures dealing with improvements to sewage and industrial waste treatment and with nutrient management on farms (see Chapter 15) are designed mainly or *inter alia* to minimise the loading of phosphorus on surface waters. An indication of the efficacy of such measures has been provided by recent studies in the Lough Conn catchment (McGarrigle *et al.,* in press).

The most intractable problem in achieving such a goal is likely to concern agricultural sources of phosphorus. The difficulty of preventing significant losses of phosphorus from farmyards and from lands used for spreading manure slurries and other wastes has been made clear in a number of research projects carried out in recent years (Tunney *et al.,* 2000; Cork County Council *et al.,* 1995). It is clear now that the more intensive types of agricultural activity, necessitating the disposal of large quantities of wastes, may not be compatible with the maintenance of good water quality, and require particularly stringent control in the catchments of rivers and lakes of high ecological quality (McGarrigle and Champ, 1999). While the inclusion of most of the

pig and poultry rearing enterprises in the EPA's Integrated Pollution Control licensing system has brought about a more systematic measure of control of these enterprises than heretofore, the continued reliance on land spreading as the ultimate method of disposal still carries significant risks and presents major problems from the point of view of enforcement of licence conditions.

The pig and poultry sectors account for only a minor proportion of the phosphorus load generated in livestock manures and the same pollution risks apply to the much greater amounts produced on the dairy and other cattle farms which remain outside the IPC system. The EU Rural Environment Protection Scheme (REPS) has some potential to address these cases by encouraging less intensive farming, although it appears that the scheme is not attracting, or cannot attract, the involvement of the larger enterprises. In addition, the concept of nutrient management planning which is part of the REPS scheme is now provided for under the Water Pollution Acts, allowing a local authority to require such planning on farms where it deems there is a risk of pollution. There is little doubt that such planning is urgently needed as the practice, which has largely obtained to date, of dealing with slurries and

other farm wastes as a disposal problem rather than as a source of nutrients for the land has led to much of the water pollution associated with agriculture. However, it must be conceded that bringing about such a change is likely to present management challenges on individual farms and will need continued support from the government advisory agencies in many cases.

The phosphorus loads from sewage and industrial wastes are much smaller than those from agriculture but are, in the main, directly discharged to waters. In addition, these discharges are continuous and may be the dominant factor of enrichment in many river reaches in the low flow periods when the run-off from land is reduced. Thus, the eutrophication potential of such wastes may be greater, per unit of phosphorus produced, than those derived for farm lands. While the appropriate phosphorus reduction strategies are best addressed on an individual catchment basis, there is an arguable case, therefore, for the provision of phosphorus removal from all sizeable waste effluents in the public and private sectors. The urban waste water treatment Directive has limited relevance in this connection as nutrient removal is required only for discharges greater than 10,000 person equivalents in the case of sensitive areas. However, phosphorus removal is now being provided for smaller discharges in the context of the Catchment Management programmes to combat eutrophication, e.g., in the Shannon catchment; this approach needs to be applied on a wider basis. The same approach is warranted for some industrial sectors, e.g., milk processing and slaughtering plants, where the waste effluents have relatively high phosphorus concentrations, comparable to those in sewage. The EPA is addressing this need in the case of those activities subject to the Integrated Pollution Control licensing system.

There are no other widespread quality problems in inland waters comparable to eutrophication. However, the localised pollution of groundwaters is a matter of concern and calls for improved management and protection of these resources. Nitrate contamination of waters appears to be increasing in the south-east of the country and this trend will need close surveillance. In some areas, there may be a requirement at this stage for the designation of vulnerable zones under the EU nitrates Directive in order to reinforce the codes of good practice already issued in accordance with that directive. In regard to potentially toxic substances in waters, the limited data available indicate that, with the exception of those in some of the older mining areas, the State's waters are not significantly affected by such contamination. This database needs to be increased and widened to cover the synthetic organic compounds, such as herbicides, imported into the State in large quantities including those known to affect the reproductive system in fish.

It is concluded that the quality of the State's inland waters remains relatively good despite the continuing erosion of this position by the spread of eutrophication. It remains to be seen whether the measures introduced in recent years to counteract this development will be sufficiently effective and, in particular, allow the targets set down in the Phosphorus Standards Regulations to be met for presently polluted waters. Such improvements will be needed in any event under the proposed EU framework Directive (EC, 1996) on water policy which, *inter alia*, sets a very demanding target of good ecological quality in all waters. The concept of good ecological quality in the draft Directive is very widely defined embracing all aspects of the aquatic ecosystem, including water quality, and will greatly extend, in particular, the range of biological indicators to be monitored.

However, it is clear that attainment of good quality as defined will demand at the least a rating of satisfactory for river water quality and mesotrophic for lake water quality when these are judged by the classifications schemes currently used in the State.

REFERENCES

Bowman, J.J., 1986. *Precipitation Characteristics and the Chemistry and Biology of Poorly Buffered Irish Lakes.* An Foras Forbartha, Dublin.

Bowman, J.J., 1991. *Acid Sensitive Surface Waters in Ireland.* Environmental Research Unit, Dublin.

Bowman, J.J., Clabby, K.J., Lucey, J., McGarrigle, M.L., and Toner, P.F., 1996. *Water Quality in Ireland 1991-1994.* Environmental Protection Agency, Wexford.

Caffrey, J.M. and Allison, J.P., 1998. Eutrophication in canals. In: Wilson, J.G. (ed.) *Eutrophication in Irish Waters*, 71-81. Royal Irish Academy, Dublin.

Caffrey, J.M. and Johnston, B., 1998. The Grand and Royal Canals: an ecological perspective. In: Moriarty C. (ed.) *Studies of Irish Rivers.* 57-76. Essays on the occasion of the XXVII Congress of *Societas Internationalis Limnologiae* (SIL). Marine Institute, Dublin.

Caffrey, J.M. and Monahan, C., 1995. *Aquatic weed management in Irish canals 1990-1995.* Office of Public Works commissioned report. Central Fisheries Board, Dublin.

CEC (Council of the European Communities), 1975. Council Directive of the 16 June 1975 concerning the quality required of surface water intended for the abstraction of drinking water in the Member States (75/440/EEC). *O. J.* L 194/26.

CEC (Council of the European Communities), 1976. Council Directive of the 4 May 1976 on pollution caused by certain substances discharged into the aquatic environment of the Community. *O. J.* L 129/23.

CEC (Council of the European Communities), 1980. Council Directive of the 15 July 1980 relating to the quality of water intended for human consumption (80/778/EEC). *O. J.* L 229/11.

CEC (Council of the European Communities), 1991a. Council Directive of 12 December 1991 concerning the protection of waters against pollution caused by nitrates from agricultural sources (91/676/EEC). *O. J.* L 375/1.

CEC (Council of the European Communities), 1991b. Council Directive of 21 May 1991 concerning urban waste water treatment (91/271/EEC). *O. J.* L 135/40.

Clabby, K.J., Lucey. J. and McGarrigle, M., 1982. *The National Survey of Irish Rivers. River Quality Investigations - Biological. Results of the 1980 and 1981 Investigations.* An Foras Forbartha, Dublin.

Clabby, K.J., Bowman, J.J., Lucey, J., McGarrigle, M.L., and Toner, P.F., 1992. *Water Quality in Ireland 1987-1990.* Environmental Research Unit, Dublin.

Cork County Council, Electricity Supply Board, ESB International, RPS Cairns Ltd., South Western Regional Fisheries Board, Teagasc and University College Cork, 1995. *STRIDE - Lee Catchment Project. Lee Valley Report May 1995.* (Unpublished report).

Cullen and Co., 1994. *Trace organic contaminants in Irish ground water.* K.T. Cullen and Co., Dublin.

DELG (Department of the Environment and Local Government), 1998. *Local Government (Water Pollution) Act, 1977 (Water Quality Standards for Phosphorus) Regulations, 1998.* Statutory Instrument No. 258 of 1998. Government Supplies Agency, Dublin.

DELG (Department of the Environment and Local Government), Environmental Protection Agency and Geological Survey of Ireland, 1999. *Groundwater Protection Schemes.* Department of the Environment and Local Government, Dublin.

DoE (Department of the Environment), 1997. *Managing Ireland's Rivers and Lakes. A Catchment-based Strategy against Eutrophication.* Department of the Environment, Dublin.

EC (European Commission), 1996. Proposal for a Council Directive establishing a framework for Community action in the field of water policy. *O. J. C* 184/20

EEA (European Environmental Agency), 1998. *Europe's Environment: The Second Assessment.* EEA, Copenhagen.

EPA (Environmental Protection Agency), 1999. *The Quality of Drinking Water in Ireland. A Report for the Year 1998 with a Review of the Period 1996-1998.* EPA, Wexford.

Flanagan, P. J. and Toner, P. F., 1972. *The National Survey of Irish Rivers. A Report on Water Quality.* An Foras Forbartha, WR/R1, Dublin.

Giller, P. S. (ed.), 1998. *Studies in Irish Limnology.* Essays on the occasion of the XXVII Congress of Societas Internationalis Limnologiae (SIL), Dublin, 9-14 August, 1998. Marine Institute, Dublin.

King, J.J., 1996a. *Channel maintenance in drained Irish catchments: experimental strategies, ecological impacts and management implications.* Ph.D. Dissertation, National University of Ireland, Dublin.

King, J.J., 1996b. The impact of drainage maintenance strategies on the flora of a low gradient, drained Irish salmonid river. *Hydrobiologia* **340**, 197-203.

King, J.J., O'Grady, M.F. and Curtin, J., in press. *The Experimental Drainage Maintenance (EDM) Programme: engineering and fisheries management interactions in drained Irish salmonid channels.* Paper presented at the XXVII Congress of Societas Internationalis Limnologiae (SIL), Dublin 1998.

Lucey, J., Bowman, J.J., Clabby, K.J., Cunningham, P., Lehane, M., MacCárthaigh, M., McGarrigle, M.L and Toner, P.F., 1999. *Water Quality in Ireland 1995-1997.* Environmental Protection Agency, Wexford.

McCumiskey, L.M., 1991. *Water in Ireland. A Review of Water Resources, Water Supplies and Sewerage Services.* Environmental Research Unit, Dublin.

McGarrigle, M. L. and Champ, W. S. T., 1999. Keeping pristine lakes clean: Loughs Conn and Mask, Western Ireland. *Hydrobiologia*, **395/396**, 455-469

McGarrigle, M.L., Champ, W.S.T., Norton, R., Larkin, P. and Moore, M., 1993. *The Trophic Status of Lough Conn. An Investigation into the Causes of Recent Accelerated Eutrophication.* Mayo County Council, Castlebar.

McGarrigle, M.L., Hallissey, R., Donnelly, K. and Kilmartin, L. *Trends in phosphorus loading to Lough Conn, Co. Mayo, Ireland.* (in press)

Moriarty, C., 1996. *Fish Kills in Ireland in 1994 and 1995.* Fishery Leaflet 169. The Marine Institute, Fisheries Research Centre, Dublin.

Moriarty, C. (ed.), 1998. *Studies of Irish Rivers and Lakes.* Essays on the occasion of the XXVII Congress of Societas Internationalis Limnologiae (SIL), Dublin, 9-14 August, 1998. Marine Institute, Dublin.

O'Donnell, C., 1996. *Pesticides in Drinking Waters. Results of a Preliminary Survey December 1994-December 1995.* Environmental Protection Agency, Wexford.

OECD (Organisation for Economic Co-operation and Development), 1982. *Eutrophication of Waters, Monitoring, Assessment and Control.* OECD, Paris.

O'Muircheartaigh, F.S., 1999 In: Whelan K.F. & O'Muircheartaigh, F.S. (eds): *Managing Ireland's Spring Salmon Stocks – the Options.* Proceedings of a Salmon Research Agency and Central Fisheries Board seminar and workshop, Dublin, 11th Sept. 1999.

Reeders, H.H., Bij de Vaate, A. and Slim, F.J., 1989. The filtration rate of *Dreissena polymorpha* (Bivalvia) in three Dutch lakes with reference to biological water quality management. *Freshwater Biology* **22**, 133-141.

Reynolds, J. D., 1998. *Ireland's Freshwaters.* Produced for the XXVII Congress of Societas Internationalis Limnologiae (SIL), Dublin, 9-14 August, 1998. Marine Institute, Dublin.

Roche, W., 1998a. *Monitoring of juvenile salmonid stocks in the Slaney catchment,1997.* Central Fisheries Board, Dublin.

Roche, W., 1998b. *The current status of two brown trout fisheries in the Fanad peninsula: 1992 and 1997 compared.* Central Fisheries Board, Dublin.

Stapleton, L. (ed.), 1996. *State of the Environment in Ireland.* Environmental Protection Agency, Wexford.

Tunney, H., Coulter, B., Daly, K., Kurz, I., Coxon, C., Jeffrey, D., Mills, P., Kiely, G. and Morgan, G., 2000. *Quantification of Phosphorus Loss from Soil to Water.* EPA, Wexford.

Toner, P.F., Clabby, K.J., Bowman, J.J. and McGarrigle, M.L., 1986. *Water Quality in Ireland. The Current Position. Part One: General Assessment.* An Foras Forbartha, Dublin.

Whilde, A. 1993. *Threatened mammals, birds, amphibians and fish in Ireland.* Irish Red Data Book 2: Vertebrates. HMSO, Belfast.

ESTUARINE AND COASTAL WATERS

Bycatch in hake fishery.

The sea waters around Ireland are generally clean and the main environmental issue relating to them is the impact of fishing activity on both target and non-target species. There is concern about some stocks of cod, hake, saithe, plaice and sole. There is concern too that the by-catch mortality of harbour porpoises in the Celtic Sea hake fishery may be greater than can be sustained by the population. The discharges from the British Nuclear Fuels reprocessing plant at Sellafield continue to result in contamination of the Irish marine environment, but exposure of humans is not considered to pose a significant health risk.

Diverse pressures come to bear on the estuarine and coastal environment, leading to impaired quality in some respects. The use of paints containing the compound tributyltin (TBT) for anti-fouling on vessels is a serious continuing problem in various parts of the world; in Ireland impacts have been increasing in general port areas and particularly in fishing ports.

In certain tidal inlets receiving organic discharges, notably a section of the Lee Estuary/Inner Cork Harbour and the estuary of the Castletown River (Dundalk), these discharges result in areas of serious deoxygenation. Surveys indicate that sustained eutrophic conditions are confined mainly to inner Cork Harbour and the Broadmeadow Estuary, County Dublin. Current and planned initiatives, notably the upgrading of national sewage treatment infrastructure (Chapter 5) are expected to bring about considerable improvements in these and other areas.

Various forms of coastal development, much of which is related to tourism and leisure activities, are increasing pressures on the coastal zone and particularly on vulnerable habitats. This is a matter of serious concern and requires a strategic and multi-sectoral response. Litter from sources both on land and at sea remains a problem which diminishes the aesthetic quality of the coast. The quality of bathing waters is generally very good. Overall, the environmental quality of Ireland's estuaries, bays and coastal waters remains exceptionally good in a European context but this quality is subject to increasing pressures and needs to be guarded.

INTRODUCTION

The waters of the north-east Atlantic largely determine the nature and composition of Ireland's coastal and offshore waters, making them among the highest quality marine waters in Europe. The open ocean is not entirely free of contaminants, however, since it receives atmospheric deposition of pollutants that have been emitted to the air (Chapter 5, Chapter 7). Closer to the shore, and particularly in certain bays and estuaries, urban and industrial effluents give rise to varying degrees of quality impairment. This may be augmented by rivers which enter tidal waters carrying large amounts of substances such as organic matter and nutrients deriving from agriculture and other activities inland.

The coastline of Ireland is heavily indented, particularly on the Atlantic seaboard. There are some 400 estuaries, of which fewer than 50 can be regarded as being of a significant size. Approximately 34 per cent of the coastline is sandy beach, with the rest predominantly rock and cliff, except for around 10 per cent mud shore, which is largely restricted to estuaries. Over half of the Irish population is now living within 10 km of the coast (Chapter 2), and most of the major towns are situated on estuaries and bays. The coastal zone also supports, in large measure, strategic sectors such as heavy industry, power generation, external trade, fisheries, aquaculture and tourism (Chapter 3). The estuarine and coastal environment is consequently subject to a wide variety of human pressures. These include inputs of organic matter, nutrients and contaminants from sources such as urban waste water, industrial discharges, riverine inflow and accidental spillages (Chapter 5), as well as the impacts of activities such as fisheries, shipping, aquaculture and tourism (Chapter 7). The fabric of the coastline itself may be physically altered by erosion or deposition, both natural and through human intervention.

The environmental quality of estuarine and coastal waters is monitored by the Environmental Protection Agency (EPA), the Local Authorities, the Marine Institute's

Fisheries Research Centre (FRC), the Department of the Marine and Natural Resources and the Radiological Protection Institute of Ireland. Additional work is carried out by other bodies including non-governmental organisations (NGOs) and educational institutes. Monitoring of the estuarine and marine environment has been heavily influenced by Ireland's commitments as a member of the European Union. Significant initiatives in the area of marine environmental monitoring and assessment have also come from the Convention for the Protection of the Marine Environment of the North East Atlantic (OSPAR Convention).

This chapter presents an overview of general environmental quality conditions in estuarine and coastal waters in the period since the previous State of the Environment report (Stapleton, 1996). Environmental aspects of the fisheries and aquaculture sectors are briefly reviewed, while discussion of general habitat quality and biodiversity is included in Chapter 12. An important source of information for this chapter was the recent assessment of the quality status of Ireland's marine and coastal areas and adjacent seas undertaken by the Marine Institute (Boelens *et al.*, 1999) as part of a wider OSPAR assessment of the waters of the north-east Atlantic.

EFFECTS OF ORGANIC WASTES AND NUTRIENTS

Regular water quality monitoring is carried out in 25 estuaries and bays around the country, including the estuaries of most of the major rivers, to assess the effects of organic matter and nutrient discharges. The surveys are carried out mainly in the summer months, the period when low water exchange and higher temperatures increase the likelihood of the occurrence of oxygen imbalance and eutrophic levels of plant growth. Winter surveys are carried out in near-shore waters as well as in offshore waters in the Irish Sea to monitor levels of nutrients in the absence of plant growth.

The results of water quality surveys over the period 1995-1997 were assessed in the latest review of water quality in Ireland (Lucey *et al.*, 1999). The findings of these surveys indicate that the general quality of estuarine and coastal waters around the country has remained high. While most major estuaries receive inputs of sewage and other wastes (Chapter 5), the majority showed no clear indications of excessive enrichment or seriously impaired environmental conditions.

However, certain areas in a few estuaries and bays continue to exhibit serious deoxygenation, including a section of the Lee Estuary/Inner Cork Harbour and the estuary of the Castletown River in the vicinity of Dundalk. A similarly affected area in the estuary of the Lee (Tralee) River was relatively small in extent.

Clear and sustained eutrophic conditions were observed only in a few estuaries. Nutrients from both riverine inflows and local discharges were present at high levels in the Lee Estuary and the Lough Mahon area of Inner Cork Harbour, and excessive phytoplankton blooms were observed regularly. Eutrophic levels of growth were also common in the Broadmeadow Estuary in North County Dublin, an impounded lagoon that consequently has a very low flushing rate which allows high plankton biomass to develop.

Intermittent pollution due to effluent discharges was observed in the Boyne, Liffey, Suir, Shannon and Garavoge estuaries. Conditions in these waters typically improved rapidly within a short distance of the affected areas, and the severity of pollution was insufficient to cause significant or prolonged disturbance to fish and other biota. There were no indications of sustained eutrophic conditions in these areas, although periodic blooms of phytoplankton were occasionally observed in some cases, notably the estuaries of the Liffey and Garavoge. Strandings of macroalgae were also noted in some of these areas, particularly on the shores of Dublin and Dundalk Bays.

Elevated growth of phytoplankton is a regular feature of the estuaries in the south and south-east, notably the estuaries of the Slaney (Box 10.1), Barrow-Nore-Suir, Blackwater and Bandon rivers, and in the Cashen-Feale, Maigue and Deel estuaries in the mid-west region. In all of these, very high chlorophyll *a* concentrations were regularly recorded during the summer months, particularly in the low-salinity reaches. However, both the areas and the volumes of water affected were limited, and associated effects such as oxygen supersaturation were generally unremarkable. It is therefore probable that the development of unusually high summer phytoplankton concentrations in the upper reaches of all of these estuaries is strongly related to their poor flushing rates (Neill, 1998), which are particularly evident in periods of lowered freshwater flows. Thus, it is not yet possible to make a definitive assessment of the

trophic status of these estuaries; it is possible that they are naturally productive areas which would occasionally exhibit high phytoplankton production rates even in the absence of significant nutrient enrichment through human activities. Nevertheless, it will be necessary to redouble current efforts to reduce nutrient inputs from diffuse sources into these estuaries and their feeder rivers, in accordance with the EU urban waste water and nitrates Directives.

Water quality in Dublin Bay was found to be high. Conditions in the Liffey/Tolka estuary were generally impaired, however, due largely to the discharge from the Ringsend sewage works, and occasional evidence of eutrophication in the form of high phytoplankton abundance was observed in the estuarine area. No signs of water-column eutrophication were observed in Dublin Bay, although as already noted, there were instead strandings of variable quantities of macroalgae on the shores each summer.

Box 10.1 Modelling Nutrients and Algae in Estuaries

Supported by the 1994-1999 environmental research programme (Chapter 1), a detailed two-year study of nutrient dynamics and algal growth in the estuarine zones of Wexford and Cork Harbours has been undertaken. The project was carried out by a consortium of Irish researchers with additional input from the EPA, the Marine Institute and the Local Authorities. Using innovative techniques, including aerial video imagery and detailed field monitoring of hydrology, water quality and ecological zonation, the project has investigated all potential sources of nutrients, rates of transport through the estuaries and the resulting patterns of phytoplankton production. High-resolution mathematical models of both estuaries were developed and validated using the results of dye-release experiments and other field data, and a Geographic Information System (GIS) user interface was constructed for each model. These models will allow prediction of the effects of different conditions of weather, river flow and nutrient inputs on algal growth and eutrophication in Wexford and Cork Harbours, greatly assisting in the ongoing management of these waters. It is hoped that this study will also provide a methodology for similar studies in other Irish estuaries.

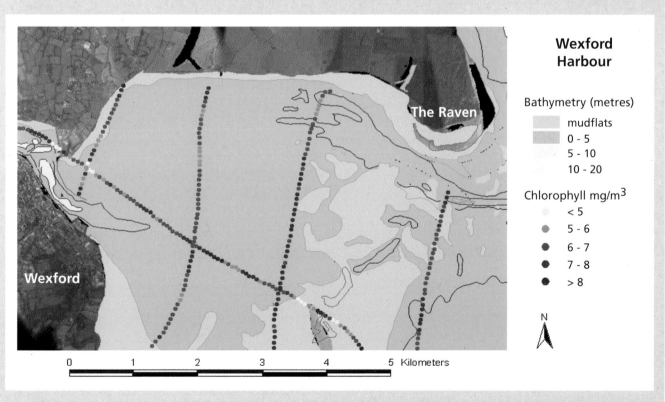

The GIS map above shows water depths (bathymetry) in Wexford Harbour and the results of aerial remote sensing of chlorophyll (an indicator of the abundance of algae in the water). The lower chlorophyll levels occur in areas of strong water movement.

Costello et al., in press.

Recent studies indicate that the fauna occupying the sediments in estuaries and bays may be experiencing only moderate, local effects of organic enrichment. Exceptions are the Liffey estuary and parts of Dublin Bay, and also Inner Cork Harbour, where quite extensive alteration of the expected sediment fauna has been found over the years (ERU, 1989; Boelens *et al.*, 1999).

Water quality was generally very high in the coastal areas surveyed. Winter nutrient concentrations, monitored by the Marine Institute in the western Irish Sea during the period 1995-1997 (M. Bloxham, pers. comm.), were, except in the vicinity of the major estuaries, broadly similar to background levels in the north-east Atlantic.

A bloom of the colony-forming Prymnesiophyte alga *Phaeocystis globosa* was observed throughout the western Irish Sea from mid May to early June 1996 (Lucey *et al.*, 1999). This caused the deposition of a mucous material, composed of decaying colonies, at a number of locations along the east coast. Excess production of a related species has been observed regularly in the English Channel and the southern North Sea over the last number of years, and has been linked to nutrient enrichment (Lancelot *et al.*, 1987; Richardson, 1989). There was no indication, however, that the 1996 *Phaeocystis* event was directly related to local nutrient inputs.

TOXIC CONTAMINANT LEVELS

Potential sources of hydrocarbons, heavy metals and synthetic organic chemical substances entering tidal waters include both licensed and, probably more importantly, accidental or unauthorised releases from industrial sources such as oil storage depots, garages, general manufacturing and mining operations. Other important sources of these materials are ports and harbours, horticulture and runoff from urban areas, notably road surfaces.

An extensive background survey of metals and chlorinated hydrocarbons in shellfish, finfish, water and sediments at a variety of locations around the coast was carried out by the FRC in the period between 1978 and 1988 (O'Sullivan *et al.*, 1991). The results showed that the general overall trend in metal levels over that period was one of stability or, in the case of more marked contamination, of reduction over time, and it was concluded that with few exceptions Irish coastal waters carried very low levels of contamination. The most recent published results for the heavy metals cadmium, copper, lead, zinc and chromium, and for chlorinated hydrocarbon concentrations, in finfish were also low and within standard and guidance values (Bloxham *et al.*, 1998; Rowe *et al.*, 1998).

Mercury concentrations in finfish from the commercial catch and shellfish from the major growing areas were also found to be low and well within the EC limits set for protection of the consumer. Concentrations of 'priority organochlorines', including the DDT group of compounds and the polychlorinated biphenyls (PCBs), in the tissues of all fish and shellfish monitored were found to be less than 1 per cent of the strictest values applied by OSPAR countries for the protection of human health. There is, however, some cause for keeping under review the body burdens of these substances present in seabirds and in seals, porpoises and other marine mammals (Boelens *et al.*, 1999).

In the early 1990s significant concentrations of the pesticide toxaphene, which is not known to have been used extensively in western Europe, were detected in a number of commercial fish species throughout the north-east Atlantic, including sites off the west coast of Ireland. The few existing national standards for toxaphene in food are contradictory and a review of European standards for toxaphene in seafood has been initiated (Boelens *et al.*, 1999).

TRIBUTYLTIN

Tributyltin has been used since the 1960s as the biocidal agent in anti-fouling paints on boats and ships. It was also used extensively on cage netting at salmon farms in the 1980s. TBT is one of a class of synthetic chemicals known as endocrine disrupters (Chapter 7), which cause changes to the normal functioning of hormones in humans and animals and can lead to physical deformation of reproductive structures and reduced reproductive success. TBT itself is known to cause masculinisation (imposex) of female molluscs, even at extremely low ambient concentrations, as well as growth retardation and deformities in both tissues and shell structure.

Studies in the 1980s revealed TBT contamination to be a widespread problem in Irish waters (Minchin and Duggan, 1986; Minchin et al., 1987), and a by-law was introduced in April 1987 prohibiting, with few exceptions, the use of TBT on vessels under 25 metres and on other structures including fish farm cages. Since 1987, regular surveys have been conducted to determine changes in contamination levels in areas with aquaculture, small boat activity and at major ports. The results are summarised in Figures 10.1 and 10.2, and indicate a general reduction in TBT contamination in the vicinity of aquaculture sites and small boat activity since 1987, although there

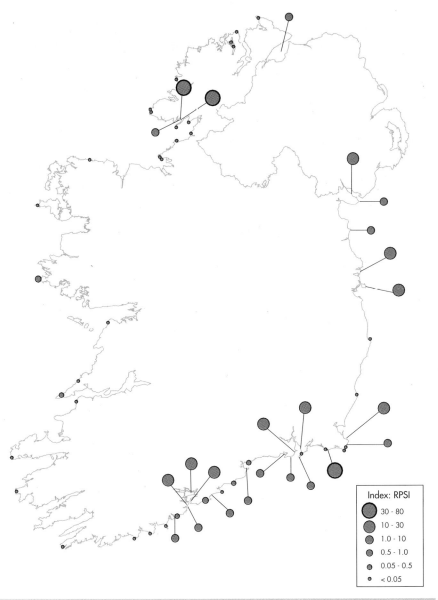

Index: RPSI

- 30 - 80
- 10 - 30
- 1.0 - 10
- 0.5 - 1.0
- 0.05 - 0.5
- < 0.05

Fig. 10.1 Prevalence of TBT-induced Imposex in Dogwhelks (after Boelens et al., 1999)

Unusually high levels of contaminants, particularly mercury and the anti-fouling agent tributyltin (TBT) (see below) were detected in the surface sediments of Bantry Harbour in the period 1994 - 1997 (Nixon, 1997). Lead levels were also unusually high in parts of the harbour and such contamination would be expected to have detrimental effects on sediment-dwelling species. Because there are no major industrial or agricultural activities in the Bantry area and the sewage discharge is relatively small, the reason for the high metal levels is not immediately clear. The TBT contamination, however, was much higher than in Kenmare Bay, and was

attributed to the use of anti-fouling paints on boats and the subsequent cleaning of these vessels (Nixon, 1997; Byrne Ó Cléirigh, 1998).

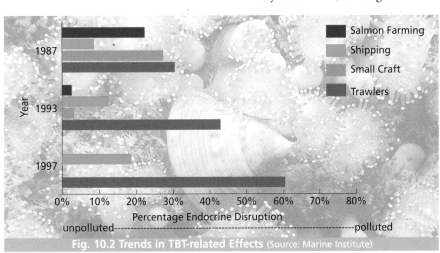

Salmon Farming
Shipping
Small Craft
Trawlers

Percentage Endocrine Disruption

unpolluted --------------------------------- polluted

Fig. 10.2 Trends in TBT-related Effects (Source: Marine Institute)

Box 10.2 Classification System for Shellfish Production Areas

The scheme of classification of shellfish production areas, operated by the Department of the Marine and Natural Resources under Directive 91/492/EEC (CEC, 1991), is as follows:

Classification	Faecal coliforms (*E. coli*) per gram of shellfish flesh	Requirements
A	Less than 3 (2.3)	None - sale for direct human consumption permitted[1]
B	3 (2.3) or greater with not more than 10% of samples exceeding 60 (46)	Purification in an approved plant for 48 hours prior to sale for human consumption[2]
C	Greater than 60 (46) and not more than 600 (460)	Relaying for a period of at least two months in clean seawater prior to sale for human consumption[2]

1 In addition must not contain Salmonella in 25 grams of flesh

2 Scientifically proven cooking methods, approved by the Standing Veterinary Committee, may obviate the necessity for purification or relaying

Note: All figures in brackets refer to E. coli.
    Although the classification is mainly based on the bacteriological quality of the shellfish, other criteria are also taken into account for the assessment.

has been an increase in other areas (Minchin *et al.*, 1995). The most contaminated areas were busy ports, especially in estuaries and bays, and where TBT paints are still applied to ships exempt from the 1987 ban. It is therefore clear that the use of TBT is a serious continuing problem in Irish waters as in other parts of the world, and research into alternative anti-fouling treatments is ongoing. The International Maritime Organisation has recently proposed an extension of the current ban to include ships up to 50 metres in length.

SHELLFISH WATERS

Classification

The Irish shellfish industry is continuing to expand at a rapid rate (Chapter 3). In order to safeguard the industry and the consumer, environmental and public health monitoring programmes are in place. Shellfish production areas are classified by the Department of the Marine and Natural Resources under the Regulations (SI No. 147 of 1996) that enforce the EC Directive laying down the health conditions for the production and the placing on the market of live bivalve molluscs (CEC, 1991). The scheme of classification

has three categories, corresponding with the criteria as laid down in the Directive, which are summarised in Box 10.2.

Currently, 58 production areas are sampled in the monitoring programme under the Directive. The most recent classification, effective from November 1998, is given in Table 10.1 along with classifications in previous review periods (Toner *et al.*, 1986; Clabby *et al.*, 1992; Bowman *et al.*, 1996). A full list of the sites with their most recent classification (M. O'Driscoll, pers. comm.) is illustrated in Fig. 10.3.

Monitoring of Contaminants in Shellfish Waters

Member States are required under an earlier EC Directive (CEC, 1979), to

monitor designated shellfish waters to ensure that the quality of the edible species is maintained or enhanced. A total of 14 areas have been designated to date under the Quality of Shellfish Waters Regulations 1994, which transposed the requirements of the Directive into Irish law. Water and shellfish samples were analysed for physico-chemical parameters and chemical contaminants at 21 sites in 1995, including the 14 designated areas (Fig. 10.3) as well as sites in Wexford Harbour, at Arthurstown (Waterford), Cork Harbour, Kenmare Bay, Tralee Bay, Aughinish (Limerick) and Lough Foyle. In 1996, Dungarvan Harbour was added to the list of surveyed areas. The water quality of the shellfish growing areas was good and complied with the requirements of the Regulations. Petroleum hydrocarbons were not observed in any of the

Table 10.1 Classifications of Shellfish Waters 1986-1998				
	1998	1991-94	1987-90	1986
Total	58*	58**	25***	13
A	26 %	55%	12%	38%
B	60%	29%	60%	54%
C	2%	3%	12%	8%

*four areas were classed as partly A and B; one as B and C; one as A, B and C
**five areas were classed as partly A and B; one as A and C; one as B and C
***four areas were not classified

the detection of harmful algal toxins is shown in Fig. 10.4.

Except in a few cases, the organisms most likely to have caused the toxicity in these instances are the dinoflagellates *Dinophysis acuta* and *D. acuminata*. These species and others have been associated with a gastroenteritis-like illness known as diarrhetic shellfish poisoning (DSP), the symptoms of which include diarrhoea and vomiting. A potentially more serious condition known as paralytic shellfish poisoning (PSP) is apparently not a general problem in Irish shellfish waters, although the causative organisms as well as PSP toxins have been recorded at low levels here in the past (McMahon, 1994).

Although other coasts in Ireland are occasionally affected, the south-west is most liable to be affected by this phenomenon (Fig. 10.4). There is no evidence that such blooms of harmful phytoplankton in the south-west are indicative of local nutrient enrichment and pollution; in fact, field studies indicate that the accumulation of toxins in shellfish in this region can be directly linked to

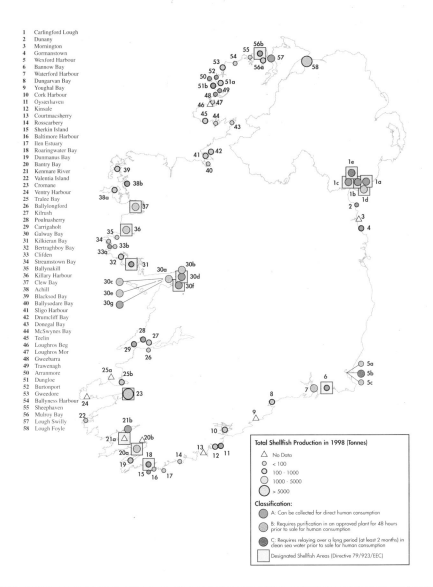

1 Carlingford Lough
2 Dunany
3 Mornington
4 Gormanstown
5 Wexford Harbour
6 Bannow Bay
7 Waterford Harbour
8 Dungarvan Bay
9 Youghal Bay
10 Cork Harbour
11 Oysterhaven
12 Kinsale
13 Courtmacsherry
14 Rosscarbery
15 Sherkin Island
16 Baltimore Harbour
17 Ilen Estuary
18 Roaringwater Bay
19 Dunmanus Bay
20 Bantry Bay
21 Kenmare River
22 Valentia Island
23 Cromane
24 Ventry Harbour
25 Tralee Bay
26 Ballylongford
27 Kilrush
28 Poulnasherry
29 Carrigaholt
30 Galway Bay
31 Kilkieran Bay
32 Bertraghboy Bay
33 Clifden
34 Streamstown Bay
35 Ballynakill
36 Killary Harbour
37 Clew Bay
38 Achill
39 Blacksod Bay
40 Ballysodare Bay
41 Sligo Harbour
42 Drumcliff Bay
43 Donegal Bay
44 McSwynes Bay
45 Teelin
46 Loughros Beg
47 Loughros Mor
48 Gweebarra
49 Trawenagh
50 Arranmore
51 Dungloe
52 Burtonport
53 Gweedore
54 Ballyness Harbour
55 Sheephaven
56 Mulroy Bay
57 Lough Swilly
58 Lough Foyle

Total Shellfish Production in 1998 (Tonnes)

△ No Data
○ < 100
○ 100 - 1000
○ 1000 - 5000
○ > 5000

Classification:

○ A: Can be collected for direct human consumption

○ B: Requires purification in an approved plant for 48 hours prior to sale for human consumption

○ C: Requires relaying over a long period (at least 2 months) in clean sea water prior to sale for human consumption

□ Designated Shellfish Areas (Directive 79/923/EEC)

Fig. 10.3 Shellfish Production Areas (Directive 91/492/EEC)

shellfish waters nor as deposits on shellfish. With the exception of elevated lead in mussels from Wexford and slightly elevated cadmium in oysters from some other areas, trace metal levels were consistently low (Bloxham *et al.*, 1998). The elevated cadmium values have been recorded consistently over a number of years, and appear not to be anthropogenic in origin (Nixon *et al.*, 1995).

Phycotoxins

Since 1984, the Fisheries Research Centre has operated a national monitoring programme for detecting the occurrence in shellfish of phycotoxins, from certain planktonic

algae (McMahon, 1994). These toxins have been associated with illness and in some cases death in humans following consumption of shellfish. There are no antidotes available for any of the toxins involved, nor can they be destroyed by cooking or processing. The monitoring programme is based on a laboratory bioassay, and samples are collected regularly from all shellfish production areas. When a production area gives a positive result for toxins, restrictions on the harvesting and sale of the shellfish are put in place under the terms of Directive 91/492/EEC (CEC, 1991). The average annual duration of closures of selected shellfish production areas arising from

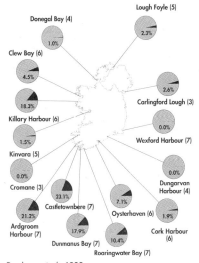

Boelens *et al.*, 1999

Fig. 10.4 Average duration (as % of the year) of closure of selected shellfish growing areas arising from detection of harmful algal toxins from 1991-1997

Numbers in brackets indicate the number of years that samples were submitted.

offshore blooms being carried into nearshore shellfish areas by landward currents (McMahon *et al.*, 1998).

The risk to Irish consumers of contracting shellfish poisoning due to phycotoxins is very small because of the efficacy of the monitoring and testing procedures in place. Regular testing, the frequency of which is weekly on a year-round basis, will continue to ensure that the risk of placing contaminated product on the market is minimised (McMahon, 1998).

BATHING WATERS

Monitoring of water quality at designated bathing areas is undertaken annually by the local authorities in accordance with the requirements of the EC Directive concerning the quality of bathing waters (CEC, 1976). The purpose of the directive is to ensure that bathing water quality is maintained, and if necessary improved, so that it complies with specified standards designed to protect public health and the environment. Since 1996, the EPA has been collating the water quality results from the local authorities and reporting these in summarised form (EPA, 1997; 1998a).

The number of designated sea water bathing areas has increased over the years to a total of 121 sites by 1998. The results for the 1998 bathing season indicate that 119 of the 121 sites complied with the mandatory standards, of which 97 complied with the more stringent guidline standards. The locations and compliance status of the bathing areas sampled during 1998 are shown in Fig. 10.5.

All but one of the bathing areas complied with the standards for total and faecal coliforms. In addition, 93.4 per cent of the sites tested complied with the National Limit Value for faecal streptococci and, while only 66 sites were tested for

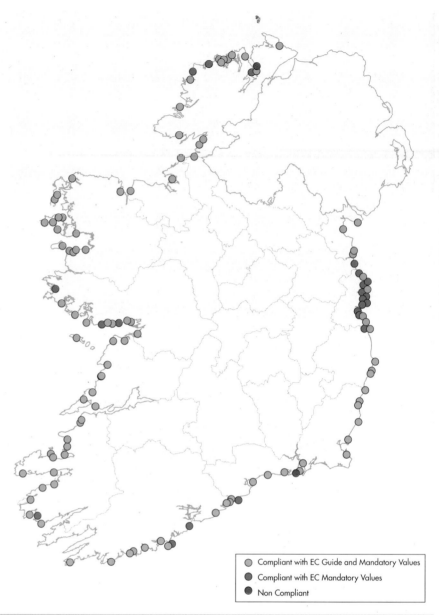

- ○ Compliant with EC Guide and Mandatory Values
- ● Compliant with EC Mandatory Values
- ● Non Compliant

Fig. 10.5 Locations and Compliance Status of Bathing Areas in 1998

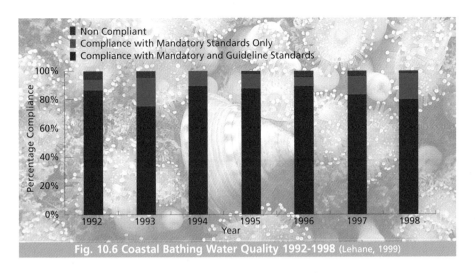

Fig. 10.6 Coastal Bathing Water Quality 1992-1998 (Lehane, 1999)

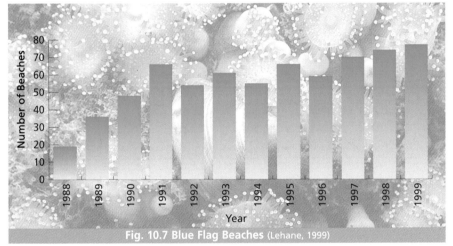

Fig. 10.7 Blue Flag Beaches (Lehane, 1999)

Analysis of bathing water in respect of the Regulations is separate from, though complementary to, the European Blue Flag Scheme (Fig. 10.7), a voluntary scheme administered in Ireland by An Taisce and at European level by the Foundation for Environmental Education in Europe. To receive a blue flag, a bathing site must, in addition to maintaining a high standard of water quality, meet specified objectives with regard to the provision of safety services and facilities, environmental management of the beach area and environmental education.

RADIOACTIVITY IN IRISH WATERS

The Radiological Protection Institute of Ireland (RPII) is the statutory authority with responsibility for monitoring radioactivity in the Irish environment. Its functions include the ongoing surveillance of the Irish marine environment, in which sea water as well as marine biota and sediments are monitored, to assess the level and impact of radioactive contamination.

The results from the continuing RPII monitoring programme show that contamination levels of radiocaesium (one of the main radionuclides discharged up to the mid-1980s) in sea water, sediments, seaweed, fish and shellfish in the Irish Sea have continued to decline since the early 1990s (Pollard et al., 1996; Long et al., 1998a). This decline was due to changes in waste handling technologies at Sellafield, which resulted in significant reductions in discharges of radiocaesium (Fig. 10.8). However, the commissioning of two new plants at the Sellafield site in the early 1990s has resulted in the discharge of certain other radionuclides, particularly technetium-99, in significant quantities. Monitoring of radioactivity by the UK Ministry of Agriculture, Fisheries and Food

dissolved oxygen, 96 per cent of these complied with the appropriate limit value.

Compliance rates for bathing waters over the period 1992-1998 are presented in Fig. 10.6. Compliance with the mandatory criteria has remained high over the period peaking at 100 per cent in 1994. Compliance with the more stringent guideline standards has decreased in the last few years and has returned towards pre-1994 levels.

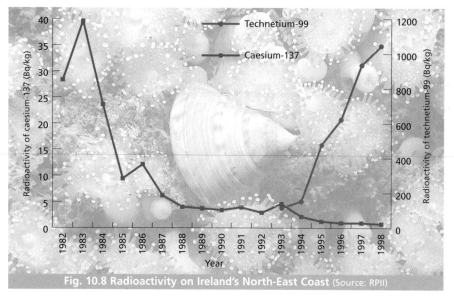

Fig. 10.8 Radioactivity on Ireland's North-East Coast (Source: RPII)

(Leonard *et al.*, 1997), shows that, by December 1994, concentrations of technetium-99 in sea water off the Irish east and north-east coasts had respectively doubled and quadrupled. By 1995, the impact of increased discharges of liquid radioactive waste was being recorded by the RPII, who reported 'enhanced' concentrations of technetium-99 in seaweeds (Figure 10.8) along the eastern Irish coastline (Pollard *et al.*, 1996); by late 1996 these effects had become a matter of serious concern to the Institute (RPII, 1997).

The consumption of fish and shellfish is the most likely route by which radiation exposure of the Irish public can occur as a consequence of radioactive contamination of the marine environment (Long *et al.*, 1998b), and external exposure to bathers and recreational water users is considered to be insignificant (Pollard *et al.*, 1996). Because of the lower radiotoxicity of technetium-99, it contributed only 15 per cent of the estimated dose due to artificial radioactive contamination of Irish seafood in 1996 and 1997, still significantly less than the 65 per cent contribution made by caesium-137. However, the ingestion dose from naturally-occurring radionuclides is many times larger, and artificial radioactivity in seafood accounts for less than one per cent of the annual

dose limit for members of the public as recommended by the International Commission on Radiological Protection.

Radiation doses due to consumption of seafood allow an estimation of the risk to the Irish public; evaluation of this risk is based on the assumption that there is a linear relationship between radiation dose and the risk of a fatal cancer. For 1996 and 1997 the risk has been calculated as one in 60 million for a typical seafood consumer (Long *et al.*, 1998a). It is clear, therefore, that the levels of radioactive contamination of the Irish marine environment do not justify misgivings on health grounds, nor warrant any modification of the habits of people in Ireland, either in respect of consumption of seafood or any other use of the amenities of the marine environment (Long *et al.*, 1998). However, as the RPII points out, any contamination of Ireland's marine environment resulting from the operations of nuclear installations in other countries is viewed as objectionable.

OIL POLLUTION

Sources of accidental oil spillages include losses from passing shipping and land-based facilities as well as offshore oil and gas installations. Reports of marine oil pollution from

all sources have been recorded since 1993 by the Irish Marine Emergency Service (IMES) of the Department of the Marine and Natural Resources. The location and extent of oil pollution from significant incidents recorded by IMES in the 1995-1997 period are given in Table 10.2.

In addition to the three incidents outlined in Table 10.2, other minor oil spills, where the amounts of oil released were very small, have been recorded in the period: 15 in 1995, 18 during 1996 and 12 in 1997 (Boelens *et al.*, 1999).

When the *Sea Empress* went aground in March 1996, some 72,000 tonnes of oil (mainly crude) were released into Milford Haven in south Wales making it the third largest oil spill to have occurred in UK waters. Some time afterwards, small amounts of the oil were washed up on the Irish coast. As it was in the form of well matured 'tar balls', there was little or no impact on the Irish coastal environment (G. Livingstone, pers. comm.). The results of monitoring, prior to and following the incident, showed no apparent effects on the plankton in the southern Irish Sea (Batten *et al.*, 1998).

As current levels of exploration and production activity in the offshore oil and gas sector are low, there has been little environmental impact from this source in Irish waters. It is known that, with the exception of accidental losses during production, the main potential hazard associated with sub-sea exploration concerns the disposal of contaminated drilling spoil close to the drilling location. With current drilling techniques, however, the risk of significant impacts from this source is thought to be minimal.

GENERAL AMENITY AND RECREATION

It is estimated that over 1.5 million Irish adults participate in various maritime and coast-based leisure

Table 10.2 Oil Pollution Incidents in Irish Waters 1995-1997				
Location	**Date**	**Tonnes**	**Cause**	**Impact**
Wicklow Harbour	15 Dec. 1995	70 (Gas Oil)	Grounding of MV Salavat Yulaev in severe weather	Slight, due to dispersal of oil; beach cleaned
Dublin Bay	21 Sep. 1996	Unquantified (small quantity)	Unknown	500 oiled birds washed ashore
Cork Harbour	04 Nov. 1997	31 (Heavy Fuel Oil)	Leakage of Irish Refining plc pipeline, Whitegate	Described in Chapter 7

Sources: Irish Marine Emergency Service (Capt. G. Livingstone, pers. comm.); EPA (1998b)

activities, giving rise to 29 million day trips per annum (Marine Institute, 1998). The coastal zone thus constitutes a major recreational amenity, particularly in the summer months. There have been improvements over the last decade in access and facilities at beaches around the coast as well as the development of increasing numbers of golf courses and marinas. A recent study of the economic value of the water-based tourism and leisure sector estimated revenue totalling £391.9 million and an equivalent full-time employment of 14,525 (Marine Institute, 1998).

However, increasing recreational use of beaches has been reported to have led to increases in litter as well as physical and ecological damage to many areas (Boelens *et al.*, 1999), particularly fragile sand dune sites where unrestricted access has contributed to the retreat of the dunes and encroachment of the high tide line. There is also potential for increasing pressures from developments such as golf links, marinas, holiday homes and caravan parks (Chapter 7). The resident populations of coastal towns and villages have also been increasing in recent times, and satellite imagery shows that the proportion of the coastal zone covered by discontinuous urban fabric (including industrial and commercial units) has increased by over 25 per cent since the mid 1980s.

It is therefore essential to intensify efforts towards management of the coastal zone. Although much of Ireland's coastline remains relatively undisturbed, there is still insufficient information by which to judge the current rate and long-term environmental implications of coastal development. The Government published a draft policy on coastal zone management in 1997 (Brady Shipman Martin, 1997) with a view to improving planning and control of coastal developments at local, regional and national level (See also Chapters 11 and 15).

LITTER AND UNAUTHORISED DUMPING ON THE COAST

The aesthetic and amenity value of the coastal zone is particularly vulnerable to degradation by litter, which can also impact adversely on wildlife. Litter on the Irish coast comes from a variety of sources, both land and sea. In the October 1997 Coastwatch Europe survey of the Irish coastline, more than 1,300 sites were examined, of which some 1,100 were in the Republic (Dubsky *et al.*, 1998a); at the time of writing, preliminary results from the October

1998 survey of 866 sites (592 in the Republic) were also available (Dubsky *et al.*, 1998b). In both surveys, large metal items and landfill material were found to be the most common form of large waste/debris. These were observed, respectively, at 26.4 and 26.3 per cent of sites around the coast in 1997, and at 29 per cent and 27 per cent of sites respectively in 1998. Household rubbish, drinks containers and plastics such as shopping bags, bottles and 'six-pack' holders were among the items regularly noted. Fewer plastic, metal and glass drinks containers were found in 1998 compared to 1997, but numbers are still much higher than in the early 1990s.

Both reports note the 'startling rise' since 1989 in the recordings of fishing-related plastic waste items, such as fragments of oyster bags, nets, floats and ropes. It is not clear how much of the overall increase is due to aquaculture activities, but shellfish and finfish farms have been identified as large contributors of litter on adjacent shores. The 1997 report

concluded by noting that, while there were some signs of progress, the greater use of powers available under the Waste Management Act (1996) and the Litter Pollution Act (1997) could ensure a considerable improvement in the quality of the coastal environment. The 1998 report observed that the number of beaches showing evidence of sewage matter has risen during the 1990s. This is apparently related to the expansion in the numbers of caravan sites and holiday homes, noted earlier, without the prior installation of adequate sewage infrastructure.

IMPACTS OF MARINE DUMPING

Licensed dumping of waste material at sea was outlined in Chapter 5. The discharge of sewage sludge from the Ringsend sewage works in an area about 14 km east of the Dublin coast after 1990 was found to have had no measurable effect on the benthic faunal assemblages of this area (Neiland, 1994), largely due to the active and dispersive nature of the area. This dumping ceased in September 1999.

Much of the dredge spoil created in Ireland derives from maintenance dredging in the various ports and harbours around the country, and the scale and frequency of disposal is generally small and involves small quantities of material. A permit to dump dredge spoil at sea is given only if no beneficial use or alternative land-based disposal option can be

identified. Heavily contaminated sediments are not licensed for sea disposal in Ireland, but must instead be disposed of on land. Impacts from the disposal of dredged material include the covering over of indigenous sediments and their resident faunal communities, and potential degradation of fish breeding and nursery areas. Fine sediments from industrial harbours may contain relatively high concentrations of metals and organics, and resuspension of this material into the water column during operations may be of concern in relation to both the dredging site and the dump site.

There has been little evidence of significant metal contamination in the area of the dump site for dredged material from Dublin Port and the adjacent pre-1990 sewage sludge dump site off Howth. There is a concern, however, that insufficient attention is paid to the selection of dumping sites for the spoil produced in the majority of ports and harbours around the country, and increased monitoring of the effects of dumping on the local biota is required (Boelens et al., 1999).

ENVIRONMENTAL ASPECTS OF FISHERIES AND MARINE AQUACULTURE

An outline of the marine food sector was given in Chapter 3, and the potential environmental pressures associated with fishing and marine farming activities were discussed

further in Chapter 7. Recent information on the state of commercial fish and shellfish stocks and on the impact of the marine food industry on non-target organisms was comprehensively reviewed as part of the assessment of Ireland's coastal waters and adjacent seas (Boelens et al., 1999). Some of the main findings relating to the environmental aspects of this industry are outlined below.

State of Fish Stocks

Information on fish landings is collated by the International Council for the Exploration of the Seas (ICES), primarily from figures reported by the fleets in the various countries. There is a recognition that these statistics are imperfect because of frequently inaccurate reporting of catches, but they nonetheless constitute the best available data on which to base estimates of stock size and allowable quotas for each species.

Many commercially important fish species are heavily exploited in the waters around Ireland. Recent ICES figures suggest that significant proportions of the total adult stocks of the main pelagic (mid water) and demersal (sea-bed) fish species, up to 60 per cent in some instances, are taken in catches. Pelagic fish, mainly mackerel, horse mackerel and herring, typically make up around two-thirds of the total fish and shellfish landings. Mackerel stocks are currently thought to be low in historic terms, but stable and within (above) safe biological limits; this is the minimum stock size below which replenishment by recruitment is likely to be insufficient to sustain a viable fishery, based on ICES models of the species concerned. Spawning stocks of horse mackerel are reported to have declined by 75 per cent over the last decade, and recruitment of this species would appear to be highly variable from year to year. There is a real concern that the fishery is not sustainable at current rates of exploitation.

Following major stock collapses due to overfishing, many herring fisheries in Western Europe were closed in the late 1970s. As a result, the stocks substantially recovered, but in recent years concern has been expressed again about many of them. The spawning stock to the west and north-west of Ireland has decreased sharply from a peak in the late 1980s, while total landings have remained relatively constant, and there appears to be a need for significant reduction in fishing pressure. The herring fishery in the waters off the south and south-west coasts is also currently outside safe limits, though the spawning stock in this area appears to be more stable (ICES, 1998).

Among the demersal species, there is concern about some stocks of cod, hake, saithe, plaice and sole. Significant reductions in quotas have recently been agreed for a number of species in the Irish Sea, notably the cod fishery. Whiting stocks are low but stable in Irish waters, and haddock stocks are currently believed to be stable or increasing. Stocks of sole in the Irish Sea are considered to be outside safe limits because of both a low spawning stock biomass and high fishing mortality, while plaice stocks are close to safe limits. Anglerfish and a number of cartilaginous fishes such as the rays and skates are also at dangerously low levels; these species are long-lived, slow growing and have very low recruitment rates, and are

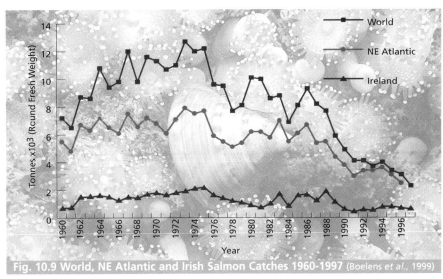

Fig. 10.9 World, NE Atlantic and Irish Salmon Catches 1960-1997 (Boelens et al., 1999)

therefore uniquely at risk from overexploitation.

The commercial salmon net fishery in coastal waters and estuaries currently accounts for around 85 per cent of the total salmon catch, with the remainder made up by rod and line angling upriver. Total nominal catches of Atlantic salmon have declined considerably over the last two decades, in Ireland and elsewhere (Figure 10.9). The most recent ICES assessment of European salmon stocks indicate that this species is close to or outside safe biological limits and a significant reduction in exploitation is required. The management of salmon stocks is problematic because of the recognised under-reporting of catches, according to the Salmon Management Task Force (1996). Changes in the

licensing system for salmon fishing and the introduction of carcass tagging are intended to partly redress this situation (Boelens et al., 1999) (see also Chapter 9).

Sea trout stocks in Ireland and elsewhere suffered a serious collapse in the late 1980s (Fig. 10.10), leading to a major controversy over the possible causes which is not yet resolved. In particular, infestation of sea trout with lice from salmon farms was blamed for the collapse. There is some evidence to support this contention, and that the control of lice infestations, particularly in the critical March-May period, may assist in promoting the recovery of sea trout stocks in affected rivers. Currently, catches of sea trout in Irish waters remain at a low level relative to those taken before the collapse occurred (see also Chapter 9).

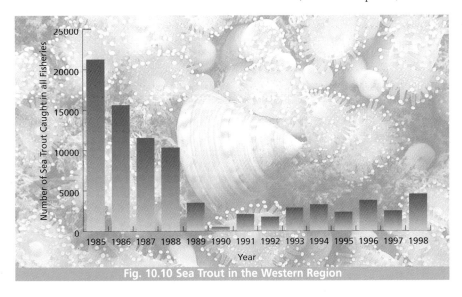

Fig. 10.10 Sea Trout in the Western Region

Impact of Fishing on Juveniles, Non-target Fish Species and Other Aquatic Organisms

Discarding of undersize and non-target fishes (Chapter 7) is a problem which has long been recognised, but information on the quantities discarded has only recently started to become available for many fisheries. It is estimated that over 15,300 tonnes of fish were discarded by the demersal fleets sampled in the waters around Ireland and the west coast of the UK in 1996. Discards of demersal fish by the Irish fleets sampled in 1996 were 9,300 tonnes compared to demersal landings of 46,000 tonnes. No figures on discarding of non target fish are yet available for Irish pelagic fisheries, but as an indication of the potential scale of the problem, recent data from trawl fisheries in the Netherlands indicate that discards amounted to 23 per cent and 13 per cent of the mackerel and horse mackerel landings respectively in 1996 (Boelens et al., 1999).

Fishing gear towed along the seabed can displace, kill or injure animals burrowed in the sediment or living on its surface, and may alter the sediment structure. The impact on benthic communities and the seabed is very much dependent on the fishing intensity, design of the gear and the sediment type. Estimates of the total area swept annually by the various gear types can provide an indication of the possible scale of disturbance. In 1994, up to 25 per cent, 22 per cent and 8 per cent of the total area of the Irish Sea bed was swept by otter trawling, beam trawling and shellfish dredging respectively. It has been shown that some areas now support clearly altered faunal communities which are adapted to the regular disturbance caused by bottom fishing; a number of species characteristic of active substrates may now be found in actively-fished parts of the Irish Sea, and the sea urchin *Brissopsis* has apparently been displaced from areas where it was previously abundant (Boelens et al., 1999).

Considerable research is being devoted to improving the design of fishing gear and modifying fishing techniques to reduce catches of unwanted species or undersized fish, to reduce the impact of demersal trawls on the benthic fauna and to avoid the problems associated with lost gear continuing to trap and kill afterwards.

Marine mammal and bird populations are adversely affected by fishing and aquaculture activities in two main ways: either through incidental capture or from competition for resources. Numerous national and international studies have demonstrated the ability of trawls and, perhaps more significantly, drift nets and other static gears to trap seals, dolphins and porpoises as well as diving seabirds such as auks, shags and cormorants.

In the case of static gear such as drift nets, the animals are probably attracted by fish caught in the nets. This habit leads to the occasional granting of licences for seal culling issued to fishermen under the Wildlife Act. This practice is not regarded as an acceptable solution in the longer term, and research is ongoing into non-harmful deterrents, similar to the ultrasonic 'seal scarers' and other methods used by fish farms.

There is considerable uncertainty concerning the significance of cetacean by-catch at the population level. A programme to assess the marine mammal by-catch of the Irish and UK bottom-set gill-net fisheries, primarily targeting hake, on the Celtic Shelf to the south-west of Britain and Ireland was conducted from 1992 to 1994. The estimated total annual by-catch is 2,200 harbour porpoises and 200 common dolphins, representing 6.2 per cent and 0.3 per cent, respectively, of their estimated populations in the Celtic Sea. While the mortality estimates should be interpreted with caution, nevertheless there is concern about the ability of the harbour porpoise population in the Celtic Sea to sustain such losses (see also Chapter 12).

There have been regular reports from Ireland and elsewhere of the entanglement of large numbers of birds in nets, and it is clear that monofilament gill- and tangle netting is largely responsible. However, the limited information available has not shown any negative effects on population sizes of the most commonly-affected species (Boelens et al., 1999).

Impacts of Mariculture

Concerns about the environmental implications of marine aquaculture were outlined in Chapter 7. The sector with the greatest impact on the environment and on other aquatic life is the production of finfish. There are currently over 30 salmon production sites, and a further three producing sea trout. This industry is located on the north and west coasts, and individual farms typically represent the largest source of nutrients and organic material entering the local aquatic environment (Chapter 5). Recent monitoring data on the state of production sites are extremely limited, but the enriching effects of fish farming were demonstrated in the 1980s in a number of sheltered, poorly-flushed inlets, such as Inner Kilkieran Bay and Mulroy Bay. However, the majority of salmon farms are now located in open bays and coastal waters, with good tidal exchange which facilitates the dispersal of wastes. Along with the regular fallowing of sites, this relocation helps to maintain good water quality, which in addition to being an important environmental objective is also a prime requirement for successful fish cultivation.

Up until the early 1990s, a number of antibiotics were regularly administered to farmed fish for the control of infectious diseases such as furunculosis and vibriosis. As a result, antibiotic residues have been detectable in the sediments beneath cages and in the tissues of wild finfish from the vicinity of fish farms (Boelens et al., 1999). Since the introduction of effective vaccines against these diseases, antibiotic use has been curtailed, and is now carried out infrequently and under veterinary license (T. Scanlon, pers. comm.). Recent research has indicated that the use of these antibiotics carries no significant risk of the encouragement of resistance in human pathogens (Smith et al., 1994).

In the past, organophosphate pesticides have been the main chemical treatment used for the control of parasites, chiefly sea lice, on farmed fish. Although these are known to be hazardous to human health and also to other aquatic life, there have been no reports of toxic effects on other organisms in either the water column or the sediments around fish farms. Other biocidal agents such as ivermectin, which has been widely used in agricultural parasite control, have recently come into use as replacements for organophosphates. Since they are administered in feed rather than as bath treatments, the quantities released to the environment are significantly smaller. These compounds are also toxic to other marine organisms in laboratory tests, but again there have been no reports of adverse effects on the biota around fish cages in Ireland. The clearance of residues of the various substances from fish flesh may take up to a month, so treatments are required to be withheld from stocks approaching market readiness.

The chemicals used in finfish culture include also copper-based antifoulants applied to the cages and nets. There are concerns that this source of contamination may be locally significant, though no information has been collected on the distribution and potential effects of copper around cage sites, as metals are not currently included in routine fish farm monitoring programmes (Boelens et al., 1999).

Rearing of salmon in sea cages inevitably involves the risk of accidental escapes, and escaped fish have been shown to be capable of surviving and breeding with wild populations (Chapter 12). For instance, studies in Irish rivers have shown that escapees are present in catches from many wild fisheries, that farmed salmon may successfully breed with wild fish and that the young fish produced may make up a substantial portion of the total recruitment in individual rivers (Clifford et al., 1998). The potential problems associated with genetic interactions between wild and reared salmon include gradual replacement of wild stocks by farmed salmon, genetic alteration of native populations, reduction in adaptation to local conditions and reduction in fitness. The effects, if any, on wild populations have not yet been identified and cannot be predicted with certainty. It is however, clear that they cannot now be prevented.

Environmental concerns associated with shellfish cultivation are largely limited to visual impacts in scenic areas (also an issue in finfish farming) and, in relation to some types of activity, possible conflicts with shore-feeding bird populations. However, intensive mussel cultivation, though not based on the addition of foodstuffs, has been reported to cause local changes in the sediments below

rafts and longlines. The sediments of inner Bantry Bay have become progressively muddier and more organically enriched as a result of mussel culture over the last number of decades (Boelens *et al.*, 1999).

IMPACTS OF CLIMATE CHANGE ON FAUNAL COMMUNITIES

Since biological communities are largely controlled by climate, one of the more likely consequences of global warming is an alteration of these communities. Some species will undoubtedly find the new conditions favourable and extend their ranges, while others will become less well adapted or less competitive, and may be pushed to local extinction. Minchin (1993) has discussed the more likely changes in distribution of a number of marine species in Irish waters. Some species occurring occasionally in Irish waters, such as the pilchard (*Sardina pilchardus*) and others introduced for commercial purposes, such as the pacific oyster (*Crassostrea gigas*), which cannot currently reproduce here because temperatures are too low, may be able to undergo population increases. Toxic algal blooms may also increase in frequency, and there is a possibility that organisms introduced accidentally, for instance in ballast waters and on ships' hulls, may become more firmly established. Some of these might be parasitic and disease-causing species, including pests for the fishing and aquaculture industries, as in the case of the introduced slipper limpet, now a serious pest on oyster beds in the southern North Sea.

MARINE RESEARCH AND DEVELOPMENT

A wide range of marine research is carried out in Ireland, by government agencies, third-level institutes and commercial companies. Much of this work is partly funded under EU programmes and co-ordinated by the Environmental Protection Agency and the Marine Institute. Recent projects have included the Biomar study, which produced a CD Rom based guide to the habitats, flora and fauna of the coastal zone throughout the island of Ireland. A number of studies are underway into nutrients and their effects, seaweed cultivation, biological pest control in aquaculture and the development of new technologies for the fishing industry, offshore fish farming and wave energy.

The Marine Institute is the national agency whose functions, as defined by the Marine Agency Act, 1991, are "to undertake, to co-ordinate, to promote and to assist in marine research and development and to provide such services related to marine research and development that in the opinion of the Institute will promote economic development and create employment and protect the marine environment". The Institute encompasses the Fisheries Research Centre and the Irish Marine Data Centre. In 1998, the Institute published a strategy containing a range of detailed initiatives for research and development in the areas of Marine Environment, Tourism and Leisure, Food and Technology, whose overall aim is to help realise the growth potential of the marine resource.

CONCLUSIONS

The environmental quality of Ireland's estuaries, bays and coastal waters remains generally high in a European context, despite substantial population growth and economic development over recent decades (Chapter 3). There is scope for further marine-based economic growth, particularly in tourism and leisure, aquaculture and exploitation of seabed resources, including offshore oil and gas, minerals and aggregates (see Chapter 7) and ocean energy. However, there is also potential for conflict of uses and environmental degradation and

damage to sensitive ecosystems if development is not properly managed.

A few areas, mostly estuarine, are affected by poor bacteriological quality, excessive organic enrichment and eutrophic pressures, because of direct municipal and industrial discharges as well as the nutrient load carried down by rivers. The impacts include loss of amenity value, possible interference with fisheries and aquaculture and some changes in the natural animal and plant communities. It is anticipated that the current and planned upgrading of national sewage treatment infrastructure and initiatives to control nutrient loss from diffuse sources (Chapter 5) will lead to significant improvements in these areas over the next number of years.

There is little doubt that the occurrence of harmful algal blooms is increasing in Irish waters as in other coastal regions around the world. While no clear link with human activities has yet been demonstrated, it is essential that the causes of these events are identified and any necessary action is taken to combat this trend (EC, 1999).

With the increasing market demand and with modern fishery capability and efficiency, there is now recognition that the exploitation of wild fisheries may be approaching unsustainable levels. Initiatives are being taken at local, national and international levels to improve the management and exploitation of wild fish and shellfish stocks. The increase in aquaculture production is expected to continue, and while this is to be welcomed, there is a need for further efforts to reduce the dependence of the industry on chemicals and to lessen the potential for adverse effects on wild fisheries and the local aquatic environment.

REFERENCES

Batten, S.D., Allen, R.S.J. and Wotton, C.O.M., 1998. The effects of the Sea Empress oil spill on the plankton of the southern Irish Sea. *Marine Pollution Bulletin* 36, pp. 764-774.

Bloxham, M., Smyth, M., Rowe, A., McGovern, E. and Nixon, E., 1998. *Trace Metal and Chlorinated Hydrocarbon Concentrations in Shellfish and Fin-fish from Irish Waters - 1996.* Fishery Leaflet 179. Marine Environmental Series 2/98. Marine Institute, Dublin.

Boelens, R.G.V., Maloney, D.M., Parsons, A.P. and Walsh, A.R., 1999. *Ireland's Marine and Coastal Areas and Adjacent Seas. An Environmental Assessment.* Prepared by the Marine Institute on behalf of the Department of Environment & Local Government and the Department of Marine & Natural Resources. Marine Institute, Dublin.

Bowman, J.J., Clabby, K.J., Lucey, J., McGarrigle, M.L., and Toner, P.F., 1996. *Water Quality in Ireland 1991-1994.* Environmental Protection Agency, Wexford.

Brady Shipman Martin, 1997. *Coastal Zone Management, a Draft Policy for Ireland.* Department of Environment and Local Government, Department of Arts, Heritage, Gaeltacht and the Islands, Department of the Marine and Natural Resources, Dublin.

CEC (Council of the European Communities), 1976. Council Directive of 8 December 1975 concerning the quality of bathing water (76/160/EEC). *O. J.* L 31/1.

CEC (Council of the European Communities), 1979. Council Directive of 30 October 1979 on the quality required of shellfish waters (79/923/EEC). *O. J.* L 281/47.

CEC (Council of the European Communities), 1991. Council Directive of 15 July 1991 laying down the health conditions for the production and the placing on the market of live bivalve molluscs (91/492/EEC). *O. J.* L 268/1.

Clabby, K.J., Bowman, J.J., Lucey, J., McGarrigle, M.L. and Toner, P.F., 1992. *Water Quality in Ireland 1987-1990.* Environmental Research Unit, Dublin.

Clifford, S.L., McGinnity, P., and Ferguson, A., 1998. Genetic changes in Atlantic salmon (*Salmo salar*) populations of Northwest Irish rivers resulting from escapes of adult farm salmon. *Can. J. Fish. Aquat. Sci.* 55, pp. 358-363.

Costello, M.J., Hartnett, M., Mills, P., O'Mongáin, E., Collier, L., Johnson, M., Nash, S., Leslie, R., Berry, A., Emblow, C., Collins, A. and McCrea, M., in press. *Quantitative modelling of the nutrient dynamics of Cork and Wexford Harbours.* Environmental Protection Agency, Wexford.

Dubsky, K., Larragy, J., Nolan, D. and Troddyn, S., 1998a. *Coastwatch Europe - Autumn 1997. Results for all Ireland.* Coastwatch Europe, Trinity College, Dublin.

Dubsky, K., Larragy, J. and Richter, K, 1998b. *Coastwatch Europe - Autumn 1998. Results for all Ireland.* Coastwatch Europe, Trinity College, Dublin.

EC (European Commission), 1999. *EUR 18592 – Harmful algal blooms in European marine and brackish waters.* Office for Official Publications of the European Communities, Luxembourg.

EPA (Environmental Protection Agency), 1997. *The Quality of Bathing Water in Ireland (1996).* Environmental Protection Agency, Wexford.

EPA (Environmental Protection Agency), 1998a. *The Quality of Bathing Water in Ireland (1997).* Environmental Protection Agency, Wexford.

EPA (Environmental Protection Agency), 1998b. *Oil Spillage from Irish Refining Plc, Whitegate, Co. Cork: 4th November 1997.* Environmental Protection Agency, Wexford.

ERU (Environmental Research Unit), 1989. *Cork Harbour Water Quality.* Environmental Research Unit, Dublin.

ICES (International Council for the Exploration of the Sea), 1998. *Coop. Res. Rep. No. 229 – Part 2.*

International Council for the Exploration of the Sea, Copenhagen.

Lancelot, C., Billen, G., Sournia, A., Weisse, T., Colijn, F., Veldhuis, M.J.W., Davies, A. and Wassman, P., 1987. *Phaeocystis* blooms and nutrient enrichment in the Continental Coastal Zones of the North Sea. *Ambio* 16:1, pp 32-37.

Lehane, 1999 (ed.). *Environment in Focus. A Discussion Document on Key National Environmental Indicators.* Environmental Protection Agency, Wexford.

Leonard, K.S., McCubbin, D., Brown, J., Bonfield, R. and Brooks, T., 1997. Distribution of Technetium-99 in UK coastal waters. *Marine Pollution Bulletin* 34, pp. 628-636.

Long, S., Pollard, D., Hayden, E., Smith, V., Fegan, M., Ryan, T.P., Dowdall, A. and Cunningham, J. D., 1998a. *Radioactivity monitoring of the Irish marine environment 1996 and 1997.* Radiological Protection Institute of Ireland, Dublin.

Long, S., Hayden, E., Smith, Ryan, T., V., Pollard, D. and Cunningham, J., 1998b. An overview of the Irish marine monitoring programme. *Radiation Protection Dosimetry* 75, Nos. 1-4, pp. 33-38.

Lucey, J., Bowman, J.J., Clabby, K.J., Cunningham, P., Lehane, M., MacCarthaigh, M., McGarrigle, M.L. and Toner, P.F., 1999. *Water Quality in Ireland 1995-1997.* Environmental Protection Agency, Dublin.

Marine Institute, 1998. *A Marine, Research, Technology, Development and Innovation Strategy for Ireland.* Marine Institute, Dublin.

McMahon, T., 1994. *Shellfish Poisoning in Ireland: Monitoring and Management. Environmental Health Officers Yearbook 1994, pp.19-22.* Environmental Health Officers Association, Dublin.

McMahon, T., 1998. Monitoring of algal toxins in shellfish. *Aquaculture Newsletter* 25: 5.

McMahon, T., Raine, R. and Silke, J., 1998. *Oceanographic control of harmful phytoplankton blooms around south-western Ireland.* In: Reguera, B., Blanco, J., Fernández, M. L. and Wyatt, T. (eds). Harmful Algae - Proceedings of the VIII International Conference on Harmful Algae. Vigo, Spain, 25-29 June 1997.

Minchin, D., 1993. *Possible influence of increases in mean sea temperature on Irish marine fauna and fisheries. Biogeography of Ireland: past, present and future.* In: M.J. Costello and K.S. Kelly (eds) Occasional Publications of the Irish Biogeographical Society No. 2, 1993, pp. 113-125.

Minchin, D. and Duggan, C.B., 1986. *Organotin contamination in Irish waters.* ICES CM 1986/F:48.

Minchin, D., Duggan, C.B. and King, W., 1987. Possible effects of organotins on scallop recruitment. *Marine Pollution Bulletin* 18: 11, pp. 604-608

Minchin, D., Oehlmann, J., Duggan, C.B., Stroben, E. and Keatinge, M., 1995. Marine TBT antifouling contamination in Ireland, following legislation in 1987. *Marine Pollution Bulletin* 30, pp 633-639.

Neiland, S., 1994. *Monitoring the environmental impact of sewage sludge dumping on the benthos.* Report of the Fisheries Research Centre, Abbotstown. Marine Institute, Dublin.

Neill, M., 1998. *A report on water quality in the Suir/Barrow/Nore Estuary 1997.* Environmental Protection Agency, Kilkenny.

Nixon, E., 1997. *Bantry Harbour Sediment Survey.* Fisheries Research Centre (Marine Institute), Dublin.

Nixon, E., McLoughlin, D., Rowe, A. and Smith, M., 1995. *Monitoring of Shellfish Growing Areas – 1994.* Fishery Leaflet 166. Marine Environmental Series 1/95. Department of Marine, Dublin.

O'Sullivan, M. P., Nixon, E. R., McLaughlin, D., O'Sullivan, M. and O'Sullivan, D., 1991. *Chemical Contaminants in Irish Estuarine and Coastal Waters, 1978-1988.* Fisheries Bulletin, No.10. Department of the Marine, Dublin.

Pollard, D., Long, S., Hayden, E., Smith, V., Ryan, T.P., Dowdall, A., McGarry, A. and Cunningham, J. D., 1996. *Radioactivity monitoring of the Irish marine environment 1993 to 1995.* Radiological Protection Institute of Ireland, Dublin.

Richardson, K., 1989. Algal Blooms in the North Sea: the Good, the Bad and the Ugly. *Dana* 8, pp 83-93.

Rowe, A., Nixon, E., McGovern, E., McManus, M. and Smyth, M., 1998. *Metal and Organo-chlorine Concentrations in Fin-fish from Irish Waters in 1995.* Fishery Leaflet 176. Marine Environmental Series 1/98. Marine Institute, Dublin.

RPII (Radiological Protection Institute of Ireland), 1997. *Annual Report and Accounts 1996.* Radiological Protection Institute of Ireland, Dublin.

Salmon Management Task Force, 1996. *Salmon Management Task Force - Report to the Minister.* Stationery Office, Dublin.

Smith, P., Hiney, M.P. and Samuelson, M.B., 1994. Bacterial resistance to antimicrobial agents used in fish farming: a critical evaluation of method and meaning. *Ann. Rev. Fish Diseases* 4, pp. 273-313.

Stapleton, L. (ed), 1996. *State of the Environment in Ireland.* Environmental Protection Agency, Wexford.

Toner, P.F., Clabby, K.J., Bowman, J.J. and McGarrigle, M.L., 1986. *Water Quality in Ireland. The Current Position. Part One: General Assessment.* An Foras Forbartha, Dublin.

CHAPTER 11

THE LAND

In recent years the ecological and visual amenity of many Irish landscapes has been seriously affected by developments such as urban sprawl, road construction, the growth of industry, commercial forestry and an upsurge in the development of holiday homes, which are overpowering some traditional villages, towns and coastal areas.

Significant afforestation has occurred in recent decades and this is planned to continue. Currently 79 per cent of Irish forests are made up of coniferous species, significantly higher than in most EU States. Poor planting design and unnatural boundaries can impact negatively on the landscape. Irish forests can potentially make a contribution to limiting emissions of greenhouse gases. The average carbon storage in Irish coniferous forests is estimated at 3.36 tonnes per hectare per annum. However, recent research has given rise to uncertainties regarding the permanence of forests to act as carbon sinks in the long term.

Peatlands once covered over 17 per cent of the land area of the State. However, now only 19 per cent of the original amount remains in a relatively untouched condition. In upland areas and on western blanket bogs, overgrazing by sheep has caused serious damage.

Intensification and specialisation of agricultural practices have impacted on the environment to a significant degree. The main concerns in this regard relate to the emission of greenhouse gases, increasing surface water pollution and the effects of overgrazing on soil and biodiversity. There is now a considerable surplus of phosphorus input to farmland over that removed in produce. Many soils are now likely to contain phosphorus at levels where losses to local streams and other surface waters will occur during periods of high rainfall, leading to eutrophication and the loss of habitats for fish.

Rising vehicle numbers and increased usage of cars have caused significant traffic congestion and noise, particularly in urban areas. While a beginning has been made on introducing pedestrian walkways and cycle lanes, there is major scope for improvement. The incidence of litter remains widespread in Ireland, despite the extent of actions undertaken by local authorities. There has been a steady rate of loss of archaeological features.

An assessment of artificial radioactivity in the terrestrial environment indicates that levels in air, water and the food chain are low and do not give rise to public health concerns. A study of critical loads and their exceedance indicates that Ireland is largely free of the threat of acidification.

INTRODUCTION

This chapter outlines the current state of the land in Ireland and considers the impacts resulting from human activity and various socio-economic activities, including agricultural practices, afforestation, and urbanisation. For the purposes of this chapter, the land is considered to include landscapes, soil, the coastal margin, upland areas, bogs and wetlands, the rural and urban environments in general and the archaeological resource. The chapter also covers degraded land and artificial radioactivity and the impacts of overgrazing by sheep. Other aspects of the land are covered elsewhere in the report and flora, fauna and habitats are considered in Chapter 12.

The pattern of land use and the shape of the landscape in Ireland are influenced by many factors including changing agricultural practices, urban expansion, rural housing patterns, economic developments in tourism and industry and mineral extraction. More recently some of the main land use changes include forestry planting, developments in road infrastructure and the location of electricity transmission facilities, telecommunication masts and windfarms (DoE, 1997; DAF, 1999). In the absence of a national land-use policy, land use in the past has been determined by tradition, market

prices of agricultural products and
the ability of an area to sustain the
most lucrative products (Heritage
Council, 1999a).

LANDSCAPE QUALITY

The quality of the landscape
influences our lives whether we live in
a city, a town or in the countryside.
Landscape is not static, but rather it
is the dynamic product of a complex
interaction between the human and
natural systems. However,
interpreting the quality of landscapes
is difficult. The aesthetic
appreciation of scenery and the
perception of landscape quality can
vary from person to person.

In Ireland, human interaction with
the environment has produced a wide
range of characteristic landscape
features and a variety of distinctive
rural landscapes, reflecting the natural
diversity of the country. Natural
landscapes, the product of geological,
climatic and biological processes with

no human influence are rare in the
world today. Yet Ireland's landscape
heritage has a wealth of natural and
cultural resources (Aalen *et al.*, 1997).
Like landscapes everywhere, they are
inevitably altered when the character
of the interaction between people and
nature changes. The distinctive
interrelationship between nature and
people, especially in long and closely
settled areas such as Ireland, is
characterised by the term 'cultural
landscape'. Cultural elements of the
Irish landscape include field and
settlement patterns, hedgerows,
buildings, archaeological and
historical monuments, woodlands,
bogs and mines (Box 11.1).

Throughout the centuries agriculture
has had a significant effect on
landscapes in Ireland. More recently,
agricultural intensification and farm
abandonment, urban expansion,
standardisation of building designs,
infrastructure development, tourism
and recreation have resulted in some
replacement of natural and regional

diversity by homogeneity. In some
cases this is accompanied by more
specific environmental degradation.
The landscape has also been affected
by commercially orientated
afforestation policies that have
resulted in the monoculture of
coniferous trees in forestry plantations.

A draft European Landscape
Convention requires that a consistent
strategic approach be adopted in
landscape protection, management
and planning. At present in Ireland,
the policy is one of designation, a
concern with sites rather than
landscapes. Existing conservation
policies are heavily concerned with
the protection of individual features,
not with the landscape as a unified
whole (Aalen *et al.*, 1997).

The Heritage Council is currently
preparing a landscape policy. Issues
to be addressed include the definition
of terms such as landscape and scenic
beauty, and the baseline landscape
characteristics upon which to base
policy. Draft guidelines on landscape
and landscape assessment for local
authorities have been prepared to
raise awareness of the importance of
landscape in physical planning and to
highlight specific requirements for
county development plans. The
proposal is to classify landscapes
according to their type, value and
sensitivity. Landscape values are the
environmental or cultural benefits
that can be derived from landscape
and include aesthetic, ecological and
historical aspects. The sensitivity of
the landscape is the extent to which it

Box 11.1 Bocage Landscape

The 'bocage' landscape of Ireland, which is an enclosed agricultural
landscape with hedgerows, is a classic example of an agricultural landscape
with a long history. Bocage landscapes, found also in Brittany and central
England, usually have a slightly rolling landform and are found mainly in
maritime climates. Being a small-scale enclosed landscape, the bocage
offers much variation in biotopes, with habitats for birds, small mammals,
amphibians and butterflies.

Whilst the bocage landscapes of Brittany and Normandy have experienced
seriously disruption, the scale of change in Ireland has been more moderate.
The major removal of enclosures has resulted from intensified farming and
the introduction of large farm machinery since the 1950s. In recent years
the spread of forest plantations has submerged field patterns in hill areas
while urban growth has obliterated them on the edge of lowland towns.

EEA, 1995; Aalen et al., 1997

can accommodate change without unacceptable loss of existing character or value (O'Leary and McCormack, 2000). The guidelines propose that local authorities map and describe landscape character areas, their values and their degree of sensitivity and establish a policy response in relation to each landscape area. The response could range from encouragement of particular types of development in some landscapes to the prohibition of any development in other landscape areas for the purposes of preservation and conservation.

Landscape Issues Relating to Wind Farms

Wind is a renewable source of energy and its use for electricity generation reduces the requirement to burn fossil fuels. Ireland has one of the richest wind energy resources in Europe, due mainly to the strength of prevailing westerly winds across the Atlantic. While this industry is relatively new in Ireland, developments in recent years (including turbine size) have seen an increase in the use of wind energy for electricity generation. Currently there are ten wind farms in commercial operation, and it is expected that wind energy developments will dominate renewable energy technology in the short term (DPE, 1999). Turbines are located in areas with significant wind resources, which tend to be in upland or coastal areas and the western and north-western parts of the country.

The potential visual impact of these farms, particularly in areas of high landscape quality should be a key consideration in deciding on their siting (Box 11.2). Guidelines for planning authorities recommend that wind turbines should not dominate landscape features, particularly views of special amenity or interest. In relation to the option of offshore wind farms, issues to be considered include possible impacts on seabirds.

GENERAL RURAL ENVIRONMENT

The rural environment in Ireland can be considered to be all areas outside of urban settlements of more than 1500 people. Approximately 42 per cent of Ireland's population live in small villages and in the open countryside. The overall rural population has remained relatively stable at around 1.5 million for some time. Between 1971 and 1996 the rural population increased by a total of 7 per cent while in the same period the urban population increased by 36 per cent. The combination of a high dependence on agriculture, the lack of diversified employment to sustain or generate off-farm income and the out-migration of those with higher levels of education has undermined the economic structure of many rural areas (DAF, 1999). Other influences on the rural environment include urbanisation and sub-urbanisation, industrial development, tourism and afforestation.

Although in many rural areas there is population decline, leading to vacant buildings, there is in some areas a demand for one-off housing to meet the needs of people working in nearby towns and cities. There is also demand to build tourist housing in scenic areas and this is overpowering some traditional villages and towns. However, the demand for housing in the countryside from those working in the cities and towns is generally regarded as unsustainable. This is because many one-off houses are served by individual septic tanks

---

Box 11.2 Physical Impacts of Wind Farms on the Land

Modern medium sized wind turbines (300-600 kW rating) are 30-40 m high, with rotors 30-35 m in diameter. Wind farms can consist of anything between 3 and 50 turbines. To ensure maximum efficiency, turbines are normally located 5-10 rotor diameters apart. Therefore, while the individual footprint of each turbine is relatively small, wind farms can occupy significant areas of land (DoE, 1996).

Wind farms also require ancillary developments such as access for construction and routine servicing, communications infrastructure for control and grid connection works (transformers, sub-stations, transmission lines, etc.). These add to the surface area required for the farm. In addition erecting, for example a 600 kW turbine, needs at least 200 m³ of concrete, while 20 tonnes of steel are needed for the foundations of a 1000 kW turbine.

Rodts, 1999

(leading to concerns for groundwater protection), there are increased road and transport costs and commuting and there is a negative impact in terms of the urban fabric of towns (DoE, 1997a).

The rural environment is a major asset and provides economic, recreational, social and cultural benefits. Sustainable development issues outlined in a strategy for rural development (DAF, 1999) identified the need to develop an optimum settlement pattern and to locate jobs in close proximity to residential areas so as to reduce pollution and congestion arising from commuting by car. The objective is to encourage smaller urban centres to become more self-sustaining, in economic, social and environmental terms. As the long-term well being of the rural environment is dependent on the sustainable use of local resources, the strategy also states that planning policy in rural areas must aim at encouraging economic developments while conserving local natural environments.

AGRICULTURAL LAND

While the majority of rural dwellers are now neither farmers nor directly dependent on agriculture, the industry remains one of the most important sectors in the rural and national economies. There has been a decline in the number of farms of almost 33 per cent between 1975 and 1995 and a consequent rise in the average size of farm holdings. The current trend for those involved in farming is to consider other options such as agri-tourism and forestry. However as the main land use in terms of area, agriculture remains the primary determinant of the rural landscape and environment (Heritage Council, 1999a).

With the highest percentage of productive grassland in Europe, Irish agriculture has relied heavily on dairy

and beef farming rather than on tillage farming. Over 90 per cent of the area farmed is devoted to pasture, silage, hay and rough grazing (Chapter 3). Cereals are grown in approximately 7 per cent of the area, with the remainder including activities such as horticulture and fruit growing.

Agriculture has experienced a considerable change over the last few decades and this has placed pressures on the farming community to concentrate, specialise and intensify production. There has been an intensification of livestock farming and a greater concentration of intensive agricultural practices particularly in the pigs, poultry, dairy, mushroom and cereal sectors. Intensification and specialisation of agricultural practices have consequently led to a rapid growth in livestock numbers. Aside from a reduction in sheep numbers since 1992, the general trend of livestock numbers is continuing to rise, leading to higher stocking densities (Chapter 3). These concentrations together with other practices, such as a reduction of out-wintering of cattle

in favour of animal housing, a switch from hay to silage feed, the increased fertilisation of the land and the landspreading of organic wastes have impacted on the environment to a significant degree. The main concerns in this regard relate to the emission of greenhouse gases, particularly methane and nitrous oxide (Chapter 4), the very significant role of excess phosphorus in increasing surface water pollution (Chapter 9), and the effects of overgrazing on soil and biodiversity, as discussed later in this chapter. Also, the agricultural contribution to total ammonia emissions in Ireland is estimated to be approximately 99.5 per cent (Chapter 4). The emissions are estimated to be equivalent to about 30 per cent of annual nitrogen fertiliser usage and have serious implications for Ireland in meeting its international obligations under the EU acidification strategy (Lee, 1999).

Agricultural developments and, in particular, intensive agriculture, have led to a reduction in semi-natural habitats throughout the countryside and to a loss of biodiversity. Estimates of hedgerow reduction are

put at 16 per cent (Webb, 1998). These issues are further discussed in Chapter 12.

Animal stocking density, age of pasture, length of grazing season and the use of heavy farm machinery can affect soil compaction. Soil compaction increases the risk of overland flow of potential pollutants from soils.

The management of waste arising from agriculture has implications for the environment, particularly in the area of water quality, as farm wastes have a high polluting potential relative to sewage or industrial waste. Of the estimated 132 million tonnes arising, approximately 65 million tonnes are collected, stored and subsequently landspread (Chapter 6). Landspreading of organic waste has a significant potential for loss to waters, particularly if it takes place outside the growing season or when weather or ground conditions are unsuitable (Chapter 5). The housing and feeding of higher numbers of livestock for extended periods in the farmyard and run-off from silage storage pits are also pollution threats (Chapter 3).

There has been a steady growth in pig production since 1989. Nationally there are 175,000 sows producing approximately 3.85 million pigs a year in Ireland. Although the pig sector accounts for approximately 5 per cent of the waste landspread in Ireland, regional concentrations of intensive pig units lead to waste disposal problems. Northeast Cork and Cavan together host approximately 38 per cent of sow numbers. In Cavan, the waste management problems are exacerbated by the fact that many pig units are sited on soils that are not ideal from a landspreading viewpoint, because of the potential for surface run-off or groundwater contamination (V. Power, pers. comm.).

Farm Film Recovery Scheme

The Waste Management (Farm Plastic) Regulations, 1997, now place obligations on manufacturers and importers of farm plastics to arrange for environmentally acceptable ways of collecting and disposing of used plastic film. It is estimated that, each year, approximately 12,000 tonnes of waste is generated from the use of plastic sheeting in the agricultural and horticultural sectors (DoE, 1997).

Health and safety concerns are already exerting pressure to discourage the practice of disposing of used plastic film by burying or burning it. This coincides with recent advances that allow plastic film to be efficiently recycled for use in other products. While presently, most of this waste is not recycled or reused, the Farm Film Recovery Scheme operated by Irish Farm Film Producers Group (IFFPG) collected 1980 tonnes in 1998. Of this, 480 tonnes was recycled in Ireland with the remainder exported for recycling (IFFPG, pers. comm.).

FOREST COVER

Mixed woodlands were once a natural feature of much of the Irish countryside. The decline in the natural forest cover of Ireland was a slow process starting in Neolithic times, with small scale clearing. As agriculture developed, large areas of

forests were burnt or cut down and the land used for grazing and planting of crops. Throughout the Medieval period Irish woodlands were increasingly exploited and by the early seventeenth century, the tree cover was decimated as a result of extensive felling for timber export. By the turn of the nineteenth century only one per cent of Ireland was under forest (Johnson, 1998).

Recent afforestation policies have significantly increased the land area under forestry, and forest cover is now estimated to be almost 9 per cent of the national territory (615,000 ha). Forest cover as a percentage of land cover is planned to increase by approximately third of a per cent each year, rising to seventeen per cent (1.2 million hectares) by 2030 (Forest Service, 1996). This proposed large-scale and rapid expansion of forestry will radically alter the landscape in many parts of the country. As it stands, however, Ireland has the lowest level of forest cover in the EU, where the average is over 30 per cent, although its recent *per capita* planting rate is one of the highest in Europe. Afforestation by county during the 1990s is shown in Fig. 11.1.

One of the limiting factors in the forestry sector has been the scarcity of suitable and affordable land. Blanket bog was used for the expansion of forestry because of its low agricultural value. Planting on blanket bog

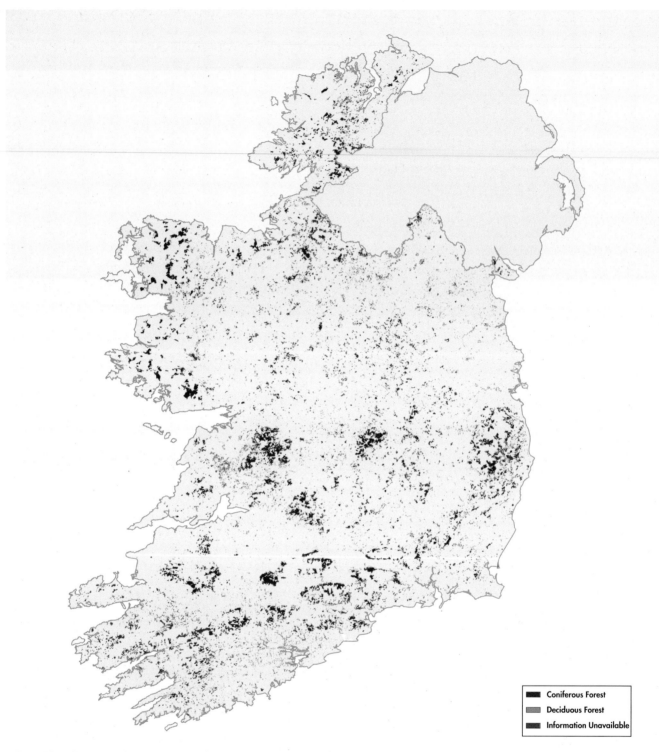

Coniferous Forest
Deciduous Forest
Information Unavailable

Fig. 11.1 Afforestation in the 1990s (Source: Forest Service)

became commonplace, peaking in the mid 1980s, and as a result the boglands and uplands of Munster and Connaught were heavily forested (Johnson, 1998). Many peatlands and other upland habitats of high conservation value have been damaged over the years as a result of inappropriate planting (Heritage Council, 1999b). While no accurate figure is available, it is estimated there are some 200,000 hectares of peatland forestry in Ireland (Farrell and Boyle, 1990). Afforestation has gradually moved to marginal agricultural land and more recently into the wet mineral lowland soils. Approximately one million hectares of wet mineral lowlands are considered to be of limited agricultural value but highly productive for forestry.

In Irish forests, the range of native broadleaves (see Chapter 12) and introduced broadleaves such as beech and sycamore are limited. The trend in past afforestation has been the predominant planting of coniferous rather than native and broadleaf

species (Fig. 11.2). Exotic species from Europe, North America and Japan proliferate. Currently 79 per cent of Irish forests are made up of coniferous species, of which over 50 per cent are Sitka spruce. The emphasis on quick-growing softwoods reflects the conditions of the Irish climate for these species, which supports rapid growth and quick returns on investment (DoE, 1997a).

As well as providing a valuable timber crop and employment, forestry provides other benefits. Forests are a valuable recreational resource and can add to the amenity of urban and rural landscape, if they are developed in a sensitive manner. They are home to wildlife, the extent of occurrence being dependent on the development stage of the crop. Forests can also assist in preventing soil erosion and controlling landslips.

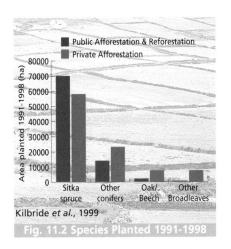

Kilbride et al., 1999

Fig. 11.2 Species Planted 1991-1998

Forests also play an important role in the carbon cycle as they have the ability to absorb large quantities of carbon dioxide from the atmosphere and to store carbon in the biomass for a lengthy period before the eventual release of carbon dioxide as timber decays or is burned. In this regard the Irish forest crops can potentially make a significant contribution to meeting Ireland's international obligations in limiting emissions of greenhouse gases. Relatively fast growing conifers can

store carbon rapidly over the short term, while slower growing broadleaf species act as longer term carbon stores, although they sequester carbon at a slower rate. The average carbon storage in Irish forests is estimated at 3.36 tonnes per hectare per annum. The rate of carbon storage by Sitka spruce is 3.6 tonnes per hectare per annum while the storage rate of oak and beech is 1.8 tonnes per hectare per annum (Kilbride et al., 1999). A change of use of land from agriculture to forestry is likely to reduce other greenhouse gas emissions, such as nitrous oxide and methane. However, uncertainties remain regarding the permanence of sequestered carbon and the capacity of forests to sustain the rate of uptake in the long term, as carbon dioxide concentrations increase.

The benefits of forestry however have to be balanced against a number of potentially adverse environmental effects. Some of the main issues include visual intrusion, impacts on water courses, loss or damage to sites of archaeological or scientific interest and the reduction in the range of flora and fauna (DoE, 1997a).

Forestry can contribute to soil erosion during the forest cycle particularly during the afforestation, harvesting and replanting stages and during road construction. Forestry plantations on peatland may pose particular problems arising from the nature of the soil. The oxidation of carbon from the peat caused by forestry development and drainage depletes

the soil. It also releases additional soil carbon into the carbon cycle, which may partly offset the carbon sequestration effect of the forestry biomass. Several studies have shown that acidification due to conifer plantations, particularly in areas of base poor geology, such as the Wicklow Mountains and west Galway-Mayo, has serious long-term effects on aquatic life (e.g., Bowman and Bracken 1993, Allott et al., 1997, Kelly-Quinn et al., 1997) (Chapter 9). The Forest Service have indicated that some of these studies were carried out on forests established before the current forest and fisheries guidelines were introduced, which addressed forest development on acid sensitive soils.

Poor drainage design can cause problems of sediment and flash flooding, which in turn can lead to aluminium stripping and leaching on poor soils (DoE, 1997a). Forestry development can also impose significant traffic loads on the road system, particularly when timber is harvested and transported to mills and processing plants.

In relation to landscape quality and biodiversity, inappropriate or insensitively placed plantations and clearfelling operations have the potential to impact negatively on the scenic quality of landscapes (Heritage Council, 1999b). Uniform, even-aged plantations are of limited biological diversity value. Imaginative forest management, incorporating different stages of the forest cycle within a forest, including open spaces and mature trees in the forest design, retaining some dead wood within the forest, and significantly increasing the proportion of native tree species (and native seed) planted within forests, will support greater biological and landscape diversity. Planting of broadleaved trees has particular value in terms of landscape, heritage, amenity and habitats. Diverse woodland stands encourage selective felling techniques, thus reducing many of the negative impacts of clearfelling.

Current forestry policy does place greater emphasis on the planting of broadleaved species, including native species, with the target for annual broadleaf afforestation set at 20 per cent of total annual afforestation. In young conifer plantations there is planting of indigenous broadleaf species, in riparian zones, roadside margins and for landscape purposes which are not recorded as such (Source: Forest Service).

The term *semi-natural* is generally used to refer to those stands of woodland that most resemble the potential natural vegetation. Ireland has only a small number of truly native trees (Chapter 12). The broadleaf forests are of the greatest conservation interest, as they provide habitat for a variety of wildlife

species. Woodland edges are important for wildlife, where there is the greatest variation in vegetation height and structure. These areas provide food, cover and nest sites for a wide variety of birds and other animals and are a limiting factor in the survival of certain species.

Box 11.3 Peatland Types

Peat is made up of the partially decomposed remains of dead plants that have accumulated in waterlogged places for thousands of years. There are two major peatland types found in Ireland, fens and bogs. Some of the main differences between these two types are as follows:

- fens are alkaline with a pH of 7 to 8. Bogs are acid with a pH of 3.2 to 4.2;
- the average peat depth in a fen is up to 2m; peat depth in a bog varies from 2 to 15m;
- the water supply for fens is from the mineral-rich ground water, while the water supply for bogs is from the mineral-poor rainwater.

Bogs can be further divided into two types; raised bogs and blankets bogs.

Raised bogs occur primarily in the midlands. At the end of the last glaciation period, 10,000 years ago, the midlands were covered by undulating glacial deposits with shallow lakes. Peat began to form in these lakes and eventually developed into dome shaped raised bogs. The bogs have an average thickness of 6 to 7 metres.

Blanket bogs are situated in upland areas such as the Wicklow and Slieve Bloom Mountains as well as in the lowlands of the western counties of Donegal, Sligo, Mayo, Galway and Kerry. Around 4,000 years ago peat began to form on the higher mountains in the country and on the lower ground of the western seaboard. Although initially forming in hollows, the peat spread out to form a blanket covering large areas. Blanket bogs have an average depth of 3.5 metres.

Foss and O'Connell, 1998

BOGS AND WETLANDS

Ireland has a considerable variety of peatlands, many of which are of international importance. They include fens, raised bogs, lowland and upland blanket bogs and several transitional types. (Box 11.3, Fig 11.3). In the national context they have an immense economic, cultural and ecological value (Foss and O'Connell, 1998).

Bogs suffer from grazing and trampling by sheep, commercial and private extraction, afforestation and agricultural reclamation. Traditional cutting of bogs by turbary over the last 400 years has had a serious impact on both raised and blanket bogs. It is estimated that approximately 68 per cent of the raised bogs and 46 per cent of the blanket bogs have been affected to some degree by this process. The introduction of large-scale, mechanised peat extraction schemes in the 1940s, afforestation

programmes commencing in the 1950s, intensification of agriculture following Ireland's entry to the European Community in 1973 have seriously depleted the area of peatland suitable for conservation (Foss and O'Connell, 1998). More recently the possibility of erosion associated with the infrastructural elements of wind farms and telecommunications installations is of increasing concern. Peatlands once covered over 17 per cent of the land area of the state. Now, only 19 per cent (220,902 ha) of that original bogland remains in a relatively untouched condition. The present distribution of peatlands is shown in Fig. 11.3.

A study in the late 1980s found that out of 66 lowland blanket bogs surveyed in Co. Mayo, 38 per cent were overgrazed and several had been almost denuded of vegetation cover (Douglas, 1994). These figures are thought to be significantly underestimated however (C. Douglas, pers. comm.). The aim of the survey was to identify Areas of Scientific Interest and therefore sites known to be significantly degraded were not considered to be of potential nature conservation interest and were excluded from this survey. The Irish Peatland Conservation Council has indicated that 50 peatland sites of conservation importance have been damaged due to overgrazing (see also Mountain Areas below).

The most serious impact on fens has been their reclamation for agricultural land, which involved drainage, fertilisation, reclamation and removal of peat. Forty-two per cent have been lost to this use, leaving 54,000 ha suitable for conservation. A number of these sites are secondary fens created by the activity of man. Examples of these are in cutaway bog areas, the margins of raised bogs, the Shannon callows and lake shores where water levels have been artificially lowered (Foss and O'Connell, 1998).

Many important peatland areas in Ireland remain as proposed Natural Heritage Areas, which currently affords them little protection against certain types of development. As a diminishing, non-renewable natural resource, it is vital that Ireland's bogs are given the protection that they so clearly need.

In addition to peatlands, wetlands include areas of marsh, reed beds, callows, swamps, turloughs, drumlin lakes, rivers and lakes. They include estuaries and sheltered intertidal bays, salt-marshes and coastal areas where the depth of water does not exceed six metres. From the middle of the last century to the present day the total area drained under various Acts and schemes amounted to over 2 million hectares or almost 30 per cent of the total area of Ireland (Heritage Council, 1999a). This drainage has in many cases resulted in damage to areas of scientific interest and to fish

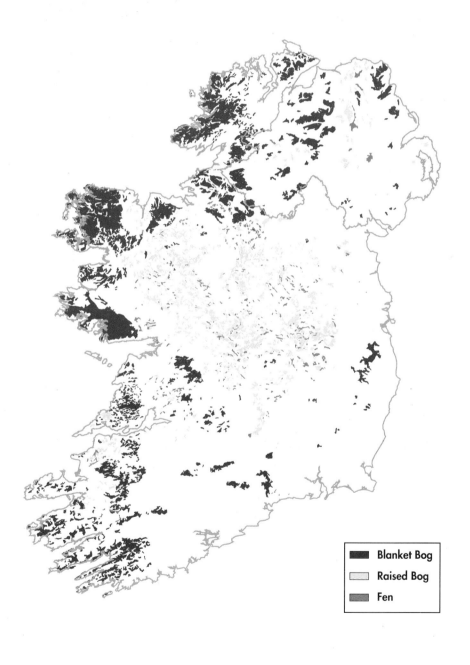

	Blanket Bog
	Raised Bog
	Fen

Fig. 11.3 Present Distribution of Peatlands (Source: IPCC)

stocks. Turloughs were particularly affected by arterial drainage schemes, primarily in the last century, but also as late as 1992 when the internationally important Rahasane Turlough in County Galway was subject to drainage operations.

MOUNTAIN AREAS

Upland or mountain areas in Ireland are considered to be those areas above 400 m above sea level. Evidence of significant erosion has been noted in the upland environment since the 1940s. The soil survey of West Donegal, completed in the late 1960s, indicated that over 4,500 hectares were affected by severe erosion (Walsh, 1997). The problem of overgrazing by sheep in the upland regions of the west of Ireland was first highlighted in the early 1990s with reported damage to important game fisheries due to excessive amounts of peat silt from eroding peatlands. Teagasc estimate that around 20 per cent of the upland area (0.3 million ha) may be affected by soil erosion to varying degrees (J. Lee pers. comm.). Overgrazing by sheep is one of the principal contributing factors, and this problem has arisen as a direct result of EU-funded incentives.

Although overgrazing can negatively affect a number of vegetation types, most attention has focused on the damage done to blanket bog, wet and heath communities and to coastal vegetation. Overgrazing on western blanket bog has resulted in a decrease in vegetation cover, a depletion of bog species, invasion by species alien to the bog habitat and erosion of peat surfaces (MacGowan and Doyle, 1996). The loss of characteristic and rare flora, such as heather, sedges and mosses, deprive wildlife of food and cover and numbers of fauna may also therefore be affected (Douglas, 1994). In addition, the eroded peat particles are washed into rivers and streams, choking up spawning beds and resulting in the condition known

(in salmonid species) as gill hyperplasia (Bleasdale and Sheehy Skeffington, 1992).

Measures to assess the damage to overgrazed areas and to establish optimum stocking densities are underway with the Commonage Assessment Survey. This Commonage Assessment Survey will survey all commonages, commencing in the West of Ireland and agri-environmental plans will be produced for each commonage. These plans will be used by REPS planners to produce individual farm plans. It is anticipated that the modifications to REPS combined with other cross-compliance controls introduced in 1998 should assist in alleviating the serious overgrazing problem (DAHGI, 1999).

Should an ideal stocking rate be adopted and observed, grazing could be maintained in those areas that have as yet suffered only minor damage. According to limited field research conducted by Dúchas, recovery of vegetation cover in experimental enclosures has been dramatic, indicating that for some areas at least, removal of sheep for an indefinite period could be effective in assisting natural regeneration, especially if the root mat is still intact on site and erosion is not too active (Heritage Council, 1999a). However, some blanket bog areas are so severely

damaged that withdrawal of sheep is unlikely to lead to a restoration of bog vegetation in either the short or medium term. Vegetation recolonisation potentials can be extremely slow, partly because of the slow growth rate of peatland ecosystems, which are naturally nutrient poor.

Tourist Trampling

Irish National Parks attract 350,000 visitors per year. The problem of trampling by walkers has been increasing over the past decade from a few isolated patches of damage to large tracks of eroded pathways in some of the more popular walking areas. The problem areas are concentrated in Wicklow, Killarney and Connemara National Parks. Tourist trampling, like overgrazing, damages the vegetation of blanket bogs (MacGowan and Doyle, 1996).

With increasing tourist numbers and an expansion of the leisure industry, the number of walkers on our hills is growing every year. The number of overseas visitors engaging in hiking or hillwalking in Ireland in 1998 was 275,000 (up by 44,000 from 1996 figures). Visitor management and the erection and maintenance of appropriate pathways are needed to ensure that lateral extension of damaged trackways is to be avoided in future.

THE COASTAL MARGIN

Around 3,000 km of the Irish coastline are classified as soft, including sandy beaches and unconsolidated glacial cliffs. Some 1,500 km of these are at risk from coastal erosion and 490 km require immediate attention (DoE, 1997a; Brady Shipman Martin, 1997). Coasts are among the most dynamic and complex of all environments and physical processes can alter the shape and character of the coastline over a short period of time. The Irish coastal zone is characterised by considerable diversity, both in natural terms and in the range and extent of human activity. The coastal zone provides economic, recreational and aesthetic benefits and access to marine resources including fisheries and aquaculture. It is an area containing many sensitive ecosystems of considerable natural value as well as geological and geomorphological features. It is also important for cultural heritage, including marine and terrestrial archaeology.

Ireland's coastal zone has been considerably developed and is under increasing pressure from further development. Since the 1970s significant stretches of the coastline, particularly in the vicinity of major settlements and on the east coast, have been substantially built up. An upsurge in the development of holiday homes, resulting from tax incentives introduced under the Seaside Resorts Scheme, has seriously affected many coastal areas.

Wave and storm action cause erosion of Ireland's coastline. It is estimated that coastal erosion causes a loss of land area of between 160 to 300 ha a year around the coast of Ireland. About 300 localities are affected mainly on the east coast. The most rapid long term erosion rate is thought to be in parts of Co. Wexford. Present erosion problems could worsen as a consequence of climate change, which may increase sea levels and the severity of storms. Flooding of low-lying coastal areas is also likely to become more frequent (Brady Shipman Martin, 1997).

Few pristine examples of sand dunes and machair (Chapter 12) currently exist and a number of important sites are currently under threat, being particularly vulnerable to developments such as golf courses and caravan parks.

Ireland's coastal zone requires special attention in order to promote its sustainable use and to address the potential conflicts arising from different uses. A draft policy for coastal zone management was published in 1997, but since then there has been little progress made in initiating a strategic approach to the sustainable management of this resource.

BUILT ENVIRONMENT

Ireland's urban fabric and the built environment generally are major resources in the country's economic development. Although a number of recent policy initiatives have focused on improving the socio-economic conditions of built up areas, many environmental problems are still intensifying. Such problems include waste management, air, noise, and water pollution, traffic congestion, the loss of open space, and the degradation of the urban landscape. A number of these issues have been covered in earlier chapters.

Urban environments have greatly changed in Ireland. In addition to the migration of people from rural to urban areas, the centres of cities and towns have been subject to depopulation resulting in the decay of the urban fabric. A distinction must therefore be made between growth in urban centres and growth on their periphery. The past trend towards less intensive urban patterns exacerbated the growth and use of private transport and has resulted in increased energy usage, emissions of air pollutants and reduced effectiveness of public transport networks (DoE, 1997a). With urban expansion, agricultural land surrounding the cities and towns as well as green space within them are subject to increasing pressure. An example of the effects of urban-isation is shown in Box 11.4.

Open space and green spaces within urban centres provide, in addition to general amenity value, various environmental benefits in terms of maintenance of biodiversity and improved air quality. They also add to the general aesthetic quality of the

11

Box 11.4 Urbanisation in Dublin

An EU study on urban environmental issues has provided some initial results on the extent and impact of urbanisation in Dublin. Between 1956 and 1998, the area of residential urban fabric in Dublin has more than doubled, while the area used for road networks increased by a factor of almost 10. The reduction of forest and semi-natural areas and agricultural areas during that time was approximately 15 per cent.

Landuse Change in Dublin 1956-1998

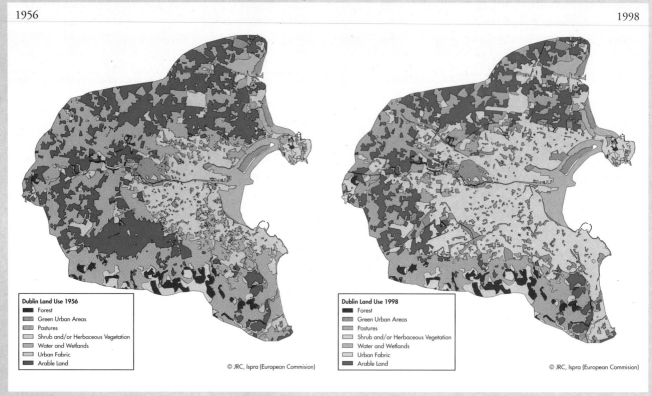

1956

1998

Dublin Land Use 1956
- Forest
- Green Urban Areas
- Pastures
- Shrub and/or Herbaceous Vegetation
- Water and Wetlands
- Urban Fabric
- Arable Land

© JRC, Ispra (European Commision)

Dublin Land Use 1998
- Forest
- Green Urban Areas
- Pastures
- Shrub and/or Herbaceous Vegetation
- Water and Wetlands
- Urban Fabric
- Arable Land

© JRC, Ispra (European Commision)

Critchley, 1999

urban landscape. With renewed emphasis on high density housing, the value of green space increases. The percentage of green space within the legally defined areas of a selection of urban centres in Ireland is illustrated in Fig. 11.4. Limerick and Cork have the highest percentage of green space, with 20 per cent and 15 per cent respectively. However, this is a difficult issue to standardise across the different towns, as opinion varies as to what may be considered green space. Boundary issues, access to green space in the peripheries, access to countryside and amenities and density of housing all differ and affect the existence and significance of the relative amount of green space.

Sustainable urban development should seek to bring redundant and derelict land and buildings back into active use. This reuses available resources and sustains the urban fabric. In addition, new residential developments in inner city areas rely on existing infrastructure such as

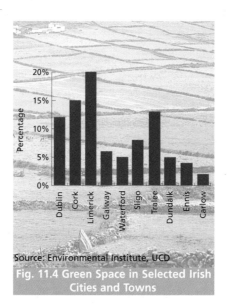

Source: Environmental Institute, UCD

Fig. 11.4 Green Space in Selected Irish Cities and Towns

water supply and roads thereby reducing the need to develop greenfield sites on the outskirts of already sprawling towns and cities. This has benefits in terms of traffic management, air pollution and maximising utilisation of existing services.

Urban Renewal Schemes were introduced in Ireland in 1985 in response to the increasing problem of dereliction and dilapidation, which had affected large inner areas of Irish towns and cities. The core objectives of the schemes were to promote urban renewal and redevelopment by promoting investment in the construction and reconstruction of buildings in designated inner city areas. The incentives introduced were primarily tax-based. In 1986, areas were designated in each of the five County Boroughs, Dublin, Cork, Waterford, Limerick and Galway. Since then, the scheme has been extended to many of Ireland's major towns. The volume of urban renewal activity as a percentage of the total land surface area of a selection of Irish urban centres is illustrated in Fig. 11.5. There is presently little quantitative data available on the environmental benefits of the urban renewal schemes.

One aspect of urban renewal to be considered is the relative proportion of construction of new buildings compared to refurbishment of existing buildings. In some cases, the construction of new buildings may intrude on the existing built environment because of different size or style. The replacement of older buildings that have an architectural or historical value can also impact negatively on the aesthetic and cultural value of the urban centres. Fig. 11.6 illustrates the levels of refurbishment in urban centres as a proportion of total urban renewal projects. The Local Government (Planning and Development) Act, 1999, which came into force in January 2000, provides a legislative framework for the protection of individual structures and areas of architectural heritage value.

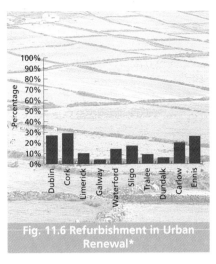

Fig. 11.6 Refurbishment in Urban Renewal*

*Percentage Refurbishment in Urban Renewal Projects in Selected Urban Centres. Source: Environmental Institute, UCD.

In times of economic growth, the demand for transport increases significantly, with most of the growth in the car-owning sector. The rise in private car ownership in the 1990s has been illustrated earlier in Chapter 3. The main impact of traffic growth is in urban areas, especially in the cities. Rising vehicle numbers and increased usage of cars have caused significant traffic congestion and noise in urban areas. For example travel times for commuters have increased in all parts of Dublin between 1991 and 1999 (see Fig. 11.7). Congestion problems have not been helped by the general lack of car sharing and pooling. A survey in 1998 showed that, of the approximately 152,000 car journeys

made on the M50 motorway each day, 80 per cent of vehicles carried just one person (NRA, 1999). Road traffic also adds to local air pollution and is a major contributor to emissions of carbon monoxide (CO), carbon dioxide (CO_2), nitrogen oxides (NO_x), volatile organic compounds (VOC) and PM_{10} (particulate matter less than 10 microns in diameter). These emissions can be damaging to human health, as well as to buildings and the natural environment (Lehane, 1999).

Transport management in urban areas requires the provision of alternatives to the use of private cars. These can include increased provision for cyclists and pedestrians, in particular, for short journeys and the improved availability of more efficient public

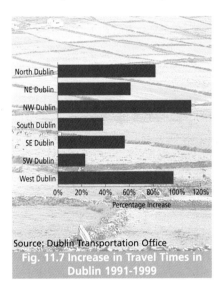

Source: Dublin Transportation Office

Fig. 11.7 Increase in Travel Times in Dublin 1991-1999

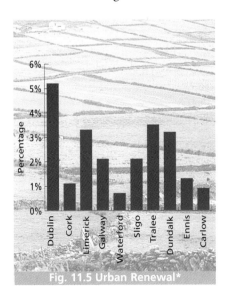

Fig. 11.5 Urban Renewal*

*Volume of Urban Renewal Activity as a Percentage of Total Surface Area in Selected Irish Urban Centres. Source: Environmental Institute, UCD.

transport. The present extent of cycle lanes and area pedestrianised in selected Irish urban centres are illustrated in Fig 11.8 and 11.9. As can be seen, there is major scope for improvement. Furthermore, it is recognised that public transport has been seriously neglected and poorly funded in the past. While new initiatives in Dublin, such as the introduction of Quality Bus Corridors, have been of benefit, there is still considerable progress to be made in the provision of a co-ordinated and effective public transport system in Irish urban centres.

The sustained growth in car availability in the next few years will generate even greater numbers of trips by cars and give rise to further congestion, air pollution and noise. It is essential to break the link between car ownership and car usage and to provide efficient alternative modes of transport.

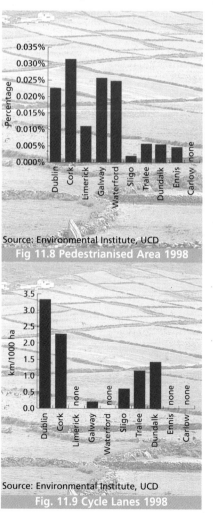

Source: Environmental Institute, UCD
Fig 11.8 Pedestrianised Area 1998

Source: Environmental Institute, UCD
Fig. 11.9 Cycle Lanes 1998

Table 11.1 Results of Litter Surveys 1995 and 1997		
Category	Percentage of Surveyed Sites in each Category	
	1995	1997
Complete absence of litter	12	10
Scattered small amounts of litter	58	57
Small accumulations of litter	25	28
Significant accumulations of litter	5	5

DoE, 1995,1997b

LITTER

Litter has for many years been a significant problem, particularly in towns and cities. The impact of litter is detrimental to tourism and other economic sectors, and damages the aesthetic quality of the environment. In recent years, national litter surveys were carried out in 1995 and 1997 at various locations around the country. The locations included cities, towns, villages, tourist areas and beaches, which were graded according to their cleanliness. The results show that the incidence of litter remains widespread in Ireland, despite the extent of clean-up operations undertaken by local authorities (Table 11.1). The most common items littered included cigarette ends and packaging, plastic bottles, paper and plastic wrappers; fast food cartons, plastic shopping bags, beverage cans and glass bottles. As many of these are light in weight, they are prone to dispersal by wind. The locations typically found to be littered are bus stops, areas close to fast food outlets, secondary schools and third level institutions, motorways and dual carriageways close to cities and towns, construction sites, recycling centres, areas serviced by open top litter bins, beaches and side streets in urban areas. The surveys noted that there tended to be less littering in areas which had good background environmental quality (DoE, 1997b).

The 1997 survey also examined the presence of items such as chewing gum, dog fouling, graffiti and overflowing bins. It found that chewing gum was present at 88 per cent of sites, dog fouling at 36 per cent and graffiti at 27 per cent of the sites. The extent of overflowing bins was not generally considered to be a serious problem (DoE, 1997b).

Local Authorities are increasingly taking a more proactive approach to combat the problem of litter in Ireland, using their extensive management and enforcement powers under the Litter Pollution Act, 1997. Increased numbers of litter wardens have been employed and the number of on-the-spot fines and prosecutions for litter violations has increased dramatically since 1997 (Fig. 11.10). In 1998 alone, local authorities spent over £26 million on street cleansing and litter warden services (DELG, 1999). However, the number of fines and prosecutions reflects not just the response to the problem but also the extent of the problem and much remains to be done before the issue of litter is dealt with effectively.

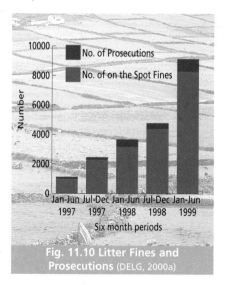

Fig. 11.10 Litter Fines and Prosecutions (DELG, 2000a)

In 1999, a national anti-litter forum was established, involving representatives of local authorities, the business and commercial sector, the educational and tourism sectors, environmental NGOs and community groups. The terms of references of the forum include reviewing the current range of initiatives designed to tackle litter pollution and identifying further measures that would bring added value to these initiatives. A national litter monitoring system has also been developed to monitor and assess local authority management and enforcement actions and to advise on litter management at a national level. Between 1997 and 1999 grants amounting to £1 million were allocated to local authorities for public education and awareness initiatives on litter (DELG, 1999).

ARCHAEOLOGICAL RESOURCE

Archaeology is a non-renewable component of Irish culture, heritage and landscape. Ireland is exceptionally rich in archaeological features with between 150,000 and 200,000 known pre-1700 AD sites and monuments (Johnson, 1998). Archaeological sites and monuments range from substantial above-ground structures to easily damaged subterranean traces of human activity. As the character of landscape change in Ireland was, by and large, gradual until the second half of the twentieth century, there has been a comparatively high rate of survival of visible archaeological sites.

An EU Convention on the protection of the archaeological heritage introduced a number of significant requirements for archaeologists and developers, including the preservation, *in situ,* of archaeological sites where feasible. Historic monuments are legally protected by inclusion in the Register of Historic Monuments. This Register will ultimately list all sites that are considered to be of archaeological significance. The system of notification however is a slow process and at present the Register only includes about 5,000 sites.

Archaeological landscapes are vulnerable to a wide range of impacts arising from landuse and development such as agricultural practices, peat extraction, afforestation, reclamation and drainage schemes and road construction.

A limited survey of monuments, carried out in 1998, covered approximately 2.2 per cent of the land area in the State. A total of 993 monuments were assessed of which 101 could not be located and 154 of which had been interfered with in some way (71 destroyed, 18 seriously damaged and 65 slightly damaged). The main reasons for the interference and destruction of these monuments are land improvement, erosion, forestry, drainage works and other various forms of development

(Johnson, 1998). The study concluded that the destruction of known archaeological monuments in Ireland has accelerated dramatically. Earthen monuments are coming under increasing pressure. Archaeological monuments set in pasture are particularly vulnerable. When calculated over the period 1994 to 1998, the notional destruction rate per decade of monuments is estimated at 4.6 per cent. This rate rises to 10 per cent when calculated over the period 1997 to 1998 and to 17 per cent when based on 1998 figures. This compares with the average destruction rate of 2.1 per cent per decade in the 140 years to 1978 (O'Sullivan *et al.,* in prep.).

GENERAL SOIL QUALITY

Soil is a dynamic, living, natural body that is vital to the function of terrestrial ecosystems. It represents a unique balance between physical, chemical and biological factors. As soil is formed so slowly in nature it can be considered essentially as a non-renewable resource of significant value for economic, ecological and heritage reasons. Soil supports the natural vegetation and where this has been altered or changed as a result of human activity it continues to support agricultural crops, horticultural crops and forests (EPA, in prep.).

Soil quality can be defined as the capacity of the soil to function as a vital living system, to sustain biological productivity, promote the quality of air and water environments, and maintain plant, animal and human health. However, of the three environmental compartments, water, air and soil, the quality of soils is the most difficult to assess in a quantitative way. It can be assessed only in relation to soil function or to the purpose for which the soil is used. The wide variety of natural soil types and characteristics and range of possible functions and uses makes setting soil quality standards more problematical than standards for air or water. Different soil types are suitable for a range of different uses depending on their properties. For example, some soils are capable of sustaining high annual yields of grass and cereals while other soils, although their production potential is low, sustain unique flora and habitats. Proposals for development of environmental quality objectives and standards for soil are presently being prepared by the EPA (EPA, in prep.).

Heavy Metal Levels in Irish Soils

A national survey of the concentration of heavy metals in soil has recently been initiated in Ireland. To date approximately one quarter of the land area in Ireland has been surveyed and the soils analysed for the concentrations of metals such as cadmium, copper, mercury, nickel, lead and zinc. The results in relation to land type are listed below in Table 11.2.

The results indicate that generally there is an absence of seriously contaminated soils in Ireland, although some areas, particularly in the west, have elevated cadmium levels. Forest soils appear to be severely depleted of nutrients including copper and zinc. Levels in excess of limit values for metals specified in the EU sewage sludge

Table 11.2. Mean Heavy Metals Concentrations by Land Use (g/g)				
Metal	Grassland	Tillage	Forest	Peat
Cd	0.52	0.76	0.29	0.35
Cu	18.0	19.1	8.7	4.9
Hg	0.1	0.11	0.15	0.13
Ni	13.4	23.3	5.5	4.4
Pb	30.0	30.3	38.1	17.6
Zn	73.1	88.6	38.0	26.2

McGrath and Murphy, 1998

Directive occur in almost a quarter of the soils, and these soils would therefore be disqualified from receiving sewage sludge. This together with the proportion of tilled soils with elevated levels and their proximity to high population centres in the east of Ireland has implications for future plans to expand sludge use in agriculture (McGrath and Murphy, 1998).

Organic Micro-pollutants

Measurements of the concentrations of organochlorine insecticides, and polychlorinated biphenyls (PCBs) in Irish soils show that while these compounds are no longer in use, elevated levels can potentially occur in soils. Mean levels were found to be generally low in agricultural soils. In contrast, levels of DDT residues in urban areas were much higher, with mean levels in soils of 0.31mg/kg (McGrath, 1998; McGrath pers. comm.).

Nutrient Levels in Soils

One of the principal environmental impacts of agriculture is the eutrophication of inland waters by phosphorus from organic wastes and chemical fertilisers. While phosphorus is important for plant growth, its over-application in the form of manures and fertilisers has important consequences for water quality (Chapter 9).

The national trends show a steady increase in soil phosphorus levels

between 1950 and 1991 as a result of a planned effort to raise soil fertility (Fig. 11.11). From 1991 to 1995 levels dropped slightly, although in recent years the trend appears to be again on the increase. A national balance for phosphorus has been developed to estimate the potential for loss of phosphorus from soil to water. In summary, there is now considerable evidence to show that a large excess of phosphorus over and above agronomic requirements is being applied to agricultural land in Ireland. A conservative estimate is that over-application of phosphorus is in the region of 40,000 tonnes per annum. This means that, on average, each hectare of farmed land in Ireland is receiving an excess of 9 kg of phosphorus each year, above that required for agronomic purposes (EPA, in prep.). Many soils are now likely to contain phosphorus at levels where losses to local streams and other surface waters will occur during periods of high rainfall.

Reducing the loss of phosphorus from lands requires the development of nutrient management plans in which the nutrient inputs are balanced with output. A reduction of 10 per cent per annum in artificial phosphorus fertiliser usage over the next five years has been set as a target in the National Sustainable Development Strategy (DoE, 1997a).

Degraded Sites

Compared to more heavily industrialised countries, Ireland has significantly fewer contaminated land

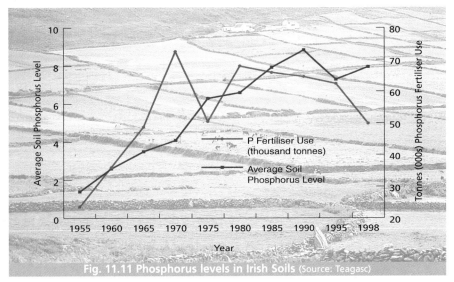

Fig. 11.11 Phosphorus levels in Irish Soils (Source: Teagasc)

problems than those of other European Countries. While at present Ireland lacks specific legislation for dealing with contaminated land, some existing legislation does provide powers to the Environmental Protection Agency and local authorities to deal with the issue.

Soil contamination generally arises as a result of spillages, leaks and improper handling of raw materials, manufactured goods and waste products. Examples of most of the common types of land contamination to be found in Ireland include old gasworks sites, waste disposal sites, disused mining sites and associated tailing ponds and leaking underground storage tanks. To date no specific national survey has been carried out to identify and register contaminated sites in Ireland. The proposed National Hazardous Waste Management Plan (Chapter 6) specifies that each local authority should maintain a register identifying sites known or suspected to have been used for the disposal of hazardous waste in the past.

RADIOACTIVITY

The Radiological Protection Institute of Ireland (RPII) undertakes a programme of monitoring radioactivity in the Irish terrestrial environment. The monitoring programme assesses the exposure to the Irish population arising from

radioactivity in the food chain and the terrestrial environment in general. It involves continuous sampling and testing of air and rain-water, sampling and analysis of drinking water, milk and other foodstuffs, and in-vivo monitoring of sheep in certain upland areas. Additionally, gaseous krypton-85 concentrations in air are measured at Clonskeagh in Dublin. The topic of radon gas has been covered earlier in Chapter 7.

Monitoring of sheep is undertaken in a limited number of upland areas and local slaughter-houses in those areas. These upland areas are in parts of the north-west, north-east and south of the country. The results for 1998 indicate that while their radiocaesium activities continue to decrease slowly, some sheep grazing these upland areas continue to have radiocaesium activities above the level considered suitable for marketing. However, before being slaughtered, sheep from these upland areas are grazed on lower pastures where their radioactivity levels decrease rapidly. The results of monitoring at local slaughterhouses indicate that regular consumption of sheep meat does not constitute a significant human health hazard.

The mean concentration of krypton-85 measured in air at Clonskeagh during 1998 was 1.46 Bq/m^3, a small increase over the 1997 and 1996 values of 1.43 and 1.3 Bq/m^3 respectively. Krypton-85 is released

to the atmosphere almost exclusively as a result of the reprocessing of spent nuclear fuel. Some of the increase can be attributed to the THORP reprocessing plant at Sellafield whose krypton-85 discharges increased from 47,000 TBq in 1996 to 99,000 TBq in 1998 as a consequence of reprocessing more spent fuel. The doses due to krypton-85 are considered by the RPII to be very low and not radiologically significant.

Overall, measurements carried out during 1998 show that the levels of radioactivity in air, water and the food chain are low and are virtually indistinguishable from global background levels. The RPII conclude that the levels of artificial radioactivity in the terrestrial environment do not give rise to public health concerns (RPII, 1999).

CRITICAL LOADS

The *critical load* is defined as an estimate of the exposure to one or more pollutants, below which significant harmful effects on specified sensitive elements of the environment do not occur according to present knowledge (Werner and Spranger, 1996). Estimates of critical loads represent the long-term carrying capacity of the environment with respect to acidification, resulting from sulphur and nitrogen deposition, or with respect to eutrophication, which may be caused by excessive nitrogen in some ecosystems. In the same way, critical levels are thresholds for pollutant concentrations in air above which crops, forests or other vegetation may suffer adverse impact.

Mapping techniques are used to determine where, and by how much, critical loads are exceeded. Over the past 10 years, a series of international workshops has developed methods for estimating critical loads and critical levels and these have been applied to map critical loads for Europe (Posch *et al.,* 1999). Ireland has had active participation in this programme.

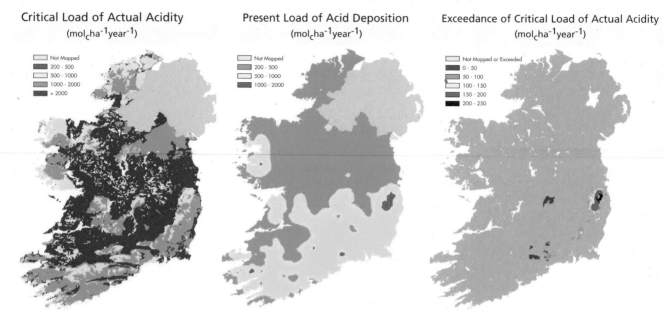

Critical Load of Actual Acidity
(mol$_c$ha^{-1}year^{-1})

Not Mapped
200 - 500
500 - 1000
1000 - 2000
> 2000

Present Load of Acid Deposition
(mol$_c$ha^{-1}year^{-1})

Not Mapped
200 - 500
500 - 1000
1000 - 2000

Exceedance of Critical Load of Actual Acidity
(mol$_c$ha^{-1}year^{-1})

Not Mapped or Exceeded
0 - 50
50 - 100
100 - 150
150 - 200
200 - 250

Fig.11.12 Critical Loads for Acidity and their Exceedances

These data on critical loads provided much of the scientific support for negotiations on the Oslo Protocol on sulphur emissions and, more recently, the Gothenburg Protocol to abate acidification, eutrophication and ground-level ozone.

The Irish critical load estimates for acidity and nutrient nitrogen are shown on Fig. 11.12 and Fig. 11.13. The acidity critical loads are based on detailed steady-state analysis for soils while empirical methods have been used to derive critical loads for nutrient nitrogen in relation to forests,

heathlands, grasslands and wetlands (Aherne *et al.*, 2000). An indication of critical load exceedance, based on typical deposition loads in the 1990s (Chapter 8), is also given. The degree of exceedance is very marginal for both acidity and nutrient nitrogen. Only two per cent of mapped soils were found to have deposition in excess of critical loads for acidity. These occur mainly in the Dublin and Wicklow mountains where low critical loads coincide with the highest load of acid deposition. A parallel analysis, using a steady-state water chemistry approach that

covered almost 200 lakes in acid-sensitive areas of the country, found that only six per cent of the lakes exceeded the critical load.

Nitrogen deposition exceeds the critical load of nutrient nitrogen over approximately 15 per cent of the mapped area and the level of excess is up to 6 kg N/ha in some areas. This is largely due to substantial deposition of nitrogen emanating from local agricultural sources of ammonia. In the long term, this suggests a potential risk of nutrient imbalance in forest plantations and possible loss of

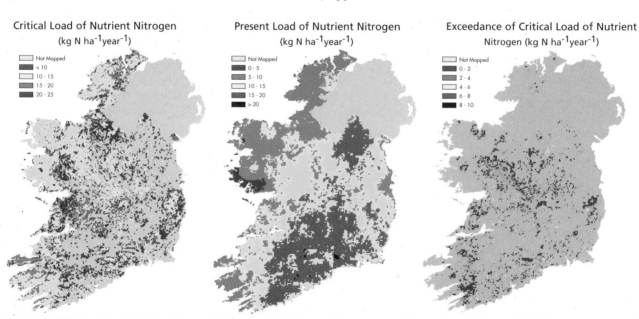

Critical Load of Nutrient Nitrogen
(kg N ha^{-1}year^{-1})

Not Mapped
< 10
10 - 15
15 - 20
20 - 25

Present Load of Nutrient Nitrogen
(kg N ha^{-1}year^{-1})

Not Mapped
0 - 5
5 - 10
10 - 15
15 - 20
> 20

Exceedance of Critical Load of Nutrient
Nitrogen (kg N ha^{-1}year^{-1})

Not Mapped
0 - 2
2 - 4
4 - 6
6 - 8
8 - 10

Fig.11.13 Critical Loads for Nutrient Nitrogen and their Exceedances

biodiversity in natural and semi-natural ecosystems. In general, the threat of ecosystem damage from acidification or nutrient nitrogen will diminish in the coming years as major decreases in the emissions of both nitrogen and sulphur foreseen under international legislation are achieved (Chapter 4).

DISCUSSION

While this chapter provides only a brief overview of the main aspects of the terrestrial environment, it is clear that the impact of human activities and economic development have affected the environment in various ways. Continuing economic growth is likely to result in increased demands being placed on the land and its resources. Urbanisation and intensification of agricultural practices have the potential to exacerbate many environmental problems. Forestry development, unless managed in a sensitive and imaginative manner, has the potential to impact negatively on the scenic quality of landscapes and the environment in general. More complete and up-to-date information is required to assess the effects of urbanisation and other developments on the coastal margin.

A National Spatial Strategy is currently being prepared and has a key objectives of identifying broad spatial development patterns for areas and establishing indicative policies in relation to the location of industrial and residential development, services, rural development, tourism and heritage (DELG, 2000b). Some particular environmental issues to be explored in the development of the strategy are as follows:

- the identification of spatial development patterns that would contribute to efficient energy usage and waste minimisation; and would reduce the impact of traffic and maximise opportunities for sustainable transportation;
- maintaining and enhancing the quality and diversity of natural and cultural heritage, including landscape;
- matching the requirements of extensive and intensive land uses in rural areas with landscape and environmental considerations. Such land uses may include renewable energy, forestry and intensive agriculture;
- identifying where balanced and sustainable urban growth is feasible.

The development of more detailed proposals for inclusion in the strategy is underway.

REFERENCES

Aalen, F.H.A., Whelan, K. and Stout, M. (eds), 1997. *Atlas of the Irish Rural Landscape.* Cork University Press, Cork.

Aherne, J., de Kluizenaar, Y., Ryan, D., van den Beuken, R. and Farrell, E.P., 2000. *Determination and Mapping of Critical Loads for Sulphur and Nitrogen and Critical Levels for Ozone in Ireland.* Environmental Protection Agency, Wexford.

Allott, N., Brennan, M., Cooke, D., Renolds, J.D. & Simon, N., 1997. *A Study of the Effects of Stream Hydrology and Water Quality in Forested Catchments on Fish and Invertebrates.* AQUAFOR Report, Vol 4. COFORD, Dublin.

Bowman, J.J. and Bracken, J., 1993. Effect of run-off from afforested and non-afforested catchments on the survival of brown trout *Salmo trutta* L. in two acid-sensitive rivers in Wicklow, Ireland. *Biology and Environment. Proceedings of the Royal Irish Academy.* 93B, pp. 143-150.

Bleasdale, A.J. and Sheehy Skeffington, M., 1992. The influence of agricultural practices on plant communities in Connemara. In: Feehan, J. (ed) *Environment and Development in Ireland.* pp. 331-336. The Environmental Institute, UCD, Dublin.

Brady Shipman Martin, 1997. *Coastal Zone Management, a Draft Policy for Ireland.* Department of Environment and Local Government, Department of Arts, Heritage, Gaeltacht and the Islands, Department of the Marine and Natural Resources, Dublin.

Critchley, M., 1999. *Monitoring Urban Dynamics (MURBANDY) - Dublin.* Final report prepared by ERA-Maptec Ltd for the European Commission, Joint Research Centre. ERA-Maptec Ltd, Dublin.

DAF (Department of Agriculture and Food), 1999. *Ensuring the Future - A Strategy for Rural Development in Ireland.* Government Publications Office, Dublin.

DAHGI (Department of Arts, Heritage, Gaeltacht and the Islands), 1999. *National Report Ireland 1998. First national report on the implementation of the Convention on Biological Diversity by Ireland.* Department of Arts, Heritage, Gaeltacht and the Islands, Dublin.

DELG (Department of Environment and Local Government), 1999. *Environment Bulletin.* Issue 43. Department of Environment and Local Government.

DELG (Department of Environment and Local Government), 2000a. *Environment Bulletin.* Issue 45. Department of Environment and Local Government.

DELG (Department of Environment and Local Government), 2000b. *The National Spatial Strategy. What are the Issues?* Consultation Paper No. 1. Department of Environment and Local Government.

DoE (Department of Environment), 1995. *National Litter Survey 1995.* Department of Environment.

DoE (Department of Environment), 1996. *Wind Farm Development. Guidelines for Planning Authorities.* Government Publications Office, Dublin.

DoE (Department of Environment), 1997a. *Sustainable Development: A strategy for Ireland.* Government Publications Office, Dublin.

DoE (Department of Environment), 1997b. *National Litter Survey 1997.* Department of Environment, Dublin.

Douglas, C., 1994. *Overgrazing in Ireland: some impacts.* Unpublished report. National Parks and Wildlife Service, Dublin.

DPE (Department of Public Enterprise), 1999. *Green Paper on Sustainable Energy.* Department of Public Enterprise, Dublin.

EEA (European Environment Agency), 1995. *Europe's Environment: The Dobris Assessment.* EEA, Copenhagen.

EPA (Environmental Protection Agency), in press. *National Waste Database Report, 1998.* Environmental Protection Agency, Wexford.

EPA (Environmental Protection Agency), in prep. *National Agricultural Phosphorus Balance.*

EPA (Environmental Protection Agency), in prep. *Environmental Quality Objectives and Standards for Soil - A discussion Document.*

Farrell, E. P. and Boyle, G., 1990. Peatland Forestry in the 1990s. 1. Low-level blanket bog. *Irish Forestry* 47(2): 69-78.

Forest Service, 1996. *Growing for the Future. A Strategic Plan for the Development of the Forest Sector in Ireland.* Government Publications Office, Dublin.

Foss, P. and O'Connell, C., 1996. *Irish Peatland Conservation Plan 2000.* Irish Peatland Conservation Council, Dublin.

Foss, P. and O'Connell, C., 1998. *The IPCC Peatland Conservation and Management Handbook.* Irish Peatland Conservation Council, Dublin.

Heritage Council, 1999a. *A Report on the Impact of Agriculture Schemes on Aspects of Irish Heritage.* Heritage Council, Kilkenny.

Heritage Council, 1999b. *Policy Paper on Forestry and the National Heritage.* The Heritage Council, Kilkenny.

Irish Energy Centre, 1998. *Energy Efficiency Indicators for Ireland - Estimates and Assessment of Trends in Energy Consumption in Ireland 1980 - 1996.* Irish Energy Centre, Dublin.

Johnson, G., 1998. *Archaeology and Forestry in Ireland.* The Heritage Council, Kilkenny.

Kelly-Quinn, M., Tierney, D., Coyle, S. and Bracken, J.J., 1997. *A study of the effects of stream hydrology and water quality in forested catchments on fish and invertebrates.* AQUAFOR Report, Vol 3. COFORD, Dublin.

Kilbride, C. M., Byrne, K. A. and Gardiner, J. J., 1999. *Carbon Sequestration in Irish Forests.* COFORD, Dublin.

Lee, J., 1999. *Securing a balance between competitive agriculture and environmental protection.* Paper presented at the Agri-food Millennium conference, Dublin. December 1999.

Lehane, M. (ed.), 1999. *Environment in Focus: A Discussion Document on Key National Environmental Indicators.* Environmental Protection Agency, Wexford.

MacGowan, F. and Doyle, G.J., 1996. The Effects of Sheep Grazing and Trampling by Tourists on Lowland Blanket Bog in the West of Ireland. In: Giller, P.S. and Myers, A.A. (eds.) *Disturbance and recovery in ecological systems,* 20-32. Royal Irish Academy, Dublin.

McGrath, D., 1998. *Persistent Organochlorines in Soils in the Republic of Ireland.* Poster presented at a Meeting of the Soil Science Society, Belfast, September 6-9, 1998.

McGrath, D and Murphy, W. E., 1998. *Geochemical Survey of Soils in the Republic of Ireland.* Poster presented at a Meeting of the Soil Science Society, Belfast, September 6-9, 1998.

NRA (National Roads Authority), 1999. *1998 Review and Programme for 1999.* National Roads Authority, Dublin.

O'Leary, T. N. and McCormack, A. G., 2000. *An Approach to Lanscape and Landscape Assessment for Local Authorities. A Report to the Department of Environment and Local Government.* MosArt Landscape and Architectural Design.

O'Sullivan, A., 1999. Ireland. In: J. Parviainen, D. Little, M. Doyle, A. O'Sullivan, M. Kettunen and M. Korhonen (eds.). *Research in forest reserves and natural forests in European countries - country reports for the COST Action E4:* Forest Reserves Research Network, pp. 145-161. Proceedings No. 16. European Forest Institute, Torikatu.

O'Sullivan, M., O'Connor, D. J. and Kennedy, L., in prep. *A survey measuring the recent destruction of Ireland's archaeological heritage.*

Posch, M., de Smet, P.A.M., Hettelingh, J-P. and Downing, R.J. (eds.), 1999. *Calculation and Mapping of Critical Thresholds in Europe : Status Report 1999.* RIVM Report No. 259101007, RIVM, Bilthoven, The Netherlands.

RPII (Radiological Protection Institute of Ireland), 1999. *Annual Report 1998.* RPII, Dublin.

Rodts, J., 1999. Eoliennes et Protection des Oiseau un Dilemme *L'homme et L'Oiseau,* 2, pp. 111-123. Belgium.

Walsh, M., 1997. *Evaluation of the Impact of Livestock on the Hill Environment.* Teagasc.

Webb, R., 1998. *The status of hedgerow field margins in Ireland. In: Environmental Management in Agriculture - European Perspective* (ed. J. R. Park), CEC, Belhaven Press, pp. 125-131.

Werner, B. and Spranger, T. (eds.), 1996. *Manual on methodologies and criteria for mapping critical levels/loads and geographical areas where they are exceeded.* Federal Environment Agency (Umweltbundesamt), Berlin, Germany.

[handwritten: Biodiversity = variability among living organisms & the ecological complexes of which they are part]

NATURAL HERITAGE AND BIODIVERSITY

Ireland's natural heritage includes a unique geological legacy, which gives the country its natural distinctiveness. Native mixed deciduous woodlands are few and small in extent, but hedgerows are a particularly prominent feature of the Irish countryside. Ireland has habitat types that are scarce or absent over much of Europe, including turloughs, shingle beaches, coastal lagoons, maërl beds, machair and a complete range of bog types of international importance.

The total number of species in Ireland has not been established for all groups of flora and fauna. The country has 30 per cent of the European lichen species and six per cent of the world's known species of mosses. Irish machair sites support what are believed to be the largest populations of petalwort, a Bern Convention and habitats Directive species. A number of plant species have become extinct in Ireland in recent times (for example, the purple spurge and the three-lobed crowfoot). Certain 'alien' species have become established, including problem species such as the giant hogweed.

The Irish freshwater crayfish population is probably the largest in Europe. Conservation projects have boosted the number of roseate terns and stabilised the number of corncrakes, but these remain under threat along with several other bird species (including the grey partridge); the corn bunting is now considered to be extinct as a breeding species. The Irish population of the lesser horseshoe bat is reckoned to exceed the total known numbers from mainland Europe. The country has the most concentrated population of otters in western Europe and one of only five known resident European populations of bottle-nosed dolphins.

Drawbacks in managing biodiversity in Ireland include the lack of data. There is no centrally co-ordinated biological records centre and no standard approach to habitat classification. Various protection measures are in place or in process to protect the country's habitats from diverse threats and impacts, including those deriving from changes and developments in the economic sectors. Certain locations merit being proposed as natural World Heritage Sites to add to the State's two existing cultural ones. Despite the slow progress in the management of the natural environment, it is concluded that aspects of the natural heritage are being better resourced than ever before.

forms (Lucey and Nolan, 1996) including the geological legacy (Box 12.1). Biodiversity may be defined as the variability among living organisms and the ecological complexes of which they are part; this includes diversity within species, between species and of ecosystems.

Ireland's natural heritage and biodiversity may be conveniently

INTRODUCTION

This chapter gives an account of the state of Ireland's natural heritage and biodiversity at the turn of the millennium. The natural heritage can be described as the inheritance of the natural environment in all its

Ireland has a rich geological heritage, with a wide diversity of rock successions covering large spans of earth history. Many geological sites are of international importance but have had no legal protection. However, since 1998 the Geological Survey of Ireland (GSI) and Dúchas - the Heritage Service have been undertaking the appraisal of geological and geomorphological sites to select, on strictly scientific criteria, those which should be designated as Natural Heritage Areas (NHAs). The programme also aims at establishing County Geological Sites, without statutory protection, which will be incorporated into County Development Plans.

One particular site of palaeontological importance stands out as a special case: a fossil trackway on Valentia Island in Co. Kerry, discovered in 1993 and subsequently purchased by the State. The site is of international importance and has been dated at older than 385 million years. About 200 prints represent the passage of a primitive four-legged vertebrate, across the soft sediment of a large river floodplain

M. Parkes, pers. comm.; Parkes and Morris, 1999.

discussed under two main headings: habitats and species. The linkage between species and their habitats is vital, as changing a habitat will usually affect the diversity of species contained within it, while a change in species number and composition may well affect the nature of the habitat. This chapter will provide a brief outline of some of Ireland's more important habitats as well as elements of the flora and fauna. It will also discuss the state of the natural environment in Ireland and how efforts to safeguard the natural heritage are progressing.

Ireland owes its natural distinctiveness to its unique geology more than anything else (Feehan, 1997). The Quaternary era, with its glaciations and post-glacial stages, has most shaped the present landscape and its flora and fauna. Despite its uniqueness the island has only one natural World Heritage Site, the Giant's Causeway in Co. Antrim.

LEGISLATIVE FRAMEWORK

In a global context the most important initiative for nature conservation is the United Nations Convention on Biological Diversity, 1992, which was ratified by Ireland in 1996. In 1998 the Department of Arts, Heritage, Gaeltacht and the Islands prepared a National Report on the Implementation of the Convention on Biological Diversity. A list of the international agreements and conventions that Ireland has

signed or ratified is given in Table 12.1

The National Biodiversity report, reviews the state of biological diversity in Ireland (habitats, species and genetic diversity) and outlines measures which are currently in place for the conservation and sustainable use of biological diversity. A report on Ireland's biodiversity, commissioned by the Department, concluded that the following general threats affect the fauna either directly or indirectly: habitat loss, pollution and introduced species (Purcell, 1996).

The principal national legislative instrument governing nature conservation in Ireland is the Wildlife Act, 1976. Recent national legislative developments include the European Communities (Natural Habitats) Regulations, 1997 and the Wildlife (Amendment) Bill, 1999. Dúchas, the Heritage Service, is the main body involved in implementing such legislation. One of the main objectives of the Wildlife (Amendment) Bill is to provide for the establishment and protection of a national network of protected areas of both natural heritage and geological importance - to be known as Natural Heritage Areas (NHAs). The Natural Habitats Regulations provide for the designation and protection of Special Areas of Conservation (SACs) under the EU habitats Directive (CEC, 1992) and for protection measures that apply to Special Protection

Table 12.1 International Action on Biodiversity*		
Title	Signed	Ratified
Bern Convention on the Conservation of European Wildlife and Natural Habitats	1979	1982
Bonn Convention on the Conservation of Migratory Species of Wild Animals	1979	1983
Agreement on Conservation of Bats in Europe (Bonn Convention)	1993	1995
Ramsar Convention on Wetlands of International Importance	1971	1984
International Convention for the Regulation of Whaling	1946	1985
Convention on Biological Diversity	1992	1996
Convention on International Trade in Endangered Species (CITES)	1974	Awaits amendment of Wildlife Act, 1976
Agreement on the Conservation of African-Eurasian Migratory Waterwild birds (AEWA) (Bonn Convention)	1996	Awaits amendment of Wildlife Act, 1976
International Tropical Timber Agreement 1994	1996	Ratification expected shortly
Pan-European Biological and Landscape Diversity Strategy	-	Endorsed 1995

Biodiversity-related Conventions, Agreements or Processes that Ireland has ratified, signed or is a party to (from Buckley, 1998).

Table 12.2 Categories of Protected Areas

Category	Objectives	Area covered (ha)	Number of sites	Protective measures
Nature Reserves	Conservation of flora, fauna and habitats	18,095	78	Statutory protection; generally State ownership
Special Protection Areas (SPAs)	Conservation of bird species and habitats of European importance	230,000	109	Statutory protection; to prevent habitat damage
Special Areas of Conservation (SACs)	Conservation of flora, fauna and habitats of European importance	~650,000	400	Statutory protection; to prevent habitat damage
Natural Heritage Areas (NHAs)	Protection of flora, fauna, habitats and geological sites of national importance	~750,000	1,100+	At present: grant assessment, financial incentive; planning laws
National Parks	Nature conservation and public use and appreciation	56,987	6	Non-statutory protection; State-owned
Wildfowl Sanctuaries	Hunting of wild birds prohibited	N/A	68	Statutory enforcement of hunting controls
Refuges for Fauna	Conservation of the habitat of named species of animals	N/A	7	Statutory protection for named species

Sources: Buckley, 1998; Duchas

Areas (SPAs) designated under the EU wild birds Directive (CEC, 1979). The habitats Directive has been the most important development for nature conservation in the EU and it provides for the establishment of a coherent ecological network of protected areas across the 15 member states, to be termed NATURA 2000.

There is a three stage procedure leading to the creation of the NATURA 2000 sites. Stage One, the selection of national lists of sites, was due for completion by June 1995 but no Member States had finalised the process some two years after that date (Grist, 1997). Stage Two - the establishment of a list of Sites of Community Importance (SCIs) - was to have been completed between June 1995 and June 1998. Stage Three - the formal designation by Member States of the adopted list of SCIs as SACs - was originally scheduled for the period June 1998 to June 2004 (Grist, 1997). At the time of writing, Ireland has transmitted 241 candidate SACs to the EU. In the European Commission's evaluation, Ireland's classification of sites (as of 10 January 2000) for NATURA 2000 was assessed as 'incomplete' for SPA classification and 'notably insufficient' for the list of SCIs.

The different categories of protected areas in Ireland, as of 1998, are given in Table 12.2 and areas proposed as NHAs, SPAs and SACs are shown in Fig. 12.1. (See also Chapter 15).

HABITATS

Of the priority habitats listed in the habitats Directive, 16 are found in Ireland (10 per cent of the total). Some examples of priority and non-priority habitats are given below.

Native Woodlands

Only very small areas of the woodlands, representing the mixed deciduous forest which dominated the post-glacial landscape, remain today in Ireland. As noted in Chapter 11, of the estimated 100,000 hectares of Ireland's broadleaved woodland, not more than 6,000 are protected for conservation (O'Sullivan, 1999). Ireland's range of native and naturalised trees is listed in Box 12.2.

A distinction must be made between native and modern forest. Plantations are poor substitutes for native woodland but they do provide niches for a number of the more common mammal and bird species, some invertebrates and fungi. Unlike Ireland's modern forests much of the tree cover in former times was in lowland areas, notably along the great river valleys. Nowadays riparian trees are regularly removed by angling interests thus compromising the habitat of species, such as freshwater sponges and the pearl mussel, which show a preference for shaded sites (e.g. Lucey, 1993; Gittings *et al.*, 1998).

Box 12.2 Native and Naturalised Tree Species in Ireland

The native and naturalised tree species in Ireland include three cherries (including blackthorn); three conifers (juniper, yew and Scots pine which was reintroduced); two birches; alder; hazel; two oaks; six species of whitebeam (including the rowan or mountain ash); hawthorn or whitethorn; ash; Wych elm; holly; spindle; buckthorn and alder buckthorn; elder; arbutus; crab apple; aspen; and willow.

Nelson and Walsh, 1993.

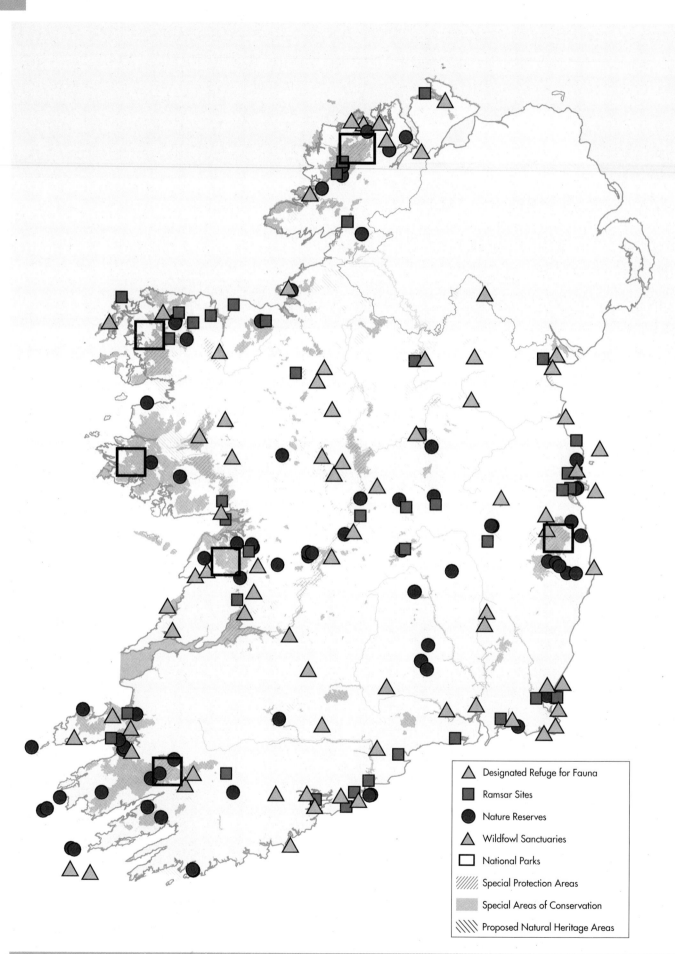

Fig 12.1 A Selection of Major Areas Designated for Conservation (Source: Dúchas)

Legend:
- Designated Refuge for Fauna
- Ramsar Sites
- Nature Reserves
- Wildfowl Sanctuaries
- National Parks
- Special Protection Areas
- Special Areas of Conservation
- Proposed Natural Heritage Areas

Under the Rural Environment Protection Scheme (REPS) planting of trees such as oak, beech, willow, birch, ash, whitethorn, blackthorn and elder is recommended for riparian zones but the planting of conifers is prohibited (DAF, 1999). A report, commissioned by the Heritage Council, on the impact of current forestry policy has identified some areas of concern (Heritage Council, 1998).

Hedgerows

Field boundaries, mainly hedgerows, are a particularly prominent feature of the Irish countryside. They act as linear strips of native woodland, providing niches for a number of common woodland plant and animal species. Hedgerows are especially important, as they act as linking corridors between habitat patches. Hedgerows forming townland boundaries and roadside hedgerows are particularly important from an ecological and cultural viewpoint. Hedgerows have suffered significant losses, largely due to their removal for agricultural purposes, particularly in arable areas. Their removal has impacted negatively on biodiversity in the wider countryside and it has also affected the cultural heritage and altered the visual landscape in those areas. The habitat quality of many remaining hedgerows may be adversely affected by maintenance operations undertaken by Local Authorities and other bodies, as well as by private landowners. Currently controls are in place that contribute to mitigating negative impacts on hedgerows. The Wildlife Act, 1976 prevents the cutting or destruction of hedgerows or other vegetation between 15th April and 31st August, and there is also guidance to ensure that the importance of roadside hedgerows for wildlife is taken into account (DAHGI, 1999).

Fen and Bog

Despite the loss of peatlands, Ireland remains unique in western Europe in

having a wide range of bog types of international importance. Active raised bog, once common in the Irish midlands, is now a relatively rare habitat. The vegetation is dominated by *Sphagnum* mosses with some vascular plants such as heathers, cottons and sundews also occurring. Threatened species include the bog orchid (*Hammarbya paludosa*) and, where mineral flushes occur, the yellow marsh saxifrage (*Saxifraga hirculis*), an Annex II species in the habitats Directive, is found.

Bog orchid (*Hammarbya paludosa*)
This small orchid grows in wet, acid, spongy bogs and is difficult to detect. It has an erratic flowering habit and can be abundant in some years. It has been recorded from more than 50 sites in the past but recently confirmed at single sites in just six counties. The apparent decline may be associated with the loss of its peatland habitat.
Source: Curtis and McGough, 1988

Based on presence in 10 km squares

Fig 12.2 Distribution of the Bog Orchid

Blanket bogs are subject to a range of adverse effects from grazing and trampling due to excessive sheep stocking, peat extraction, afforestation and agricultural reclamation (Douglas, 1998). Among the threatened species are the slender cottongrass (*Eriophorum gracile*) and Mackay's heath (*Erica mackaiana*). Both active raised and blanket bogs, are priority habitats under the habitats Directive.

In total 32 raised bog, 47 blanket bog and 39 fen sites considered to be of prime ecological importance have been proposed as candidate SACs. Of particular concern, has been the continuation of turf cutting on raised bogs of ecological importance resulting in a further decline of approximately 10 per cent in the area of original uncut surface area in the last decade (J. Ryan, pers. comm.).

Calcareous fens occur in limestone areas subject to a permanently high water table where the vegetation typically consists of a complex of sedge communities (Ó Críodáin and Doyle, 1997) dominated by the black bog rush (*Schoenus nigricans*) and purple moor grass (*Molina caerulea*).

Turloughs

Turloughs are temporary water bodies on Carboniferous limestone and are characteristic features of the western third of Ireland. They are typically associated with swallow-holes through

which they fill and empty through the local groundwater system. A total of 43 turloughs has been proposed as Special Areas of Conservation (SACs).

The chief threats to turloughs are land drainage and pollution. Drainage in the nineteenth century eliminated many of the great turloughs of east Galway and more recent schemes have also had effects, where seven sites of importance for Greenland white-fronted geese and Bewick and whooper swans were drastically affected (Reynolds, 1996). Two turloughs are designated as Special Protection Areas and one, in Co. Galway, is protected in a Nature Reserve (DAHGI, 1999). One of the best known is Rahasane turlough (275 ha) in east Galway which was the site of first discovery of the shrimp *Tanymastix stagnalis* in Britain and Ireland. Among the characteristic flora of turloughs the black moss *Cinclidotus fontinaloides* may be seen on rocks or boulders. Because of their unique ecological features, turloughs possess characteristic vegetation and aquatic faunal communities. Their conservation requires sensitive management of the regional catchment, both surface and underground (Reynolds, 1996). A recent study, carried out by the Office of Public Works (OPW), of the

flooding in south Galway has greatly increased knowledge on the hydrology and biology of these systems.

Freshwater Habitats

Lakes are vitally important for breeding and wintering wildfowl. Twenty eight lakes, covering approximately 75,000 hectares, almost half the total area of Irish lakes, are waterfowl sites designated as SPAs. A number of other lakes are listed as candidate SACs. Two lakes in Kerry, the habitat of the endangered natterjack toad, are Nature Reserves and some additional lakes are conserved in National Parks (DAHGI, 1999). In addition the Grand and Royal canals have been identified as proposed NHAs.

In general, Irish rivers and lakes (Chapter 9) are still capable of supporting salmonids (*Salmo salar and S. trutta*). The salmon is a listed species in the habitats Directive and the Irish authorities are required to propose sites for its protection. Despite Ireland being one of the most important areas in the EU for salmon rivers, the list and extent of the proposed sites appears extremely limited.

Some smaller lakes and ponds have disappeared or shrunk due to drainage, for example Loughs Iron and

Annaghmore. Certain salmonid lakes in poorly-buffered, upland areas in west Galway and Mayo have been affected by acidification from commercial conifer plantations. Artificial acidification, attributed to afforestation, has also been measured in a feeder stream to Glendalough Lake Upper in Co. Wicklow (Bowman and Bracken, 1993; Lucey *et al.*, 1999). However, pollution, especially from diffuse agricultural sources, is the main threat (Chapter 9).

Coastal and Marine Habitats

With a coastline of 7,100 km, including offshore islands, Ireland is well endowed with marine and coastal ecosystems. Habitats of international importance include the west coast maërl beds (Box 12.3) and limestone pavements with the sea urchin *Paracentrotus lividus* (Wilson and Lawler, 1996). The only marine locality designated as a National Nature Reserve is Lough Hyne. Irish sand dunes are species-rich habitats for plants and invertebrates and 168 sand systems have been catalogued (DAHGI, 1999). Vulnerable plants include sea pea (*Lathyrus japonicus*) and lesser centaury (*Centaurium pulchellum*) and seaside centaury (*C. littorale*) in Northern Ireland. With regard to vascular plant species associated with dunes, as many as 26 are under threat, of which three are probably extinct, one endangered and six vulnerable. In south Kerry, dune pools and margins are important spawning and feeding areas for the natterjack toad.

Box 12.3 Maërl Communities

Deposits of calcareous red algae (maërl) form a rare habitat with a rich associated fauna. Seven free-living maërl species are known to occur in Irish marine waters with some species forming deep deposits (maërl beds) that are harvested for agricultural and horticultural use. The faunal richness of maërl beds has recently been assessed and more than 70 per cent of the species recorded were crustaceans; of which over 85 species have been identified, illustrating the taxonomic richness of this biotype. Some rarely recorded isopods, such as *Munna* cf *petiti* which is only known with certainty from three locations in the Mediterranean, and *Cymodoce* spp., were identified among the Crustacea.
Marine Institute, 1999

Machair is a rare habitat found only on the west coast between Galway Bay and Malin Head. It is a mosaic of dunes, grassland and wetland,

grazed by sheep and cattle and is an important habitat for three vulnerable bird species: corncrake, dunlin and red-necked phalarope. Irish sand dunes and machairs are listed in the habitats Directive as priority habitats and are highly vulnerable to human pressures. The main threats include caravan parks, football pitches, beach houses, agricultural intensification, sand quarrying and conversion to golf courses. Few pristine examples of sand dunes and machair currently exist, because so many have been degraded. A number of important sites are currently under threat. Since 1997 the best examples have been listed as candidate SACs. Four sand dune systems are protected in Nature Reserves, covering 1,352 hectares (DAHGI, 1999).

Shingle beaches (including the strand line) are significant invertebrate habitats. Characteristic plant species of vegetated sites include couch (*Elymus* spp.), spear-leaved orache (*Atriplex prostrata*), sea mayweed (*Tripleurospermum maritimum*), curled dock (*Rumex crispus*), sea milkwort (*Glaux maritima*) and sea beet (*Beta vulgaris*). Threatened plant species include the sea pea (*Lathyrus japonicus*) and oysterplant (*Mertensia maritma*); another species, the purple spurge (*Euphorbia peplis*) is now

extinct in Ireland. Sandy beaches can be important feeding areas for waders because of the productive invertebrate populations. Tern species nest and roost on shingle beaches (e.g. little tern) while common seals and harbour seals haul up on remote sandy beaches in southern and western areas. The main threat to this habitat is the widespread and illegal removal of shingle and sand for building.

Coastal lagoons are also identified as priority habitats in the habitats Directive and surveys were carried out in 1996 and 1998 of the 92 sites in the national inventory. The sites are mainly situated on the south and west coasts. It appears, from the study, that aquatic flora and fauna are rich compared with other regions of western Europe (Healy and Oliver, 1998; Healy, 1999). Among the biota, stoneworts and insects in particular were well represented. Overall 53 species of plants, 220 species of aquatic fauna (invertebrates and fish) and 209 Carabidae and Staphylinidae (Coleoptera) were recorded from lagoon shores. Following these surveys Irish lagoons are now known to be of European and international conservation importance and 38 lagoons in 25 sites are being proposed as SACs.

Table 12.3 Estimated Number of Species

Insects	Amphibians	Reptiles	Freshwater fish	Birds	Mammals	Vascular plants
~16,000	3	2*	27	140-168**	31(42)***	1341

*Including slow-worm
**Represents resident, passage migrant, summer visitor and winter visitor species which occur regularly
***Including regularly occurring marine species　　　　　　　(See text for other groups)
Webb et al., 1996; Ashe et al., 1998; DAHGI, 1999; O. Merne, pers. comm.

SPECIES

A prerequisite to any conservation policy or strategy is to establish the number of species occurring and ascertain their status. While the number of species for all groups in Ireland has not been established the known figures or estimates have been computed for some and these are listed in Table 12.3. Unlike habitats no Irish species have been given priority designation in the habitats Directive.

Box 12.4 Lower Plants

Petalwort (*Petalophyllum ralfsii*) is a small liverwort found in coastal dune slacks and machairs. It is listed in the Bern Convention and the habitats Directive. It occurs in scattered localities along the western seaboard, from Kerry to Donegal, as well as some dune sites in Dublin. A survey in 1997-98 identified that four of its 13 former stations have been lost: two to agricultural intensification, one to golf course development and the only known inland site to competition from vascular plants in a disused quarry. Many of the older records, including a small population in Kerry not seen since 1890, were re-found during the survey. Nine new localities were also discovered and it now appears that its most important sites in Ireland are the machairs of Galway and Mayo. Furthermore, these machairs support what are thought to be the largest populations of this species in the world. All 18 populations in the Republic are within proposed NHAs.
N. Lockhart, pers. comm.

Stoneworts are a separate class (Characeae) of the green algae (Chlorophyta). They grow entirely under water and some species can tolerate strongly brackish conditions. They are deemed to be so important and vulnerable that they are the subject of a Red Data Book for Britain and Ireland. Ten species are listed as being endangered in Ireland while *Tolypella prolifera*, has already become extinct during this century. Many stonewort species prefer calcium-rich but nutrient-poor situations and parts of the Grand and Royal canals provide such conditions. Canal maintenance and heavy boat traffic in the canals can be threats to these plants. The contraction of the Characeae flora was a feature of the eutrophication effects of Lough Sheelin. Recent surveys of lagoons and coastal lakes have identified one species new to Ireland and rediscovered another, *Chara muscosa*, which was believed to have become extinct.
Stewart and Church, 1992; Champ, 1998; Roden, 2000

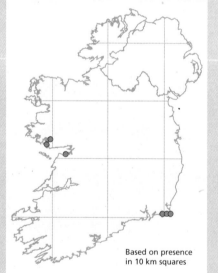

Foxtail stonewort (*Lamprothamnium papulosum*)
This stonewort grows in brackish lagoons with salinities in the range 1-3 per cent. It is protected under the Flora Order (1999). Having recently been recorded from two new sites, both high salinity lagoons, it is now known from five locations. Its saline lagoon habitat is threatened, *inter alia*, by land reclamation, water pollution and changes in salinity; the latter occurs at one of its sites, Lady's Island Lake in Co. Wexford, from the regular cutting of the sand bar which separates the lake from the sea.
Sources: Stewart and Church, 1992; Hatch and Healy, 1998

Flora (Plants)

Algae are a diverse group found largely in freshwater and marine habitats. Some are unicellular but many, such as seaweeds are multicellular plants. To date, a total of 524 species of macro-algae and 181 species of phytoplankton has been recorded from the Irish marine environment (DAHGI, 1999). Algae can cause problems in both fresh water and sea water. The group formerly known as blue-green algae are now classed among the bacteria (cyanobacteria).

There are an estimated 700-1,000 species of freshwater desmids (green algae) and 25 known stoneworts; the latter figure is equivalent to about 10 per cent of the known species world-wide. Examples of lower plants are given in Box 12.4.

Fungi (e.g., mushrooms, moulds, rusts and yeasts) are simply-organised organisms lacking green colouring matter (chlorophyll) and hence unable to photosynthesise. They need organic material to grow and are normally found on decaying matter. As a group the fungi are apparently a neglected area for study in Ireland and while some 3,500 species have been recorded it is believed that the true figure is much greater; one estimate (7,800) would give Ireland about 0.5 per cent of the world's fungal flora (DAHGI, 1999). What is known of Irish fungal diversity is largely due to work undertaken, in the 1980s, to catalogue the species.

Several rare European lichens are found in Ireland. Ireland has 30 per cent of the total number of European taxa which, compared with other flora groups, is a relatively high proportion and is probably attributable in part to the reasonably good air quality. A total of 1050 taxa has been recorded of which 34 are believed to be threatened European species (Seaward, 1994; DAHGI, 1999). The only lichen listed in the

Irish Natural Habitats Regulations is the 'reindeer moss' (*Cladonia* subgenus *Cladina*).

Ireland, because of its moist climate, has a flora rich in mosses and liverworts. These bryophytes do not possess vascular systems or roots and are classed among the so-called lower plants. Although some parts of the country have been well studied, such as Killarney and Ben Bulben, the full Irish bryological flora distribution is imperfectly understood. The number of species recorded for Ireland is 533 mosses and 226 liverworts which represents respectively 6 per cent and 3 per cent of the known bryophytes world-wide (DAHGI, 1999). Eighteen species of bryophytes are now legally protected in the Republic under the Flora (Protection) Order, 1999, two of which (*Petalophyllum ralfsii* and *Drepanocladus vernicosus*) are also listed on Annex II of the habitats Directive. The only bryophytes listed in the Irish Natural Habitats Regulations are *Leucobryum glaucum* and *Sphagnum* species (peat mosses).

Ferns and their allies (Pteridophytes) are the most primitive of the higher plants. Although they possess vascular systems and produce roots they are spore-producing and do not produce flowers and fruit. The clubmosses (*Lycopodium* spp.) are listed in the Irish Natural Habitats Regulations. Some examples of rare vascular plants are given in Box 12.5.

The total vascular flora, including well established introductions and hybrids has been given as 1,341

Box 12.5 Vascular Plants

Meadow Saffron: The decline of this wetland species, also known as the autumn crocus (*Colchicum autumnale*), is apparently a result of loss of habitat due to intensive agriculture and drainage. It is now regarded as one of the most endangered species of wild flora in Ireland. It was once locally common in the Nore valley where it occurred in old damp meadows and on river banks; elsewhere its only other recently recorded sites were in one area of County Limerick (as well as County Armagh where it has become naturalised). It was last recorded at the Limerick site, formerly an old pasture, in 1995 but has not been seen since then; ownership of the site changed hands and the land was subsequently ploughed. The remaining County Kilkenny habitats are threatened by the construction of a bypass.

The plant contains a toxin, known as colchicine, and there have been occasional instances of fatalities to livestock although it is generally avoided by animals. Despite its toxicity it has long been used as a treatment for gout and is still considered an important plant from a pharmaceutical point of view. This aspect together with its rarity and threatened status should make its conservation a major objective.

Curtis and McGough, 1988; C. Ó Críodáin, pers. comm.; S. Reynolds, pers. comm.

Oyster Plant: Also known as the shore-wort, the oyster plant (*Mertensia maritima*) is a perennial of shingle beaches and gravelly seashores. It was previously recorded from eight counties on the north and east coasts but underwent a gradual decrease in range over the past century and has recently been confirmed from Donegal, Antrim and Down. Climatic factors are usually given as the reason for its decline. However, other factors may also be implicated and shingle removal, particularly at one site, is seen as the greatest threat with grazing by sheep reported in the past from all extant sites. It is a protected species through the Flora Protection Order 1999.

Curtis and McGough, 1988; Farrell and Randall, 1992

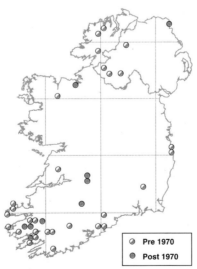

| ⬤ | Pre 1970 |
| ⬤ | Post 1970 |

Based on presence
in 10 km squares

Killarney fern (*Trichomanes speciosum*)
This beautiful small fern occurs in dark, sheltered places with a humid atmosphere such as near waterfalls. In Britain it is extremely rare and just one site in England remains. Collecting, chiefly in the 19th century, has been responsible for its decline in some areas such as in south-west Ireland.
Sources: Curtis and McGough, 1988; Merryweather and Hill, 1992.

Fig 12.3 Distribution of Killarney Fern

(Webb *et al.*, 1996). The distribution of vascular plants has changed as a result of changes in agricultural practice (particularly intensification of farming) and land-use (e.g. afforestation and building development) while many alien species, previously unknown, have become widespread in the countryside. Under national legislation, particular plants can be protected under a Flora Protection Order. Under such an Order it becomes an offence to cut, uproot or

damage these plants unless licensed. Under the Flora (Protection) Order, 1999, 70 vascular plants are listed as protected as are 14 mosses, four liverworts, including *Petalophyllum ralfsii*, two stoneworts and one lichen (*Fulgensia fulgens*). There are no flowering plants listed in the Irish Natural Habitats Regulations but the two species (*Najas flexilis* and *Saxifraga hirculus*) listed in the habitats Directive are among those in the above Order.

Among the rare and threatened aquatic plants some examples are worth mentioning. The river water-crowfoot (*Ranunculus fluitans*) has to date not been found in the Republic but is recorded for one river in Co. Antrim in Northern Ireland (Hackney, 1992). There is some doubt as to the validity of historical records for the three-lobed crowfoot (*Ranunculus tripartitus*), whose habitat is generally acidic and unpolluted lakes. It had been

'recorded' from five sites in the south-west up to 1988 (Curtis and Harrington, 1987; Curtis and McGough, 1988) but has, according to some, become extinct (Preston and Croft, 1997) in the meantime. However, the soft hornwort (*Ceratophyllum submersum*) has been added to the Irish flora after being first found in 1989 (Smith and Wolfe-Murphy, 1991) and the floating water-plantain (*Luronium natans*) has been rediscovered (Rich *et al.*, 1995); neither species is listed in the Flora (Protection) Order, 1999. The latter is considered by some Irish botanists not to be a native species. Other species, such as the opposite-leaved pondweed (*Groenlandia densa*) and the slender naiad (*Najas flexilis*) which is vulnerable to eutrophication (Preston and Croft, 1997), have been discovered at new localities. *L. natans* and *N. flexilis*, are protected under the Bern Convention and the habitats Directive. Another protected species, the triangular club-rush

(*Schoenoplectus triqueter*), which is known from only two vice-county divisions, Clare and Limerick, was recently confirmed living in the estuary of the River Maigue (Reynolds, 1997a).

Among alien species, the Japanese knotweed (*Reynoutria japonica*), Indian balsam (*Impatiens glandulifera*) and giant hogweed (*Heracleum mantegazzianum*) are, because of their large size and invasive habit, most easily recognised. Many others, however, for a variety of reasons go largely unnoticed. Surveys carried out at the ports of Dublin and Foynes, recorded 66 and 41 species respectively of established and casual alien plants (Reynolds, 1997b). The alien aquatic fern (*Azolla filiculoides*) is occasionally recorded in Ireland but any spread is usually checked by colder winters and it is unlikely to become a pest species unless a warming of the climate and increases in winter temperatures occur (Lucey, 1998). A minor *Azolla* bloom

Based on presence in 10 km squares

Giant hogweed (*Heracleum mantegazzianum*) Introduced in the 19th century, as a garden ornamental, it has become naturalized in many places particularly along the banks of rivers. Because of its photoxicity it can be a health hazard and can also cause environmental problems. Such is the cause for concern in some quarters that a nationally co-ordinated control, and ultimate eradication, strategy has been recommended for this invasive alien.
Sources: Wyse Jackson, 1989; Lucey, 1994; Wade et al., 1997; Caffrey, 1999.

Fig 12.4 Distribution of Giant Hogweed

occurred on the River Barrow, at and upstream of Graiguenamanagh, in the autumn of 1999 (Lucey, 1999a).

Fauna (Animals)

While efforts have been made to determine Ireland's entire fauna, from protozoans and sponges to mammals, further work is needed to provide a reasonable estimate of the total number of species. The insect component alone is thought to comprise some 16,000 species of which 1,499 are recorded as aquatic (Ashe *et al.*, 1998). The elements of the country's fauna that remain to be discovered chiefly comprise invertebrate animals.

Invertebrates do not have a high profile when it comes to conservation. The Irish invertebrate species listed in the habitats Directive are: the freshwater pearl mussel (*Margaritifera margaritifera*); the white-clawed crayfish (*Austropotamobius pallipes*); the Kerry slug (*Geomalacus maculosus*); three marsh snails (*Vertigo* spp.) and one butterfly, the marsh fritillary (*Euphydryas aurinia*). The crayfish,

Box 12.6 Freshwater Invertebrates

Pearl Mussel: Unlike many other molluscs this mussel requires clean, cool, well-oxygenated water free from mud and suspended matter. Also unusual for a mollusc, it is found chiefly in soft water. It is a declining species throughout Europe and has become extinct in some places in Ireland. The causes are various and include destruction by pearl fishers, physical changes to the habitat and pollution. The species is particularly vulnerable because of its unusual longevity (one hundred years or more) and slow reproduction (Lucey, 1993; Kerney, 1999) The hard-water form which occurred in the main channels of the Suir and Barrow up until relatively recently is now restricted to a 10 km stretch of the Nore (Moorkens and Costello, 1994). The known distribution, based on 10 km squares, is given below.

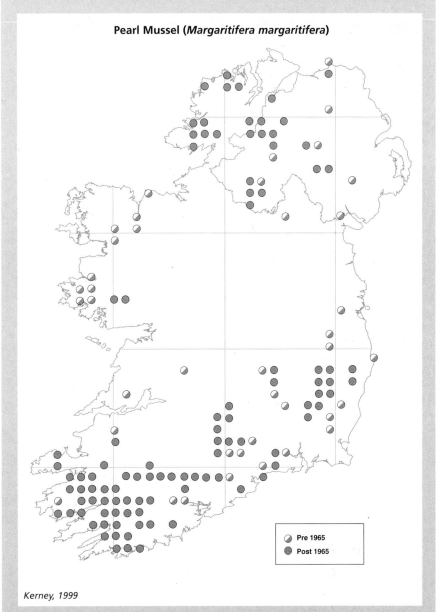

Pearl Mussel (*Margaritifera margaritifera*)

Pre 1965
Post 1965

Kerney, 1999

Freshwater Crayfish: The crayfish, which is not native to Ireland, is relatively common and widely distributed in limestone rivers and lakes but is under threat from a lethal fungus (*Aphanomyces astaci*) disease which has devastated stocks throughout Britain and Europe and which may have been responsible for the collapse of some Irish lake populations. The Irish crayfish populations, however, probably constitute the largest reservoir of the species in Europe.

Lucey, 1999b; Lucey and Nolan, 1996

pearl mussel and Kerry slug are large invertebrates which are protected in Ireland through national and international law. Of the three species, the mussel is the most vulnerable (Box 12.6). The Kerry slug is common over a considerable area in the south-west where it lives among rocks, in heather moorland and rough pasture or more rarely in oak woods on moss-covered timber. There is no evidence that it is declining (Platts and Speight, 1988). Four species of the Vertiginidae family of tiny land snails, which show strong affinities for wetlands or marshy ground, are listed in the habitats Directive. Three of these occur in Ireland *Vertigo angustio*r (a declining species, considered vulnerable in Ireland), the rare *V. moulinsiana* and the endangered *V. geyeriis*. *V. lilljeborgi* is also quite rare in Ireland but is not listed in the Directive. The main threats are from drainage, afforestation or other changes in land use which reduce the size of their habitat (Cawley, 1996; Kerney, 1999; O'Sullivan, 1999). Twenty three SACs are being proposed for these species by Dúchas.

A survey of butterflies was carried out in the summer months between 1995

and 1999. In order to get an accurate true representation of butterfly numbers monitoring needs to be carried out for several years as some species are affected by weather conditions: lower than normal numbers of the small tortoise shell (*Aglais urticae*) were found in the summer of 1999. As well as the known resident butterfly species, three more migrant species usually arrive from abroad each year giving a total of 28 species. Loss of habitat due mainly to agricultural practices is thought to be causing a decline in their numbers in Ireland (D. Nash, pers. comm.).

Of the resident species, six may be considered vulnerable due to their very limited and fragmented geographical distribution or their dependence on restricted specialised habitats. The six species (the large heath *Coenonympha tullia,* the pearl bordered fritillary *Bolaria euphrosyne*, the marsh fritillary *Eurodryas aurina* - an Annex II species under the habitats Directive - the brown hairstreak *Thecla betulae*, the dingy skipper *Erynnis tages* and the small blue *Cupido minimus*) are, as is the case elsewhere in Europe, under threat from changes and trends in land use (B. Aldwell, pers. comm.). These changes include loss of traditional meadows, major drainage of bogs and wetlands, intensive sheep grazing, loss of sand dunes, the removal or severe cutting of field hedges and scrub and the use of chemicals in agriculture. The large heath butterfly occurs on wet peat moors and bogs and has suffered major habitat loss (D. Nash, pers. comm.) (Fig 12.5).

Modern world-wide plant material movement has resulted in the introduction and establishment of several exotic invertebrate pests to Ireland including the New Zealand flatworm (*Artioposthia triangulata*). The movement of honeybees has also led to the establishment of the parasite *Varroa jacobsoni*. These pest

species have mainly been introduced from other EU countries, where they have become established and not from their native areas. Other exotic insect and mite introductions encountered in recent years include the serpentine or Florida leafminer, the South American leafminer, the western flower thrips, the sweet potato whitefly, the lupin aphid and the Colorado beetle (R. Dunne, pers. comm.).

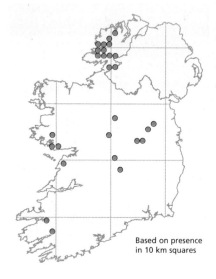

Based on presence in 10 km squares

Large heath (*Coenonympha tullia*)
Between 1995 and 1999 it was recorded from 27 of the 820 squares searched. It has suffered major habitat loss due to the exploitation of our raised and blanket bogs.
Source: D. Nash, Dublin Naturalist's Field Club

Fig 12.5 Distribution of Large Heath

The fish species listed in the Irish Natural Habitats Regulations are the lampern or river lamprey (*Lampetra fluviatilis*), pollan (*Coregonus autumnalis*), allis shad (*Alosa alosa*), twaite shad (*Alosa fallax*) and salmon (*Salmo salar*) in fresh water.

Box 12.7 Fish

Arctic Charr (Salvelinus alpinus): An indigenous species which was formerly widespread and abundant but has become rare in most places. It is restricted to cool, stony, unpolluted lakes. Although considered to be endangered in Europe it is not listed in the habitats Directive. The fish has become extinct in some lakes in Ireland since the beginning of the century with the most recent extirpation, from Lough Conn in County Mayo confirmed since 1996. There has also been a collapse of populations in Loughs Corrib and Leane. The main threats are eutrophication, acidification and over-fishing. Among the conservation measures that have been proposed are control of water pollution (primarily from agriculture and forestry) as well as the possible banning of smolt-rearing and cage-rearing of other salmonids in their waters. Its current known distribution is shown in the map.

Whilde, 1993; Champ, 1998

Lampreys: Three species of lamprey occur in Irish waters: the sea lamprey (*Petromyzon marinus*), the river lamprey (*Lampetra fluviatilis*) and the brook lamprey (*Lampetra planeri*). All three species are known to spawn in Irish rivers or streams and are listed in the habitats Directive. Lampreys were once widespread in Europe but stocks have declined in recent years although this has not been quantified for Irish populations. Water quality is implicated in the demise of populations as well as the impediment by weirs and dams to upstream and downstream migration. Nevertheless, Irish populations appear to be still widespread and are in a position to make an important contribution to the conservation of European stocks. To conserve Irish lamprey populations, however, the known spawning grounds and larval habitats need to be protected and maintained. Nine SACs have been proposed for these species.

Kurz and Costello, 1999; F. Marnell, pers. comm.

Basking Shark (Cetorhinus maximus): This shark is known to occur off the coasts of Antrim, Dublin, Waterford, Wexford, Cork, Kerry, Galway, Mayo and Donegal. It was hunted off the Irish coast for hundreds of years mainly for its oil. Between 1947 and 1975 some 12,400 were killed off Achill Island. Thousands (4,442 in 1984) were taken by Norwegian shark fishermen off the south-east coast during the 1980s. The Achill fishery closed in 1975 after annual catches had dropped to less than 100. A national survey, carried out in 1993, showed little sign of recovery of stocks in the heavily fished areas. Since 1998 basking sharks in UK waters have been given full protection under legislation. As yet no such protection has been afforded them in Irish territorial waters.

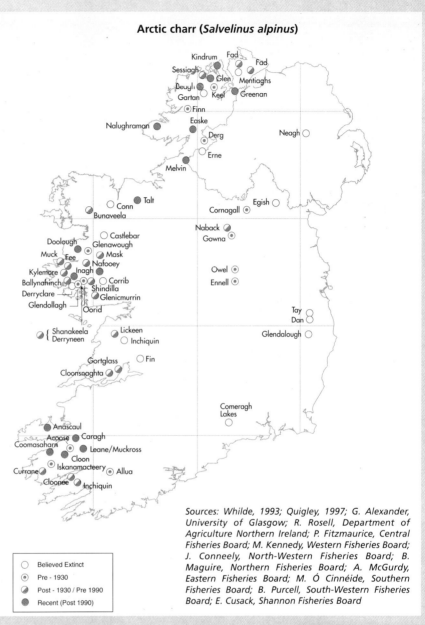

Arctic charr (*Salvelinus alpinus*)

Sources: Whilde, 1993; Quigley, 1997; G. Alexander, University of Glasgow; R. Rosell, Department of Agriculture Northern Ireland; P. Fitzmaurice, Central Fisheries Board; M. Kennedy, Western Fisheries Board; J. Conneely, North-Western Fisheries Board; B. Maguire, Northern Fisheries Board; A. McGurdy, Eastern Fisheries Board; M. Ó Cinnéide, Southern Fisheries Board; B. Purcell, South-Western Fisheries Board; E. Cusack, Shannon Fisheries Board

○	Believed Extinct
◉	Pre - 1930
◑	Post - 1930 / Pre 1990
●	Recent (Post 1990)

Maitland (1996) concluded that active conservation management was needed for the arctic charr (*Salvelinus alpinus*) and smelt *(Osmerus eperlanus)* in addition to the pollan and shads.

Two amphibian species, the natterjack toad (*Bufo calamita*) and the common frog (*Rana temporaria*),

are listed in the Irish Natural Habitats Regulations (1997). The smooth newt (*Triturus vulgaris*) is the only tailed amphibian found in Ireland and has received less attention. Unlike these other two amphibian species, whose origins in Ireland are unclear, the newt is considered an old native. A detailed survey, carried out between 1993 and 1995, showed a widespread distribution although it was not found in Donegal, Fermanagh or Tyrone and except for a location near Bantry in Co. Cork was apparently absent from the south-west. Newts

appear to be widespread but uncommon in Ireland and require suitable ponds as well as undisturbed terrestrial habitats for their continued survival (Wilson, 1986; Marnell, 1996; 1998a; 1998b).

The two reptile species, the common lizard (*Lacerta vivipara*) and slow-worm (*Anguis fragilis*), occurring in Ireland have been little studied and details regarding their status are lacking. From anecdotal evidence it would appear that the lizard is less common than previously. The slow-worm, which is a legless lizard, appears to have been introduced into the Burren in Co. Clare relatively recently where it was first recorded in the 1970s but it is not known if it has become established in other areas or how successfully it has become naturalised. Another species the green lizard (*Lacerta viridis*), which occurs naturally in southern Europe and the Channel Islands, was introduced also to the Burren in 1958; eight males and seven females were released and one was found in 1962. It appears to have died out thereafter and has not been seen since (Cabot, 1965; F. Marnell, pers. comm.). Some species of marine turtles occur in Irish waters from time to time.

All bird species are afforded protection under the Wildlife Act and the wild birds Directive.

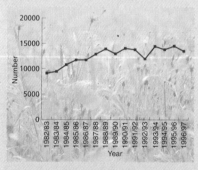

Greenland White-fronted Goose numbers 1983-1997
J. Wilson, pers. comm.

Conservation projects over the past decade have boosted population numbers of rare species such as the roseate tern and stabilised numbers of the corncrake. In the west, the numbers of red grouse and apparently also merlin and hen harrier, have been adversely affected by overgrazing of habitats by sheep. Surveys have also shown a recent decrease in certain local populations of wetland species, such as the redshank, snipe and the

Box 12.9 Threatened Countryside Birds

Grey Partridge: The native grey partridge (*Perdix perdix*) is now an extremely rare species which has been recorded in recent times from eight counties (Galway, Kildare, Longford, Louth, Offaly, Tipperary, Wexford and Wicklow). The remaining wild birds, appear to be split between two populations, at Boora in Co. Offaly and Lullymore in Co. Kildare. Since 1995 partridges have declined in most parts of their range in Europe and the 1998 breeding season was one of the worst on record in the UK. The decline in Irish populations is part of a world-wide trend the specific reasons for which have not been entirely established. It is believed that the removal of hedgerows together with the use of insecticides and herbicides, which have reduced the abundance of insects and the weed species, are responsible for lower chick survival. It has been shown that predators significantly affect nesting hen and chick survival rates. Dúchas is supporting a conservation strategy which involves predator reduction in the core area, habitat improvement by the creation of suitable nesting and brood rearing cover as well as monitoring the species response to the habitat measures.
Whilde, 1993; B. Kavanagh, pers. comm.; O'Gorman, 1998

Corn Bunting: This bird was classed, in the Red Data Book, as a rare and endangered resident species breeding at only a handful of sites mostly on the west coast. In 1998, the Heritage Council commissioned a survey of its status. Based on the results of this survey, during which no wild birds were located in the traditional strongholds of the species, the Heritage Council now considers this species as being extinct as a breeding species in Ireland. A single specimen was seen in north Donegal in the summer of 1999.
Whilde, 1993; Heritage Council; O. Merne, pers. comm.

Corncrake: Corncrakes are now regarded as globally endangered chiefly due to intensification of farmland management. In Ireland there had been a long-term decline in the summering population. The Corncrake Grant Scheme (CGS), whereby landowners were paid to delay grass mowing and encouraged to do centre-out cutting, was first introduced in 1992. The aim of the programme is to conserve corncrakes in the Shannon Callows (between Athlone and Portumna), north-west Mayo and parts of the north Donegal coast and islands where mowing was already fairly late. The scheme has apparently arrested and reversed the long-term decline in numbers. The number of calling males has increased or stabilised in all the areas with Inishbofin and Tory Islands doing particularly well (Table 12.4).
Source: Dúchas

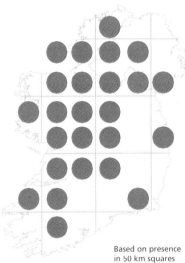

Based on presence in 50 km squares

Pine marten (*Martes martes*)
Believed to be an old native species this carnivore has suffered greatly at the hands of man: it was hunted for its pelt in the 16th and 17th centuries when the destruction of its habitat, the natural forests, was also occurring. Its numbers are now increasing and its recent expansion in range has been such that it is considered to be secure particularly since the laying of the poison strychnine has been banned.
Sources: Whilde, 1993; Mitchell-Jones et al., 1999; T.J. Hayden, pers. comm.

Fig 12.6 Distribution of Pine Marten

curlew but in particular, and unexpectedly, the lapwing. Although this collapse may have been caused by four consecutive years of April flooding, the chief factors for overall wader population declines are the loss of wetlands and nest predation (D. Norriss, pers. comm.). D'Arcy (1999) includes the following species among the threatened wild birds: corn bunting, corncrake and partridge (Box. 12.9), quail, grouse, roseate and little tern, twite, chough, barn owl, nightjar, merlin and hen harrier.

Ireland, including its inshore waters, is home to 42 mammal species. Those listed in Annex II of the habitats Directives are the otter (*Lutra lutra*), bottle-nosed dolphin (*Tursiops truncatus*), lesser horseshoe bat (*Rhinolophus hipposideros*), grey seal (*Halichoerus grypus*) and common seal (*Phoca viulina*). Examples of two mammals are given in Box 12.10.

In Irish waters, to date, 23 species of cetaceans have been recorded, 11 of which are regularly sighted. These include harbour porpoise, common dolphin, striped dolphin, bottle-nosed dolphin, white-sided dolphin, white-

Area	1994	1995	1996	1997	1998
Inishbofin Island	12	27	15	12	15-17
Tory Island	8	12	21	18-20	19
Donegal, Mayo, Shannon Callows	129*	174*	184*	148-150*	149-153*
Total	149	213	220	178-182	183-189

Table 12.4 Corncrake Numbers in Certain Areas

Based on counts in 1994-98 period
*Core area totals
Source: Dúchas

Lesser Horseshoe Bat (*Rhinolophus hipposideros*): Ireland has nine bat species, the rarest being the lesser horseshoe which is confined to an area along the west and south-west coasts. Its Irish population is estimated to be 12,000 bats which is thought to exceed the total known population from mainland Europe. It is already rare in much of Europe, reduced by disturbance during hibernation, loss of habitat and chemical treatment of roof timbers. The largest maternity roost in Europe (428 counted in 1998) is in an old building adjacent to Dromore National Nature Reserve in Co. Clare. The Heritage Council purchased the building in 1998 to protect this roost and to promote pride in Ireland's heritage. It is proposed to develop a management plan for the site and to restore the building, as a model for bat conservation in Ireland.
Whilde, 1993; McAney, 1994; O'Sullivan, 1994; McGuire, 1998

Otter (*Lutra lutra*): The otter is also listed in the habitats Directive. Ireland has the densest populations of otters in western Europe and these occur in freshwater and coastal habitats. Otters are widespread throughout Ireland and appear to be thriving. Unlike in other countries they live within city limits and an increase in numbers is evident for the Greater Dublin area. Dúchas has proposed 37 SACs for the protection of otters.
Whilde, 1993; Lunnon, 1996; F. Marnell, pers. comm.

The impact of the fishing industry on cetacean populations, notably harbour porpoises in the Celtic Sea, has been referred to in Chapter 10. Impact, both directly through entanglement and from competition for resources, is one of the most sensitive issues affecting the management of a cetacean sanctuary. There is concern within Europe that bottle-nosed dolphin numbers have declined considerably in the last few years and studies have suggested that calves are being born infertile in the Irish Sea due to contamination with organochlorines (Berrow, 1990; Rogan and Berrow, 1995).

DISCUSSION

No terrestrial landscape has remained unaltered or unaffected since the arrival of humans in Ireland. The physical and biotic world has been so strongly modified by human agency that the resulting landscape is a synthesis of natural and cultural elements (Aalen, 1997). With few exceptions, the bulk of the native terrestrial fauna has suffered range contraction and population fragmentation due, in large measure, to habitat loss and to the impacts of an increasingly mechanised agricultural system (Purcell, 1996). Over the centuries various species have been introduced by humans to Ireland. While the extinction of species can occur as a result of climatic changes (e.g. lemmings, the

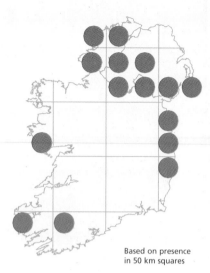

Based on presence in 50 km squares

Red deer (*Cervus elaphus*)
One of six species occurring and the only one present before the last Glacial maximum but it may have become extinct and also have been introduced by man. It was relatively abundant and widespread in the middle ages but was hunted almost to extinction by the middle of the 19th century. Since then reintroduction to Donegal, from Britain, and escapes from deer parks have led to a number of distinct populations, which can be shown scientifically to differ from a Co. Kerry wild population.
Sources: Mitchell-Jones et al., *1999; T.J. Hayden, pers. comm.*

Fig 12.7 Distribution of Red Deer

giant Irish deer and the reindeer), human influence can be cited as the main cause in the recent past. Some examples of extinctions and introductions are given in Fig. 12.8

Human influences, such as fire and grazing by livestock, have also helped to shape the landscape. Paradoxically this has been in part responsible for creating one of the jewels in the Irish landscape, the Burren in Co. Clare,

beaked dolphin, Risso's dolphin, killer whale, pilot whale and minke whale. Although the Worldwide Fund for Nature (WWF) has included the harbour porpoise among its 10 most endangered faunal species it is by far the most common cetacean in Irish waters and is usually found close inshore. South-west Ireland is considered to be a breeding ground (Berrow, 1990; Rogan and Berrow, 1995). The Shannon estuary hosts a resident population of bottle-nosed dolphins; one of only five known resident populations in Europe.

which would revert to scrub if winter grazing by cattle of the pavements ceased (Nelson, 1991).

Not all grazing effects, however, have benefited the Irish landscape. Overgrazing caused by the gross overstocking of sheep has been identified as one of the most important threats to habitats and biodiversity in Ireland. As discussed in Chapter 11, the effects of overgrazing have been most marked along the western seaboard, but no upland area has escaped and it can be said that sheep are inappropriate on the dwarf shrub communities in nearly all upland areas (R. Harrington, pers. comm.). The original Rural Environment Protection Scheme (REPS) was not successful in redressing the overgrazing problem. It is anticipated that the modifications to REPS combined with the introduction of the SAC programme, Commonage Framework Plans and the introduction of further cross-compliance controls in 1998 should greatly assist in alleviating the serious overgrazing problem (DAHGI, 1999).

The European Commission has decided to make an application to the European Court of Justice against Ireland for non-respect of the European Union's wild birds Directive. The decision concerns the failure to curb sheep overgrazing, particularly in the west of Ireland,

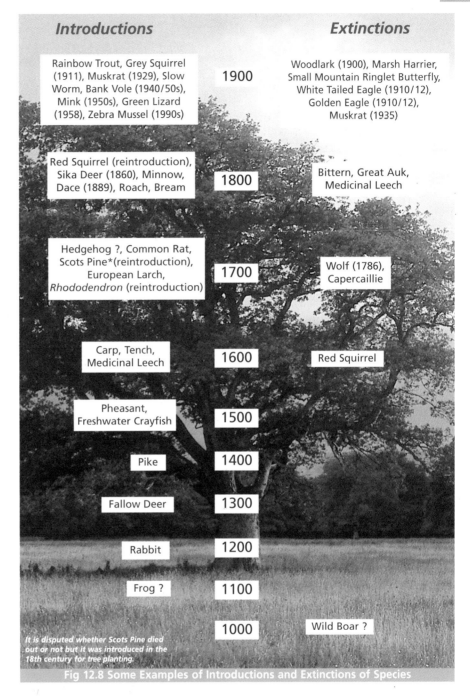

Introductions		Extinctions
Rainbow Trout, Grey Squirrel (1911), Muskrat (1929), Slow Worm, Bank Vole (1940/50s), Mink (1950s), Green Lizard (1958), Zebra Mussel (1990s)	1900	Woodlark (1900), Marsh Harrier, Small Mountain Ringlet Butterfly, White Tailed Eagle (1910/12), Golden Eagle (1910/12), Muskrat (1935)
Red Squirrel (reintroduction), Sika Deer (1860), Minnow, Dace (1889), Roach, Bream	1800	Bittern, Great Auk, Medicinal Leech
Hedgehog ?, Common Rat, Scots Pine*(reintroduction), European Larch, *Rhododendron* (reintroduction)	1700	Wolf (1786), Capercaillie
Carp, Tench, Medicinal Leech	1600	Red Squirrel
Pheasant, Freshwater Crayfish	1500	
Pike	1400	
Fallow Deer	1300	
Rabbit	1200	
Frog ?	1100	
	1000	Wild Boar ?

It is disputed whether Scots Pine died out or not but it was introduced in the 18th century for tree planting.

Fig 12.8 Some Examples of Introductions and Extinctions of Species

leading to serious damage to Ireland's largest SPA, the Owenduff-Nephin Beg Complex in Co. Mayo, as well as wider loss of the habitat of the red grouse.

REPS has provision for payments to farmers and landowners where areas fall within NHAs, SACs or Commonages (DAF, 1999). Among the objectives of REPS are to establish farming practices and production methods that reflect the increasing concern for conservation, landscape protection and wider

Table 12.5 Damaging Activities in Coastal Protected Areas			
Activity	**Impact (per cent)***		
	NHA	**SAC**	**SPA**
Grazing	46.0	73.0	35.5
Dumping	40.2	56.2	35.5
Water polluting activities	28.9	37.5	42.0
Littering	26.6	35.9	63.0
Agricultural improvement	26.0	39.0	26.6
Natural spread of unwanted species	25.4	32.8	42.2
Building/Civil engineering	21.8	37.5	26.6
Drainage	18.9	31.0	24.4
Infill/Reclamation	18.3	21.8	44.4
Fertiliser application/drift	17.0	29.0	11.1
Camping/caravanning	16.5	34.0	6.6
Other Recreation	16.5	29.0	15.5
Removal of beach material	15.9	23.4	15.5
Aquaculture	13.6	14.0	20.0
Golf	13.0	29.0	17.7
No observable impacts	5.9	1.5	0.0

*Percentage of proposed designated coastal sites subject to impacts
Neff, in press

environmental problems as well as to protect wildlife habitats and endangered species of flora and fauna (Box 12.11).

In the period between 1960 and 1990 the production of silage became widespread (Chapter 3). The indoor wintering of cattle and the need to conserve fodder, particularly silage, and the change from hay to silage making have led to a loss of both plant and animal diversity from hay meadows.

Dúchas has initiated an inter-sectoral resource management project including restoration ecology and the reinstatement of habitats. Restoration ecology projects are underway to develop economic alternatives to existing upland use and overgrazing problems through the use of traditional cattle breeds and reinstatement of native woodlands. The issue of extensive cattle grazing in particular the over-wintering of cattle on standing crop vegetation is part of this initiative (R. Harrington, pers. comm.).

Ecological corridors (which can vary from a 5 metre-wide roadside strip to a kilometres-wide landscape) have been recommended as a solution to the fragmentation of European habitats and their potential for habitat and species conservation in Ireland has been reviewed (Good, 1998). Examples of man-made ecological corridors are the canals and railways.

A study of coastal sites, carried out on behalf of the Heritage Council (Neff, in press), showed that not only were many non-designated areas virtually beyond recovery but that many of the proposed designated areas already had significant impairment. Table 12.5 shows the percentage of sites subject to the 15 most common damaging activities in coastal NHAs, SACs and SPAs as a whole. The study found that agricultural practices account for the major impacts with grazing effects the most significant.

There have been success stories in the last decade such as the conservation of the remaining peatlands and the stabilisation of corncrake numbers. Yet in both of these examples some, or all, of the financial support came from outside Ireland.

Ongoing Dúchas projects and programmes relate *inter alia* to a wide variety of species and habitat surveys, management plans for sites, including SACs and SPAs, zoning estuarine SPAs for aquaculture, database development, monitoring and remote sensing in the terrestrial, freshwater and marine environments. The Heritage Council, as well as carrying out its own work programme, sponsors research work on all aspects of the national heritage including the natural environment. One of the

Box 12.11 Rural Environmental Protection Scheme and Biodiversity

The objective of the measure in REPS covering the natural heritage is to retain certain listed habitats and to control commercial farming practices on these areas in the interests of wildlife (flora and fauna) and conservation generally. The habitats to be retained are: callows, turloughs and other seasonally flooded areas; marshes and swamps; peatlands (including raised bog, cut-over bog, blanket bog or moors and fens); sand-dunes, foreshore and sea-shore; machairs; eskers; natural or semi-natural vegetation; woodlands; scrubland; lakes, ponds, rivers and streams; field boundaries/margins, hedgerows and stonewalls; old buildings inhabited by protected species such as barn owls and bats; disused quarries and such workings which have become habitats.

Under the scheme the following practices cannot be carried out in such areas:
- afforestation;
- land improvement works including drainage;
- ploughing and re-seeding;
- interference with the free-flow of waters to "swallow holes" in turloughs;
- removal of sand and gravel from foreshore and sea-shore;
- commercial turf cutting on unexploited bog;
- burning of growing vegetation on land between April 1st and August 30th.

Source: DAF, 1999

Government's millennium projects has included the planting of a million oak trees throughout the country and the enhancement and conservation of native woodlands.

One further aspect of natural heritage and biodiversity is genetic diversity. Little is known about genetic variation in the wild in Ireland and genetic diversity below the species level has received little attention. The exceptions, of course, are in plant and animal husbandry where species and varieties have been changed over the years to increase yield. This should not be confused with DNA manipulation in farmed situations. There is much concern among the public regarding genetically modified organisms (GMOs) as discussed earlier in Chapter 7.

Ireland's booming tourism industry (Chapter 3) poses a threat to the island's natural heritage and biodiversity. What were regarded as remote places some 50 years ago have now become accessible to the tourist and tripper. Most tourists are attracted by the landscape and there must be a case for at least one natural World Heritage Site designation in the Republic of Ireland. Prospective candidates could include the Burren in Co. Clare and Valentia Island in Co. Kerry to accompany Newgrange in Co. Meath and Skellig Michael in Co. Kerry which were designated as cultural sites, in the UNESCO World Heritage List, respectively in 1993 and 1996.

CONCLUSIONS

It has not been possible, except in general terms, to assess Ireland's biodiversity. We do not know precisely what it entails. Inadequate data is a serious problem in Ireland. Among the main problems faced by researchers is how to measure biological diversity and there is an urgent need to define a common methodology to evaluate the various forms of biodiversity. Furthermore, in the Republic of Ireland there is no biological records centre. There is a strong case for a centrally co-ordinated approach to the collection and collation of species records in Ireland, particularly for lower plant groups such as fungi and algae (Neff, 1996). A properly resourced central records database for all plant and animal groups is essential if species diversity is to be properly monitored.

The absence of a standard approach to habitat classification has been identified as a key area for concern in relation to co-ordination of data collection on wildlife and the natural environment. The Heritage Council has been endeavouring to develop a standard approach to habitat classification and to provide standard guidelines for recording, classifying and describing Irish wildlife habitats (Heritage Council, in prep).

The putting in place of the structures for protection of the natural heritage and biodiversity in Ireland has been slow to progress. However, what has been achieved here in the past was with much less resources, pro rata, than in most other EU Member States. Although it should have been anticipated, an additional factor leading to delays in, for example, the notification of SACs to the European Commission, is the due process of appeals. Perhaps the best barometer on which to judge the extent of commitment to conservation is by the amount of monies allocated. Direct spending by Dúchas on nature conservation was under £7 million in 1993 but by 1998 the allocation was almost £25 million (DAHGI, 1999). While a large portion of the budget is currently used to compensate landowners the increase in spending does reflect the seriousness with which the natural heritage and biodiversity are now regarded. Equally to be welcomed is the more transparent and open approach adopted in recent years to nature protection in which the public is being better informed. It could therefore be concluded that aspects of the natural heritage are, at the beginning of this new millennium, being better resourced than in the past.

REFERENCES

Aalen, F.H.A. 1997. The Irish rural landscape: synthesis of habitat and history. In: F.H.A. Aalen, K. Whelan and M. Stout (eds.) *Atlas of the Irish rural landscape*, pp. 4-30. University Press, Cork.

Ashe, P., O'Connor, J.P. and Murray, D.A. 1998. A checklist of Irish aquatic insects. *Occasional publication of the Irish Biogeographical Society.* 3, pp. 1-80.

Berrow, S. and Heardman, C. 1994. The basking shark *Cetorhinus maximus* (Gunnerus) in Irish waters - patterns of distribution and abundance. *Biology and Environment. Proceedings of the Royal Irish Academy.* 94B, pp. 101-107.

Berrow, S. and Heardman, C. 1995. Basking sharks *Cetorhinus maximus* Gunnerus, stranded on the Irish coast. *Irish Naturalists' Journal.* 25, p. 152.

Bowman, J.J. and Bracken, J. 1993. Effect of run-off from afforested and non-afforested catchments on the survival of brown trout *Salmo trutta* L. in two acid-sensitive rivers in Wicklow, Ireland. *Biology and Environment. Proceedings of the Royal Irish Academy.* 93B, pp. 143-150.

Buckley, P. 1998. Legislation and protected areas for the conservation of biological diversity. In: Deevey, M.B. (comp.). *Irish heritage and environmental directory 1999.* pp. 13-30. The Heritage Council & Archaeology Ireland, Bray.

Cabot, D. 1965. The green lizard, *Lacerta viridis*, in Ireland. *Irish Naturalists' Journal.* 15, p. 111.

Caffrey, J. 1999. The hogweed hazard. *Technology Ireland.* March, pp. 16-18.

Cawley, M. 1996. Notes on some non-marine Mollusca from Co Sligo and Co Leitrim, including a new site for *Vertigo geyeri* Lindholm. *Irish Naturalists' Journal.* 25, pp. 183-185.

CEC (Council of the European Communities), 1979. Council Directive of 2 April 1979 on the conservation of wild birds (79/409/EEC). *O. J.* L 103/1, 25 April 1979.

CEC (Council of the European Communities), 1992. Council Directive of 21 May 1992 on the conservation of natural habitats and of wild fauna and flora (92/43/EEC). *O. J.* L 206/35, 22 July 1992.

Champ, W.S.T. 1998. Phosphorus/chlorophyll relationships in selected Irish lakes: ecological consequences and suggested criteria for ecosystem management. In: Wilson, J.G. (ed.) *Eutrophication in Irish waters*, pp. 91-105. Royal Irish Academy, Dublin.

Curtis, T.G.F. and Harrington, T.J. 1987. A second station for *Ranunculus tripartitus* DC. in Kerry (H1). *Irish Naturalists' Journal.* 22, p. 204.

Curtis, T.G.F. and McGough, H.N. 1988. *The Irish red data book. I. Vascular plants.* Stationery Office, Dublin.
D'Arcy, G. 1999. *Ireland's lost wild birds.* Four Courts Press, Dublin.

DAF (Department of Agriculture and Food), 1999. *Rural Environment Protection Scheme: Agri-Environmental Specifications.* European Commission: Implementation of Council Regulation (EEC) No. 2078/92.

DAHGI (Department of Arts, Heritage, Gaeltacht and the Islands), 1999. *National Report Ireland 1998. First national report on the implementation of the Convention on Biological Diversity by Ireland.* Department of Arts, Heritage, Gaeltacht and the Islands, Dublin.

Douglas, C. 1998. Blanket bog conservation. In: O'Leary, G. and Gormley, F. (eds.) *Towards a conservation strategy for the bogs of Ireland*, pp. 205-222. Irish Peatland Conservation Council, Dublin.

Farrell, L. and Randell, R.E. 1992. The distribution of *Mertensia maritima* (L.) Gray, Oyster plant, in Ireland. *Irish Naturalists' Journal.* 24, pp. 135-140.

Feehan, J. 1997. The heritage of the rocks. In: Foster, J.W. and Chesney, H.C.G. (eds.)

Nature in Ireland: a scientific and cultural history, pp. 3-22. Lilliput Press, Dublin.

Gittings, T., O'Keefe, D., Gallagher, F., Finn, J. O'Mahony, T. 1998. Longitudinal variation in abundance of a freshwater pearl mussel *Margaritifera margaritifera* population in relation to riverine habitats. *Biology and Environment: Proceedings of the Royal Irish Academy*, 98B, pp. 171-178.

Good, J.A. 1998. *The potential role of ecological corridors for habitat conservation in Ireland: a review.* Irish Wildlife Manuals, No.2. Dúchas, The Heritage Service, Dublin.

Grist, B., 1997. Wildlife legislation - the rocky road to special areas of conservation surveyed. *Irish Planning and Environmental Law Journal.* 4, pp. 87-95.

Hackney, P. (ed.) 1992. *Stewert & Corry's Flora of the North-east of Ireland.* Institute of Irish Studies, The Queen's University, Belfast.

Hatch, P. and Healy, B. 1998. Aquatic Vegetation of Irish Coastal Lagoons. *Bulletin of the Irish Biogeographical Society.* 21, pp. 2-21.

Healy, B. 1999. *Survey of Irish Coastal Lagoons: background, description and summary.* Dúchas, The Heritage Service, Dublin.

Healy, B. and Oliver, G.A. 1998. Irish coastal lagoons: summary of a survey. *Bulletin of the Irish Biogeographical Society.* 21, pp. 116-150.

Heritage Council, in prep. *A Guide to Ireland's Habitats.* Heritage Council, Kilkenny.

Heritage Council, 1998. *Impact of current forestry policy on aspects of Ireland's heritage.* A report prepared by Environmental Resources Management for the Heritage Council, Kilkenny.

Kerney, M. 1999. *Atlas of the land and freshwater molluscs of Britain and Ireland.* Harley Books, Colchester in association with the Conchological Society of Great Britain and Ireland.

Kurz, I. and Costello, M.J. 1999. *An outline of the biology, distribution and conservation of lampreys in Ireland.* Irish Wildlife Manuals, No.5. Dúchas, The Heritage Service, Dublin.

Lucey, J. 1993. The distribution of *Margaritifera margaritifera* (L.) in southern

Irish rivers and streams. *Journal of Conchology.* 34, pp. 301-310.

Lucey, J. 1994. Records of the giant hogweed, *Heracleum mantegazzianum*, along southern Irish rivers and streams with a revised distribution map for the region. *Bulletin of the Irish Biogeographical Society.* 17, pp. 2-6.

Lucey, J. 1998. *Azolla filiculoides* Lam. (water fern) in fresh and brackish water in E. Cork (v.c. H5). *Irish Botanical News.* 8, pp. 5-7.

Lucey, J. 1999a. River bloom generates much interest. *Kilkenny People.* 17 September, p. 20.

Lucey, J. 1999b. A chronological account of the crayfish *Austopotamobius pallipes* (Lereboullet) in Ireland. *Bulletin of the Irish Biogeographical Society.* 23, pp. 143-161.

Lucey, J., Bowman, J.J., Clabby, K.J., Cunningham, P., Lehane, M., MacCárthaigh, M., McGarrigle, M.L. and Toner, P.F. 1999. *Water quality in Ireland 1995-1997.* Environmental Protection Agency, Wexford.

Lucey, J. and Nolan, K. 1996. Natural heritage. In: Stapleton L. (ed.) *State of the Environment in Ireland*, pp. 160-183. Environmental Protection Agency, Wexford.

Lunnon, R. 1996. Otter *(Lutra lutra* L.) distribution in Ireland. In: Reynolds, J.D. (ed.) *The conservation of aquatic systems*, pp. 111-116. Royal Irish Academy, Dublin.

Maitland, P.S. 1996. Threatened fishes of the British Isles, with special reference to Ireland. In: Reynolds, J.D. (ed.) *The conservation of aquatic systems*, pp. 84-100. Royal Irish Academy, Dublin.

Marine Institute, 1999. *Ireland's marine and coastal areas: an environmental assessment.* Prepared by the Marine Institute on behalf of the Department of Environment & Local Government and the Department of Marine & Natural Resources, Ireland. Marine Institute, Dublin.

Marnell, F. 1996. Aspects of the population ecology of smooth newts *Triturus vulgaris* L. at a pond in County Dublin. *Biology and Environment: Proceedings of the Royal Irish Academy.* 96B, pp. 113-116.

Marnell, F. 1998a. Discriminant analysis of the terrestrial and aquatic habitat determinants of the smooth newt *(Triturus vulgaris)* and the common frog *(Rana*

temporaria) in Ireland. *Journal of Zoology, London.* 244, pp. 1-6.

Marnell, F. 1998b. The distribution of the smooth newt, *Triturus vulgaris* L., in Ireland. *Bulletin of the Irish Biogeographical Society.* 22, pp. 84-96.

McAney, C.M. 1994. The lesser horseshoe bat in Ireland - past, present and future. *Folia Zoologica*, 43, pp. 387-392.

McGuire, C. 1998. Survey of lesser horseshoe bats *Rhinolophus hipposideros* (Bechstein) and other bat species in north Co Clare, Ireland. *Irish Naturalists' Journal.* 26, pp. 43-50.

Merryweather, J. and Hill, M. 1992. The fern guide: an introductory guide to the ferns, clubmosses, quillworts and horsetails of the British Isles. *Field Studies.* 8, pp. 101-188.

Mitchell-Jones A.J., Amori, G., Bogdanowicz, W., Kryπtufek, B., Reijnders, P. J., Spitzenberger, F., Stubbe, M., Thissen, J.B.M., Vohralík, V. and Zima, J., 1999. *The Atlas of European Mammals.* T. & A.D. Poyser, London.

Moorkens, E.A. and Costello, M.J. 1994. Imminent extinction of the Nore freshwater pearl mussel *Margaritifera durrovensis* Phillips: a species unique to Ireland. *Aquatic Conservation: Marine and Freshwater Ecosystems* 5, pp. 363-365.

Neff, J. 1996. *Biodiversity in Ireland: a review of species diversity in the Irish flora.* For the Heritage Policy Unit of the Department of Arts, Culture and the Gaeltacht, Dublin.

Neff, J. in press. *Irish coastal habitats: a study of impacts on designated conservation areas.* Heritage Council, Kilkenny.

Nelson, E.C. 1991. *The Burren: a companion to the wildflowers of an Irish limestone wilderness.* Boethius Press, Aberystwyth and Kilkenny.

Nelson, E.C. and Walsh, W. 1993. *Trees of Ireland.* Lilliput Press, Dublin.

Ó Críodáin, C. and Doyle, G. 1997. *Schoenetum nigricantis*, the *Schoenus* fen and flush vegetation of Ireland. *Proceedings of the Royal Irish Academy.* 97B, pp. 203-218.

O'Gorman, C. 1998. *Home range and habitat use by the endangered Grey Partridge (Perdix perdix) in the Irish Midlands.* A report submitted to the University of Dublin in partial fulfilment of the requirement to transfer to a Doctoral degree in Zoology. Royal College of Surgeons in Ireland, Dublin.

O'Sullivan, A. 1999. Ireland. In: Parviainen, J., Little, D., Doyle, M., O'Sullivan, A., Kettunen, M. and Korhonen, M. (eds.). *Research in forest reserves and natural forests in European countries – country reports for the COST Action E4: Forest Reserves Research Network*, pp. 145-161. Proceedings No. 16. European Forest Institute, Torikatu.

O'Sullivan, P. 1994. Bats in Ireland. *Irish Naturalists' Journal. Special Zoological Supplement*, pp. 1-21.

Parkes, M. and Morris, J. 1999. Protecting our geological heritage. *Irish Scientist Year Book.* 7, p. 76.

Platts, E.A. and Speight, M.C.D. 1988. The taxonomy and distribution of the Kerry slug *Geomalacus maculosus* Allman, 1843 (Mollusca: Arionidae) with a discussion of its status as a threatened species. *Irish Naturalists' Journal.* pp. 22, 417-430.

Preston, C.D. and Croft, J.M. 1997. *Aquatic plants in Britain and Ireland.* Harley Books, Colchester.

Purcell, P. 1996. *Biodiversity in Ireland: an inventory of biological diversity on a taxonomic basis. Fauna.* Report submitted to the Heritage Policy Unit, Department of the Arts, Culture and the Gaeltacht, Dublin.

Reynolds, J.D. 1996. Turloughs, their significance and possibilities for conservation. In: Reynolds, J.D. (ed.) *The conservation of aquatic systems,* pp. 38-46. Royal Irish Academy, Dublin.

Reynolds, S. 1997a. Report for Co. Limerick (v.c. H8), 1996. *Irish Botanical News.* 7, pp. 39-42.

Reynolds, S. 1997b. Alien plants at Foynes Port, Co. Limerick (v.c. H8), 1988-1994. *Watsonia.* 21, pp. 283-285.

Rich, T.C.G., Kay, G.M. and Kirschner, J. 1995. Floating water-plantain *Luronium natans* (L.) Raf. (Alismataceae) present in Ireland. *Irish Naturalists' Journal.* 25, pp. 140-145.

Roden, C. 2000. *A survey of coastal lakes in Cos. Galway, Mayo, Sligo and Donegal.* Report to the Heritage Council, Kilkenny.

Rogan, E. and Berrow, D. 1995. The management of Irish waters as a whale and dolphin sanctuary. In: Blix, A.S., Walløe, L. and Ulltang, Ø. (eds.) *Developments in Marine Biology. 4. Whales, seals, fish and man.* pp. 671-81. Proceedings of the International Symposium on the Biology of Marine Mammals in the Northeast Atlantic. Tromsø, Norway, 29 November-1 December, 1994. Elsevier, Amsterdam.

Seaward, M.R.D. 1994. Vice-county distribution of Irish lichens. *Biology and Environment. Proceedings of the Royal Irish Academy.* 94B, pp. 177-194.

Smith, S.J. and Wolfe-Murphy, S.A. 1991. *Ceratophyllum submersum* L. soft hornwort, a species new to Ireland. *Irish Naturalists' Journal.* 23, pp. 374-376.
Stewart, N.F. and Church, J.M. 1992. *Red data books of Britain and Ireland: Stoneworts.* Joint Nature Conservation Committee, Peterborough.

Wade, M., Darby, E.J., Courtney, A.D. and Caffrey, J.M. 1997. *Heracleum mantegazzianum*: a problem for river managers in the Republic of Ireland and the United Kingdom. In: Brock, J.H., *et al.*

(eds) *Plant invasions: studies from North America and Europe,* pp. 139-151. Backhuys Publishers, Leiden.

Webb, D.A., Parnell, J. and Doogue, D. 1996. *An Irish Flora.* Dundalgan Press.

Whilde, A. 1993. *Threatened mammals, wild birds, amphibians and fish in Ireland. Irish Red Data Book 2: Vertebrates.* HMSO, Belfast.

Wilson, J.P.F. 1986. The post-glacial colonisation of Ireland by fish, amphibians and reptiles. In: Sleeman, D.P., Devoy, R.J. and Woodman, P.C. (eds.) *Proceedings of the Postglacial Colonisation Conference, pp. 53-58.* Occasional publication of the Irish Biogeographical Society, No. 1.

Wilson, J.G. and Lawler, I. 1996. Irish marine habitats. In: Reynolds, J.D. (ed.) *The conservation of aquatic systems,* pp. 47-55. Royal Irish Academy, Dublin.

Wyse Jackson, M. 1989. Observations on the Irish distribution of a plant with serious public health implications: giant hogweed (*Heracleum mantegazzianum* Sommier and Levier). *Bulletin of the Irish Biogeographical Society.* 12, pp. 94-111.

PART V

Environmental Protection and the Future

CHAPTER 13

IRELAND'S ENVIRONMENT: THE MAIN ISSUES

The main environmental issues in Ireland are eutrophication of inland waters, the increase in the amounts of waste, the deterioration of the urban environment and allied transport problems and the need to reduce emissions of greenhouse gases. Depletion of natural resources is a further matter of concern. These problems are a product of the increased economic activity of the last thirty years and mirror similar though earlier changes in other countries. However, the scale of the problems here is still moderate and, in general, the quality of the Irish environment remains relatively good and compares favourably with that of other EU States.

INTRODUCTION

Ireland is favoured by a number of circumstances which mitigate or lessen the potential impacts of environmental pressures. These include the predominance of westerly winds originating as clean air masses over the Atlantic, a high rainfall and a population density that, in European terms, is still relatively low. To these natural advantages one might add the poorly developed industrial and agricultural activities that obtained until the 1960s. It is not surprising, therefore, that the health of the natural environment became a matter of public concern in Ireland only in recent decades and that systematic monitoring and other investigations on a national basis commenced as late as the 1970s. Since that time, developments in the agricultural and industrial sectors, in particular, as well as increases in population and urbanisation have created a greater potential for environmental damage. As has been shown in the preceding chapters, this potential has been realised in several cases and parallels, to some extent, that which happened at an earlier stage of the twentieth century in most other European States.

A further factor that changed the status of environmental matters in Ireland was the accession of the State

to the then European Economic Community in 1972. This not only led to the acquisition of financial aids for economic development, particularly in the agricultural sector, but also required the State to adhere to various directives dealing with environmental quality and allied matters. This in turn prompted further investigation and monitoring and, in addition, fostered a public interest in and concern for environmental quality. It is possible that Ireland would have suffered greater damage to its environment, comparable to that which affected some other fast developing states in

the same period, were it not for its membership of the European Union.

While much play has been made about the State's currently high rate of development, it must not be forgotten that this largely reflects the relatively low base from which it commenced. In terms of infrastructure such as roads and public transport, the wealth of the State still lags behind many of its European neighbours while the scale of industrial development, the overall intensity of agriculture and the population density also remain moderate compared to the position in the latter countries. Consequently, the threat to the environment that such factors generate also remains relatively modest. It is worth noting too that the late development of much of the industrial sector here, as well as the lack of those basic resources, such as coal and iron, which facilitate the more polluting types of industrial activities, has greatly reduced the importance of that sector as a threat to the Irish environment when compared to its

past impact in most other EU States. However, industrial development is still a controversial matter in many areas of the country and many are not convinced that it can operate in a benign manner, especially in rural areas (see Box 13.1).

In general, therefore, the pressures on the Irish environment, while increasing significantly in the last thirty years, have not reached and perhaps are now not likely to reach, the intensity that they had already achieved in the first part of the twentieth century in many other countries of Europe. Thus the requirement for many aspects of the Irish environment is the maintenance of existing high quality conditions or the elimination of the relatively minor degree of deterioration that has occurred. In some cases, the latter aim may be as difficult to achieve as the restoration to an acceptable condition of highly polluted or otherwise disturbed environments and may not be justifiable on cost grounds. It is worth noting that environmental monitoring and investigations commenced in the State before pressures increased significantly from the relatively low level characteristic of the first part of the century. Thus, Ireland may have documented those initial phases of environmental deterioration that occurred much earlier in the more industrialised and heavily populated areas of Europe and which have, perhaps, gone largely unrecorded. This is particularly the case for inland surface waters where there has been a notable decline in quality over the last 30 years but where conditions remain, in general, better than those in most of the other Member States of the EU.

The following sections review the main issues of current concern in the environmental area, based on the material presented in the foregoing chapters. These concerns have been identified by McCumiskey (1998) as follows: the eutrophication of inland surface waters; the disposal of waste; the urban environment and transport; and the reduction of greenhouse gas emissions. To these might be added the depletion of natural resources which is starting to emerge as a significant environmental issue. Future perspectives in relation to these matters are dealt with separately in Chapter 16. Firstly, however, the question of human health must be addressed as this will always be the chief concern where the integrity of the environment is threatened, especially by pollution.

HUMAN HEALTH

Public health in Ireland, like that in other developed states, is greatly improved compared to the situation even 50 years ago, and the main threats now come from personal habits in regard to factors such as diet, use of cigarettes and alcohol and exercise. In general, environmental pollution would not now be viewed as a major threat to health although modern life has brought some potentially new threats, the risks from

---

Box 13.1 Industry and the Rural Environment

Compared to most other Member States of the EU, Ireland is still largely a rural country with a relatively small fraction of the land surface given over to urban and industrial activities. Apart from the processing of agriculture produce, the extent of industrial activities in the rural areas was limited up to recent decades. This has changed since the 1960s with the locating of a variety of manufacturing plants in areas previously devoted solely to farming. While the scale of such development remains modest compared to the situation in the more heavily industrialised states of the EU, it has changed the perception of the areas involved in respect of environmental purity. Often, this perception is not helped by industrial accidents which, while not having a significant impact on the environment, may lead to a lack of confidence among the local population in the management of the plant. The following are examples of the several investigations undertaken in recent years to address such concerns.

Askeaton Animal Health Investigations: These investigations were carried out between 1995 and 1998 to determine the causes of serious animal health problems on two farms in the Askeaton area of Co. Limerick. There were reports of similar problems on 25 other farms and, in addition, concerns were expressed regarding human health. An opinion had formed locally that environmental pollution was involved and the main focus, in this respect, was on the nearby alumina production plant. While the final report on the investigations is not available at the time of writing, interim reports (EPA, 1995, 1997a, 1998a) state that evidence has not been found which would substantiate the suggestion that environmental pollution is involved. Arising from this investigation, a protocol was drawn up to ensure an early and structured response to investigating similar situations in future (EPA, 1997b).

Farm at Clonmel: The owner of a farm in the vicinity of a pharmaceutical plant near Clonmel, Co. Tipperary, reported animal and human health problems on his property in the early 1980s. Investigations carried out by various agencies did not establish a clear connection between emissions from the factory and the effects described. Subsequently the farmer sought damages in the courts against the owners of the plant. The case was rejected by the High Court but won on appeal to the Supreme Court and substantial damages were paid. The Supreme Court, in considering evidence that certain waste containment practices at the plant had been defective, took the view that, on the balance of probability, its emissions were implicated in the health problems on the farm.

Sentinel Herd Scheme, Cork: In view of the build up of industrial activity in the Cork Harbour area in the 1970s and 1980s, the local authority instigated a scheme to monitor key animal health indicators in a number of local dairy herds. The scheme has now been taken over by the EPA following the introduction of the Integrated Pollution Control licensing system which is required for the types of industries involved. To date, there have been no indications from the monitoring of any adverse impacts on animal health arising from the industrial activity.

which have yet to be fully evaluated. However, where direct impacts of environmental pollution on human health do occur, they are still likely to arise mainly from contamination of waters and air.

Contamination of water supplies caused major problems for public health in many European countries in the past and continues to do so in large areas of the developing world today. In Ireland, incidents in recent years involving the water supplies to Naas in Co. Kildare and Nenagh in Co. Tipperary illustrated the severe disruption to daily life that arises when such vital services are rendered unfit for use. These were localised events and, in view of the general abundance of clean water in Ireland, it is somewhat unexpected that recent reports on the quality of drinking water in the State have recorded significant breaches of the EU limits, in particular that for faecal coliforms. This is largely a problem with the privately operated group schemes and reflects contaminated source waters or poor treatment or a combination of these factors. The sources for most of these private supplies are groundwaters and, as has been shown by the monitoring programmes undertaken in recent years (Chapter 9), the presence of faecal coliform in such waters is not uncommon and indicates a risk of illness in consumers. It is noted that co-ordinated efforts are presently in train to address this problem, the solution to which involves the protection of sources and proper maintenance of draw-off and treatment facilities.

The quality of the public supplies is much more satisfactory and clearly there would be advantages in having a greater proportion of the population served by the public system, wherever this is feasible. However, even the public supplies may be affected by emerging problems such as the presence of algal toxins in waters drawn particularly from eutrophic waters or the

formation of potentially carcinogenic substances, such as chloroform, in the treatment of water from similar sources. In addition, there are new risks arising from micro-organisms such as the protozoan *Cryptosporidium* which have caused major episodes of human illness in the UK and USA. Large sales of bottled water and other anecdotal evidence suggest that there is a measure of distrust in some segments of the population regarding the wholesomeness of the public supplies, perhaps arising in part at least from the publicity surrounding the defects in the private supplies. Protection of sources and the provision of rigorous treatment will, therefore, be increasingly important considerations in the supply of this basic service.

The health risk from air pollution arises mainly in the larger urban areas and here the bans on the sale of bituminous coal in a number of these areas, introduced in the 1990s, have had a major impact in reducing the levels of particulate matter in the air, especially in Dublin. There was some evidence prior to the ban that increased morbidity and deaths were occurring at times of high pollution levels in the Dublin area, as had been recorded in many other large European cities earlier in the century, most notably in London in the 1950s. Similarly, the potential threat from lead in air, to children in particular, has been greatly reduced by the phasing out of leaded petrol. The EU Framework Directive on

ambient air quality assessment and management, introduced in 1996, is now setting additional and more stringent standards for air quality and, as shown in Chapter 8, there are indications that some of these limits would not be achieved under existing conditions in the urban areas. Of particular note in this context is fine particulate matter (PM_{10}); research indicates that it is particulates of this size and smaller which are most likely to cause the respiratory and related illnesses associated with air pollution. Fuel combustion in vehicles is a major source of these pollutants and any improvements required will have implications, therefore, for road traffic (see below).

Other common risks to human health arising from environmental pollution are bathing in natural waters and consumption of shellfish. The bathing waters of the State appear to present little risk, based on current EU criteria (see Chapter 10) although there has been some questioning of the efficacy of the faecal coliforms as indicator organisms used to assess the likelihood of the presence of pathogens. The risk from the consumption of shellfish arises mainly where live organisms, such as oysters, are eaten. Shellfish waters appear to be in a less satisfactory state than bathing waters as, for most of the production areas, prior purification of the molluscs must be provided before they are offered for sale (see Table 10.1, Chapter 10). There have been some cases of sickness in consumers in recent years involving oysters taken from Irish waters, a development which is clearly inimical to the promotion of the shellfish rearing industry as one for which Irish waters are particularly suited. Conditions in some of these shellfish areas, and bathing areas, will be improved by the sewage treatment plants presently under construction in all of the major coastal towns (see Chapter 5).

The importance of other forms of environmental contamination for human health is less well understood so that it is difficult to assess the risks they present. Concern has been expressed regarding the large number of synthetic chemicals now in use and the lack of information on the toxicity of many of these substances (EEA, 1999a). A particular concern has arisen in recent years regarding the apparent capability of certain chemicals to influence the activity of the hormones controlling the reproductive system or to induce cancers (see Chapter 7). While such effects have not yet been clearly demonstrated in humans there are suspicions that certain trends, e.g., decreasing sperm counts reported in some countries, may be a manifestation of the phenomenon. Besides pollutants, other aspects of the environment, particularly noise and odours, may create nuisance for sensitive individuals and this in turn can induce stress with adverse implications for personal health.

In general, the role, if any, of these and other environmental disturbances

in public health problems remain to be assessed in any detail in Ireland but it is reasonable to assume that as the State approaches the level of development of its European partners they will become matters of increasing concern. However, it may be difficult to identify any links between environmental quality and human health due to confounding factors and the length of time needed for some adverse effects to develop (EEA, 1999b).

EUTROPHICATION OF INLAND WATERS

The eutrophication of rivers and lakes probably represents the most serious environmental pollution problem currently affecting the State. This assessment is a recognition of the relatively large proportion of the surface waters affected and the fact that the position is continuing to worsen. While the intensity of the effect, as pointed out in Chapter 9, is moderate in many cases, the resulting changes in the aquatic ecosystem are inimicable to the game fish populations endemic in most Irish waters. The presence of healthy populations of these fish is an important indicator of the overall quality of the surface waters and the suitability of these resources for various uses.

Eutrophication of waters is, perhaps, a classic example of the impact of economic development on the environment. In most cases, excess phosphorus is the primary cause of the

problem and is contributed to, in this respect, by nearly all sectors of economic activity, domestic, public, industrial and agricultural. Besides the main sources, such as discharges of sewage and industrial wastes and the losses from agricultural land, fish farming, forestry development and even road building and other types of land disturbance may lead to phosphorus enrichment of waters on a local level. As the scale of economic activity increases, the potential sources of phosphorus loss to waters also increase, e.g., through increased use of detergents and fertilisers.

Estimates (see Chapter 5) suggest that agriculture is responsible for by far the largest input of phosphorus to inland waters, accounting for 73 per cent of the total (Fig. 13.1). This is not surprising in view of the fact that the amount (96,000 tonnes) of phosphorus generated annually in livestock manures and silage wastes is over 30 times greater than the equivalent amount in the combined municipal and industrial waste loads. The impact of the residual agricultural load that enters waters may be mitigated to some extent by the fact that much of it is likely to be discharged from the land during the periods of high rainfall in winter and spring and flushed relatively rapidly from the river systems. In addition, the forms in which the phosphorus is lost from agricultural land may not all be immediately available for

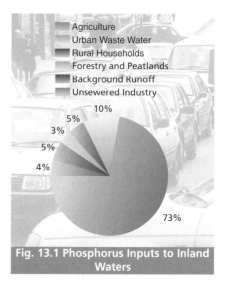

Agriculture
Urban Waste Water
Rural Households
Forestry and Peatlands
Background Runoff
Unsewered Industry

10%
5%
3%
5%
4%
73%

Fig. 13.1 Phosphorus Inputs to Inland Waters

uptake by algae and other aquatic plants. There is a need for investigations to determine the fate of this phosphorus and its full significance as a potential stimulator of plant growth in rivers and lakes.

There is little doubt, however, that, as shown by water quality surveys, agriculture is a major cause of the increasing eutrophication. It has been estimated that, on a national level, the inputs of phosphorus to farming are greater than its removal in produce and that, as a consequence, the soil content of the nutrient is in many cases above that required for plant needs. In such situations, excessive loss of phosphorus from the soil is likely to occur, especially in periods of high rainfall. In addition, there is evidence that losses directly from farmyards are

a further important source of the nutrient. Minimising such losses of phosphorus requires, therefore, a management approach that treats farm wastes as a nutrient source rather than a waste disposal problem. This means matching the amounts of waste spread on the land and the timing of the spreading with crop needs for nutrients and cutting back on the use of artificial fertilisers where these are unnecessary. In addition, it requires efficient interception and secure storage of farmyard wastes.

It is perhaps inevitable that increased productivity of farm land will lead to some increase of the productivity of the waters draining the land, and it may not be possible to maintain these waters in their pristine state in such circumstances, even with rigorous

controls on waste management. This suggests that the preservation of waters of high ecological quality will only be accomplished by restrictions on the more intensive type of farming in the surrounding catchments, a policy which seems justified, for instance, in the case of the large western lakes, such as Mask and Corrib. Failure to do so is likely to lead to situations like Lough Sheelin in Co. Cavan, a renowned trout lake which has been badly impacted by the development of pig farming, in particular, in its catchment since the early 1970s and where control measures have not been effective.

The combined discharges from urban waste water treatment plants and unsewered industry contribute some 14 per cent of the phosphorus load to inland water (Fig. 13.1). While this is a relatively small fraction, it is likely that in many cases such discharges have a relatively greater potential to cause eutrophication than do the inputs from agriculture. As pointed out in Chapter 9, the fact that such discharges enter waters directly and continuously means that, in many cases, they are likely to be major enriching factors during periods of low flow and high temperatures when plant growth is most favoured. Furthermore, run-off from land at such times is likely to be greatly reduced. There is a strong case, therefore, for the incorporation of phosphorus removal in all significant treatment plants discharging to inland waters in order to ensure that the loads are minimised at critical periods. It is arguable that this might be a more profitable use of resources than the provision of secondary treatment to all of the coastal towns and cities. It is now part of the price that must be paid if the State's rivers and lakes are to retain their status as primarily game fish waters and will be needed, in any event, if the water quality targets in the proposed EU directive on water management are to be met.

WASTE

The production of waste materials has always been an inevitable side-effect of economic activity – witness the midden heaps left by medieval communities – but has become one of the defining characteristics of the modern, consumerist society. Waste, in this context, excludes the water borne discharges from sewerage systems and industries and the emissions of gaseous and other materials to the atmosphere. The latter, if properly pre-treated, are diluted to harmless levels in the environment after discharge. However, solid or semi-solid wastes such as domestic refuse, industrial waste materials and manures from livestock cannot be dealt with in this manner and require disposal, as appropriate, by landfilling, incineration or by land spreading. These disposal routes all carry a risk of environmental damage as well as leading to nuisance. Waste is now a major concern in all countries in Europe where it is estimated that the total amount generated increased by nearly 10 per cent in the early 1990s (EEA, 1999b).

The information given in Chapter 6 shows that some 80 million tonnes of waste were generated in the State in 1998. However, this figure is distorted by the fact that 80 per cent of the total is accounted for by agricultural wastes, mostly manures and dirty water from farmyards. These wastes are dealt with mainly at farm level and, while implicated in water pollution as discussed above, are not normally considered in the context of the waste problem as generally understood. The same might apply to the sludges from sewage and water treatment, which amounted to over 0.5 million tonnes in 1998, although much of this material is currently sent to landfills. Sewage sludge will increase in volume considerably in future years as treatment plants, for the coastal towns in particular, come on stream. Since

dumping at sea is no longer a disposal option for this material, it is now necessary to pre-treat the sludge sufficiently to allow safe application to land as fertiliser; this is already in train in Dublin where sludge from the present primary plant is being thermally dried and pelletised in preparation for application to land. Widespread application of sewage sludge to agricultural land may give rise to problems of public acceptability of the produce from such land; however, it is worth noting that the quantities of sludge requiring land disposal now and in the future are very small compared to the amounts of agriculture waste produced.

The bulk of the remaining 15.5 million tonnes produced in 1998 was made up of industrial manufacturing waste (4.9 million tonnes), mining and quarrying waste (3.5 million tonnes), municipal waste (i.e. domestic and commercial waste and street cleaning waste) (2.1 million tonnes) and construction and demolition waste (2.7 million tonnes). In all of these sectors, the main disposal method is landfill. It is now clear that this approach will not be sustainable in the longer term given the quantities of waste being generated and the difficulty in providing new facilities due to public objections. In addition, targets set by EU directives and declared national policy preclude the continuance of the current scale of reliance on this mode of disposal.

In general, efforts to date to deal with the situation in Ireland by means of minimising waste production, recycling or otherwise reducing the volume of waste have met with little or only minor success, although for some of the schemes now in operation such a conclusion may be premature. It would appear that the State, in this as in many other areas of environmental concern, is following the same trend set in other, more developed countries of Europe and that little change can be expected in the immediate future. Despite the expression of much public concern on the matter, especially resistance to the development of new landfills or to other methods of disposal such as incineration, there is little indication of a widespread attempt, either at public or private level, to reduce the amounts of waste generated. While this may be due partly to the lack of the necessary opportunities or back-up needed and to the varying economics of recycling, it is clear that the problem is not being addressed in a radical enough manner. There is a need for a national infrastructure of waste recycling and disposal facilities.

The aspects of the waste problem that probably impact most on the public mind are poorly operated landfills and litter. The former can cause much local nuisance through odours and vermin as well as pollution of ground and surface waters. Experience or reports of such impacts are probably part of the reason why there is so much resistance to the development of landfills in new areas. Considerable improvements are now required in the operation of landfills under the scheme of licensing by the EPA introduced by the Waste Management Act of 1996 but it remains to be seen whether this will be sufficient to allay public misgivings. However, with the requirement to reduce the amounts of waste going to landfills, there will be a need to consider other forms of disposal, including incineration. While this technique is widely used in other European countries, it is clear from the response to several proposals that public resistance to its use here will be difficult to overcome. This resistance seems to be concerned mainly with the possibility of the generation of dioxins and related compounds and the consequent risk of contamination of the local environment.

While problems with the management of landfills and other facilities are the responsibility of public bodies, littering is a result of personal behaviour and it appears that a large segment of the population contributes directly to the image of the "throw away society". The extent of littering has been rightly termed a national disgrace and is one of the unfavourable features of the country raised by foreign visitors. The chewing gum spattered pavements of cities and towns do not suggest that the attitude of the younger generation will lead to any future improvement. The littering problem is largely facilitated by factors such as the widescale use of packaging for consumer goods and the proliferation of fast food outlets; it appears that those measures currently in force that might control such factors are not sufficiently stringent. Ultimately, the resolution of the problem requires a change of individual attitudes to bring about that heightened sense of civic responsibility that seems to be more

prevalent in other European countries. In order to achieve this, there may be a need for a greater use of penalties as well as an ongoing education process.

THE URBAN ENVIRONMENT AND TRANSPORT

Ireland has become an urbanised society later than most other European countries, the majority of the population still being classified as rural in 1961. However, with nearly 60 per cent of the current population now living within urban areas, the position is fast approaching that of most of our neighbours. Thus the quality of the urban environment is a matter of concern for the majority of the people living in the State. This applies particularly to the Dublin urban area, which holds nearly one third of the national population and which is the only such area in the State comparable in size to the major cities of Europe.

Urban life has many conveniences such as ease of access to services and entertainment facilities. However, increased urbanisation creates the need for the movement of large numbers of people and goods within and between cities and towns for work and social purposes, and this can be accommodated only by good public transport services and a properly designed road system. Failure to provide such facilities is one of the main reasons for the deterioration in the quality of the

urban environment. The concentration of large numbers of people in confined areas together with supporting infrastructure and industry creates problems such as air pollution, street congestion and noise, which are all immediately attributable to vehicular traffic. These conditions induce stress and are liable to impact directly on health. The problems are exacerbated in many cities by the fact that the inner core of streets date from a much earlier age and are unsuited for the movement of large numbers of vehicles.

All of these problems are now present to a greater or lesser extent in Ireland, especially in the Dublin area; they seem destined to continue and increase until, in particular, further limitiations are imposed on private car drivers and the planned improvements to public transport are fully achieved. The development of large and often distant suburbs and the more recent increase in car ownership has led to a much greater private use of the road system with consequent clogging of main routes and increasing journey times between home and work location. Furthermore, access to parking is now difficult in the city area and requires many drivers to start their work day much earlier to increase their chances of gaining a parking space. This has led to an extension of the period over which high traffic densities occur with increasing noise disruption to residents near main roads. Increased

car use also has implications for air quality and as pointed out above, there is evidence that ambient levels of some vehicle-produced pollutants are likely to be in excess of the new, more stringent EU standards for the protection of human health. In addition, there is an economic penalty in terms of time lost due to long periods spent in slow moving traffic.

Efforts to reduce car use in urban areas have had some success recently but cannot have substantial impact until convenient alternatives are made available for a much greater proportion of commuters. The building of new roads does not offer a long-term solution as traffic tends to increase and take up the expanded capacity. This is a particular feature of the large bypasses built around towns which, although intended to divert through traffic from the urban core, tend to be dominated by local traffic making use of such roads in the course of relatively short journeys. While this can be countered by the imposition of toll charges, it is clear from the reaction of interested parties that such a move would be strongly resisted.

CLIMATE CHANGE AND GREENHOUSE GASES

The probability of changes in climate due to increases of carbon dioxide and other gases in the atmosphere is, unlike many other environmental issues, a matter of concern for all of the world's states. While there is no clear-cut evidence that the major problems likely to arise from these changes are presently manifest, there is a consensus that the quantities of the greenhouse gases in the atmosphere have increased due to anthropogenic emissions, that global surface temperatures have increased by between 0.3 and 0.6 degrees C since the late nineteenth century and that the balance of evidence suggests a discernible human influence on

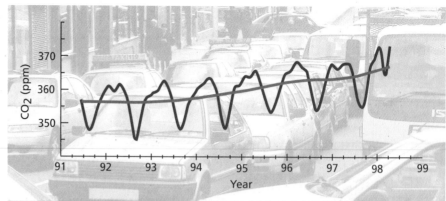

Fig. 13.2 Annual Variation and Increasing Trend in Carbon Dioxide Concentrations Levels (since 1991) at Mace Head (Source: G. Jennings, UCG, pers. comm.)

global climate (IPCC, 1995). It is interesting to note that the long-term records of carbon dioxide concentration at Mace Head Co. Galway reflects the global increase (Fig. 13.2).

In view of the scale of the problems that may arise from climate change, e.g,. land inundation due to a rise in sea levels, changes in rainfall patterns and extensions of the ranges of disease-carrying insects, the costs of not reacting appropriately to the situation may be very high. On the other side of the argument is the consideration that the economic impacts of undertaking the necessary measures to reduce the emissions of the gases are likely to be enormous for most States. There is no doubt that the matter presents a major test of the adherence of the world's community to the precautionary principle in dealing with potential environmental problems and, specifically, a

commitment to the international targets agreed for reductions of greenhouse gas emissions.

Ireland has one of the higher emissions of greenhouse gases in Europe per capita, a situation attributable in part to the limited capacity for hydropower development and a policy not to avail of nuclear power. This means that energy generation is almost totally dependent on fossil fuels and is responsible for nearly 30 per cent of the national emissions of the gases. The high per capita figure also arises from the relatively large number of cattle in the country, the methane generation from which, together with the nitrous oxide lost from agricultural land, accounts for one third of the total of greenhouse gas emissions in the State, when expressed in terms of carbon dioxide equivalent (see Chapter 4). Together, energy generation, agriculture and traffic, account for

over 70 per cent of national emissions of greenhouse gases.

In the context of the Kyoto agreement, Ireland was assigned a target of restricting increase in greenhouse gas emissions to 13 per cent by the 2008-2012 period on the base year of 1990 (see Chapter 4). Estimates show, however, that by 1998 there had already been an 18 per cent increase in net emissions compared to 1990 while those forecast for the 2008-2012 period are as much as 30 per cent greater than the base year emissions. Thus, it appears that the State is now in a position where rather than restricting increases it must achieve reductions in the current level of emissions in order to meet the target set for the 2008-2012 period. Most of this quicker than expected change is attributable to increases in the outputs from energy production and, particularly, the transport sector. In the latter case, the unprecedented growth in car ownership has been a major factor. Car ownership is still below average EU levels so that it is likely to continue its increase in the absence of significant disincentives (see Chapter 16).

Efforts to curtail the increase in emissions have been insignificant to date. For instance, there has been very limited development of renewable energy sources, such as wind power, and even this has been met with a negative public reaction in several areas; this does not suggest an easy passage for the large scale installations which may be necessary in future. Furthermore, the current availability of "sinks" for carbon dioxide in the State is limited because only those forests planted since 1990 are included in relation to the Kyoto commitments. However, this may change if the proposed high planting rates are achieved (see Chapter 16).

Clearly, the situation presents a dilemma for the State; the concession to Ireland of a further increase in emissions, despite the requirement for an overall reduction in the EU's output, and the considerably improved economic situation here, means that little sympathy can be expected from other Member States if the allowed target is not respected. Furthermore, the fact that the economy is still in a strongly growing mode suggests that there will be little appetite in either the private or public spheres for any radical measures which may apply a significant brake on development. Nonetheless, there is a need for immediate action in order to reduce the pain of meeting the accepted target.

PROTECTION OF NATURAL RESOURCES

Natural resources have come under much greater pressure in the last two centuries owing to industrialisation and urbanisation and the associated increase in populations. More recently, changes in agriculture have had a similar impact. Besides the depletion of minerals, coal and oil and other finite resources, these developments may adversely affect the continued use of potentially renewable resources such as water and fisheries. In addition, they are likely to reduce or even eliminate the habitats of certain flora and fauna leading in some cases to extinction of species.

It is obvious that some of these impacts are not completely avoidable and a certain level of environmental disruption must be accepted as part of the price to be paid for better living and working conditions and for the overall prosperity of society. The change of use of agricultural land to housing and roads, the damming and abstraction of water from rivers and the combustion of fossil fuels are all examples of exploitation of natural resources for which there are no realistic alternatives at present. Thus, it is not reasonable to expect that modern life can have a totally benign impact on natural resources; the aim must be to minimise this impact and to seek alternatives to disruptive developments wherever feasible.

Ireland's main natural resources of economic importance are its agricultural land and its inland and coastal waters and their fisheries. To these might be added the scenic landscapes and indigenous flora and fauna; although of less direct economic significance than the foregoing, these too would be considered by most people as important aspects of the Irish environment. While the country is perhaps not as poorly endowed as once thought with reserves of extractable minerals and fossil fuel sources, these are generally not of the same relative magnitude as those found in many other European countries.

All of these resources and others have been exploited to a greater or lesser extent since man first arrived in the island. The natural forest cover, which once dominated the landscape, was greatly reduced in extent by the

end of the seventeenth century and had shrunk to around 1 per cent of the land by the beginning of the twentieth century. In addition, it is clear from many investigations that the land surface in most areas of the country has been greatly changed, albeit in some cases improved, through the centuries by agricultural activities, particularly in the late eighteenth and early nineteenth centuries when the population increased rapidly and nearly all available land was exploited for the cultivation of food crops. Thus, it is unlikely that there are any substantial tracts of the Irish territory that can be said to be in their natural state and even the most prized landscapes have a large element attributable to man-induced changes.

Relatively low economic activity in the first half of the twentieth century moderated the impact of urban development on the State and it is only in the last 40 years or so that cities and towns have spread significantly over adjacent agricultural land through the development of large suburbs. However, this is now a prominent feature of the State's cities and towns, of Dublin in particular, and many rural areas and their villages in the vicinity of the larger urban centres have now been engulfed by housing estates and industrial development and their identity largely obliterated. In other areas, the rural character has been diminished by ribbon building along

main roads radiating from the nearby urban centre.

The coastal zone, in particular, has been significantly impacted by development, especially in the vicinity of ports and urban areas. Besides economic use, this zone is important for many leisure and recreational activities and there is continual pressure to increase the facilities supporting such activities in these areas. This includes the proliferation of privately built holiday homes and the State-supported development of holiday villages. Such developments have led to adverse changes in the character of the nearby existing settlements and to conflicts with the need for the protection of natural features such as sand dunes and the habitats of various animal and plant species. In addition, the coastal zone in some areas of the country is subject to natural erosion processes.

Agriculture has been the main factor shaping the Irish landscape up to recent times and has in general produced a pattern that is attractive to local and foreign visitors. This pattern has been eroded in some areas by the increase in field size and the removal of hedges, although not on the scale seen in other countries in Europe.

The accelerated development of commercial plantations of trees, especially those composed exclusively

of coniferous species, has also changed the appearance of the landscape in many cases and for the worse in the opinion of many people. Exploitation of the large lowland bogs since the 1940s, while greatly beneficial to the State, has removed a large proportion of these very characteristic features of the Irish midlands.

All of these changes to the land surface have adverse implications for the habitats of a number of native species of flora and fauna; in some cases, they have led to virtual extinction of sensitive species. Such changes may also lessen the attractiveness of the landscape to visitors and may threaten the future success of tourism in the most affected areas.

Water resources are, in general, only moderately exploited in Ireland; as explained in Chapter 9, abundant rainfall and relatively low population density means that the State has a high availability of water on a national basis. However, there is a potential shortfall in the eastern part of the country, which has a combination of the lowest rainfall and the greatest population, and this has already manifested itself in some localised areas. The use of the existing sources supplying Dublin is approaching full capacity and further significant growth of the metropolitan area may involve tapping new sources much further afield, e.g., the Shannon. However, as pointed out in Chapter 7, there is a very large loss from the distribution system in Dublin through leakages; the need for improvements in this situation has been identified and remedial action is in train.

Sea fisheries are the main natural, biological resources of economic importance to the State. There is evidence (see Chapter 10) that the exploitation rates of some of the fin-fisheries are now at unsustainable levels with a large proportion, in some cases the bulk, of the standing stock of adult fish been removed in the fishing season. In addition, there is evidence of mortality of large numbers of juvenile fish taken as a bycatch. Such exploitation rates and juvenile mortality threaten the ability of the fish population to reproduce itself and are thus unsustainable.

Adequate protection of all of these natural resources requires a planning approach to their use that takes a comprehensive view of the factors involved rather than one which focuses on particular issues. This is particularly needed in relation to the use of the land where there are many competing needs, some of them potentially in conflict. Protection of natural resources is probably the area in which the principle of sustainability is of particular relevance but also the one where its application presents the greatest challenge.

OTHER CONCERNS

The foregoing issues correspond in general to those raised by the public in recent surveys (EPA, 1998b). However, there are several other matters of environmental concern that do not figure above for various reasons. Perhaps the most outstanding is the potential contamination arising from the Sellafield nuclear processing plant in Cumbria, UK, the proximity of which to the Irish east coast has caused much concern in the populations living in that area. Undoubtedly it is this concern which leads to the Irish population's perception (Lehane, 1999) of the threat from nuclear power being much greater than that held by the inhabitants of other European states, despite not having such a facility here. Although the contamination of the western Irish Sea, due to discharges from the Sellafield complex, has diminished considerably in recent years and is unlikely to present a threat to consumers of sea food (see Chapter 10), the acceptability of even this low

level of contamination has been rightly questioned; however, the possibility of serious accident looms much larger in the public consciousness. Unlike the issues raised above, the main problem in this case is the lack of direct control by the Irish authorities.

The use of genetically modified organisms (GMOs) and their products has become a controversial issue in Ireland within a short period and has been highlighted in particular by the objections to the growth trials of GM crop species which have taken place in a number of areas. From the environmental point of view, it is the possible cross contamination of other crop or weed species with foreign genetic material which is the chief concern. This possibility has been heightened in particular by organic farmers who claim that the use of GM crops in the vicinity of their holdings will pose a risk of such contamination and thus harm the clean image which they claim for their produce. All of these concerns are mirrored in other countries in Europe and now appear to be emerging in the US which up to now has made large-scale use of GM crops. There is a measure of uncertainty now over the further use of genetic modification, at least for use in plants grown in the general environment, and public resistance to the techniques, if it remains unchanged, is likely to continue this uncertainty.

It is noted that emissions from industry continue to be regarded by the public as a significant environmental problem (see Chapter 2). This is somewhat at variance with the improvements that have been achieved in recent years following the introduction of the Integrated Pollution Control licensing system, with its emphasis on emission reduction and on waste minimisation and recovery. In addition, industry, aside from one or two categories, is now a minor contributor to greenhouse gas emissions. It is possible that public attitudes to the sector are largely influenced by problems with odours, which have been a problem with several industries in recent years, notably with rendering plants. Public attitudes may also be influenced by the animal health problems reported in a number of areas in recent years and attributed by locals to industry. The Askeaton case, referred to above, has attracted much public attention in this regard. Overall, of the main sectors of the economy having adverse impacts on the environment, industry is probably now the least damaging.

In addition to the challenge to reduce the national emissions of greenhouse gases, the State is also facing the need to cut back substantially its production of those gases giving rise to acidification of the environment and the production of ozone, principally sulphur dioxide, nitrogen

oxides and ammonia (see Chapter 4). This need arises from the international examination of the problem of acidification in Europe undertaken by the UN and the EU. The proposed emission "ceilings" for the above gases which have emerged from the extensive modeling exercises carried out on behalf of the UN and EU will require substantial reductions of emissions in Ireland, particularly of sulphur dioxide. This has implications for the power generation sector in particular. As in the case of the greenhouse gases, agriculture is also a large contributor to the emissions of acidifying gases, in this case due to the ammonia released from manures.

CONCLUSIONS

Ireland remains a country with a relatively clean environment and one largely free of the residue of past industrial pollution, which afflicts many other European countries. This is as much a result of favourable circumstances pertaining to past pressures on the environment as it is to protective measures. In addition, membership of the EU has helped to highlight the need for environmental protection in the State. However, there are now clear signs that the State is drawing down its capital of good

environmental conditions and following the pattern of deterioration that has characterised many of the early industrialising States. As pointed out above, the more rigorous control of industry introduced in recent years has significantly lessened the potential of that sector to cause environmental damage. Greater efforts will now be needed in other sectors, especially energy production, agriculture and transport, if further deterioration is to be avoided and the aims of the Government's policy on sustainable development are to be achieved.

REFERENCES

EEA (European Environment Agency), 1999a. *Chemicals in the European Environment: Low Doses, High Stakes?* The EEA and UNEP Annual Message 2 on the State of Europe's Environment. EEA, Copenhagen.

EEA (European Environment Agency), 1999b. *Environment in the European Union at the turn of the century.* Environmental Assessment Report No. 2. EEA, Copenhagen.

EPA (Environmental Protection Agency), 1995. *Investigation of animal health problems at Askeaton, Co. Limerick.* Interim Report to September 1995. EPA, Wexford.

EPA (Environmental Protection Agency), 1997a. *Investigation of animal health problems at Askeaton, Co. Limerick.* 2nd Interim Report (October, 1995 to December, 1996). EPA, Wexford.

EPA (Environmental Protection Agency), 1997b. *Protocol for the investigative approach to serious animal health/human health problems.* (Prepared by the EPA with Department of Agriculture and Food, Department of Health/Health Boards and Teagasc). EPA, Wexford.

EPA (Environmental Protection Agency), 1998a. *Investigation of animal health problems at Askeaton, Co. Limerick.* 3rd Interim Report (January to December, 1997). EPA, Wexford.

EPA (Environmental Protection Agency), 1998b. *Irish Citizens and the Environment: A Cross-national Study of Environmental Attitudes, Perceptions and Behaviours.* Report prepared by the Social Sciences Research Centre UCD. EPA, Wexford.

IPCC (International Panel on Climate Change), 1995. *Second Assessment Report: Climate Change 1995.* UNFCCC.

Lehane, M. (ed.), 1999. *Environment in Focus – A Discussion Document on Key National Environmental Indicators.* EPA, Wexford.

McCumiskey, L. M., 1998. Environmental Protection in the Future: The Main Challenges. In: *Engineering - The Key Profession - creating wealth, protecting health and sustaining the environment.* Proceedings of the IEI Annual Conference 1998. Institute of Engineers of Ireland, Dublin.

CHAPTER 14

ENVIRONMENTAL ECONOMICS

In many countries the use of economic instruments, such as taxes, charges, deposit and refund schemes and subsidies makes a positive contribution to improving the efficiency and effectiveness of environmental policy. A number of such instruments has been in operation in Ireland for some time but their use is not widespread. Ireland has traditionally levied high taxes on mineral oils and on cars. For example, in 1998, receipts from excise duty on petrol and oils totalled £1,028 million. However, there is considerable scope to reform the Irish fiscal system to address the key environmental challenges facing Ireland, to meet international obligations and to apply more fully the polluter pays principle. Such measures could include appropriate cost recovery for the provision of water, waste collection and disposal and waste water treatment, a landfill tax and an excise tax on the sale of fertilisers to discourage overuse. Options to promote energy efficiency and to limit greenhouse gas emissions include a carbon/energy tax on the sale of fossil fuels and emissions trading.

Total capital investment in water and sanitary services in the period 1994-1998 amounted to £689 million with a further £275 million provided for in 1999. Expenditure on heritage has also increased over that period. Expenditure under the basic REPS scheme between 1994-1998 amounted to £217.6 million. Total expenditure on the environment by other socio-economic sectors is, however, more difficult to quantify.

An EC evaluation of the Cohesion Fund in Ireland indicates that while investment in waste water treatment infrastructure has been substantial, Ireland's progress in the implementation of the urban waste water treatment Directive has been slow, principally because of the long lead times for such projects. Evaluating the impact of Structural Funds in Ireland is hampered by a lack of comparable and comprehensive data and there is a clear need to develop indicators to track environmental impacts and to identify the environmental dimensions within various operational programmes.

INTRODUCTION

This chapter reviews various economic aspects of the environment, including the use of economic instruments to facilitate a longer term re-focusing of environmental policy. European Union and other international developments are considered along with related national developments in this area. An overview of the EU financial support mechanisms is given, together with an evaluation of their environmental impact in Ireland. The chapter also addresses expenditure at a national level on environmental services, and on heritage and by the various key sectors of the economy. The application of economic instruments in Ireland is reviewed and proposals for extending their scope are discussed.

INTERNATIONAL DEVELOPMENTS

European Union

The Amsterdam Treaty (CEC, 1997), strengthened the position of the environment in the European Union. It placed the protection of the environment and the achievement of a sustainable pattern of development at the core of the EU's objectives for the future. The Treaty specifies that environmental protection requirements must in the future be integrated into European policies and actions with a view to promoting sustainable development.

A follow-up strategy prepared by the European Commission (CEC, 1998a) outlined the ways in which such policy integration could be achieved. Using as an example the policy package Agenda 2000 (which includes proposals for the reform of the agriculture and Cohesion policies), the strategy outlined how improved use of the EU financial mechanisms could contribute to policy integration. The key proposals in this regard are as follows:

- environmental protection and improvement to be established as objectives, under Structural Funds round 2000-2006, to ensure the funds make a positive contribution to sustainable development;
- enhanced financial support to be provided for projects of particular environmental importance;
- for projects over 50 Million ECU there should be a more systematic scrutiny in regard to environmental protection;
- for the rural development programme under the Common Agricultural Policy, a substantial amount of funds would be reserved for actions with direct environmental benefits. Other projects under this programme should be compatible with environmental objectives;
- Member States to put in place a partnership involving environmental bodies to integrate environmental protection requirements in Structural Fund programmes.

The *Fifth Action Programme on the Environment*, entitled "Towards Sustainability" has made explicit the need for market based and other economic instruments to facilitate a longer term re-focusing of environmental policy in Member States. Such instruments include environmental taxes and charges, fiscal incentives and subsidies. However, since its implementation in 1992, there has been little progress in their use at an EU level. Following a

review of the action programme, the European Parliament and the European Commission agreed on how to strengthen its implementation (CEC, 1998b). As a key priority, the EU reaffirmed its commitment to develop and encourage a more extensive mix of instruments to bring about substantial changes in current trends and practices. In relation to the development of market based and other economic instruments as a means of implementing environmental policy, particular attention is to be given to:

- environmental accounting;
- examining constraints on the introduction of economic instruments;
- the use of environmental charges;
- identifying and reforming subsidy schemes which adversely affect sustainable production;
- encouraging the application in Member States of the concept of environmental liability;
- using voluntary environmental agreements to pursue environmental objectives while respecting competition rules;
- encouraging the use of fiscal instruments to achieve environmental objectives.

Priority is also to be given to improving the use of the EU financial support mechanisms as a means of supporting sustainable development. This includes better integration of environment considerations in development projects and an evaluation of the impact of these mechanisms on the environment.

EU Financial Support Mechanisms

Structural Funds

The Structural Funds are the EU's primary financial instruments and are aimed at promoting better economic and social balance across the European Union. The funds, which are used to finance development in Ireland, comprise:

- European Regional Development Fund (ERDF), which includes investment in infrastructure aimed at environment protection;
- European Social Fund (ESF), which includes support for training in the environment;
- the European Agricultural Guidance and Guarantee Fund (EAGGF), which includes environmentally friendly farming, rural development and the conservation of rural heritage;
- the Financial Instrument for Fisheries Guidance (FIFG), which includes support to achieve a sustainable balance between fishery resources and exploitation.

The aim of the Structural Funds is to concentrate the support where it is

most needed. Rather than looking at individual projects proposed by Member States, the priorities and issues of a whole region are examined and comprehensive programmes are developed. Any measure financed by the EU Structural Fund mechanism must be co-financed by the Member State.

Cohesion Fund

The Cohesion Fund was established in 1993 with the purpose of strengthening the social and economic cohesion of the European Union. With a budget of some 15 billion ECU for the period 1993-1999, it aims at assisting those countries with a per capita Gross National Product (GNP) of less than 90 per cent of the EU average. At the time of application, the fund applied to four countries: Ireland, Spain, Portugal and Greece.

Unlike the Structural Funds, the Cohesion Fund assists individual projects as opposed to programmes. It co-finances projects in two fields, environment and transport, and focuses on large infrastructural projects in these areas. In Ireland, the main environmental themes to which the Cohesion Fund contributes are:

- Water Resource Management - improving drinking water supply and improving water conservation;
- Waste Water Treatment: - meeting Ireland's commitment under the

urban waste water treatment Directive;
- Integrated Catchment Management: protecting key river catchment areas.

The aim of the funds is to target environmental projects linked to the implementation of European Policies and more specifically to the themes of the EU Fifth Action Programme on the Environment. One important environmental dimension that affects all Cohesion Fund investments (both environment and transport) is that the project appraisal procedures are designed to ensure that each project complies with EU environmental policies and legislation as well as being consistent with national strategies and programmes.

Since the introduction of the Cohesion Fund, Ireland has benefited greatly in terms of environment and transport developments. By the end of 1999, a total of 107 projects were approved for Cohesion Fund assistance, with EU funding amounting to £1,178 million (Table 14.1) (DoF, 1999a).

Roads investment co-financed by the fund resulted in the provision of 71 km of motorway, 157 km of single carriageway, 47 km dual carriageway and 5 km of three lane carriageway. Rail investment resulted in 355 km track renewal as well as bridge renewals and improvements to level

crossings. On the environmental side, investment (including structural fund assistance of £96 million) supported 163 major water and sewerage schemes, one landfill, a waste baling station and the development of number of river catchment monitoring and management systems (DoF, 1999a).

Community Financial Instrument for Environment (LIFE)

Introduced in 1992, the Community Financial Instrument for Environment (LIFE) contributes to the development and implementation of EU environmental policy by financing demonstration projects in Member States. The budget for the period 1996-1999 (the second phase of the instrument) amounted to 450 million ECU. Two particular areas of activity addressed under LIFE are:

LIFE-Environment: which provides support for innovative and demonstration projects designed to promote sustainable development in industrial activities and land use planning and support for preparatory measures designed to implement EU policy measures and legislation.

LIFE-Nature: Support of measures for protection of endangered species and habitats.

Table 14.1 Cohesion Fund Assistance in Ireland 1993-1999	
Category	Cohesion Fund Contribution (£million)
Transport	
Road	441.8
Rail	111.8
Ports	32.3
Airports	2.4
Sub-total Transport	*588.3*
Environment	
Water Supply	197.7
Waste Water	377.2
Solid Waste	7.9
Habitats	1.6
Technical Assistance	5.5
Sub-total Environment	*589.9*
Total	**1,178.2**

DoF, 1999a

Unlike the Cohesion and Structural Funds, funding under LIFE is open to any person or company in the EU. Between 1992 and 1998 a total of 23 projects have been funded in Ireland under LIFE-Environment, with a total EU funding of almost £8.7 million. In 1999, an additional four Irish projects were successful in securing European funding totalling over £1 million.

Organisation for Economic Cooperation and Development (OECD)

The OECD, consisting of 29 member countries (including Ireland), provides a forum to develop economic and social policy. Some of the basic premises of the OECD are that economic activity is fundamentally linked to environmental quality and that economic and environmental policies cannot be made in isolation. The OECD has been at the forefront of studies on the potential use of economic instruments for environment policy and on the progress made in various Member Countries in integrating the economy and the environment.

The OECD has concluded that economic instruments, such as those outlined in Box 14.1 can make a positive contribution to improving the efficiency and effectiveness of environmental policy. In comparison to the more traditional "command and control" approaches, they could in principle reduce the economic costs of achieving a given level of environmental protection. They may stimulate growth in pollution abatement technologies, as they provide incentives to reduce pollution. In the cases of taxes and charges, revenue raised through these instruments could be used for financing other environmental policy measures or for developing environmental infrastructure or reducing taxes in other areas (OECD, 1997a.)

However, the environmental benefit of subsidies is not as clear. Many subsidies can generate either a negative or positive environmental effect depending on what they subsidise and how they are targeted. For example, subsidies for agriculture under the Common Agricultural Policy, such as the sheep headage payment and ewe premium, have had an unintended detrimental effect on the environment in Ireland, particularly in relation to overgrazing of mountain areas (See Chapter 11). On the other hand, public funding for rail and the public transport infrastructure can promote a modal shift away from private transport which can have significant environmental benefits.

In addition to encouraging the use of economic instruments for environmental policy, the OECD stresses that greater efforts are needed to evaluate the effectiveness and efficiency of the instruments in actual practice. This would contribute to improving future policy by identifying the circumstances in which the most appropriate economic instruments could be applied in the most effective manner (OECD, 1996).

NATIONAL DEVELOPMENTS

National Sustainable Development Strategy

The National Sustainable Development Strategy (DoE, 1997) has the aim of ensuring that economy and society in Ireland can develop to their full potential within a well protected environment. To achieve this objective, environment, economic and social policies must be mutually supportive. In relation to environmental economics, some of the key strategic actions proposed in the strategy include:
- supporting EU approaches which advocate a shift of the tax burden away from labour towards polluters;
- development of suitable economic instruments including:
  - resource pricing
  - green taxation measures
  - exploration of market based instruments such as emission trading;
- maintaining a substantial environmental infrastructure investment programme to underpin sustainable economic and social development;
- pursuing active labour market policies to promote cleaner production and environmental management and auditing;
- promoting and encouraging the development of environmental industry.

Box 14.1 Examples of Economic Instruments for Environmental Policy

Charges/Taxes
- Emission Charges: based on quantity/quality of discharged pollutants
- User Charges: payments for collection of waste or treatment of effluents
- Product Charges: charges on products that are polluting in the manufacturing or consumption phase or for which a disposal system has been organised

Subsidies
- Grants: non-repayable forms of financial assistance
- Soft Loans: loans with interest rates below market rates
- Tax Allowances: tax exemptions and rebates

Tradeable Emission Permits

Deposit and Refund Systems
- Surcharges on potentially polluting products
- Deposit-refund on short cycle goods (packaging and batteries)
- Deposit-refund on durables (e.g. cars)

OECD, 1997a

National Development Plan 1994-1999

One of the primary objectives of the National Development Plan (1994-1999) was to enhance economic performance through sustainable growth and development. The plan states that a well maintained environment offers an important opportunity for competitive advantage in the development of the agriculture, food and tourism sectors and the promotion of branded Irish products. It identified that a sound environment must be maintained as the natural resource base and guarantor of these activities.

The National Development Plan included strategies and policies to be assisted by the EU Structural Funds, and other European initiatives. It formed the basis of the negotiations between the Irish Government and the European Commission which in turn led to the finalisation of Ireland's Community Support Framework. The new National Development Plan (2000-2006) is considered mainly in Chapter 16.

Community Support Framework 1994-1999

The Community Support Framework (CSF) is a legal agreement between the European Commission and the Irish Government. It outlined the purpose and priorities for the use of some £5 billion provided to Ireland under the Structural Fund Mechanism over the six years between 1994-1999 (The CSF does not include Cohesion Fund projects). Building on the National Development Plan, the CSF set strategic goals and targets to the year 2000. The priorities of the CSF are covered in nine Operational Programmes as follows:
• industrial development;
• agriculture, rural development and forestry;
• fisheries;
• tourism;
• transport;
• economic infrastructure;
• environmental services;
• human resources development;
• local urban and rural development.

Operational Programme for Environmental Services 1994-1999

The Operational Programme (OP) for Environmental Services details the sub-programme and measures agreed between Ireland and the EU in the use of Structural Funds for investment in environmental services. The OP outlined a phased programme of infrastructural development for water supply, sanitary services, waste disposal and coastal protection over the six year period. A total of £101 million was allocated to this OP.

Environmental Accounts

The Irish national accounts provide a framework in which national economic data are presented in a consistent and reliable manner. However, it has been recognised that the national accounting framework gives an incomplete picture of the economic activity in the country as, among other matters, the effects of pollution are not taken into account. At EU level there have been various suggestions for mechanisms to address this issue, including the development of satellite environmental accounts to supplement the main national monetary accounts. Owing to difficulties in dealing with environmental accounts purely in monetary terms, there has recently been a shift towards using physical environmental data which quantifies the negative impacts of sectors, such as households and industry, and places them alongside the beneficial impacts in terms of employment and their contribution to the economy.

The first set of satellite environmental accounts for Ireland was produced in 1999 (CSO, 1999), and focused on four environmental themes; global warming potential, acid rain precursors, eutrophication and solid waste arising. The contribution of various economic sectors to these themes was set against the numbers at work and the contribution to GDP. A brief outline of the main findings of this pilot exercise is given below (Table 14.2).

Table 14.2 Compilation of Pilot Environmental Accounts under Four Environmental Themes						
Sector	Global warming potential (%)	Acid rain Precursors (%)	Eutrophication potential (%)	Solid waste arising (%)	Numbers at work (%)	Contribution to GDP (%)
Agriculture, forestry, fishing	29.30	49.48	62 to 72		12.04	8.53
Fuel, power, water (FPW)*	1.42	0.54		3.35	1.12	1.82
Industry excl. FPW	23.00	20.40	11 to 15	65.76	26.36	35.08
Transport*					3.85	3.42
Total Services excl. transport	18.99	10.81	11 to 15	17.51	56.63	51.15
Residential	27.29	18.77	5 to 7	11.93		
Unclassified				1.45		
Total	100.00	100.00	100.00	100.00	100.00	100.00

Notes: * Emmissions from electricity and transport are attributed to users of electricity and transport.
Figures refer to the year 1994, except for solid waste arising which are for 1995 (and are for non-agricultural wastes).
There are uncertainties in the figures for eutrophication.

CSO, 1999

The accounts show that the agricultural sector is a principal contributor to the national totals of global warming potential, acid rain precursors and eutrophication. In terms of numbers of persons employed and contribution to GDP, the sector has a disproportionate role in this regard. Industry as a whole contributes proportionally less to these three themes, has greater numbers employed and contributes significantly more to GDP. The residential sector (households) is also a key contributor to global warming potential mainly through the use of electricity and transport. For the waste theme, industry is the main contributor, but it should be noted that the assessment focused only on non-agricultural waste.

Further updates and refinement of the satellite environmental accounts for Ireland are expected in the coming years.

EXPENDITURE ON ENVIRONMENT SERVICES AND HERITAGE

Total expenditure on environmental services and on heritage can be difficult to estimate as such expenditure is not always identifiable in the national accounts. Environmentally related expenditure is often linked to or contained in other social or economic expenditure.

Expenditure on Environmental Services

In the past number of years, economic growth, tourist numbers and levels of residential development have greatly exceeded the predictions outlined in the National Development Plan. As a result there was increased demand for both water services and waste water treatment facilities and major capital investment in water and sanitary services was required. Total capital investment in water and sanitary services in the period 1994-1998 amounted to £689 million with a further £275 million provided for in 1999. The bulk of this investment has been EU co-financed through Structural Funds and the Cohesion Fund (DELG, 1999a).

In addition to capital investment, local authorities must also fund operating and maintenance costs associated with the water and sewage schemes. Local authority estimates show that current expenditure on water supply and sewerage amounted to over £170 million in 1998. This is expected to rise to nearly £190 million by the year 2000 as sewage collection and treatment schemes required to comply with the urban waste water treatment Directive are completed.

Expenditure on waste collection and disposal services provided by local authorities is estimated at £390

million over the period 1994-1998. With the introduction of a licensing regime for waste management facilities, it is likely that the costs and expenditure associated with such activities will increase substantially in the coming years (DELG, 1998).

The investment in environmental services over the period 1994-1998 is illustrated in Fig. 14.1

Fig. 14.1 Investment in Environmental Services (DELG, 1999a)

Expenditure on Heritage

The bulk of State expenditure on heritage is channelled through the Department of Arts, Heritage, Gaeltacht and Islands, where it is used for specific explicit heritage functions. However, there are also various activities under the remit of other Government Departments which, although not primarily concerned with heritage, may include heritage related projects. An example of this is the EU LEADER II programme which is focused on rural development but offers possibilities for funding specific heritage projects. It can be difficult to define where expenditure on heritage begins and ends. For example, in regard to tourism and heritage, a question arises as to whether heritage expenditure includes facilitating public access to heritage areas and properties or confined solely to preserving and maintaining them (Heritage Council, 1999).

In general, expenditure on explicit heritage functions includes provision

of funds for the maintenance, protection, improvement and/or restoration of the following:

- the natural environment, inland waterways, foreshores and harbours;
- national monuments and heritage buildings;
- archaeological and genealogical resources and designated heritage archives and records.

It also includes the purchase of public land, heritage buildings, heritage artefacts and the establishment of museums and heritage centres. The annual expenditure on heritage between 1995-1998 is shown in Fig. 14.2.

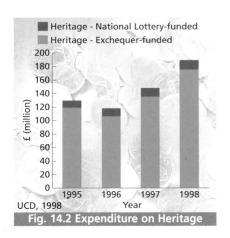

Fig. 14.2 Expenditure on Heritage

ENVIRONMENTAL EXPENDITURE BY KEY SECTORS

Although investment in environmental infrastructure and on heritage can be estimated, total expenditure on the environment is more difficult to quantify. This is mainly because much of the data are not readily available and because it is not always clear what constitutes environmental expenditure. This information gap is presently being addressed by the EPA, which has funded a research fellowship in this area. A brief overview of environmental expenditure across a number of socio-economic sectors is outlined below.

Agriculture

Owing to the dispersed nature of the agricultural sector, it is difficult to

ascertain either the total level of expenditure or the magnitude of environmental protection expenditure. In recent years, however, both the EU and national Government have instituted a number of programmes aimed at creating incentives for farmers to maintain and improve the rural environment.

The rural environmental protection scheme (REPS) is the primary agri-environmental measure in Ireland. Expenditure under the basic REPS scheme between 1994-1998, amounted to £217.6 million (Fig. 14.3), with an additional £73.6 million allocated under two supplementary measures (DAF, 1999).

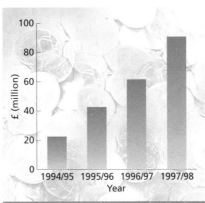

Fig. 14.3 Expenditure Under Basic REPS Scheme 1994-1998 (DAF, 1999)

Under the Control of Farmyard Pollution Scheme, participants receive grant aid towards the provision of animal housing, waste storage facilities, fodder storage facilities and associated farmyard facilities, with

farmers submitting investment proposals for particular projects. Entry into the scheme was suspended in the mid 1990s due to over subscription, but was reintroduced in 1999. Approximately £132 million was allocated in grant aid under the scheme to some 15,570 applicants between 1995 and mid-1999 (Source: Department of Agriculture, Food and Rural Development).

Energy

The energy sector in Ireland is largely publicly owned through a number of semi-state bodies and therefore most (if not all) environmental protection expenditure forms a subset of expenditure by the public sector. This will change as the Irish electricity market is gradually opened up to competition over the next three years. There is increased importance being placed on energy conservation as part of Ireland's commitments under the Kyoto agreement. The pursuit of such a policy is leading to a substantial increase in the level of funds being invested in environmental protection and energy conservation activities.

The Alternative Energy Requirement programme aims at doubling the capacity of renewable energy electricity plants to 10 per cent of total capacity by the year 2000. This is to be accomplished by a mixture of grant aid and price support and an investment of £160 million was predicted between 1998 and 2000 (DPE, 1998).

Under the Energy Efficiency Investment Support Scheme (EEISS), approximately £8 million in grants was allocated between 1994 and 1999. In addition, approximately £18 million was spent by grant recipients in co-funding of projects. The Energy Audit Grant Support Scheme (EAGS) was launched in 1994 to encourage industry and the commercial sector to identify energy saving opportunities. A total of £900,000 was allocated in grants between 1994 and 1998 and approximately £1.35 million was spent by the recipients (DPE 1999).

Expenditure on awareness programmes by the Irish Energy Centre is approximately £600,000 per annum. It is estimated that awareness efforts in the domestic sector will result in annual savings of some £5.8 million per year (DPE, 1999).

Industry

A report to Enterprise Ireland on the value of the environmental services sector in Ireland estimated environmental expenditure in Ireland to be approximately £982 million for 1998 (Ecotec, 1999). It would be reasonable to assume that this figure would have exceeded £1 billion by 2000. The expenditure is almost equally divided between capital investment and services (Table 14.3).

While it is difficult to estimate the total spin off of the manufacturing sector to the environmental industry, the combined capital investment of the sector in projects supported by Ireland's development agencies, IDA Ireland, Shannon Development and Enterprise Ireland now exceeds £1 billion. It is safe to estimate that the resulting spend on environment related activities could be as high as £200 million (P. Doherty, pers. comm.).

The Cleaner Production Pilot Demonstration Programme within the Environmental Services OP is a good example of integration of environment within the industry sector and has demonstrated a clear demand for this type of support provided it is clearly linked with improving overall environmental performance and competitiveness. The programme was established in 1997 to promote a more environment friendly approach to production in the manufacturing and service industries in Ireland. Fourteen companies were involved with a total investment of £1.7 million (including EU funding up to 40 per cent). Each company set environmental objectives and targets to be achieved in the demonstration project. The projects, which are now complete, have shown good results - both in environmental benefits and cost savings (EPA, 1998).

Transport

The OP for Transport envisaged a total expenditure of over £2,600 million (of which some £1,100 million was EU co-financed). It is difficult to ascertain what percentage of this expenditure can be attributed to environmental protection, due to the conflicting environmental effects of much of the transport investment. However, £356 million of the planned expenditure was earmarked for the Dublin Transportation Initiative (excluding road development) and public transport most of which should have a positive environmental impact.

Under the National Development Plan (2000-2006) a capital provision of £430 million has been made for the construction of the surface element of the proposed LUAS light rail network and a contingency provision of £500 million made for the construction of the underground section and a longer term rail development programme.

Tourism

A total of £2.5 million over the period 1998-1999 was allocated for some 20 pilot projects under the *Tourism and Environment Initiative* (DTSR, 1997). This initiative proposed funding of tourism-led projects which enhance management of the interface between tourism and

Table 14.3 Environmental Expenditure in Environmental Services Sector (Ecotec, 1999)			
	Capital Expenditure (£M)	Services Expenditure (£M)	Total (£M)
Air Pollution Control	37.0	32.6	69.6
Water & Wastewater	423.3	275.0	698.3
Waste Management	40.5	126.4	166.9
Contaminated Land	0.8	2.9	3.7
Marine Pollution Control	1.1	0.9	2.0
Energy Management	2.8	2.2	5.0
Noise & Vibration Control	3.0	0.3	3.3
Environmental Monitoring & Instrumentation	8.4	6.6	15.0
Environmental Contracting & Engineering Services	0.0	17.6	17.6
Total	516.9	464.5	981.4

Table 14.4 Areas for Positive Action Toward Sustainability

Step	Action Area
Business as usual	• Enhancing and maintaining visual environmental quality • Ensuring adequate environmental infrastructure is available • Ensuring environmental awareness and adjustment programmes for SMEs • Supporting the development of eco-industries
Minimisation	• Encouraging the application of clean and cleaner technologies • Supporting energy conservation, materials reuse and recycling • Supporting developments on brown-field sites • Supporting developments on sites which are already served by road/utilities/rail infrastructure
Laying the basis for sustainability	• Supporting innovation in new "green" products/services/processes • Supporting the production/use of renewable energy/materials • Encouraging economic sectors with little environmental impact • Supporting environmentally responsible transport • Supporting use of information technology for sustainability • Encouraging awareness in consumers and tourists • Spatial planning to reduce environmental impact • Development planned to encourage "industrial ecology"

ERM, 1999

the environment in Ireland. They include projects to measure carrying capacity, visitor management, the exploration of new tourism routes and access control mechanisms for sensitive locations. The results of these pilot projects will be used to develop a range of procedures to measure, correct and revise sustainable tourism programmes, including the Irish Tourist Board's Tourism Development Plan 2000-2006.

EVALUATION OF ENVIRONMENTAL EXPENDITURE

The Irish CSF (1994-1999) and its associated OPs were recently assessed to identify their environment and sustainable development focus and the impact of investment on the environment (ERM, 1999). In assessing the sustainable development focus, the budgetary resources within OPs were set against three scenarios; business as usual, minimisation, and laying the basis for sustainability. The potential actions within OPs for each of these steps are shown in Table 14.4.

It was estimated that approximately 4 per cent of the total expenditure within the Irish CSF could be linked to business as usual, 3 per cent to minimisation and 4 per cent to laying the basis for sustainability. While the remainder (89 per cent) is classed as having no clear contribution to the environment or sustainability, it must be noted that the Human Resources and Industry OPs do not contain sufficient information to classify expenditure in this context. Despite this limitation, it is estimated that approximately 1.15 billion ECU within the Irish CSF has some environmental protection or sustainable development focus. This figure excludes expenditures on environmental infrastructures from the Cohesion Fund and other EU initiatives (ERM, 1999).

In terms of the actual impacts of the CSF on the environment, only tentative conclusions could be drawn as there is a general absence of comparable and reliable data on which to base the assessment. Within several OPs a number of potential impacts (both positive and negative) can be identified. The mid-term

review of the CSF (Honohan, 1997) also indicated that the environmental effects of expenditure under the CSF are mixed. The Operational Programme (OP) for environmental services, which accounted for only 2 per cent of the total CSF investment in Ireland, could be said to have resulted in environmental improvements. However, there is insufficient evidence to determine if it provides best value for money. The environmental impact of other OPs such as agriculture, fisheries, transport and economic infrastructure varied - ranging from actual harm and missed opportunities to real improvements. One of the reasons for this is that expenditure was primarily planned with other objectives although within the overall concept of sustainable development. Some of the main impacts are discussed briefly below.

Agriculture, Rural Development and Forestry OP

The measures under this OP that most affect the environment are the control of farmyard pollution and compensatory headage allowance schemes.

The environmental benefit from the Control of Farmyard Pollution Scheme resulted in a decline in fish kills due to agricultural activities. However, priority for funding was given to those operating under the REPS scheme, who theoretically should have been operating to good practices. Therefore, the actual environmental benefits may not have been as significant as if priority had been based on the risk of pollution from farms (Honohan, 1997).

The compensatory headage allowance scheme is explicitly social in purpose and has been partially successful in achieving its aim of maintaining rural populations in marginal farming areas. However, the scheme led to gross overstocking of sheep and combined with the EU-wide Ewe Premium Scheme resulted in overgrazing and damage to many uplands areas of Ireland (Chapter 11) (Heritage Council, 1999).

Transport OP

The measures in the Operational Programme for Transport include investment in both road and rail infrastructure. These measures have potentially both positive and negative environmental impacts. The increased usage of transport, particularly road transport, which is promoted by the OP clearly has a

detrimental effect. On the positive side, environmental considerations have been addressed to some extent in major infrastructural projects through environmental impact assessment. It was concluded that the OP has not incorporated environmental considerations in a systematic way into either the design or implementation of the programme (Honohan, 1997).

Economic Infrastructure OP

Measures under this aspect of the CSF include the Energy Efficiency Investment Support Scheme (EEISS) and the Renewable Energy Measure. The EEISS provides grants to projects aimed at improving energy efficiency. With such energy savings, there is also an associated environmental benefit. However, little information is available to determine the

magnitude and significance of these environmental benefits. The renewable energy measure, which promotes the use of renewable energy sources, has a clear environmental benefit, particularly in reducing the emission of carbon dioxide. However the peat-fired power station proposed under the OP could have an adverse effect on the environment through increased CO_2 emission and the risk of siltation of rivers. It will also have implications in relation to Ireland's commitments under the Kyoto Protocol on climate change.

Overall the CSF could be said to have had an environmental focus in terms of the range of measures within its OPs. However, the visibility of the environment in the implementation and monitoring of the CSF is weak and needs to be improved. There is a clear need to develop indicators to track environmental impacts and to identify the environmental dimensions within OPs (ERM, 1999).

Environmental Benefits of the Cohesion Fund

A report by the European Commission (EC) in 1999 evaluated the approach adopted in Ireland in the use of Cohesion Funds to further EU and national environmental policies. The report noted that while the Cohesion Fund investment in waste water treatment infrastructure has been substantial, Ireland's progress in the implementation of the urban waste water treatment

Directive has been slow. This is principally due to the long lead time taken to bring projects from the design stage through to completion (Berg, 1999).

An overhaul is now underway in relation to water resources management within Ireland where water conservation is the central goal. The EC concluded it is unlikely that such a radical approach would have been undertaken without the Cohesion Fund. However, the EC highlighted that the absence of direct domestic user charges for water is at variance with the water conservation strategy and this needs to be addressed.

The Fund has also helped improve environmental management structures and systems in Ireland, for example the Lough Ree and Lough Derg catchment management and monitoring system. The EC indicate that this project has been innovative in the way it fostered partnerships between national, regional and local bodies in the implementation and management of a project to address an environmental issue. Such an approach is consistent with the key principle of shared responsibility for environmental protection.

ECONOMIC INSTRUMENTS

A number of economic instruments for environmental protection, such as taxes, charges and subsidies, have been in operation in Ireland for some time. The use of such instruments however is not widespread. The Government is now developing a more concerted approach in this regard, in the interests of sustainable development and the application of the polluter pays principle. The role of the taxation system in environmental policy has been given further recognition in the 1996 and subsequent budgets, which included taxation measures that have environmental benefits. Such measures included:

- the car scrappage scheme, which was extend until the end of 1997;
- increased Vehicle Registration Tax for cars with an engine capacity above 1400 cubic centimetre capacity;
- a three year improved capital allowance for farm pollution control.

In addition, an Interdepartmental Group on Environmental Taxation is undertaking a review of options for adopting environmental taxation measures in future budgets. This work will involve two approaches:
- removing anomalies in the current system of tax and subsidies to ensure the structure of the system does not have significant adverse effects on the environment;
- developing new measures to secure more environmentally friendly behaviour across the economic sectors.

Strategic options include pricing of resources and services, emissions trading and product and emissions charges. In the design of these instruments, particular attention must be paid to environmental effectiveness, economic efficiency, public acceptability and correct targeting of the measures. Some examples of the economic instruments presently being applied for environmental protection are reviewed briefly below.

User Charges

In some areas local authorities charge for the provision of sewerage services and for solid waste removal. Industrial effluent discharged to municipal waste water treatment plants is charged in most areas and is generally volume based. A survey in 1996 indicated that 31 of the 88 local authorities levied separate charges for domestic waste water services (Barrett *et al.,* 1997). In all cases these charges were fixed and not volume based. With regard to waste collection and disposal, many households pay either a low charge or no charge for this service. Waste charges levied on industry are often well below the true economic cost of managing their waste. In 1998, local authorities estimated that £80 million would be spent in the collection and disposal of waste, while a total of only £38 million would be recovered in landfill gate receipts and waste charges (DELG, 1998)

Charges in many urban areas are also levied on infrastructure use. Examples include parking meters and disks and pay-for-use car parks. The revenue raised per annum is now approximately £1 million, and local authorities are now required to spend this revenue on road related projects (Barrett *et al.,* 1997).

Administrative Charges

The main administrative charges applied in Ireland for environmental purposes relate to licensing and monitoring fees. Fees for applications for an IPC or waste licence are payable to the EPA and are designed to recover the costs to the Agency of processing licence applications and the revision of licences. For IPC licences the levels of fees are scaled according to the type and size of the operation so as to avoid placing an undue burden on small to medium enterprises. For waste licence applications, higher fees are levied on disposal operations. Annual monitoring charges are also levied by the EPA on IPC and waste licensees. The charges are designed to cover the costs of ongoing monitoring of the licensed facility by the EPA.

Environmental Taxes

Ireland has traditionally levied high taxes on mineral oils and on cars. It is estimated that over 65 per cent of the cost of a litre of petrol and about 35 per cent on the cost of a car is tax (DoF, 1999b).

Vehicle Registration Tax (VRT), which is payable on first registration of a vehicle, is graded according to the cubic capacity of the engine and favours smaller cars. The current VRT structure is as follows:

- cars up to 1400 cc – 22.5 per cent
- cars from 1401 to 2000 cc – 25 per cent
- cars greater than 2001 cc – 30 per cent
- all commercial vehicles (vans, trucks and lorries) are charged a flat rate of £40.

It is estimated that VRT paid on cars amounted to approximately £40 million in 1997 with an additional £22 million collected in VAT. VRT collected on commercial vehicles in 1998 amounted to £1.8 million (DoF, 1998a).

Excise duty on fuel varies by fuel type and unleaded petrol and LPG have been taxed at lower rates than leaded petrol. As a result, the switch from leaded to unleaded petrol was very pronounced and annual average sales of unleaded petrol as a percentage of total petrol sales continued to rise throughout the 1990s. Since January 2000, leaded petrol is no longer on sale in Ireland. In 1998, receipts from excise duty on petrol and oils totalled £1,028 million.

Excise duty on fuel used by public transport can be rebated and charges to the public for the use of public transport are not subject to VAT. These tax differentiations are designed to promote the use of public transport. However the high rate of taxation on vehicle purchase and on fuels has not stemmed the growth in the purchase of cars and the use of motor fuel (Chapter 3).

Subsidies

Subsidies include grants, loans with interest rates below market rates and tax exemptions and rebates. Various subsidies are given to firms to undertake environmental audits and towards industrial education in environmental management and energy use. The agri-tourism grant scheme provides grant aid to farmers and rural dwellers towards the cost of upgrading or enlargement of heritage and interpretative centres. A capital allowance scheme for farmers who incur expenditure on pollution control measures was introduced in 1997 and a new scheme of grants for protected buildings was introduced in 1999 at a cost of £3.9 million. In addition, grants totalling £6 million were made available in 1999 for the improvement of individual water supplies which are not connected either to a public or group water scheme. At the time of writing, the maximum grant allowable is £1,600 per house (DELG, 1999b).

Grant aid allocated to local authorities for public education and awareness initiatives on litter amounted £1 million between 1997 and 1999. A total of £2.1 million in grants was approved in 1998 for private sector projects to improve the management and recovery of hazardous waste.

The 1998 Finance Act introduced a tax relief for corporations making investments in renewable energy projects. The relief applies to wind, hydro, solar and biomass energy projects and is estimated to cost the Exchequer £5 million annually. Tax relief is available for maintenance, repair and reconstruction work of buildings of scientific, historical or architectural interest. The building however must allow for reasonable access by the public. An estimated cost of this relief is about £400,000 per annum (DoF, 1998b).

Tax relief is also available for urban renewal projects in designated areas (Chapter 11) and in 1999, tax incentives were introduced for the rejuvenation of designated smaller towns and villages where the population is between 500 and 6,000. The seaside resorts scheme and associated tax breaks, introduced in 1995, has come in for much criticism as it led to the upsurge of holiday homes where infrastructure may be inadequate (Chapter 11).

The Finance Bill 2000 provides for the continuation of the excise duty concession for diesel fuel used in buses, but only in respect of low-sulphur diesel.

Deposit-refund Schemes

Deposit-refund schemes operate by imposing an additional charge on an item at the time of purchase, which is refunded when the item or its container is returned. The application of such schemes in Ireland remains very limited. Over the past number of years some supermarket chains have operated an indirect refund scheme on plastic bags. For each bag re-used a donation is made to a charity or local school.

Environmental Agreements

Environmental agreements are an emerging force in the international policy arena. They are defined as commitments undertaken by firms and sectors resulting fom negotiations with public authorities (Box 14.2). While more than 300 such agreements are in place in European countries, only two have been established in Ireland. The first was formed in 1996 between the Department of Environment and Local Government, IBEC and Repak Ltd. Repak, a non-profit company established by industry, operates a recovery scheme for packaging waste. Since commencing its operation in 1997, over 500 companies have become involved in the initiative, contributing a total of £2.2 million by the end of 1998. Member companies have collected, separated and recycled over 71,000 tonnes of packaging waste arising in their own premises.

The recent environmental agreement between the Government and the Irish Detergents and Allied Products Association will provide for the phasing-out of phosphate based domestic laundry detergent products and should contribute to the reduction of phosphorus inputs to freshwaters.

Enforcement Incentives and Liability Insurance

The enforcement incentives include non-compliance fees and performance bonds. Also included are fines and damages, which are sometimes decided by the courts. Payments of insurance bonds for the rehabilitation of mines is allowable against tax. This presently costs the Exchequer approximately £1 million per year.

Anomalies

There are a number of anomalies in the Irish fiscal system that appear to be in conflict with the polluter pays and user pays principles. As noted earlier in the report, eutrophication of surface waters is a serious problem in Ireland caused by the over application of nutrients, including

artificial fertilisers. However Ireland, unlike other EU Member States, has a zero VAT rate on the purchase of fertilisers.

Ireland currently applies a reduced rate of VAT on energy products, including electricity, but VAT on insulation materials, energy audits and energy conservation work is presently charged at the standard rate.

ECONOMICS AND THE ENVIRONMENT

A comprehensive review of the tax system and application of the polluter pays principle in Ireland has been recently undertaken (Barrett, et al. 1997). The study concluded that while the principle has been applied to some degree, there is considerable scope to reform the Irish fiscal system to apply the principle in a more comprehensive and concerted manner. Some economic based instruments used for the application of the polluter pays principle have been discussed earlier in this chapter.

However, the Tax Strategy Group under the auspices of the Department of Finance has indicated that the introduction of environmental taxes present a number of difficulties. They may be ineffective in curbing consumption, especially if there are stronger factors such as income growth or particular consumer preference. They may adversely impact on those with low incomes and if they are too general or imprecisely targeted they may not

sufficiently address the environmental problem (DoF, 1998a). Outlined below are a number of suggestions for the reform of fiscal policy to tackle some of the key environmental challenges facing Ireland.

Climate Change

Economic instruments, which give a price signal to encourage energy efficiency and to limit CO_2 emissions, are essential if Ireland is to meet its international obligations. One policy option is to use market mechanisms, such as eliminating subsidies to fossil fuels. A second option is emissions trading, where companies are granted permits setting an emissions cap. These permits can be a tradable commodity between companies and countries. However, monitoring and enforcement costs related to carrying out of trades in such a system may be high (DPE, 1999).

Box. 14.2 Environmental Agreements at EU Level

One of the key elements of the EU climate change strategy is to reduce carbon dioxide emissions from cars. In this context, the EU in 1998 negotiated an environmental agreement with the European automobile industry. Under the terms of the agreement, the industry commits itself to reducing the average carbon dioxide emissions to 40g CO_2/km for new cars by 2008, which will represent a 25 per cent reduction on 1995 new car emissions. Similar agreements have also been reached with the Japanese and Korean motor industries. However, these measures are not expected to compensate for the increase in traffic growth.

There is also an option to impose a carbon tax, raising revenue that could be invested in renewable energy, or used to lower other forms of tax (DoF, 1999b). Carbon taxes provide an incentive for emissions reduction through placing a price on carbon. Usually this is achieved through a tax on the sale of fossil fuels with the tax rate varying with the carbon content of the fuel. Under such a system coal and peat would have a higher charge per unit of utilisable energy than would oil and gas. (Barrett, *et al.* 1997). To promote energy efficiency, VAT on heating fuels and power could be raised to the standard rate, in line with other EU Member States. However, as industry can recover VAT, the burden would fall mainly on domestic users.

Increases in energy prices could particularly affect low income households and therefore consideration would need to be given to introducing compensatory social welfare measures.

Water Quality

To address the problem of eutrophication of surface waters in Ireland arising from the over application of nutrients, in particular artificial fertilisers (Chapter 9), a tax based measure could be imposed on fertilisers to discourage over-use. The Tax Strategy Group does not recommend increasing VAT on fertilisers, as farmers can recover their input costs. However, the sale of fertilisers could be subject to a new excise type tax, which would not be refundable and should impact on consumption (DoF, 1998a). The sale of agri-chemicals could also be subject to a charge to discourage over-use. The revenue gained could be used to cover the costs of environmental monitoring and education (Convery and Rooney, 1998).

Urban Environment and Transport

There have been relatively few developments in the area of tax incentives for less polluting vehicles or in the area of noise control of road transport. The 1999 budget restructured the Vehicle Registration Tax rates for cars to favour the purchase of smaller cars, which are generally more fuel efficient. However, this measure is fairly crude and tax provisions based on vehicle emissions would be preferable. There is a strong case to increase the VRT on goods vehicles, especially heavy goods vehicles. A proposal from the Tax Strategy Group suggests an increase in VRT to £100 for light goods vehicles and to £300 for heavy goods vehicles (DoF, 1999b).

Attempts to reduce the costs of congestion could include road tolls, increased charges for urban parking, the removal of tax benefits for building multi-story car parks and providing tax deductions to those who commute by public transport (Barrett, *et al.* 1997).

With regard to fuel prices, it can be argued that the true price of unleaded petrol is the leaded petrol rate, as the former was originally lower to encourage use. Now that leaded petrol has been phased out, the rate for unleaded petrol could be raised to its true level. This could mean an increase of 6.5 pence per litre (DoF, 1999b).

Waste

As noted earlier in the report, increasing amounts of waste are being disposed to landfill. To ensure that landfill is correctly priced to reflect its environmental cost and to promote a more sustainable approach to waste management, there is potential to introduce a landfill tax. In the UK there is evidence to suggest that such a tax has an effect, particularly on commercial and industrial waste. The most marked change has been the drop in the amounts of construction and demolition waste disposed to landfill. By discouraging the landfilling of inert waste, the tax can also support the recycling of aggregate (DoF, 1998a).

It is estimated that approximately 1.26 billion plastic bags are consumed in Ireland each year. Most of the product consumed is ultimately landfilled as part of the household waste stream. A recent study recommends that a charge in excess of 3 pence per unit be levied to reduce their consumption. For administrative purposes, the study recommended a supply-based levy, targeting manufacturers and wholesalers.

Depletion of Natural Resources

The ESRI recommend that full cost recovery should be implemented gradually for the provision of environmental services (e.g., water supply, waste collection and disposal and waste water treatment). Ideally the charges should be volume based to provide incentives to consumers and producers to reduce waste arisings and water use (Barrett, *et al.* 1997, Convery and Rooney, 1998). Since water charges were abolished in 1996 domestic charges have been consolidated in the general tax system. In terms of the polluter pays principle, there is now a degree of inequity whereby industrial and commercial users of water resources are required to pay directly but domestic consumers of water are not (ERM, 1999).

Employment in Environmental Services

Environmental industry is defined as those firms who provide goods or services for activities such as air pollution control, waste water treatment, waste management, contaminated land and water remediation, environmental research, noise and vibration control, environmental monitoring and general environmental consultancy (OECD, 1997b). At a European level it was estimated that employment in environmental industries in the EU amounted to just over one and a half million jobs in 1994. In addition, the EU estimated in 1997 that a further two million people are employed in environment related jobs in areas such as renewable energy, waste recycling and nature and landscape protection (Ecotec, 1997).

In Ireland there are approximately 225 companies providing environmental services. These companies employ a total of 1,700 personnel. A further 2,000 persons are employed in the public sector provision of waste management, water and waste water treatment. This gives a total of 3,700 persons

employed in the public and private sector provision of environmental services (Ecotec, 1999)

The EU has indicated that there is great potential for increased employment in the environmental sector. For example, it is estimated that, through investment of up to 180 million ECU, over a half a million jobs could be created in the EU in the field of renewable energy by the year 2020. In Ireland, the potential for major job creation in environmental industry is somewhat limited due to the size of the country and economy. However, as clean technology is a relatively new market, it is a potential growth area and thus affords a significant opportunity for enterprise (Hunt, 1997).

CONCLUSIONS

Economic instruments can make a positive contribution to improving the efficiency and effectiveness of environmental policy. While a number of economic instruments for environmental protection have been in operation in Ireland for some time, their use is not widespread. There is, therefore, considerable scope to reform the Irish fiscal system to address the key environmental challenges facing Ireland, to meet international obligations and to apply more fully the polluter pays principle.

The evaluation of the impact of investment, including Structural Funds and other EU financial support measures is hampered by a lack of comparable and reliable information. There is a clear need to develop and apply indicators to track environmental impacts and to identify the environmental dimensions within operational programmes. More information is required on expenditure on the environment by industry and other economic sectors.

REFERENCES

Barrett, A., Lawlor, J and Scott, S., 1997. *The Fiscal System and the Polluter Pays Principle: A Case Study of Ireland.* Ashgate Publishing Ltd., England.

Berg, J. P., 1999. *The Cohesion Fund & the Environment: Ireland.* European Commission, Directorate-General for Regional Policy and Cohesion, Brussels.

CEC (Council of the European Communities), 1997. *Treaty of Amsterdam Amending the Treaty on European Union, the Treaties Establishing the European Communities and Certain Related Acts.* Office for Official Publications of the European Communities, Luxembourg. ISBN 92-828-1652-4.

CEC (Council of the European Communities), 1998a. *Communication from the Commission to the European Council, on Partnership for Integration: A Strategy for integrating Environment into EU Policies.* COM (98)333.

CEC (Council of the European Communities), 1998b. On the Review of the European Community Programme of Policy and Action in Relation to the Environment and Sustainable Development "Towards Sustainability". Decision no. 2179/98/EC of the European Parliament and the Council. *O. J.* L 275.

Convery, F. J. and Rooney, S. (eds.). 1998. *Making Markets Work for the Environment.* Environmental Institute, University College Dublin.

CSO (Central Statistics Office), 1999. *Pilot Environmental Accounts.* Report Compiled by Sue Scott, Economic and Social Research Institute. Stationery Office, Dublin.

DAF (Department of Agriculture and Food), 1999. *Evaluation of the Rural Environmental Protection Scheme.* Department of Agriculture and Food, Dublin.

DELG (Department of Environment and Local Government), 1998. *A Policy Statement. Waste Management, Changing Our Ways.* Department of Environment and Local Government, Dublin.

DELG (Department of Environment and Local Government), 1999a. *Water & Sewerage Services Investment Programme. Annual Report 1998.* Department of Environment and Local Government, Dublin.

DELG (Department of Environment and Local Government), 1999b. *Environment Bulletin.* Issue 42. Department of Environment and Local Government, Dublin.

DoE (Department of Environment), 1997. *Sustainable Development A Strategy for Ireland.* Stationery Office, Dublin.

DoF (Department of Finance), 1998a. *Tax Strategy Group Papers – TSG 98/41.* Department of Finance, Dublin.

DoF (Department of Finance), 1998b. *Tax Strategy Group Papers – TSG 98/13.* Department of Finance, Dublin.

DoF (Department of Finance), 1999a. *National Development Plan 2000-2006.* Stationery Office, Dublin.

DoF (Department of Finance), 1999b. *Tax Strategy Group Papers – TSG 99/51.* Department of Finance, Dublin.

DoF (Department of Finance), 1999c. *Tax Strategy Group Papers – TSG 99/41.* Department of Finance, Dublin.

DPE (Department of Public Enterprise), 1998. *Results of the Third Alternative Energy Requirement Competition.* Press Release, April 1998. Department of Public Enterprise.

DPE (Department of Public Enterprise), 1999. *Green Paper on Sustainable Energy.* Department of Public Enterprise, Dublin.

DTSR (Department of Tourism, Sport and Recreation), 1997. *Tourism and Environment Initiative.* Report Prepared for the National Monitoring Committee by Fitzpatrick Associates.

Ecotec, 1997. *Data Collection on Eco-industries in the European Union. Final Report to Eurostat.* Ecotec Research and Consulting Ltd., UK.

Ecotec, 1999. *Environmental Services Sector – A study for Enterprise Ireland.* Ecotec Research and Consulting Ltd., UK.

EPA (Environmental Protection Agency), 1998. *Cleaner Production Pilot Demonstration Programme.* Report prepared by Byrne Ó Cléirigh, EPA, Wexford.

ERM (Environmental Resource Management), 1999. *Environmental Evaluation of the Irish CSF.* A Report to the Environment Coordinating Committee for the Community Support Framework for Ireland. ERM, Dublin.

Heritage Council, 1999. *A Report on the Impact of Agriculture Schemes and Payments on Aspects of Ireland's Heritage.* Heritage Council, Kilkenny.

Honohan, P. (ed.), 1997. *EU Structural funds in Ireland: a Mid-term Evaluation of the CSF 1994-1999.* Economic and Social Research Institute, Dublin.

Hunt, S., 1997. *Report of the Taskforce on Enterprise and the Environment.* KPMG Management Consulting, Dublin.

OECD (Organisation for Economic Cooperation and Development), 1996. *Integrating Environment and Economy – Progress in the 1990s.* OECD, Paris.

OECD (Organisation for Economic Cooperation and Development), 1997a. *Evaluating Economic Instruments for Environmental Policy.* OECD, Paris.

OECD (Organisation for Economic Cooperation and Development), 1997b. *Environmental Policies and Employment.* OECD, Paris.

UCD (University College Dublin) Graduate School of Business, 1998. *Expenditure on Heritage at National Level.* Heritage Council, Kilkenny.

CHAPTER 15

MANAGING AND PROTECTING THE ENVIRONMENT

Environmental policy and legislation in Ireland have for some time been driven by European and global developments. A key consideration in current environmental policy is the integration of environmental issues into wider social and economic development. The goal of this approach is to ensure that development is sustainable, thus ensuring that future generations experience a quality of life similar to, if not better than, our own.

This chapter aims at evaluating whether Irish society is responding adequately to the pressures that exist on our environment. This evaluation has found that, whilst there have been significant advances in the development of environmental policy and legislation in the State, key deficiencies still remain (e.g., in relation to coastal zone management policy and natural heritage legislation). Future developments in these areas are pending and a national greenhouse gas abatement strategy is near completion. There has been successful application of measures to reduce particular forms of air pollution (e.g., control of smoke and lead pollution) and the growth in integrated licensing of industrial and waste facilities and in environmental management systems is to be welcomed. However, there remains an urgent need to apply measures to tackle effectively problems relating to greenhouse gas emissions, water quality (particularly eutrophication), waste generation and management, urban development and transport, and aspects of marine resources and natural heritage management and protection.

INTRODUCTION

Where problems exist with environmental quality, such as those outlined in previous chapters of this report, then responses are required to address these problems so that environmental quality can be protected and, where there is evidence of degradation, improved. This chapter outlines the main responses to the various pressures that exert an impact on the state of the environment and, as far as possible, evaluates these responses to determine their effectiveness.

There have been several key developments since the publication of the last State of the Environment report (Stapleton, 1996), such as the enactment of the Waste Management Act, 1996, and the publication of the National Sustainable Development Strategy (DoE, 1997a). Policy and legal instruments provide a framework for environmental protection. Key responses are considered here both from a sectoral perspective and from an environmental perspective. In addition, given the interconnections between sectors and between environmental media, the importance of an integrated approach to environmental management is highlighted and a framework for integrated environmental management and protection is presented.

POLICY INSTRUMENTS – RECENT DEVELOPMENTS

Global Policy

Global policy in relation to the environment in the past twenty years has been driven largely by the various international agreements and work programmes arising out of the work of the United Nations Environment Programme (UNEP). International policy on environmental issues is also developed by the Organisation for Economic Co-operation and Development (OECD). It may be noted that an environmental performance review of Ireland by the OECD is due to be published in 2000.

The principal global policy instrument in relation to environmental protection and sustainable development is Agenda 21 and the associated agreements signed at the Earth Summit in Rio de Janeiro in 1992, i.e., the Convention on Climate Change (Chapter 4), the Convention on Biological Diversity, the Forest Principles and the Rio Declaration (or Earth Charter), which outlines a set of principles linking future social and economic progress to global environmental protection.

World leaders from over 165 countries reviewed progress on the implementation of the Rio agreements at the Earth Summit+5, in New York in 1997. Unfortunately the outcome of this summit was not as successful as had been hoped. While the leaders agreed that the planet's health was generally worse than ever, there were no major breakthrough commitments, largely because of North-South differences on how to finance sustainable development globally. A programme was adopted for the Further Implementation of Agenda 21 containing a number of elements aimed at providing a basis for progress in the future. Key elements of this programme and other relevant initiatives agreed included measures to deal with issues relating to production and consumption (i.e., eco-efficiency), climate change, freshwater scarcity, forests, desertification and poverty eradication.

European Policy

The Fifth Action Programme on the Environment, *Towards Sustainability*, set the EU policy framework up to the year 2000 by committing the Union to a sustainable development strategy. A review of the Action Programme carried out from 1995 onwards indicated that the EU is making limited progress in reducing many pressures on the environment (EC, 1997). The review resulted in a renewed commitment by the Community to the achievement of the Programme's objectives. The European Commission submitted a global assessment of the implementation of the Programme to the European Parliament and the Council in 1999, accompanied by proposals for the priority objectives and measures that will be necessary beyond 2000.

> **Box 15.1 The Challenge of Integration of the Environment into other Policies**
>
> The real challenge facing the Community is to find a way of developing action that meets all of its objectives in an integrated way. This is the challenge of sustainable development, a concept too often perceived as purely environmental, but which brings together concerns for social and economic development alongside protection of the environment. The current pattern of economic development too often entails conflicts between development and environment; this cannot be permitted to continue. The development of new technologies and practices shows that we have the know-how to find solutions to some of these problems. Solutions are frequently shown to be not only cost effective for industries concerned but also generating broader benefits to the economy through the creation of value added and employment, thus providing a genuine double dividend. However achieving the desired results will require more far-reaching behavioural and policy changes in many sectors of society (EC, 1998b).

The need for integration of environmental concerns into all policy areas has been rising up the political agenda since the Maastricht Treaty. Integration was reinforced in 1997 by the Amsterdam Treaty, which underlines its importance and defines it as a way to achieve the general goal of sustainable development (Chapter 14). Other recent European initiatives promoting integration of environmental and economic policy include Agenda 2000, adopted by the March 1999 Berlin European Council and the European Community Biodiversity Strategy adopted in 1998 (EC, 1998a). The European Commission advanced the concept of integration in a 1998 strategy document (Box 15.1). The European Council has given a mandate to prioritise the integration process in the transport, energy and agriculture sectors, and in the areas of development, internal market and industry.

National Policy

General

The most significant recent policy development in relation to environmental protection and sustainable development at national level was the publication of the National Sustainable Development Strategy (DoE, 1997a). Other significant developments included the publication of strategies against eutrophication (DoE, 1997b) and on waste management (DELG, 1998), and a proposed plan for hazardous waste management (EPA, 1999a). Additional policy developments expected in the near future include a National Greenhouse Gas Abatement Strategy, a National Spatial Strategy, a National Biodiversity Plan, a

National Heritage Plan and a National Coastal Zone Management Policy.

The National Sustainable Development Strategy aims at providing a comprehensive analysis and framework that will allow sustainable development to be taken forward in a more systematic manner. A number of initiatives are outlined to allow for better supporting structures for sustainable development. Actions are described within strategic sectors (agriculture, forestry, marine resources, energy, industry, transport, tourism and trade) to integrate environmental concerns with economic activity. One of the key objectives of the Strategy is to secure the widest possible participation and involvement through the implementation of Local Agenda 21 (Box 15.2). Some aspects of policy relating to the key environmental challenges (Chapter 13) are set out below.

Box 15.2 Local Agenda 21

As part of the commitment to the Earth Charter signed at the United Nations Conference on Environment and Development at Rio de Janeiro in 1992, each local authority in the State is expected to initiate a process that will result in the development of a Local Agenda 21 for its area. A Local Agenda 21 is a blueprint for sustainable development at a local level, built through consultation with and in agreement with the local community. The Government requested all local authorities to complete a Local Agenda 21 for their areas by 1998 (though there has been some slippage on this date). Each local authority has since designated a Local Agenda 21 officer. The designated officers also constitute regional networks. In addition, each regional network has at least two representatives on a national network, which is chaired by the Department of the Environment and Local Government.

Reducing Eutrophication

Government measures to prevent pollution of fresh waters as well as for integrated land and water management and development are detailed in the policy document *Managing Ireland's Rivers and Lakes - A Catchment Based Strategy Against Eutrophication* (DoE, 1997b). Key measures suggested in the Strategy include the following: setting of targets and standards for water quality; catchment water quality management planning; further implementation of the urban wastewater treatment Directive (CEC, 1991a) and freshwater fish Directive (CEC, 1978); agri-environment schemes; promotion of the Code of Good Agricultural Practice (DAFF and DoE, 1996); farm surveys; nutrient management planning; integrated pollution control licensing; control of domestic effluent treatment systems; restrictions on the phosphorus content of detergents; the increased use of statutory powers by local authorities; and increased monitoring and research.

Preventing and Managing Waste

The Government recently launched a major strategy *Waste Management: Changing Our Ways* (DELG, 1998). The strategy is grounded on the internationally recognised waste management hierarchy, which favours in order of preference: prevention, minimisation, reuse, recycling, energy recovery and, finally, environmentally sustainable disposal of waste only where it cannot be prevented or recovered. This initiative signalled Government determination to move away from landfill as the primary means of waste disposal. The strategy sets recycling and recovery targets for achievement over a 15-year time-scale. The policy statement emphasises the key role of local authorities in changing Irish waste management practice, considers the implementation of the polluter pays principle and recognises the importance of economies of scale when planning for waste infrastructure. It is clear however, that the State still has a considerable way to go before policy targets are reached (Chapter 6). The development of the National Waste Database, with national level information available for 1995 and 1998, and the proposed National Hazardous Waste Management Plan (see below) provide essential information for implementation of future waste management policy.

The proposed National Hazardous Waste Management Plan (EPA, 1999a) tackles issues relating to hazardous waste prevention, management and disposal. The EPA will amend the proposed plan in response to feedback from the public and other interested parties and will publish a National Plan in 2000. Implementation of the Plan will require involvement by State agencies, Government Departments, the EPA, local authorities, industry, agriculture and the general public in promoting waste prevention/minimisation and finding alternative solutions to disposal. The Plan will be reviewed at least every five years and will seek to provide a practicable, economical and environmentally sound solution to the management of the State's hazardous wastes (Chapter 6).

Urban Environment

Government policy on the urban environment has been developing in a number of areas. Urban transport policy in Dublin has been implemented largely through the Dublin Transport Initiative but the rapid increase in road traffic volume in recent years has required additional measures (see section on Transport). In addition guidelines on strategic planning in the Greater Dublin Area (BSM, 1999) and residential density (DELG, 1999a) have been published which aim at integrating land use and transportation policy. The Government intends to publish a National Spatial Strategy by the end of 2001, which will aim at providing for the management of regional and urban development within the State (Chapter 11).

Control of Greenhouse Gases

A National Greenhouse Gas Abatement Strategy is being developed to provide a framework for achieving the necessary greenhouse gas emissions reductions required under the Kyoto agreement, and to prepare the State for more ambitious commitments that will be required after 2012. The Strategy will most probably include cross-sectoral economic instruments and specific sectoral policies and measures to reduce emissions. It is widely recognised that action is required to be taken by all sectors as early as possible, and in a sustainable manner, if commitments under the Kyoto

agreement are to be met (Chapters 4 and 16).

Conserving Natural Resources

A National Biodiversity Plan is being drawn up in accordance with Article 6 of the Rio Convention on Biological Diversity. The Plan is considered to be one of the most important means of delivering the Convention on Biological Diversity at a national level. The Plan will review the status of biological diversity in the State (habitat, species and genetic diversity) and assess the adequacy of the measures currently in place for the conservation and sustainable use of biological diversity. The aim of the Plan will be to integrate the conservation and sustainable use of biological resources into all sectoral and cross-sectoral plans, programmes, and policies. It is expected that the Plan will be published in 2000.

In addition, a National Heritage Plan is being developed to produce, for the first time, an integrated plan for the State's national heritage. The aim is to provide for the protection, conservation, management and preservation of the State's natural heritage (in the context of the National Biodiversity Plan); archaeological heritage; architectural, artistic and historic heritage; natural and cultural landscapes; inland waterways; and documentary and archival heritage. The Plan is to be published in 2000.

The Government issued a national policy statement on the release of genetically modified organisms to the environment in October 1999 (DELG, 1999b) to address concerns in this area (Chapter 7). This followed a period of national consultation and debate on *GMOs and the Environment*. The policy statement accepted the conclusions and recommendations of the chairing panel, stating that national policy must be balanced in terms of

environmental protection and socio-economic considerations. The Government stated that it intends to follow a positive but precautionary approach on releases of GMOs to the environment, with the primary emphasis on precaution, based on scientific risk assessment and management.

In relation to the coastal zone, effective management is extremely difficult given the range of Government Departments, agencies and organisations involved and the complex national and international legislative framework, much of which is structured on a single medium or sectoral basis and so does not promote integrated policy. In order to address this problem, a Draft National Coastal Zone Management policy document was published for comment (BSM, 1997) and was followed by a public consultation seminar in 1998. Mechanisms to promote greater co-ordination among the various statutory agencies and other interested parties active in the coastal area, as well as procedures to avoid or, where necessary, resolve conflicts of use are addressed. These are to be finalised in a forthcoming National Coastal Zone Management Policy. This Policy is particularly urgent given increased leisure, tourism and developmental pressures on the fragile coastal environment and predictions of significant sea-level rise and increased coastal erosion in the future.

LEGISLATIVE INSTRUMENTS

Recent Developments Internationally

Ireland is subject to a number of international conventions that deal with environmental protection and sustainable development. Recent Conventions that the State has ratified, signed or is a party to are listed in Box 15.3.

Recent Developments in European Legislation

Environmental law in Ireland is greatly influenced by European legislation. Major developments in European environmental legislation since 1995 include Directives relating to the following:

- integrated pollution prevention and control (CEC, 1996a),
- ambient air quality assessment and management (CEC, 1996b),
- the control of major accident hazards involving dangerous substances or 'Seveso II' (CEC, 1996c),
- the assessment of the effects of certain public and private projects on the environment (CEC, 1997),
- the contained use of genetically modified micro-organisms (CEC, 1998a),
- the quality of water intended for human consumption (CEC, 1998b),
- the landfill of waste (CEC, 1999a) and
- solvents (CEC, 1999b).

While implementation of these and other European Directives has improved the State's environmental performance, the European Commission has also taken legal action against the State relating to environmental concerns (e.g., in relation to the waste Directive (CEC, 1975) and amending Directives, the EIA Directive (CEC, 1985) and the

---

Box 15.3 Recent International Conventions

- Convention on Access to Information, Public Participation in Decision-making and Access to Justice in Environmental Matters, which was signed at Aarhus, Denmark in 1998 (Chapter 1).
- OSPAR Convention for the Protection of the Marine Environment of the North-east Atlantic - signed in 1992 and ratified in 1997 (Chapter 10).
- Protocols, under the 1979 United Nations Economic Commission for Europe (UNECE) Convention on Long-range Transboundary Air Pollution (CLRTAP), on Persistent Organic Pollutants, Heavy Metals and on Further Reduction of Sulphur Emissions (known as the 'Oslo' or 'Second Sulphur Protocol') were signed in 1998.
- The UNECE Protocol to CLRTAP to abate acidification, eutrophication and ground-level ozone was signed in Gothenburg in 1999 (Chapter 4).
- The Kyoto Protocol to the United Nations Framework Convention on Climate Change was signed by Ireland, along with the other EU member states, in 1998. It has not yet been ratified (Chapter 4).

---

habitats Directive (CEC, 1992a)). In addition, the Commission has indicated that it intends to take legal action against the State in relation to the drinking water Directive (CEC, 1980) and the wild birds Directive (CEC, 1979).

Recent Developments in National Legislation

Planning and Environmental Impact Assessment (EIA)

Planning and EIA legislation continues to evolve at both a European and national level (Box 15.4). Recent amendments extend and clarify the list of developments requiring EIA; they enable a person who is required to submit an EIS in respect of a proposed development to request the competent authority concerned to provide an opinion on the information to be contained in it; they set out the procedures to be followed in the case of a proposed development on an environmentally sensitive site or likely to have significant effects on the environment in another Member State; and they include indicative parameters for assessing whether a project is likely to have a significant

---

Box 15.4 Recent Developments in Planning and Environmental Impact Assessment Legislation

At European level, the original EIA Directive (CEC, 1985) was amended in 1997 (CEC, 1997). The latter was transposed into Irish law mainly by the European Communities (Environmental Impact Assessment) (Amendment) Regulations, 1999 and the Local Government (Planning and Development) Regulations, 1999.

The Government has recently published the Local Government (Planning and Development) Bill, 1999, which aims at introducing formally the concept of sustainable development into national legislation. The Bill also aims at consolidating all the planning Acts and much of the EIA legislation into one piece of legislation, in order to benefit users of the planning system. However there has been some concern from NGOs that certain proposals within the Bill may restrict public participation in the planning process (O'Sullivan, 1999).

A recent ruling at the EU Court of Justice that Ireland had failed to apply correctly the 1985 EIA Directive (case C-392/96) may also have implications for Irish EIA legislation. The Court ruled that Irish authorities had exceeded their discretion in implementing the EIA Directive by only laying down size thresholds for EIA, in this case for afforestation, peat cutting and land reclamation projects, without taking into account the nature, location and cumulative effects of projects. The court ruled that even small projects might be deemed to have significant impacts if located in an environmentally significant area.

---

impact on the environment. While these amendments improve the EIA process, the Directive has been criticised in a number of areas, including failure to incorporate formally early public participation or post-project monitoring in the EIA process (Sheate, 1997).

The most recent EIA Directive (CEC, 1997) specifically refers to the concept of sustainable development, but gives no guidance as to how the sustainability of a proposal should be assessed through EIA. Whilst EIA, when used wisely, is an important tool in assisting in the sustainable development of the economy, it is constrained by the fact that the EIA Directive only provides for project-based assessments (Fry, 1999). In this context, the European Commission adopted in 1996 a Proposal for a Directive on the Environmental Assessment of Plans and Programmes (i.e., Strategic Environmental Assessment or SEA). The purpose of the SEA proposal is to ensure that the environmental consequences of plans and programmes are identified and assessed before adoption, with public participation included in the process, thus contributing to a more transparent planning process and to the goal of sustainable development. In Ireland this could lead to assessment of the environmental effects of, for example, development plans. The draft SEA Directive is at an advanced stage at European level.

Pollution Prevention/Control

The principal domestic Acts governing the prevention and control of pollution in the State are the Local Government (Water Pollution) Acts, 1977 and 1990, the Air Pollution Act, 1987 and the Environmental Protection Agency Act, 1992. Recent developments of note include the Waste Management Act, 1996, the Litter Pollution Act, 1997, the Phosphorus Regulations, 1998, and various legislation relating to the marine environment.

Waste and Litter

The Waste Management Act, 1996 has radically altered the regulation of solid waste management in the State (Chapter 6). Under the Act, local authorities are responsible for regulating the collection and movement of waste within the State, with the exception of the importation of waste into the State, which is regulated by the EPA. The Act nominates the EPA as the licensing authority for all significant waste disposal and recovery activities. Eight regional waste strategy studies have been completed and most local authorities have either published, adopted or are in the process of adopting waste management plans (Fig. 15.1). The EPA is responsible for the preparation of a national hazardous waste management plan (see above).

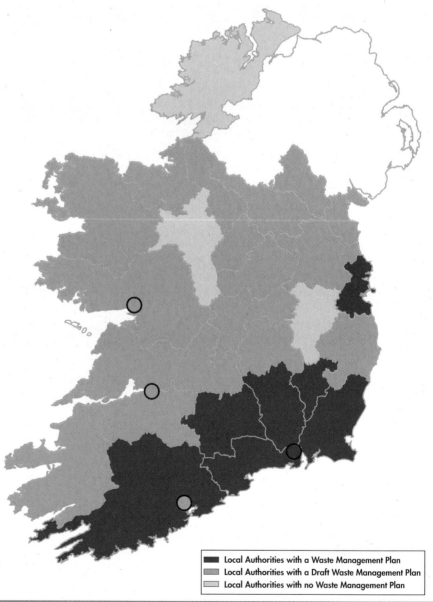

■ Local Authorities with a Waste Management Plan
▦ Local Authorities with a Draft Waste Management Plan
▨ Local Authorities with no Waste Management Plan

Fig. 15.1 Local Authorities with Waste Management Plans

The Litter Pollution Act, 1997, provides local authorities with enhanced enforcement powers to tackle litter and requires each local authority to prepare a litter management plan for its own area. The plan must set out objectives and measures aimed at litter prevention, control and awareness, and there must be consultation with local community and voluntary interests before a plan is adopted by the Council members. Most local authorities have adopted, or are in the course of finalising litter management plans.

Eutrophication

The Local Government (Water Pollution) Act, 1977 (Water Quality Standards for Phosphorus) Regulations, 1998, have been introduced under the requirements of the dangerous substances Directive (CEC, 1976) to deal with the increasing problem of eutrophication of the State's lakes and rivers (Chapter 9). The Regulations require that water quality be maintained or improved by reference to biological quality rating/trophic status or phosphorus concentrations. Where water quality is deemed unpolluted, the regulations require that the existing quality of rivers and lakes be maintained. Where quality has been found to be unsatisfactory, the regulations require that the water be improved by 2007 at the latest for waters surveyed by the EPA in the period 1995-1997 and within a maximum timeframe of ten years for waters first surveyed after 1997. The degree of improvement required is based on the existing quality and standards prescribed by the regulation. A six year extension to the period allowed to reach compliance for a certain water body is permissible in exceptional circumstances. Local authorities have primary responsibility for ensuring that the standards set by the Regulations are met. They were required to submit a report to the EPA in 1999 setting out measures to

be taken to meet the prescribed standards. This is to be followed up by a report to the Agency on the implementation of these measures by 31 July 2000 and every two years thereafter until 2008. The EPA must publish progress reports including such recommendations it considers appropriate by 31 March 2001 and every two years thereafter until 2009.

Marine Environment

Recent legislation introduced to prevent marine pollution includes the following: the Dumping at Sea Act, 1996, which strictly limits the types of substances that can be dumped at sea and provides for rigorous control of residual disposals (Chapter 5); the Fisheries (Amendment) Act, 1997, and the Fisheries and Foreshore Act, 1998, which provide for a comprehensive new licensing procedure for aquaculture activities; the Sea Pollution (Amendment) Act, 1999, which deals with procedures relating to oil pollution incidents at sea; and regulations introduced in 1997 under the Sea Pollution Act to give effect to parts of the MARPOL Convention for the prevention of pollution from ships. The Government has also recently published the Fisheries (Amendment) Bill, 1999, which includes proposals for significant changes to the structure, management and organisation of the inland fisheries services and the establishment on a statutory basis of a National Salmon Commission.

Conserving Natural Resources

The principal national legislative instrument governing nature conservation in Ireland is the Wildlife Act, 1976. Recent significant developments in natural heritage legislation in the State include the publication of the European Communities (Natural Habitats) Regulations, 1997, and the Wildlife (Amendment) Bill, 1999. The European Communities (Natural Habitats) Regulations, 1997, provide for the designation and protection of Special Areas of Conservation or SACs (under the habitats Directive), and for the protection measures that apply to Special Protection Areas or SPAs (designated under the wild birds Directive). Irish law largely anticipated both Directives in respect of direct species protection and the relatively minor adaptations required in respect of such species protection were introduced either under the existing Wildlife Act, in the case of the wild birds Directive, or by way of the 1997 Regulations in the case of the habitats Directive (DAHGI, 1998). The habitats and wild birds Directives provide a framework for the conservation of fauna and flora and their habitats including the establishment of NATURA 2000, which is a network of sites for the conservation of species and habitats that are of European importance.

It has been noted with concern for some time that many habitats important at a national level have

received limited protection under national legislation. The Wildlife Amendment Bill, 1999, aims at amending many of the provisions of the Wildlife Act, 1976, which had relatively weak habitat/site protection measures. Objectives of the Bill include the following: provision for the establishment and statutory protection of a national network of protected areas of both wildlife and geological importance - to be known as Natural Heritage Areas (NHAs); the improvement of various measures for the conservation of wildlife species and their habitats; the strengthening of penalties for contravention of the Wildlife Act; ratification of certain international

agreements; and the introduction of further measures relevant to hunting and trade. The Bill also aims at strengthening the protective regime for SACs by ensuring that protection will in all cases apply from the time of notification of proposed sites.

The Planning and Development Bill, 1999, proposes a number of significant changes to Planning Authority duties and powers relevant to protection of the environment and biodiversity. For example, it is proposed that mandatory objectives for the conservation and protection of the environment, including the protection of sites that are designated as European sites, must be included in County Development Plans. It is proposed that an assessment must be included in the Plan on the likely significant environmental effects of the Plan. It is further proposed that local authorities will have new powers to designate landscape conservation areas where planning controls may apply to developments that would normally be exempted. Local authorities may also produce Local Area Plans (for any area with a population in excess of 1,500) and regional authorities may produce plans for their areas. There are also provisions that turbary (peat extraction) and initial planting of forests would no longer be exempt from planning control.

Owing to concerns about potential risks to human health and the environment from GMOs, the EU has passed legislation relating to the contained use of genetically modified micro-organisms (GMMs) (CEC, 1990a, 1998a) and deliberate release of GMOs (CEC, 1990b). The original EU Directives (CEC, 1990a, CEC, 1990b) have been transposed into Irish law (under the Genetically Modified Organisms Regulations, 1994 to 1997). EU Member States are required to transpose the 1998 Directive on contained use of GMMs, amending the 1990 Directive (CEC, 1990a), by June 2000. Irish Regulations also cover GM animals and plants used in containment.

STRATEGIES AND TOOLS

Environmental management and protection tools generally evolve from legislative and policy instruments, which provide an overall framework within which environmental management can proceed. Recent developments in the area of policy and legislation have been outlined above. Examples of key strategies and tools available in Ireland for environmental management and protection are summarised in Table 15.1, along with the sectors and media affected. As can be seen, many of these tools can be described as both multi-sectoral, in that their application affects more than one sector of society, and multi-media, in that their application is designed to have effects on more than one environmental medium. This highlights the interconnections between the various tools available and the need for an integrated approach to environmental management.

Integrated Environmental Management and Protection

In recent years, there has been a growing trend towards the adoption of an integrated approach to

Table 15.1 Key Strategies and Tools

RESPONSES	Agriculture	Forestry	Marine	Energy	Industry	Transport	Tourism	Trade	Municipal	Water	Air	Soil	Landuse/Landscape*
Policies and Strategies													
National Sustainable Development Strategy	✓	✓	✓	✓	✓	✓	✓	✓	✓	✓	✓	✓	✓
Waste Management: Changing Our Ways	✓	✓	✓	✓	✓	✓	✓	✓	✓	✓	✓	✓	✓
Growing for the Future - Forestry Strategic Plan		✓								✓	✓	✓	✓
Catchment-based Strategy Against Eutrophication	✓	✓			✓				✓	✓		✓	✓
Guidance Tools													
Codes of Good Agricultural Practice	✓	✓			✓				✓	✓		✓	✓
Teagasc agricultural guidelines	✓	✓			✓				✓	✓		✓	
Forestry Guidelines		✓								✓		✓	
EPA Guidelines on Landfill and BATNEEC notes	✓			✓	✓				✓	✓	✓	✓	✓
Planning Tools													
Groundwater Protection Schemes	✓	✓			✓			✓		✓		✓	✓
Catchment Management Planning	✓	✓	✓	✓	✓		✓		✓	✓		✓	✓
Phosphorus Regulations Measures Reports	✓	✓			✓		✓			✓		✓	✓
Forest Inventory and Planning System		✓								✓		✓	✓
Local Authority Waste Management Plans	✓			✓	✓	✓	✓	✓	✓	✓		✓	✓
Air Quality Management Plans				✓	✓	✓			✓		✓		
County Development Plans	✓	✓	✓	✓	✓		✓		✓	✓	✓	✓	✓
Environmental Impact Assessment	✓	✓	✓	✓	✓	✓	✓		✓	✓	✓	✓	✓
Licensing Control and Enforcement Tools													
Environmental Legislation	✓	✓	✓	✓	✓	✓	✓	✓	✓	✓	✓	✓	✓
Integrated Pollution Control and Waste Licensing	✓			✓	✓					✓	✓	✓	✓
Single media licensing by Local Authorities (for water and air)					✓				✓	✓	✓		
Licensing and Control of GMOs	✓				✓			✓				✓	✓
VOC Emissions Control					✓	✓				✓	✓	✓	
Monitoring Tools													
EPA and local authority monitoring programmes	✓	✓	✓	✓	✓	✓	✓		✓	✓	✓	✓	✓
Dúchas monitoring of designated areas	✓	✓	✓	✓	✓	✓	✓	✓	✓	✓	✓	✓	✓
Environmental Protection Tools													
Urban waste water treatment					✓		✓		✓	✓			✓
Nutrient Management Planning	✓	✓			✓					✓		✓	✓
Rural Environment Protection Scheme	✓									✓		✓	✓
Control of Farmyard Pollution Scheme	✓									✓		✓	✓
Environmental Management Systems				✓	✓					✓	✓	✓	✓
Cleaner Production				✓	✓					✓	✓	✓	✓
Traffic Reduction Measures						✓				✓	✓		✓
Catalytic converters						✓					✓		
Energy conservation / alternative energy				✓	✓					✓	✓		
Protected sites / species	✓	✓	✓	✓	✓	✓	✓	✓	✓	✓	✓	✓	✓

including natural heritage and biodiversity

environmental protection and management in Ireland. Integrated pollution control (IPC) licensing of industry was introduced in 1994 and now most industrial and manufacturing activities with significant pollution potential are controlled through IPC. The integrated licensing approach has been extended to the control of all significant waste disposal and recovery activities following the enactment of the Waste Management Act, 1996. There has also been a significant growth in the adoption of an environmental management systems approach, both at individual company level and at institutional level. The integrated approach recognises the need to consider all aspects of the environment so that media such as air and water are not being protected at the expense of other media such as soil and land.

IPC Licensing

IPC licensing focuses on the elimination or reduction of waste and emissions of all kinds at source having regard to the principle of best available technology not entailing excessive cost (BATNEEC). Under IPC, a single licence is issued for one activity to cover all aspects relating to the risk of environmental pollution. As expected, there has been a strong growth in the number of companies controlled through IPC since 1994 (Fig. 15.2 and Fig. 15.3) with 409 licences issued by December 1999. Ultimately, all new and existing industrial and manufacturing facilities in the State with significant pollution potential will be subject to IPC licensing.

Regulation and enforcement of IPC licences provide a dynamic operating procedure within which progressive environmental improvements can be achieved. Two essential ingredients of the licensing system are the Environmental Management System (EMS) and the Annual Environmental Report (AER). The EMS is the engine that drives

continual improvement of environmental performance, with each licensee required to establish and implement an EMS so that measurable objectives and targets can be set to minimise and, where practicable, eliminate adverse environmental effects. The AER, in conjunction with independent assessment by the EPA, provides detailed information on the environmental performance of the activity concerned. A Pollution Emissions Register (PER) is also included in the AER where required by the licence (Box 15.5). Examples of pollution reduction, solvent reduction, waste reduction and energy and water use initiatives undertaken by licensees during 1998 (EPA, 1999b) illustrate the dynamic nature of IPC and show how the process goes well beyond simply controlling emissions. Where licensees are found to be out of compliance with a licence condition, appropriate action is taken to bring the licensee back into compliance either through the issuing and follow-up of notices or, where there is an inadequate response to notices served, through prosecution (EPA, 1999b).

The EPA has also organised a successful cleaner production pilot demonstration programme under the Environmental Monitoring R&D sub-programme of the Environmental Services Operational Programme 1994-1999 (Chapter 14). Waste and energy reduction values achieved by the 14 participating companies were very impressive; for example, the typical reduction achieved in hazardous waste generation was 50-80 per cent. The total economic benefit of the cleaner production initiatives undertaken in this pilot demonstration programme is conservatively estimated at £700,000 per year (Byrne Ó Cléirigh, 1999).

Waste Licensing

Licensing of waste activities by the EPA under the Waste Management

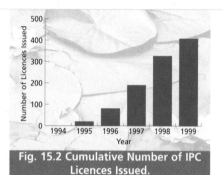

Fig. 15.2 Cumulative Number of IPC Licences Issued.

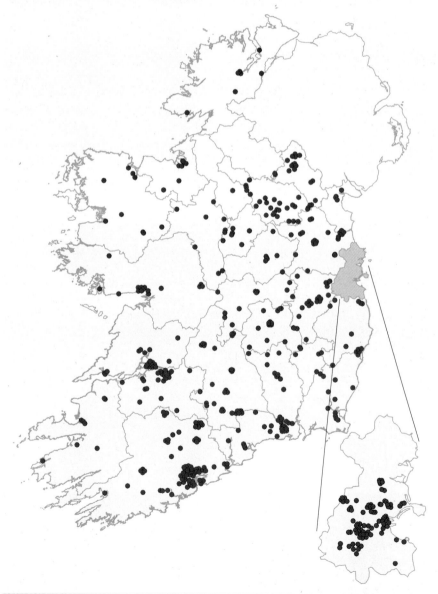

Fig. 15.3 Distribution of IPC Licensed Activities in Ireland

Box 15.5 Control of Hazardous Substances

Control of the vast number of chemical substances in use is difficult, and it is necessary therefore to adopt a policy of prioritisation, based on identifying those substances of greatest risk to humans and the environment. For instance, the main EU Directive intended to control discharges of dangerous substances to water (CEC, 1976) prioritises in its List I a number of pesticides and chlorinated solvents, as well as the metals cadmium and mercury, the toxicity and persistence of which are relatively high. A recent development under this Directive was an Informal Priority Setting (IPS) scheme relating to substances likely to enter the aquatic environment, which has resulted in two priority lists of about 230 substances. It is proposed that the water framework Directive when enacted will replace the dangerous substances Directive. In preparation for the water framework Directive, the European Commission recently proposed a priority list of 32 substances (EC, 2000a). An ongoing project undertaken by the Clean Technology Centre in Cork as part of the EPA environmental research programme (Chapter 1), aims at producing a priority list of substances which are believed to be relevant in an Irish context, with an emphasis on the aquatic environment.

In relation to air, the CLRTAP Protocol on Persistent Organic Pollutants (Box 15.3) establishes a list of 12 named pesticides and PCBs to be eliminated from production and use, with restrictions on the use of several others. Reductions of national emissions of a number of additional listed substances (including polycyclic aromatic hydrocarbons and dioxins and furans) are required, referenced to a specified base year. The CLRTAP Protocol on Heavy Metals will require reductions of harmful emissions of the metals cadmium, lead and mercury, to be achieved by applying best available techniques (BAT) and emission limit values. The recently adopted solvents Directive (CEC, 1999b) aims at preventing or reducing emissions of volatile organic compounds and the potential risks to human health.

Industrial emissions of hazardous materials are largely controlled through the IPC licensing procedure. The Pollution Emissions Register (PER), required as a condition of the majority of IPC licences, details how much of a tracked substance ends up in product, is recycled or is released to the environment. It is expected that both the quality and quantity of PER reporting will improve in coming years and that it will provide a valuable tool in estimating and controlling losses of certain substances to the environment.

In industry, substitution of dangerous solvents or active ingredients by less hazardous substances has had considerable environmental, health and safety benefits. It is important, however, that chemical substitution does not shift the source of environmental pressure and become detrimental to another area of the environment. An example of such an unintended effect can be found in changes in the chemicals used in dipping of sheep to treat against ectoparasites, such as scab, which has resulted in the use of alternative chemicals (synthetic pyrethroids) which are highly toxic to the aquatic environment.

emission limits, are required to establish and implement an Environmental Management System (EMS) and to prepare an Annual Environmental Report (AER). While it is too early to make any specific judgements about the relative impact of waste licensing, it is clear that the introduction of the licensing system is resulting in significantly increased investment. Standards of waste management are undoubtedly rising and will continue to rise.

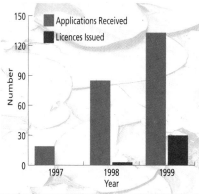

Figure 15.4 Cumulative Number of Waste Licence Applications and Licences Issued

Environmental Management Systems

There has been strong growth in the adoption of Environmental Management Systems (EMS) in Ireland, with over 300 in place and at least as many again being implemented. The primary drivers behind companies installing an EMS are the requirements of IPC and waste licensing, company interest in setting up an EMS voluntarily, local authority licensing and the 'supply-chain driver', i.e., large companies requiring that their suppliers have an EMS in place. Grant schemes to promote environmental efficiency and installation of EMSs amongst small and medium sized indigenous Irish manufacturing industries are provided by Enterprise Ireland.

The EPA is the first regulatory body in Europe to insist on an EMS as a mandatory licence condition, appropriate to the nature and scale of

Act commenced in May 1997. By the end of 1999, 133 applications had been received with 30 licences granted (Figure 15.4). Ultimately all significant waste disposal and recovery activities in the country will be licensed. Applications for waste licences are determined by the Agency on the basis of a single integrated licence (as for IPC) that deals with emissions to all environmental media, in addition to

the environmental management of the facility. All related operations carried on by the applicant in, on or adjacent to the facility are taken into consideration. Given the specific nature of waste activities such as landfilling, the Agency has the power to control the entire life cycle of an activity, from the construction phase through to closure and aftercare. Waste licensees, in addition to being required to comply with strict

the activity concerned. Large manufacturing industries are increasingly moving towards the adoption of accredited EMSs (such as ISO 14001 or the Eco-Management and Audit Scheme (EMAS)), particularly where increased competitiveness through cost savings and enhanced public image can be achieved as a result of better environmental management (Figure 15.5). The National Accreditation Board (NAB) and the EPA produced a guidance document in 1997 on harmonisation of the requirements of integrated licensing and accredited EMSs (NAB and EPA, 1997). This initiative is the first of its type in Europe and is being widely recognised for the benefits it brings in terms of cost savings, improved reporting and increased public recognition of a company's environmental efforts (Hussey, 1998; Maclean, 1998). It is consistent with the EU drive towards achieving increased coherence between the various legislative instruments in the environmental field at the level of the individual member states. Proposals for a revised European Commission Scheme - known as EMAS II - are being considered at present, to enhance the effectiveness, credibility and public awareness of the Scheme based on the experience of implementing EMAS I.

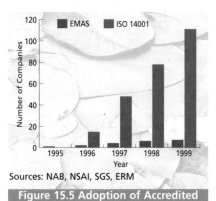

Sources: NAB, NSAI, SGS, ERM

Figure 15.5 Adoption of Accredited Environmental Management Systems

The EPA also actively encourages an EMS approach to environmental management in general, including matters such as catchment management planning, the operation of waste water treatment plants and evaluating the environmental performance of local authorities. The growth in the adoption of an EMS culture in Ireland is to be welcomed and every effort should be made to continue to encourage developments in this area, both in the public sector and the private sector.

Genetically Modified Organisms – Licensing and Control

The Department of the Environment and Local Government is responsible for national policy in the GMO area. The EPA is the competent authority for implementing the GMO Regulations, which includes consideration of notification for GMO use in the State. The EPA may consult the National Advisory Committee on Genetically Modified Organisms on any aspect of its functions under the GMO Regulations. The Committee consists of 12 members nominated by both Government and non-Governmental organisations (NGOs) and is re-appointed every three years.

In Ireland, GMO activities are considered under the headings of: (a) contained use and (b) deliberate release. Containment is provided either by physical barriers, or by a combination of physical barriers, together with chemical and/or biological barriers. Deliberate release of GMOs into the environment means any intentional release into the environment of a GMO without provisions for containment. There are two different types of deliberate release covered by the Regulations and these are for (i) research and development purposes - field trials and (ii) placing GMO products on the market. The EPA maintains a Register of GMO Users in the State and this is available for public inspection. Up to end of 1999, there were 89 entries on the Register. More than 90 per cent of the GMO users in the State fall under the category of contained uses.

Protecting Water Quality

The principal planning tool for protecting the quality of water resources in Ireland is the power of a local authority to make and implement a water quality management plan (Fig. 15.6). Extensive powers also reside in the Local Government (Water Pollution) Acts, 1977-90, in relation to licensing, monitoring and enforcement. However, it is clear that the availability of these powers has not prevented the gradual deterioration of water quality in the country, particularly through eutrophication.

It is now widely acknowledged that the principal cause of eutrophication is diffuse or non-point source pollution, principally of agricultural origin (Chapter 9; Lucey *et al.*, 1999). Past water quality management plans tended to concentrate on controlling and reducing point source inputs and did not, to any significant extent, address diffuse sources of pollution. There is also little evidence that water quality

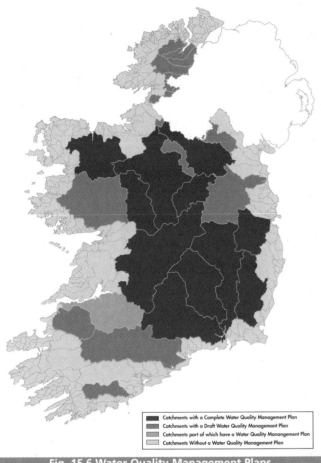

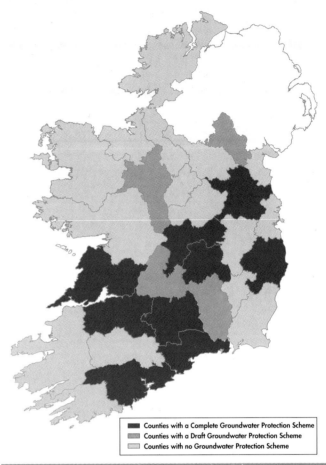

Catchments with a Complete Water Quality Management Plan
Catchments with a Draft Water Quality Management Plan
Catchments part of which have a Water Quality Management Plan
Catchments Without a Water Quality Management Plan

Counties with a Complete Groundwater Protection Scheme
Counties with a Draft Groundwater Protection Scheme
Counties with no Groundwater Protection Scheme

Fig. 15.6 Water Quality Management Plans

Fig. 15.7 Groundwater Protection Schemes

management plans have been subject to the necessary review and modifications required of a dynamic planning process, even though revision was viewed as an integral part of the legislation adopted (Fanning *et al.*, 1999).

The restriction of water quality management planning to the protection of surface waters has also meant that groundwater quality has not been afforded the same level of statutory protection. Groundwater protection schemes, have been developed by several county councils in association with the Geological Survey of Ireland (Figure 15.7) and more are in preparation, based on published guidance (DELG *et al.*, 1999). In addition, a number of measures for the protection of groundwater are being pursued in the context of the Rural Water Programme. While these initiatives will go some way to protecting groundwater, a more integrated

approach to surface water and groundwater planning can lead to a higher level of environmental protection.

All existing water quality management plans are to be reviewed in the next ten years and this revision will have to take into account the objectives and measures recommended in the Government strategy document against eutrophication (DoE, 1997b), as well as the requirements of the Phosphorus Regulations, 1998 (see above) and relevant EU Directives. In addition, these plans will have to take into account the requirements of the draft water framework Directive when enacted. All recent water quality management plans, strategies and monitoring schemes are now addressing the issue of diffuse sources of pollution in some detail. Projects are underway for the establishment of systems for the management and monitoring of water quality in

relation to Loughs Derg, Ree and Leane and the rivers Boyne, Liffey and Suir, with Government and European funding.

The status of urban waste water treatment in the State was reviewed in Chapter 5. Under the urban waste water treatment Regulations, the majority of agglomerations (i.e., population equivalents between 2,000 and 15,000) will have to have secondary treatment by the end of 2005. More stringent requirements, in terms of treatment and/or timeframe, apply to large agglomerations or agglomerations discharging into sensitive areas. The National Development Plan 2000-2006 provides for the investment of some £2.5 billion in water and waste water infrastructure with the major portion being assigned to waste water treatment facilities. Sludge arisings from urban waste water treatment plants are thus expected to increase. Reuse of sewage sludge (e.g., in agriculture and forestry), in compliance with the Waste Management (Use of Sewage Sludge in Agriculture) Regulations, 1998, is the preferable option (O'Leary and Carty, 1998).

A recent assessment of drinking water quality in the State found that while public water supplies are generally satisfactory (although problems exist in certain areas), a significant proportion of group water schemes are cause for concern (EPA, 1999c). A systematic evaluation of all group schemes commenced in 1999 through a partnership agreement between the Local Authorities, the National Federation of Group Water Schemes and the Government. This should lead to the identification of specific problem areas and help in the identification of solutions. The EPA recommends effective disinfection of drinking water supplies and appropriate siting and control of silage pits, slurry tanks and septic tanks to improve the quality of supplies (EPA, 1999c). New regulations introduced in 1999 strengthen the legal basis for addressing quality problems in private group water schemes, and require improvements within the framework of Strategic Rural Water Planning. These Regulations are a response to European Commission concern about the legal position governing quality-deficient private group water schemes. These Regulations, however, are a temporary measure and more comprehensive provisions in relation to group water schemes are expected in the forthcoming Water Services Bill. The adoption of the new drinking water Directive (CEC, 1998b) is of major significance and will have far-reaching implications. Within the next five years there will be a major change in the nature and extent of the monitoring of drinking water throughout the country and the EU at large (EPA, 1999c). Designation of nitrate vulnerable zones under the nitrates Directive (CEC, 1991b) is pending.

Protecting Air Quality

Ambient smoke, SO_2 and lead levels in urban areas of the State are now at very low levels due to the introduction of a series of measures to control their emissions (Chapter 8). However, insufficient monitoring of other air pollutants has hampered adequate assessment of the State's air quality (McGettigan, 1998). The EPA has been assigned the role of implementing the EU Directive on ambient air quality assessment and management in the State. Under this Directive, the first daughter Directive sets stringent legal limit values for SO_2, NO_2, PM_{10} and lead, which are to be met within 10-15 years (CEC, 1999c). Future daughter Directives will address ozone, benzene, carbon monoxide, polyaromatic hydrocarbons and some heavy metals. Ireland and all other Member States must take steps to comply with the new limits, monitor and assess air quality on the basis of common methods and criteria, and ensure that adequate information on ambient air quality is made available to the public (Chapter 8). The EPA has finalised a national air quality monitoring programme which takes full account of the requirements of the new legislation. This will require an increased monitoring frequency for a wider range of parameters in a greater number of locations around the State. In addition, local authorities in the Dublin area have recently published an air quality management plan under the Air Pollution Act, 1987. The success of measures to address emissions to air is addressed in Chapters 4 and 8.

Protecting Soil Quality

While Ireland has fortunately escaped the legacy of significant soil contamination experienced by many industrialised countries, it is clear that a proportion of soils in Ireland are either managed inappropriately (e.g., by over-application of nutrients) or are under threat of degradation (e.g., by overgrazing or peatland development). Pressures on soils principally arise from the following: intensive agriculture; industrial organic waste disposal; drainage; commercial forestry; peat extraction; mining; and urbanisation and infrastructure development. Many of the activities affecting soil functions also have the potential to cause deleterious effects on surface water and groundwater resources and biodiversity.

Legislation relating directly to soils and soil protection is generally poorly developed at national level and at European level, with a few exceptions (e.g., Germany, Netherlands). However, in many cases existing air, water and conservation legislation affords protection indirectly to soils, and soils are specifically addressed in environmental impact assessment legislation. A number of agreements, protocols and codes of good practice have been developed in relation to soil protection both at international and national levels (e.g., the European Soil Charter (EC, 1972), World Soil Charter (UN, 1981), the Code of Good Agricultural Practice (DAFF and DoE, 1996), Forestry and Fisheries Guidelines (Forest Service, 1991)). It is necessary that soil quality in Ireland should be maintained and, where necessary improved, through the adoption and application of appropriate environmental management practices. This will require effective application of existing legislation and codes of practice and the eco-auditing of relevant policies and programmes, such as those relating to agricultural grant schemes, forestry development, industrial and urban development and peat extraction for the energy sector.

Protecting Biodiversity

Primary Biodiversity-related Designations

The Department of Arts, Heritage, Gaeltacht and the Islands distinguishes two categories of protected areas in the State:

- one comprising sites set aside primarily for nature conservation, which are generally unpopulated with no significant economic activities, e.g., National Parks and Nature Reserves; and

- a much larger category of sites which are designated at a national (NHAs) and European (SPAs/SACs) level for their biodiversity importance, but where sustainable economic activities also take place.

In recent years progress has been made in establishing, or proposing for designation, a range of protected areas (i.e., NHAs, SPAs and SACs) for biodiversity. Approximately 1,100 sites of national ecological and geological importance have been proposed by Dúchas for designation as NHAs. However NHAs have no legislative basis until the Wildlife Amendment Bill is enacted and consequently receive limited legal protection at present, except where developments are covered by the Planning Acts. Despite Government and EU Policy to only grant-aid developments in these areas that are compatible with protecting the environment, concern has been expressed that some proposed NHAs may already have been affected by damaging activities (Hickie, 1997).

The transposition of the habitats Directive (CEC, 1992a) into Irish law in 1997 was a major step forward in protection of European (NATURA 2000) sites in Ireland. Until 1997, SPAs designated under the wild birds Directive (CEC, 1979) received relatively limited legal protection under Irish legislation. With the Habitats Regulations now in force, it is expected that SPAs and SACs threatened by development will be safeguarded from damaging activities. However, in comparison to most other European countries, Ireland has currently designated a relatively low proportion of its national territory as SPAs or proposed Sites of

Community Importance (pSCIs - an intermediary stage before full SAC status) (Figure 15.8). A recent assessment of the Irish conservation designation lists indicates that the State's SPA list is incomplete and the pSCI list is notably insufficient (EC, 2000b). Concern has also been expressed over the number of complaints which the European Commission has received relating to a wide range of potentially damaging activities in Irish SPAs (or sites requiring such protection) (Ó Briain, 1999). Indeed, the European Commission is pursuing legal action against the State in relation to the habitats Directive (Cashman, 1999) and has indicated that it intends to pursue legal action in relation to the wild birds Directive (Chapter 12).

Limited resources and the SAC appeals process are considered to have delayed NATURA 2000 site designation. Increased funding for nature conservation in the State should help address some of these and other issues relating to biodiversity protection and management (Chapter 12). Dúchas is currently developing management plans for Ireland's SPAs and candidate SACs, which should provide for effective management of these areas

and maintain and enhance the value of the sites, particularly for the species or habitats for which they are designated. It is expected that the process of designating candidate SACs will be completed in 2000 and that approximately 400 sites (or 9 per cent of the national territory) will be designated.

Statutory Nature Reserves are regarded as the most rigorous mechanism in Ireland for the protection of ecosystems and species of flora and fauna, as almost all damaging activities can be legally prevented in Nature Reserves. Concern has been expressed about

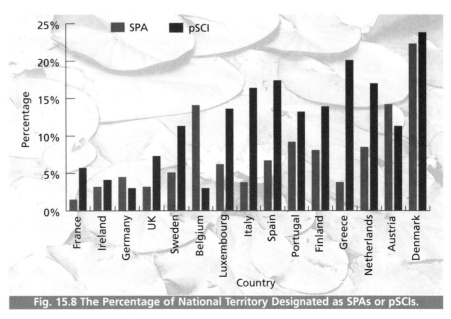

Fig. 15.8 The Percentage of National Territory Designated as SPAs or pSCIs.

Note: Based on the total terrestrial and marine surface area designated in relation to the terrestrial surface area of the Member State as of 08/03/00 (EC, 2000b).

the extent and monitoring of the Nature Reserve network, though its value in protecting habitats which may otherwise have been damaged or destroyed is recognised (Hickie, 1997). The area of land designated as National Parks in Ireland has increased by approximately 18,000 ha since 1996 (to a total of 57,000 ha). This includes the designation of a sixth National Park in the Owenduff/Nephin area of Co. Mayo in 1999, comprising 9,700 ha. The National Park designation appears to have achieved its aims of balancing nature conservation with public recreation and appreciation reasonably well, despite some problems with encroachment of livestock, infestation with exotic species such as *Rhododendron ponticum* and controversial visitor centre proposals in the Burren and the Wicklow Mountains (Hickie, 1997). To date only the Killarney National Park has a published management plan (OPW, 1990),

although plans are in preparation for the other National Parks. Other categories of areas designated for biodiversity in the State (e.g., Ramsar sites, Refuges for Fauna, Wildfowl Sanctuaries) are outlined in Chapter 12.

Other Conservation Measures

Less than 10 per cent of the Irish countryside has a formal nature conservation designation. Outside protected areas, biodiversity conservation is not generally the dominant priority. Nevertheless, it is necessary to maintain, and where possible enhance, in so far as possible, biodiversity in the broader countryside. Changes in farming practices and development pressures are thought to be the main factors exerting increasing threats to biological diversity in the State, causing deterioration in the quality of habitats and even their destruction.

As stated earlier, nature conservation countrywide is primarily put into effect through the Wildlife Act, 1976, which has been difficult to enforce effectively due to deficiencies in the Act and lack of resources. The Wildlife (Amendment) Bill, 1999, aims at addressing many of these deficiencies (see above). The Planning Acts also afford some protection for wildlife on a national basis, for example through the EIA regulations. Local authorities (and other national bodies) may have a

significant positive influence on local biological diversity, through wildlife friendly management of public areas, roadside margins, etc. and planting of native species and seed stock. Other measures important for protection of biodiversity countrywide include legal protection of species and specific conservation programmes (Chapter 12), the compilation of Red Data Books on an all-Ireland basis on species under threat and various measures to preserve genetic diversity (DAHGI, 1998).

There are a number of designations which, though not primarily made for the direct protection of biological diversity, contribute to its conservation. The most important of these in terms of biodiversity are development controls (e.g., Areas of Special Control and Special Amenity Area Orders), water quality designations and land managed under the Rural Environment Protection Scheme (REPS). Other relevant designations are generally of limited extent (Tree Preservation Orders, the UNESCO World Heritage Sites).

Several types of designations are available to local authorities to protect the environment and, *inter alia*, biodiversity. Planning authorities may designate 'Areas of Special Control' in County Development Plans to designate land where stricter planning controls apply to protect scenic landscapes, amenities and areas of ecological value. Planning authorities may also make Special Amenity Area Orders (SAAOs), on the grounds of outstanding natural beauty, special recreational value or a need for conservation, and Conservation Orders, for the conservation of threatened flora or fauna. The SAAO allows planning authorities to control development without the need for compensation and to control certain developments that are normally exempted. SAAOs are considered more effective than zoning Areas of Special Control in County

an Roinn Ealaíon, Cultúir ↑ Gaeltachta

GLENGARRIFF NATURE RESERVE

NO FIRES

NO LITTER

Development Plans (Hickie, 1997). However, to date, only two SAAOs have been made (for North Bull Island and for the Liffey Valley in Co. Dublin - one is also proposed for Howth) and no Conservation Order has ever been made. This is a matter of some concern, as SAAOs would appear to be the best existing designation for protecting 'green belts' that are subjected to intense development pressure. Changes proposed in the Planning and Development Bill, 1999, will have significant consequences for the duties and powers of planning authorities to protect the environment and biodiversity (see section on Legislation). However, included in these changes is the proposal that nature conservation will not be an objective of Special Amenity Area Orders (SAAOs) in the future, proposing that this objective is more appropriate to other specialised designations.

There are a number of existing and proposed designations to protect water quality, which may have benefits for biodiversity. These include the designation of 22 Salmonid Waters under the freshwater fish Directive and the designation of 10 water bodies as Sensitive Areas under the urban waste water treatment Directive. The EPA has proposed that the objective for all surface waters should be salmonid water quality, except where otherwise classified by a competent authority due to particular local conditions (EPA, 1997). Work is ongoing at a European level on a draft water framework Directive, which aims at protecting and enhancing the status of aquatic ecosystems (including their ecological quality), and the terrestrial ecosystems and wetlands that depend on them.

REPS is the main countrywide agri-environmental incentive scheme, which is seen as a potentially important instrument for nature conservation, though this scheme has

a number of deficiencies (Box 15.6). Despite the large uptake of REPS particularly in ecologically significant areas (and predictions of further increases in future uptake), over two-thirds of the utilisable agricultural area in the State is not presently farmed under REPS. Large-scale intensive farming activities, which may potentially have a large impact on the environment, are significantly

under-represented in REPS. It has been suggested that the provision of financial incentives to encourage farmers, who are unsuited to participation in the existing REPS, to maintain, manage and restore heritage sites and habitats (including hedgerows) on farms may provide an effective means of aiding conservation in the wider countryside (Heritage Council, 1999a).

Box 15.6 Rural Environment Protection Scheme (REPS)

Introduced in Ireland in 1994 under Council Regulation 2078/92 (CEC, 1992b), REPS constitutes the primary agri-environmental measure nation-wide. The scheme aims at rewarding farmers for carrying out their farming activities in an environmentally friendly manner and at bringing about environmental improvement on farms. Aside from the Wildlife Act, 1976, it is one of the principal mechanisms for protecting wildlife habitats both inside and outside conservation designated areas. Currently, approximately 31 per cent (or 1.5 million ha) of the utilisable agricultural area is being farmed under REPS guidelines (Fig. 15.9). It is anticipated that participation in REPS will rise significantly as a result of recent revisions to provide for increased payments to farmers in Natural Heritage Areas (including SACs and SPAs) and commonages.

A recent Government evaluation of REPS indicated that it was having positive environmental and socio-economic impacts, including reducing fertiliser use on farms and increasing awareness of environmentally sensitive farming practices (DAF, 1999). The review does, however, identify the need for better evaluation procedures and indicators. While Teagasc and other organisations have undertaken studies on aspects of the Scheme, the lack of adequate baseline information in REPS plans and the absence of a formal country-wide environmental monitoring programme of representative farms make it very difficult to assess the environmental benefit of REPS nationally. Thus it is important that a system for baseline data collection and monitoring be established.

Commonage framework plans, in the process of being drawn up by Dúchas and the Department of Agriculture, Food and Rural Development, should provide valuable ecological data for evaluating the success of REPS in future years in restoring and managing these fragile systems. Concerns have been expressed about the ecological expertise of REPS planners and the competitive pressures under which they operate the scheme (Heritage Council, 1999a). It is important that there is a clear and transparent mechanism for monitoring and evaluating the scheme. As REPS is one of the principal mechanisms to meet conservation objectives in national (NHAs) and European (SACs and SPAs) sites, appropriate ecological management of these areas under REPS is essential.

The requirement since 1998 for cross-compliance between REPS and the Headage and Ewe Premium Schemes in areas degraded by overgrazing (and the subsequent extension of this requirement to all commonages), the development of Commonage Framework Plans and the introduction of the SAC programme, are positive developments and should help address the overgrazing brought about by these sheep payment schemes. However, it appears incongruous that one scheme, REPS, makes payments to farmers in degraded areas, to counteract the negative effects of other schemes - the Ewe Premium and Headage Payment Schemes. It would be far more desirable that environmental objectives would be an integral part of all relevant agricultural grant schemes.

A SECTORAL ANALYSIS

In the National Sustainable Development Strategy the Government set out Action Programmes for sustainability for the following sectors: agriculture, forestry, marine resources, energy, industry, transport, tourism and trade. Examples of key tools and strategies available for implementing these programmes are outlined earlier in Table 15.1. This section reports on progress in relation to key elements of the Action Programmes. The challenges ahead for each sector are considered in Chapter 16. While a sectoral analysis is worthwhile in itself, it is important to appreciate the cross-linkages and inter-relationships that exist between sectors in relation to their potential impacts on the environment. Thus, integrated environmental protection and management requires that a multi-sectoral approach be adopted, for instance, when dealing with the key environmental challenges that were outlined in Chapter 13.

Agriculture

Since the publication of the National Sustainable Development Strategy, there has been some progress in introducing measures to improve agricultural sustainability, though there is still considerable work to be done. For example, cross compliance is now required between REPS and the Headage and Ewe premium

schemes, as previous measures failed to prevent overgrazing in vulnerable upland areas (Box 15.6). Targets for uptake of REPS have largely been met and the number of farmers in the scheme is expected to continue to increase (Fig. 15.9). In contrast, entry into the Control of Farmyard Pollution (CFP) scheme and the related Improvement of Dairy Hygiene Standards scheme was suspended in 1996, due to over subscription, and was not reintroduced until 1999. Participants in both schemes are required to follow an approved nutrient management plan (Chapter 16) or participate in REPS. Despite considerable expenditure on the CFP scheme (Chapter 14), the occurrence of inadequate farm slurry storage facilities is still widespread (Chapter 5).

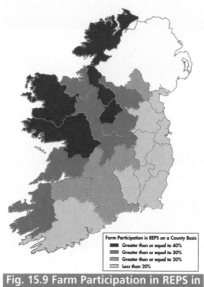

Fig. 15.9 Farm Participation in REPS in 1999

Significantly, Teagasc has issued revised guidelines on use of phosphorus and potassium fertiliser, which considerably reduce the recommended phosphorus application rates (Teagasc, 1998). IPC licensing of large-scale intensive pig and poultry operations has been introduced and a farm plastic recovery scheme is also in place. However, comprehensive guidance on sustainable agriculture by the Department of Agriculture, Food and Rural Development is still outstanding.

Forestry

Forestry may have both positive and negative impacts on the environment and the relevant issues include water resources, water quality, acidification, biodiversity, landscape and climate change (Chapter 11; O'Halloran *et al.*, 1996). Environmental considerations are taken into account for forestry grant approval, with State Agencies and local authorities consulted where environmental concerns arise. Since most afforestation only proceeds with grant aid, this has been a reasonably effective means of control (Hickie, 1997). Grant aid is precluded where plantations may impinge on listed and designated sites, and local authorities are consulted on all afforestation over 25 hectares in size. However, concern has been expressed that areas of biodiversity, landscape and heritage value outside of protected areas, such as marginal agricultural land, are at risk of over-development from commercial forestry (Heritage Council, 1999b).

The Local Government (Planning and Development) Bill proposes that initial planting of forests will no longer be exempt from planning permission given that afforestation can have significant environmental effects. Development by the Forest Service of Geographical Information System-based planning tools such as the Indicative Forestry Strategy and the recently developed Forest Inventory and Planning System (FIPS) should help guide the location and character of future afforestation to ensure it is in harmony with the environment. Appropriate strategic planning of forestry is particularly important given the rapid expansion of forestry envisaged in Government policy (DAFF, 1996).

Many of the actions recommended in the National Sustainable Development Strategy to ensure sustainable forestry have not yet been completed. Forestry legislation remains under review and the National Forest Standard is still under development by the Forest Service. The National Forest Standard will entail a Code of Best Forest Practice, embracing Forestry Guidelines (on fisheries, landscape, archaeology, biodiversity, harvesting, etc.) and criteria for sustainable forest management. In this context it is worth noting that Coillte Teoranta has produced a Sustainable Forest Management Framework and intends to develop a Management System to translate the Framework into practice (Coillte, 1999). The draft consultation guidelines for planning authorities on designation of areas sensitive to forestry development have yet to be finalised. While the requirement for EIA for new afforestation has been reduced to 70 hectares as promised in the National Sustainable Development Strategy, this threshold has been criticised by the European Commission. The European Court of Justice recently ruled that Ireland failed to apply correctly the 1985 EIA Directive in this area.

Marine Resources

There has been a significant number of international and national legislative developments in the marine sector since 1996 (see Legislation section). These developments have aimed at improving the prevention and control

of certain potentially polluting activities in the marine environment, dealing with areas such as oil pollution, dumping at sea and aquaculture. The ongoing upgrading of urban waste water treatment plants will also have positive benefits for marine water quality. In addition, the development of aquaculture zoning plans by Dúchas in Special Protection Areas, as part of site conservation plans, should help to minimise the environmental impact of mariculture operations at these sites. Other activities ongoing to address marine and coastal issues include the following: the provision of port reception facilities for ship waste; monitoring of bathing water quality and the operation of the Blue Flag Scheme in relation to quality of beaches; the Coastwatch Europe survey; and local authority programmes to combat coastal erosion. The publication of an environmental strategy for offshore oil and gas exploration is still outstanding.

The principal instrument within the EU to secure the long-term rational development of marine fisheries is the 1983 Common Fisheries Policy (CFP). A combination of Total Allowable Catches (TACs)/quotas, technical conservation measures (such as controls on fishing gear, area and time of fishing, minimum landing sizes, selectivity of gear) and multi-annual guidance programmes (to control catching capacity and fishing effort of the combined European Community fleets), is aimed at reducing and controlling fishing mortality rates, minimising discards and by-catch, and generally improving marine ecosystems. However, stocks of fish, such as cod, saithe, plaice, sole and northern hake, are at present considered by the International Council for Exploration of the Seas (ICES) to be close to or outside their safe biological limits in certain waters around Ireland and therefore give cause for concern. In addition, discarding of juvenile fish

and non-target species is perceived to be a continuing problem in many fisheries (Boelens *et al.*, 1999). Future strategies to address these issues and other problems are discussed in Chapter 16.

In relation to inland fisheries, the Government is implementing a Salmon Management Strategy on a phased basis, to ensure sufficient salmon return to their native rivers to spawn and that the surplus is shared equally between legitimate interests. It is crucial that this Strategy is successful as nominal overall Irish salmon catch is currently at historically low levels (Boelens *et al.*, 1999). Conservation regulations were introduced in 1997 as the first phase of the new management regime. A key element of the second phase is the introduction of a salmon tagging scheme, as proposed in the Fisheries (Amendment) Bill, 1999. Measures to address the sea-trout collapse include a policy of 'Single Bay Management', put in place to introduce new and better husbandry practices on fish farms. The Single Bay Management concept has been shown to be successful in reducing sea lice loads on farm fish (Boelens *et al.*, 1999). Improved catchment management planning in various rivers and introduction of the Phosphorus Regulations, 1998, should also help protect inland fisheries and reduce chemical inputs to the aquatic environment.

Energy

Progress in meeting sustainable development targets for the energy sector has been relatively poor. Greenhouse gas emissions from the energy sector continue to increase (Chapter 4) and renewable energy comprises only approximately 6 per cent (or c.307 MW) of total installed electricity generating capacity (Irish Energy Centre, 1999a, 1999b), which falls short of the Government target of 10 per cent by the end of 1999 (DoE, 1997a). This is despite

incentives for development of alternative and renewable energy, e.g., under the EU THERMIE program, EU Interreg funding in Border areas and a series of four Government operated 'Alternative Energy Requirement' schemes. In 1998, the Government introduced tax relief for corporate equity investment in renewable energies and the Irish Energy Centre operated a Renewable Energy Feasibility Study Grant Scheme to stimulate renewable energy projects (Chapter 14). As a further support to the developing renewables sector, the Electricity Regulation Act, 1999 allows all electricity customers to purchase electricity that is produced using a renewable or alternative form of energy from February 2000.

In relation to energy efficiency, Ireland participates in the EU SAVE programme and the Irish Energy Centre provides grant-aid and advice to energy users in the industrial, institutional, and commercial sectors to facilitate reduced energy use in these sectors through schemes such as the Self Audit and Statement of Energy Accounts Scheme and the Energy Efficient Investment Support Scheme (Chapter 14). Revised Building Regulations were introduced in 1998 to enable energy saving in space heating of buildings thus reducing CO_2 emissions. Ongoing integrated pollution control licensing for larger industries and activities can lead to more efficient use of energy. IPC licensing requirements will come into operation for the existing energy sector on a phased basis from September 2000.

Industry

As discussed above, the ongoing application of IPC licensing, cleaner production technology and environmental management systems to industry, and the extension of these management tools within industry, represent the primary responses for sustainable industrial development. Local authorities must regulate industry that does not come under the remit of the EPA (generally through the issuing and enforcement of single media licences).

Additional initiatives introduced for managing and reducing industrial impacts on the environment include the following: a number of Enterprise Ireland grant schemes to improve the environmental performance of small and medium sized indigenous manufacturing industries; the annual Better Environment Awards for Industry; and the setting up and funding of REPAK, a private organisation, by users of large volumes of packaging to promote the

recycling of packaging waste (Chapter 6). In addition the European Eco-labelling Scheme, which promotes the design, production, marketing and use of products that have a reduced environmental impact during their entire life-cycle, has awarded eco-labels to over 200 products at present. This scheme provides consumers with better information on the environmental impact of products and aims at encouraging preferential consideration of eco-labelled products in purchasing decisions.

Transport

The rapid growth of the transport sector presents a considerable environmental challenge to Ireland's sustainable development. Measures to reduce reliance on private cars have failed to check the rapid increase in private car ownership and use (Chapter 3). This is despite increased investment in public transport under the Operational Programme for Transport 1994-1999 and in the Dublin Transport Initiative (Box 15.7). The construction of bypasses and improvement in roads has relieved problems in some areas. There are however continuing problems of traffic congestion, noise and pollution, which threaten the environmental and social fabric of many of our cities and large towns. In addition, whilst major infrastructure investments generally require the use of environmental

Box 15.7 Dublin Transport Initiative (DTI)

The Dublin Transportation Office was established as a corporate body in 1995 to co-ordinate and monitor the implementation of the DTI strategy (DTI, 1995), to make recommendations for an implementation programme and to review the strategy at least once every five years. By the end of 1998 a total of £320 million had been spent on DTI measures, the bulk of which relates to road projects. Progress has been reported on the DTI strategy across a number of fronts to date, including improvements in public transport (both bus and rail) and in facilities for cyclists and pedestrians, as well as significant investment in traffic calming and traffic management (DTO, 1998).

However, despite these improvements, overall progress on the implementation of the DTI strategy has fallen well short of expectations and this, coupled with increased demand for travel in the Strategy area, led to the preparation of a Short Term Action Plan to address immediate needs (DTO, 1998). The Plan was designed to accelerate the implementation of those elements of the DTI Strategy that could be completed in the period up to 2000. It focused on public transport enhancement, traffic management, parking policy and cycling facilities, and also included a comprehensive public information campaign to promote sustainable transport choices.

The DTI strategy and DTO short term action plan initiatives include:
- LUAS, the Dublin Port Tunnel and the completion of the Dublin C-Ring;
- 12 Quality Bus Corridors (by end 2000);
- An additional 150 buses (by end 1999);
- Additional rolling stock for the DART and lengthening of 12 station platforms;
- Extension of DART to Malahide, Co. Dublin and Greystones, Co. Wicklow;
- 47 additional suburban railcars;
- Upgrading of Maynooth-Clonsilla rail line;
- 160 kilometres of cycle tracks (by end 2000);
- Pilot park and ride facilities;
- Improved traffic management and enforcement.

impact assessment procedures, some recent development projects have proved particularly controversial e.g., the widening of the N11 through the Glen of the Downs and the possible impact of the proposed Kildare bypass on the ecology of Pollardstown Fen. The National Development Plan 2000-2006 contains proposals for significant further infrastructural development in the transport sector. The Government has stated that it will eco-audit individual operational programmes within the Plan. It is important that these eco-audits are carried out at a strategic level to ensure sustainable transport development. At a time of increasing pressure on the environment from the transport sector it is important that unsustainable demands are not placed on our natural heritage.

The Government has phased out the use of leaded petrol since 1 January, 2000 with only small amounts (0.5 per cent of total petrol sales) permitted for specialist vehicles (e.g., vintage cars). Since 1993 all new cars with petrol engines sold in the State have catalytic converters (which reduce vehicle emissions). Vehicle testing is being phased in under European legislation (CEC, 1996d), commencing with pre-1992 cars in the year 2000, followed by all 1992-96 cars in 2001, and all 4 year old cars and eligible older cars in 2002. Tests of emissions are specifically incorporated in the test. Recently introduced tax incentives for more fuel efficient cars and cleaner fuels are discussed in Chapter 14. The potential for success of these and other measures in combating air

pollution from transport is discussed in Chapter 16.

Tourism

Tourism and recreation can exert significant pressure on the environment, particularly in sensitive areas (Chapter 7; Chapter 12). In order to address these pressures, the Department of Tourism, Sport and Recreation has allocated £2.5 million for some 20 pilot 'Tourism and the Environment' projects, in partnership with local authorities, state agencies and the private sector. The projects, which were initiated in 1998, aim at demonstrating how particular problems affecting tourism and the environment might be dealt with, thus supporting tourism development while at the same time sustaining the environment on which it is based (Chapter 14).

Fifteen areas in the west of Ireland have been awarded the 'Beatha' quality mark, in recognition of their unspoilt environments that are being managed in a sustainable manner. This initiative was launched in 1995 and is jointly financed by the EU Life Programme and Eco-Lipead NASC Teo, a partnership of various interested agencies (NASC, 1998).

The European Blue Flags Scheme, operated in Ireland by An Taisce, promotes high standards of

environmental protection for beaches while at the same time catering for the needs of visitors through the provision of environmental information (Chapter 10). Facilities at 17 locations on the Shannon, Grand Canal and Barrow Navigation Systems have been provided by local authorities to cater for river cruisers fitted with appropriate storage and pumping facilities for waste water. Boats operating on the Shannon are required to have storage tanks fitted (ENFO, 1999). The Marine Institute has recently produced a number of publications on water-based tourism and leisure (e.g., Marine Institute, 1997, 1998a, 1998b, 1999). Further policy and action is required to ensure sustainable tourism and leisure growth, particularly in the coastal zone.

Trade

Ireland is strongly dependent on trade (Chapter 3). In order to ensure that Irish exports are sustainable, Irish products and services must demonstrate a high degree of environmental awareness and protection (Chapter 16). Equally Ireland must ensure that the goods and services that it imports do not adversely affect the environmental and socio-economic sustainability of other countries, e.g. through the application of fair trade policies. The Government's Statement of National Trade Policy aims at taking account

of the objectives of Agenda 21, with particular attention to the needs of developing countries (DETE, 1998). The policy presses for action in the World Trade Organisation (WTO) and elsewhere to ensure that trade expansion is compatible with the principles of sustainable development. Ireland has not yet ratified the Convention on International Trade in Endangered Species (CITES), however there are provisions to do so in the Wildlife (Amendment) Bill, 1999. In practice, however, the main provisions of the CITES Convention have been implemented in the State (DoE, 1997a).

FRAMEWORK FOR INTEGRATED ENVIRONMENTAL MANAGEMENT AND PROTECTION

Ireland is, in many ways, staking its claim as a clean country with a high quality environment. Agriculture, tourism and marine resources, in particular, depend for their continued development on a clean environment. Integrated environmental management will provide one part of the framework for sustainable economic development in Ireland.

The Environmental Protection Agency has proposed the integration of a number of environmental management tools, namely

environmental quality objectives (EQOs), environmental quality standards (EQSs) and environmental and socio-economic indicators, to help plan for sustainable natural resource management (Clenaghan *et al.*, 1999). EQOs describe the intended *use* of environmental media or the desired quality of the media (i.e., water, air, soil and land, including natural resources such as minerals and flora and fauna). By setting EQOs we are deciding the boundaries or limits, based on the extent of our current scientific understanding, within which development is sustainable, i.e., we are setting a 'Sustainability Target'. Sustainability targets or EQOs are quantified through the application of EQSs (medium-specific standards for chemical, physical or biological parameters). Indicators are then required to measure progress towards the sustainability target.

EQOs and EQSs for environmental media establish the framework within which the sustainability of various sectors can be measured (Figure 15.10). This *resource management framework* can guide sectors in dealing effectively with environmental issues, such as eutrophication. To ensure that a sector is sustainable, emission limit values or environmental management plans may be applied. Indicators can then be used to track progress.

It is intended that the proposed framework will allow complementary 'top-down' and 'bottom-up'

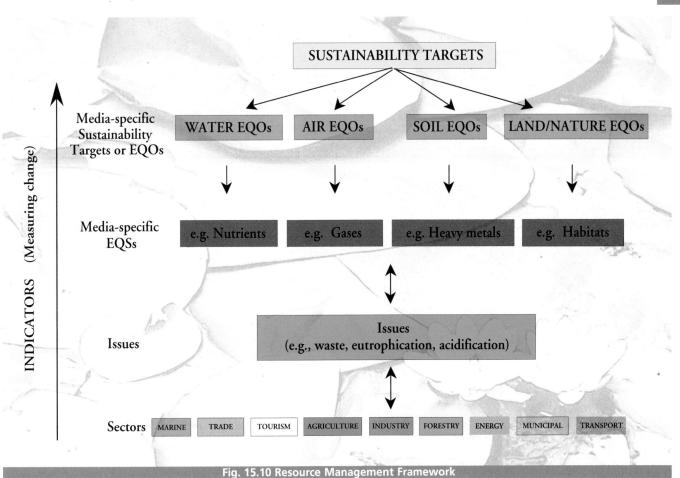

SUSTAINABILITY TARGETS

Media-specific Sustainability Targets or EQOs

WATER EQOs | AIR EQOs | SOIL EQOs | LAND/NATURE EQOs

Media-specific EQSs

e.g. Nutrients | e.g. Gases | e.g. Heavy metals | e.g. Habitats

Issues

Issues (e.g., waste, eutrophication, acidification)

INDICATORS (Measuring change)

Sectors | MARINE | TRADE | TOURISM | AGRICULTURE | INDUSTRY | FORESTRY | ENERGY | MUNICIPAL | TRANSPORT

Fig. 15.10 Resource Management Framework

approaches to sustainable environmental resource management. The publication of the Phosphorus Regulations, 1998, is an example of a 'top-down' approach. The 'bottom-up' approach allows complex issues to be addressed in a sectoral or cross-sectoral context, whether at a local, catchment or national scale. For example, such a cross-sectoral approach is presently being adopted to combat eutrophication in the Lough Conn Catchment.

Sustainability targets, EQOs and EQSs need to be developed for all media to enable full implementation of the proposed model. To date, surface water is the sole medium for which proposed EQOs and EQSs are currently being considered in a manner consistent with this model (EPA, 1997), though a number of standards exist for air quality in national and international legislation. Considerable work is required to identify sustainability targets for all media and to assign appropriate

EQOs and EQSs. Typical EQOs that might be considered for various environmental media are presented in (Table 15.2). The Environmental Protection Agency Act, 1992, empowers the EPA to specify and publish quality objectives for any environmental medium.

Work is also ongoing at national and international level on indicator development (Lehane, 1999). Changes in environmental and sectoral indicators inform us of the

Table 15.2 Examples of Objectives where EQSs may be Established

Water	Air	Soil	Land-use/ Landscape
drinking	health	agricultural	urban
fisheries	noise	horticultural	residential
bathing	odour	residential	agricultural
shellfish		recreational	industrial
boating		commercial	national park
agriculture		industrial	wilderness
amenity			protected area
			tourism

'ebb and flow' of the impact of human activities on the environment. However, in the absence of clearly defined targets, it is difficult to estimate the net worth of moving in any particular direction and, thus, setting priorities. Targets based on the sustainability of our natural capital may be the rudder that will keep the ship of sustainable development on course.

CONCLUSIONS

Integration of environmental concerns into national policies and sectoral programmes is a key requirement for sustainable social and economic development in Ireland. Recent developments in this regard include the establishment of structures and mechanisms intended to facilitate co-operation and consultation among Government Departments and between Government Departments and other interested parties. These include the Green Network of Government Departments, *Comhar* (the National Sustainable Development Partnership) and the Inter-Departmental Biodiversity Steering Group. In addition, the recent introduction on a pilot basis of eco-auditing of legislative proposals, plans, programmes and policy statements in specific sectoral areas by Government Departments is a positive development (DELG, 1999c). The wider application of eco-auditing within Government would be in line with the aim of the National Sustainable Development Strategy, which undertook to develop

a Strategic Environmental Assessment system for major sectoral plans and programmes within three years, and in line with European developments in this area. Eco-auditing or SEA is vital for the achievement of sustainable development at a national level in Ireland.

At a sectoral level it is clear that certain sectors are exerting unsustainable pressures on the environment. As noted in Chapter 13, water quality is declining, greenhouse gas emissions and waste generation continue to increase, certain habitats and species are under increasing threat, and the impact of transport, particularly in urban areas, is of concern. Whilst, there has been significant progress made in relation to national environmental policy and legislation (e.g., in the areas of water quality and waste), at the time of writing deficits remain in other areas (e.g., in relation to biodiversity, greenhouse gases and coastal zone management). It is expected that these deficits will be addressed.

Of course to be successful, policy and legislation needs to be implemented effectively. For example, in relation to water quality many of the tools to tackle the problems are already in place. However, reversing the decline in water quality requires application of these tools, and appropriate resource allocation and effort (particularly at the catchment level). Significant future investment in public transport and waste infrastructure (including measures to prevent, recycle and reuse waste) will

be required to achieve sustainability in these areas. In relation to planning and urban development, the full integration of adequate infrastructural requirements within the planning process (e.g., waste, sewage and, where necessary, public transport infrastructure), is urgently required. In addition, action needs to be taken to counteract the proliferation of unsustainable low density housing (Chapter 16).

Whilst the quality of the Irish environment is relatively good, there have been some disturbing signs of deterioration in recent years. Failure to implement measures to protect certain aspects of the environment could, in the past, be partly excused through lack of understanding and resources. However, such an excuse does not presently apply to most issues. We now have the knowledge, and the financial and technical resources, to rectify most of the mistakes of the past and to endeavour to create a sustainable future.

REFERENCES

Boelens, R.G.V., Maloney, D.M., Parsons, A.P. & Walsh, A.R., 1999. *Ireland's Marine and Coastal Areas and Adjacent Seas: An Environmental Assessment.* Prepared by the Marine Institute on behalf of the Department of the Environment and Local Government and the Department of the Marine and Natural Resources. Marine Institute, Dublin.

BSM, 1997. *Coastal Zone Management. A Draft Policy for Ireland.* Prepared by Brady Shipman Martin on behalf of the Department of the Environment and Local Government, Department of Arts, Heritage, Gaeltacht and the Islands and the Department of the Marine and Natural Resources, Dublin.

BSM, 1999. *Strategic Planning Guidelines for the Greater Dublin Area.* Prepared by Brady Shipman on behalf of local authorities in the Greater Dublin Area, the Dublin and Mid-East Regional Authorities and the Department of the Environment and Local Government, Dublin.

Byrne Ó Cléirigh, 1999. *Cleaner Production Pilot Demonstration Programme. Synthesis Report.* Environmental Protection Agency, Wexford.

Cashman, L. (1999). *Safeguarding the quality of Irish freshwaters: the role of some key EC Directives.* Written paper presented at Shannon Waters in Crisis seminar, 22 November 1999, Athlone, Ireland.

CEC (Council of the European Communities), 1975. Council Directive of 15 July 1975 on waste (75/442/EEC). *O.J.* L 194/39.

CEC (Council of the European Communities), 1976. Council Directive of 4 May 1976 on the pollution caused by certain substances discharged into the aquatic environment of the Community (76/464/EEC). *O.J.* L 129/23.

CEC (Council of the European Communities), 1978. Council Directive of 18 July 1978 on the quality of fresh waters needing protection or improvement in order to support fish life (78/659/EEC). *O.J.* L 222/1.

CEC (Council of the European Communities), 1979. Council Directive of 2 April 1979 on the conservation of wild birds (79/409/EEC). *O.J.* L 103/1.

CEC (Council of the European Communities), 1980. Council Directive of 15 July 1980 relating to the quality of water intended for human consumption (80/778/EEC). *O.J.* L 229/11.

CEC (Council of the European Communities), 1985. Council Directive of 27 June 1985 on the assessment of the effects of certain public and private projects on the environment (85/337/EEC). *O.J.* L 175/40.

CEC (Council of the European Communities), 1990a. Council Directive of 23 April 1990 on the contained use of genetically modified organisms (90/219/EEC). *O.J.* L 117/1.

CEC (Council of the European Communities), 1990b. Council Directive of 23 April 1990 on the deliberate release into the environment of genetically modified organisms (90/220/EEC). *O.J.* L 117/15.

CEC (Council of the European Communities), 1991a. Council Directive of 21 May 1991 concerning urban waste water treatment (91/271/EEC). *O.J.* L 135/40.

CEC (Council of the European Communities), 1991b. Council Directive of 12 December 1991 concerning the protection of waters against pollution caused by nitrates from agricultural sources (91/676/EEC). *O.J.* L 375/1.

CEC (Council of the European Communities), 1992a. Council Directive of 21 May 1992 on the conservation of natural habitats and of wild flora and fauna (92/43/EEC). *O.J.* L 206/35.

CEC (Council of the European Communities), 1992b. Council Regulation of 30 June 1992 on agricultural production methods compatible with the requirements of the protection of the environment and the maintenance of the countryside (2078/92). *O.J.* L 215/85.

CEC (Council of the European Communities), 1996a. Council Directive of 24 September 1996 concerning integrated pollution prevention and control (96/61/EEC). *O.J.* L 257/26.

CEC (Council of the European Communities), 1996b. Council Directive of 27 September 1996 on ambient air quality assessment and management (96/62/EEC). *O.J.* L 296.

CEC (Council of the European Communities), 1996c. Council Directive of 9 December 1996 on the control of major-accident hazards involving dangerous substances (96/82/EEC). *O.J.* L 10/13.

CEC (Council of the European Communities), 1996d. Council Directive of 20 December 1996 on the approximation of the laws of the Member States relating to roadworthiness tests for motor vehicles and their trailers (96/96/EC). *O.J.* L 46/1.

CEC (Council of the European Communities), 1997. Council Directive of 3 March 1997 amending Directive

85/337/EEC on the assessment of the effects of certain public and private projects on the environment (97/11/EC). *O.J.* L 73/5.

CEC (Council of the European Communities), 1998a. Council Directive of 26 October 1998 amending Directive 90/219/EEC on the contained use of genetically modified micro-organisms (98/81/EC). *O.J.* L 330/13.

CEC (Council of the European Communities), 1998b. Council Directive of 26 November 1998 on the quality of water intended for human consumption (98/83/EC). *O.J.* L 330/32.

CEC (Council of the European Communities), 1999a. Council Directive of 26 April 1999 on the landfill of waste (1999/31/EEC). *O.J.* L 182/1.

CEC (Council of the European Communities), 1999b. Council Directive of 11 March 1999 on the limitation of emissions of volatile organic compounds due to the use of organic solvents in certain activities and installations (1999/13/EEC). *O.J.* L 85/1.

CEC (Council of the European Communities), 1999c. Council Directive of 22 April 1999 relating to limit values for sulphur dioxide, nitrogen dioxide and oxides of nitrogen, particulate matter and lead in ambient air (1999/30/EEC). *O.J.* L 163.

CEC (Council of the European Communities), 1999d. Council Regulation (EC) of 17 May establishing common rules for direct support schemes under the common agricultural policy (No. 1259/1999). *O.J.* L 160/113.

Clenaghan, C., Crowe, M. & Carty, G. 1999. *Measuring Progress towards Sustainable Development. A Discussion Document.* Environmental Protection Agency, Wexford.

Coillte, 1999. *Coillte's Forests. A Vital Resource.* Coillte.

DAF, 1999. *Evaluation of the Rural Environmental Protection Scheme. Operated under Council Regulation 2078/92.* Department of Agriculture and Food, Dublin.

DAFF, 1996. *Growing for the future. A Strategic Plan for the Development of the Forestry Sector in Ireland.* Department of Agriculture, Food and Forestry, Dublin.

DAFF and DoE, 1996. *Code of Good Agricultural Practice to Protect Waters from Pollution by Nitrates.* Department of Agriculture, Fisheries and Food and Department of the Environment, Dublin.

DAHGI, 1998. *National Report Ireland. First National Report on the Implementation of the Convention on Biological Diversity by Ireland.* Department of the Arts, Heritage, Gaeltacht and the Islands, Dublin.

DELG, 1998. *A Policy Statement. Waste Management: Changing Our Ways.* Department of Environment and Local Government, Dublin.

DELG, 1999a. *Residential Density. Guidelines for Planning Authorities.* Department of Environment and Local Government, Dublin.

DELG, 1999b. *National Consultation on Genetically Modified Organisms and the Environment. Policy Statement.* Department of Environment and Local Government, Dublin.

DELG, 1999c. *Eco-auditing of Policies.* Environment Bulletin No. 43. Department of Environment and Local Government, Dublin.

DELG, EPA and GSI, 1999. *Groundwater Protection Schemes.* Department of Environment and Local Government, Environmental Protection Agency, Geological Survey of Ireland.

DETE, 1998. *Trade Policy Statement.* Department of Enterprise, Trade and Employment, Dublin.

DoE, 1997a. *Sustainable Development. A Strategy for Ireland.* Department of the Environment, Dublin.

DoE, 1997b. *Managing Ireland Rivers & Lakes: a Catchment-Based Strategy Against Eutrophication.* Department of Environment, Dublin.

DTI, 1995. *Dublin Transportation Initiative: Final Report.* Stationery Office, Dublin.

DTO, 1998. *Transportation Review and Short-Term Action Plan.* Dublin Transportation Office, Dublin.

EC, 1972. *European Soil Charter.* Resolution (72) 19. Adopted by the Committee of Ministers on 30 May 1972 at the 211th meeting of the Ministers' Deputies.

EC, 1997. *Towards Sustainability.* European Commission, Brussels.

EC, 1998a. *Communication of the European Commission to the Council and to the Parliament on a European Community Biodiversity Strategy* (COM(98)42). Brussels.

EC, 1998b. *Partnership for Integration. A strategy for Integrating Environment into EU Policies.* Cardiff – June 1998. COM(1998) 333 final. Communication from the Commission to the European Council. Commission of the European Communities, Brussels.

EC (European Commission), 2000a. *Proposal for a European Parliament and Council Decision establishing the list of priority substances in the field of water policy.* COM(2000)47 final, Brussels.

EC (European Commission), 2000b. European Commission Website. Directorate General Environment.

ENFO, 1999. *Sustainable Tourism.* Environmental Information Service, Dublin.

EPA, 1997. *Environmental Quality Objectives and Environmental Quality Standards. The Aquatic Environment. A Discussion Document.* Environmental Protection Agency, Wexford.

EPA, 1999a. *Proposed National Hazardous Waste Management Plan.* Environmental Protection Agency, Wexford.

EPA, 1999b. *Report on IPC Licensing and Control 1998.* Environmental Protection Agency, Wexford.

EPA, 1999c. *The Quality of Drinking Water in Ireland. A report for the year 1998 with a*

review of the period 1996-1998. Environmental Protection Agency, Wexford.

Fanning, A., Crowe, M., Carty, G. and Clenaghan, C. 1999. *Water Quality Management Planning in Ireland.* Environmental Protection Agency, Wexford.

Forest Service, 1991. *Forestry and Fisheries Guidelines.* Forest Service, Dublin.

Fry, J. 1999. Can EIA deliver sustainable development? *Irish Planning and Environmental Law Journal* 6(1), 17-21.

Heritage Council, 1999a. *Policy Paper on Agriculture and the National Heritage.* Heritage Council, Kilkenny.

Heritage Council, 1999b. *Policy Paper on Forestry and the National Heritage.* Heritage Council, Kilkenny.

Hickie, D., 1997. *Evaluation of Environmental Designations in Ireland.* Heritage Council, Kilkenny.

Hussey, J., 1998. Environmental Management Systems: the Current Position. *Environmental Management Ireland* 14(2), 12-15.

Irish Energy Centre, 1999a. *Energy Update. The Irish Energy Centre Renewable Energy Information Office Newsletter.* Issue 10. The Irish Energy Centre Renewable Energy Information Office, Bandon, Co. Cork.

Irish Energy Centre, 1999b. *Planning Update. No.1.* The Irish Energy Centre Renewable Energy Information Office, Bandon, Co. Cork.

Lehane, M. (ed.), 1999. *Environment in Focus. A Discussion Document on Key National Environmental Indicators.* Environmental Protection Agency, Wexford.

Lucey, J., Bowman, J.J., Clabby, K. J., Cunningham, P., Lehane, M., MacCárthaigh, M., McGarrigle, M. L. and Toner, P.F., 1999. *Water Quality in Ireland 1995-1997.* Environmental Protection Agency, Wexford.

McGettigan, M., 1998. *Air Quality Monitoring. Annual Report 1997.* Environmental Protection Agency, Wexford.

Maclean, I., 1998. IPC Licensing. *Environmental Management Ireland* 14(2), 17-18.

Marine Institute, 1997. *National Survey of Water Based Leisure Activities.* Marine Institute, Dublin.

Marine Institute, 1998a. *Water Based Tourism and Leisure: Facts at your fingertips.* Marine Institute, Dublin.

Marine Institute, 1998b. *A Marine Research, Technology, Development and Innovation Strategy for Ireland.* Marine Institute, Dublin.

Marine Institute, 1999. *Investment Programme 2000-2006 for the Water-based Tourism and Leisure Sector in Ireland.* Marine Institute, Dublin.

NAB and EPA, 1997. *Joint audit and report process for EMAS and IPC in Ireland. Guidance Document for participating companies and EMAS verifiers.* National Accreditation Board / Environmental Protection Agency.

NASC, 1998. Beatha – the mark of environmental quality. *Environmental Management Ireland* 4(4), 22-25.

Ó Briain, M., 1999. The Birds Directive, 20 years on. *Wings* No. 15, 12-13. Birdwatch Ireland.

O'Leary, G. and Carty, G., 1998. *Urban waste water discharges in Ireland. A report for the years 1996 and 1997.* Environmental Protection Agency, Wexford.

O'Halloran, J., Giller, P.S., Clenaghan, C., Wallace, J. & Koolen, R., 1996. Plantation forests in river catchments: disturbance and recovery. In: *Disturbance and recovery of*

ecological systems. Giller, P.S. & Myers, A. A. (eds.), pp. 68-83. Royal Irish Academy, Dublin.

OPW, 1990. *Killarney National Park. Management Plan.* The Office of Public Works, Government of Ireland, Dublin.

O'Sullivan, J., 1999. 1999 Planning Bill. *Wings* No. 15, 9. Birdwatch Ireland.

Sheate, W.R., 1997. The Environmental Impact Assessment Amendment Directive 97/11/EC – A small step forward? *European Environmental Law Review*, pp. 235-243.

Stapleton, L. (ed.) 1996. *State of the Environment in Ireland.* Environmental Protection Agency, Wexford.

Teagasc, 1998. *Nutrient advice for phosphorus and potassium fertiliser.* Teagasc, Johnstown Castle, Wexford.

UN, 1981. *World Soil Charter* (C81/27). Food and Agriculture Organisation of the United Nations. Rome.

CHAPTER 16

FUTURE OUTLOOK

The possibility exists of a sustained long-term boom in the global economy, but this is dependent on advances in international co-operation, including co-operation on the environment. One pointer towards the potential for sustainable growth is the general shift in developed countries from manufacturing towards service industries, which have lower impacts on the environment.

In Ireland, gross national product (GNP) is forecast to increase by around 5 per cent per annum over the next five years. By the year 2011, the population is expected to exceed four million persons. Over the next decade there will be a need for 45,000 or more dwellings per year, an unprecedented level of house building, which underlines the need for careful land-use planning integrated with environmental protection. The National Development Plan provides for major investment in infrastructure, including environmental infrastructure. The pilot eco-audit of the Plan points out that care will be needed to ensure that unsustainable elements of growth do not occur under the Plan. Upgrading of infrastructure for waste management and waste water treatment is now an urgent need.

In many of the strategic sectors of the Irish economy there is significant potential for further growth and change, and this poses clear threats to the environment. Projected growth levels in transport, energy and forestry are highly significant, and sustainable development in these sectors will be a major challenge. Agriculture already features strongly as a source of pressure on the environment, for example in relation to eutrophication and greenhouse gas emissions. Environmental challenges for the marine resources sector include ensuring sustainable levels and methods of fishing and developing environmentally friendly aquaculture. Environmental issues will continue coming to the fore in tourism and trade. As with the other sectors, industry will need to integrate environmental considerations fully into policy and decision-making. This can be a win-win outcome, conferring business advantages by making Irish products and services environmentally friendly in line with growing market sentiment internationally.

Environmental awareness in Ireland must be raised significantly so that in daily life citizens take the environment into account in the way that they manage their homes, use transport and make consumer choices. The continuing widespread litter problem underlines the need for action to raise environmental awareness.

INTRODUCTION

Clearly the relationship between economic growth and the environment is complex. Pressures on the environment can increase with economic activity but alternatively more efficient methods of production can reduce both natural resource use and emissions to the environment. Balancing economic development with the environment requires, among other things, increased eco-efficiency.

Eco-efficiency aims at de-coupling economic activity from resource use and pollutant release. Put more simply it means getting more from less and breaking the link between economic growth and environmental damage. Indicators of eco-efficiency represent the 'use of nature' in society and the economy. Monitoring eco-efficiency on the macro level (e.g., for sectors and whole economies) is necessary in order to assess whether sustainability is being achieved (Moll and Gee, 1999).

An initial assessment of eco-efficiency in Ireland on the macro-level was made in the 1999 EPA report on key national environmental indicators (Lehane, 1999). This has been updated for this report with more recent information on some aspects and is presented in Fig. 16.1.

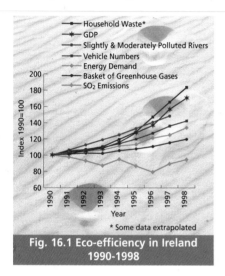

Fig. 16.1 Eco-efficiency in Ireland 1990-1998

The purpose of Fig. 16.1 is to show the trends in a number of key indicators in relation to the trend in gross domestic product (GDP). It is clear that the increase in the amounts of household waste has been matching or exceeding GDP growth. A number of the other indicators are increasing at different rates, generally somewhat slower than GDP; this is termed relative de-linking from GDP. Among the selected indicators, only in the case of sulphur dioxide has there been no general increase (in fact some reduction); this is termed an absolute de-linking from GDP, and is

clearly the more desirable outcome for the environment.

The overall trend is thus one of pressures on the environment increasing at varying rates as GDP increases, and this must raise concerns for the future. Hence there is a need to focus on future projections and their implications, which is the subject of this chapter. The objective is to assess emerging and intensifying environmental problems.

THE GLOBAL ECONOMY

A 1998 OECD conference concluded that the world was on the threshold of a tantalising opportunity - the possibility of a long sustained boom. A confluence of forces - particularly the transition to the knowledge society, the emergence of a global economy, and the pursuit of environmental stability - could propel huge improvements in wealth and well being worldwide. For this to happen there must be major advances in international co-operation on the environment (OECD, 1999a).

The potential for sustainable growth is evidenced by a shift in the balance away from manufacturing towards services, by technological potential for energy efficiency, by prospects of telework and teletrade, and by global affluence facilitating investment in the environment. It may take decades, however, to change energy infrastructures, urban settlements, the

construction of dwellings, transport systems, industrial capital stock, consumer technologies, values and attitudes – all of which tend to lock societies into energy intensive patterns (Michalski et al., 1999). Hence it has been argued (Lipietz, 1999) that any long-term boom

- will be constrained principally by ecological sustainability;
- must be based on the 'earth' factor, especially sustainable energy;
- will be fuelled by research and investment in energy-saving and environment-friendly technologies;
- will be guided by new forms of environmental regulation.

In developing the outlook in relation to the environment in Europe (EEA, 1999a) the assumption on macro-economic development was that the European GDP would increase by between 2.0 and 2.5 per cent a year in the period 2000 to 2010.

THE IRISH ECONOMY

The ESRI (Duffy et al. 1999) suggests the Irish economy is fully wound up and moving very fast but that over the next decade it is likely to unwind gradually and eventually return to the EU average rate of growth after 2010. A growth rate for GNP over the next five years of around 5 per cent a year was projected. (This compares with real GNP growth of 8.1% in 1998, 7.25% estimated for 1999, and 6.5 % projected for 2000). However, there remains the danger that either external shocks or domestic mistakes could put this scenario at risk. There will be a gradual shift from high technology manufacturing to market services, especially internationally traded services. The need for a high level of investment, especially in public physical infrastructure and housing, will limit the resources available for consumption. Over the next decade, there will be a continuing need for 45,000 or more new dwellings a year. The ESRI review concludes that a series of environmental taxes and charges are needed (see Chapter 14).

The total investment under the
Economic and Social Infrastructure
Operational Programme will be
£17,610 million as follows:

	£ million
National Roads	4,700
Public Transport	2,234
Water and Waste Water	2,495
Coastal Protection	35
Energy	146
Social and Affordable Housing	6,000
Health Capital	2,000

The public transport provision
includes, in the Greater Dublin
Area, implementation of the light
rail network LUAS, and investment
in suburban rail, the bus service,
traffic management measures and
cycling facilities. There will also be
investment in public transport
outside Dublin.

Investment in water and waste water
infrastructure will include the following:
• all outstanding schemes
  required under the urban waste
  water treatment Directive;
• water supply for urban areas,
  including measures against
  leakages;
• extending lake and river
  catchment protection;
• water and sewerage services for
  the development of land.

THE NATIONAL
DEVELOPMENT PLAN
2000-2006

A brief summary of the overall levels
of investment in the National
Development Plan 2000-2006 was
given in Chapter 1. The bulk of the
investment will be in economic and
social infrastructure (Box 16.1), in
employment and human resources
and in the productive sector. There
will be mainstreaming of
environmental considerations.

At least 50 per cent of all new jobs
from greenfield projects are planned
for the Border, Midland and Western
(BMW) Region. Modernisation of

the fishing fleet will be supported.
There will be increased investment in
research, technological development
and innovation (RTDI), in
agriculture, food, marine resources
and the environment (Box. 16.2).
Research and promotion will embrace
energy efficiency, carbon dioxide
abatement, and alternative energy.

The Environmental Research
Programme (£20 million) will aim at
measuring the impact of economic
development and contributing to the
sustainable use of natural resources.
It will complement research in
forestry, agriculture and marine
resources and will act as a focus for
integration of environmental
concerns into sectors. Projects may
involve networks for data, long term
monitoring sites, and the
development of systems, models,
instruments and techniques.

In addition, the Plan refers to the
possible establishment of a National
Environmental Research Unit or
centre of excellence (£5 million)
possibly incorporated into the
Environmental Protection Agency,
with priority programmes including:
• integrated environmental
  assessment;
• environmental management
  systems;
• information systems development;
• air pollution and acidification;
• waste prevention and
  management guidance.

Additional regional infrastructural
investment will include rural water
supply, waste management (£650
million) and urban and village renewal.
In the productive sector there will be
investment in micro-enterprises,
tourism, fisheries, forestry and rural
development. A pilot Eco-audit of the
Plan was undertaken (Box 16.3).

TECHNOLOGY

The future directions of technology
may have positive or negative impacts
on the environment. Internationally,

uncertainty applies not just to future
technical breakthroughs but also to
the range of applications of existing
breakthroughs, in particular what
may prove to be radical innovations
known as general-purpose
technologies. Such technologies now
in place include, for example, the
internal combustion engine and the
computer. There may be some
technology in its early stages of
development at present that will
emerge as one of the twenty-first
century's influential general purpose
technologies (Lipsey, 1999).

The Pilot Eco-audit notes that
economic and social development,
together with investment of the
order contained in the Plan, has
unavoidable implications for the
environment. Without
appropriate integration measures
there would be impacts on, among
other things, water and air quality,
biodiversity, patterns of land use,
energy consumption and waste
production. This places a premium
on the pursuit of policies that
promote economic efficiency, less
intensive resource use and less
environmental stress. Overall, the
environmental dimension is
addressed through the following:
• a National Spatial Strategy;
• better integration of land use
  and transport;
• enhanced eco-efficiency of
  transport;
• support towards meeting
  climate change policy objectives;
• assistance towards sustainable
  agriculture;
• improvements in water supply
  and waste water treatment;
• integrated waste management;
• environmental research.
The possibility of the emergence of
some unsustainable patterns of
development within the Plan
cannot be excluded, and therefore
measures will be taken so that the
environmental dimension is fully
integrated into the further stages
of programme planning and into
implementation. Indicators of
environmental performance will be
developed.

In 1998 the Irish Council for Science, Technology and Innovation (ICSTI) undertook a *Technology Foresight* exercise for Ireland. The time horizon for the exercise was set at 2015. The overview report (ICSTI, 1999) emphasised the importance of knowledge as one of the main drivers of prosperity and well being. It recommended that Ireland should become a centre of excellence in information and communication technologies (ICT) and biotechnology niches.

The importance of sustainable development policy was recognised. Inevitably, ecological and environmental considerations would increasingly inform and modify areas as diverse as school curricula, production, manufacturing and building processes, the use of natural resources, transport and energy. Future technological development would have to contribute to achieving greater competitive and environmental sustainability. The current low level of 'ownership' of environmental concern by Irish enterprises results in products and services that are not future-proofed against a sudden shift in market sentiment, based on broad environmental considerations. Significant market opportunity would arise for Irish enterprises that proactively operate on environmental principles. The report emphasised the need for Government, consumers and producers in Ireland to develop a shared understanding of the trade off involved in real, effective environmental policies.

DEMOGRAPHIC AND SPATIAL ASPECTS

Population and labour force projections have been prepared recently (CSO, 1999). The projections use three sets of assumptions for fertility, one for mortality and two for migration trends. Two distinct sub-periods are distinguished. For the period to 2011, Table 16.1 gives the range of the projections for the total population, suggesting that it is likely to exceed four million in the second half of the present decade. Migration assumptions account for most of the difference between the highest and lowest population projections. The labour force is projected to increase from 1.62 to 1.9 million or more by 2011.

Table 16.1 Projected Population 2001-2011	
Year	**Range (000 persons)**
2001	3,808 - 3,836
2006	3,938 - 4,052
2011	4,014 - 4,255
CSO, 1999	

The CSO report notes that the more distant the projection period the greater the uncertainty. The total projected population for the period 2016 to 2031 is given in Table 16.2.

Table 16.2 Projected Population 2016-2031	
Year	**Range (000 persons)**
2016	4,040- 4,423
2021	4,039 - 4,561
2026	4,009 - 4,672
2031	3,955 - 4,768
CSO, 1999	

The National Spatial Strategy will be a strategic spatial planning tool for the country as a whole. It will develop a dynamic conception of the Irish urban system, together with its links to rural areas. Its challenges include maintaining a competitive position while assisting in the development of the regions and ensuring that the principles of sustainable development are applied. In the recent consultation paper (DELG, 2000) an indicative list is presented of issues to be addressed in the strategy. This includes issues relating to the environment (see Chapter 11).

Challenges Ahead

The projected increases in population are likely to concentrate in urban areas and their hinterlands and in the coastal zone, thereby adding to pressures in these areas. Strong population growth is likely to continue in the Dublin region, putting pressure, for example, on water resources. Across Ireland there are already pressures on infrastructure for waste management (Chapter 6) and wastewater treatment (Chapter 5), with increased congestion and pollution from transport (Chapters 4 and 8), and loss of green belts and wildlife habitats (Chapters 11 and 12).

Minimising potential impacts on the environment from dealing with the housing crisis is crucial, and coherent integrated policies must be developed at local and national levels. Proposals in the Planning and Development Bill, 1999, to require environmental assessment of County Development Plans are to be welcomed and are in line with developments at European level in relation to the strategic environmental assessment Directive (see Chapter 15).

The projections underline the need for the integration of policies on land-use planning, transport, energy and the environment. An integrated land-use/transportation strategy should maximise the use of available urban derelict sites in order to reduce the uptake of land of agricultural or wildlife value and to reduce the environmental impacts of transport. Appropriate management of urban waste waters will play an integral role in meeting requirements under the forthcoming water framework Directive. With several large new waste water treatment plants coming on-stream (Chapter 5), the proper treatment and disposal of large amounts of sewage sludge is a further important issue. Approaches such as anaerobic digestion of suitable wastes need to be exploited where possible and the increase in production of household and commercial waste will need to be tackled at source.

AGRICULTURE

The white paper on Rural Development notes that although the economic character of rural areas is no longer synonymous with agriculture, the sector remains the single most important contributor to the economic and social viability of rural areas (DAF, 1999).

Agriculture policy is largely determined by the Common Agricultural Policy (CAP). The outcome of the Agenda 2000 negotiations sets the framework for the immediate future. This will include linking environmental protection requirements to direct support payments to farmers (Hamell, 1999). EU enlargement and international trade negotiations will also have a considerable bearing. Promoting quality output, improving consumer assurance, and environment friendly production will be essential (DAF, 1999).

The Government is committed to the continuation of the Rural Environment Protection Scheme (REPS) (see Chapter 15). The Government's strategy includes farm-based diversification and alternative enterprises, e.g., organic production and forestry. There will be continued support for environmental protection, and safeguard conditions will be included in various agriculture support schemes.

The National Development Plan notes that while the importance of primary agriculture to the economy has reduced in line with the trend in all industrialised countries, agriculture remains more important to the Irish economy than it is to the other 14 Member States. Its contribution to GDP is twice the EU average. The Plan recognises the need for an integrated rural policy, including the environment.

Challenges Ahead

The OECD (1998) has stated that regulation has increased in areas such as food safety and quality, genetic modification, pollution control and animal welfare and that such regulation may create impediments to international trade unless these issues are addressed in a multilateral framework.

In Ireland, both REPS and the Control of Farmyard Pollution Schemes have resulted in relatively large expenditure (Chapter 14) on environmental protection and further increased expenditure is proposed. Whilst these schemes have the potential to make a significant contribution to ensuring sustainable farming, it is important that a formal system is put in place to monitor their effectiveness, with a view to improving their value. The uptake of REPS is uneven across the country, and is least in many of the areas where agricultural contributions to eutrophication are greatest. This and broader biodiversity considerations underline the need for a range of measures for environmental protection outside of REPS areas.

It is a matter of serious concern that many Irish soils contain nutrient levels far in excess of that required agronomically, placing Irish

waterways under increasing threat from diffuse agricultural pollution. It is imperative that appropriate farm management is practised and nutrient management planning is more widely applied in problem areas for the benefit of the farmer and the environment (see Box 16.4).

The prevention of pollution arising from farmyards is important and the proper management and utilisation of slurries needs to be promoted and supported at all levels, with the objective of ensuring that their resource potential is fully used in a sustainable manner and their capacity to cause environmental damage is minimised.

The need for control and reduction of emissions of greenhouse gases (methane, nitrous oxide) and acidifying substances (ammonia) from agriculture is very likely to have major implications for this sector in the future. The Kyoto Protocol, the Gothenburg (multi-pollutant multi-effects) Protocol and the proposed EC Directive on national emissions ceilings aim at reducing production of these and other gases (Chapter 4). These international agreements and Ireland's forthcoming National Greenhouse Gas Abatement Strategy (see later) may require significant changes in farm management practices.

Box 16.4 Nutrient Management Planning

Nutrient management planning is advocated in the Government's Catchment Based Strategy against Eutrophication and is promoted by Teagasc through its Farm Advisory Service. A local authority can require nutrient management planning under the Local Government (Water Pollution) Acts where it is considered necessary in the interests of water quality protection.

Nutrient management planning involves an area by area assessment of the amounts of manure, slurry or inorganic fertiliser that should be applied based on soil type and nutrient status, crop nutrient requirements and the nutrient content of the proposed fertiliser.

Currently nutrient management planning is being applied through REPS and in the catchment monitoring and management schemes for Loughs Erne, Derg, Ree and Leane and the Rivers Liffey, Boyne and Suir. Cork County Council has introduced bye-laws in relation to agricultural practice, which contain provisions for nutrient management planning in three river catchments. In addition, nutrient management planning is obligatory in respect of IPC licensed intensive pig and poultry units.

FORESTRY

National policy on forestry is to support the development of a sustainable forestry industry that has a balance of species, to recognise the key role of farm families in forestry, and to insist on proper maintenance as a condition of drawing down premia (DMNR, 1998). The goals for future forestry were outlined in the Government Strategic Plan for the Development of the Forestry Sector in Ireland (DAFF, 1996). The document deals with the development of the forest sector up to 2015, and also gives an outline projection to 2035. The targets imply that in each three-year period about a further 1 per cent of the total land area of the country will be afforested.

The White Paper on Rural Development states that compatibility with the protection of the environment is a basic principle of the forestry programme and refers to controls in relation to fisheries, archaeology and the landscape (DAF, 1999). The main elements of the Government strategy for forestry include the following:

- to increase the productive forest area to 1.2 million hectares;
- to increase the diversity of species;
- to ensure compatibility with the environment;
- to encourage the provision of public access to forests;
- to promote a range of forest-based processing industries;
- to promote research and development, to include environmental concerns;
- to develop a comprehensive inventory and planning system (to include environmental data).

The National Development Plan states that the industry offers considerable scope for expansion and that the development of forestry, on a certain scale and in a particular manner, can contribute to sustainable economic and social well being compatible with the protection of the environment. Expenditure will be geared towards, *inter alia*, better knowledge of environmental issues.

Challenges Ahead

The balance of forest ownership in the State is changing, as the private sector (in particular farmers) becomes increasingly involved. The forest estate is predominantly Sitka spruce, an exotic conifer species, though the emphasis in forestry guidelines and conditions for grants is now on greater diversity. However, the target of 20 per cent for planting of broadleaves in the Government Strategic Plan (DAFF, 1996) is considered much lower than the EU planting average (Heritage Council, 1999). Imaginative forest management needs to be developed (Chapter 11) to support greater biological and landscape diversity in tandem with the production levels required in commercial forestry. Such forest management will contribute to attaining the goal of sustainable forestry envisaged at the UN Earth Summit in 1992. Increased commercial planting of native hardwoods may also help ultimately to relieve pressure on tropical forest resources about which there is much global concern.

In addition, effective measures are needed to prevent the exacerbation of surface water acidification from forestry, particularly in areas of base poor geology (Chapters 9 and 11). This is likely to require radical measures, such as restriction on planting and replanting of evergreen trees in certain categories of river catchment. The potential of forests in respect of carbon sequestration will need to be realised. An integrated environmental strategy for forestry must ensure that all factors are taken into account. The proposal for a National Forests Standard (Chapter 15) is important in this context.

MARINE RESOURCES

The elements of the Government's policy for marine resources (DMNR, 1998; DAF, 1999) include the following:

- setting out a coherent strategy and maximisation of the long-term contribution of the fisheries sector;
- developing aquaculture in a fair, equitable and environmentally-conscious way;
- protecting the Irish coast through Coastal Zone Management;
- continued support for inland fisheries;
- maximising processing;
- preserving and protecting the marine environment;
- implementation of effective RTDI.

The National Development Plan notes that the industry has an important role in sub-regional distribution of economic activity and employment. In particular it sustains remote coastal communities where there are few economic alternatives. Aquaculture production is important in the west and northwest. National policy will continue to balance the objectives and parameters of EU Common Fisheries Policy with the potential to develop the sector in coastal regions.

The Marine Institute has evaluated the development potential in the marine food sector. The Institute estimates that the implementation of its RTDI programme along with private investment from industry and support from State agencies will lead, over a 5 year period, to an increase in sectoral turnover of £100 million and an increase in employment of up to 1,000 jobs. Further growth is expected also in water-based tourism and leisure and marine technology (Marine Institute, 1998).

Challenges Ahead

Action at the international level is essential for sustainable management and protection of the marine and coastal environment. The concerns relating to the sustainability of certain fish stocks and to the effects of by-catch of juvenile fish and non-target species have been noted in earlier chapters. New regulations agreed by the Council of Fisheries Ministers in October 1997, and which come into effect from January 2000, are designed to improve the effectiveness of existing technical conservation measures and thus minimise the capture of juvenile fish. In addition, EU fisheries ministers voted in June 1998 to introduce a ban on drift-net fishing for tuna to reduce by-catch of marine mammals such as dolphins, which will come into effect in January 2002. However, cetacean (particularly harbour porpoise) by-catch mortality in other fisheries is

still a matter of some concern (Chapter 10). EU funded research is currently underway to assess methods of reducing the impact of demersal trawls on benthic marine organisms.

The Irish Government is also involved in co-operating with the British Government on managing and monitoring the Beaufort Dyke and other weapons dumping sites. Ireland has presented papers to OSPAR on the problems caused by dumped munitions, which will form the basis for future actions on the subject.

A Government Task Force reported in 1999 on the extent and impact of the dumping by Britain of radioactive waste around the British coastline. Following agreement at the International Maritime Organisation (IMO) Assembly in November 1997, to make mandatory the code that governs the transport by sea of irradiated nuclear fuels, the Government is developing improved reporting arrangements.

As discussed in Chapter 15 the Government is preparing a National Coastal Zone Management Policy. There is a pressing need for coherent action in this area, not least because of the rapidly increasing developmental, tourism and recreational pressures on the coast and a predicted increase in coastal erosion.

ENERGY

In the coming decades the world energy sector will face increasingly complex challenges – economic, geopolitical, technological and environmental. Energy demand will grow at a time when tight limits are being placed on greenhouse gas emissions, leading to greater interest in alternative energy. Meeting some of the challenges will require long lead times, as they are related to physical infrastructure (OECD, 1999b).

In Ireland, the Green Paper on Sustainable Energy contains energy projections to 2010 on a business as usual scenario. In relation to the supply of the total primary energy requirement (TPER), the projections to 2010 indicate:
- some reduction in coal;
- a significant reduction in peat;
- an increase in oil by about one third;
- more than doubling of natural gas;
- an approximate doubling of renewable energy.

The projections were for TPER to grow a further 37 per cent by 2010 over the 1998 figure (DPE, 1999). In relation to total final consumption (TFC) the projections indicate substantial increases in the industry, residential, transport and services sectors. Further work on energy projections for Ireland has been undertaken subsequently for the purposes of the forthcoming National Greenhouse Gas Abatement Strategy.

The projected more than doubling of gas input to electricity generation follows an international trend, due largely to the current wide availability of cheap natural gas coupled with its lower emissions level relative to other fossil fuels. In relation to indigenous natural gas, the positive results of tests carried out on the Corrib field off the west coast, while requiring further evaluation, appear to have demonstrated enough reserves to begin development feasibility studies. Clearly the availability of gas from the Corrib field would reverse the declining trend in the contribution of indigenous reserves.

In relation to renewables, the potential wood biomass resource for electricity and heat production in Ireland is large. Energy from municipal waste can also contribute to renewable energy in Ireland. There is scope to expand low cost solar thermal technology, as the total installed surface is well below the potential resource. Geothermal energy is only a modest resource in Ireland. The principal use at present for heat pumps is in the commercial buildings sector (Source: Irish Energy Centre).

Ireland also has one of the best onshore and offshore wind energy resources in Europe. In many areas, particularly along the west coast, wind resources are being widely evaluated with a view to installing more wind farms. The prospects for the wind energy sector in the medium term indicate that it can exceed the output level obtained by hydropower stations by 2005 (Source: Irish Energy Centre).

Wind power can now compete with the price of fossil fuel based electricity in many countries and the proportion of wind power is rapidly increasing in Europe. About 10 per cent of Denmark's electricity consumption is now met by wind power (Auken, 1999).

Challenges Ahead

Integrated energy planning across all sectors is imperative if Ireland is to satisfy its own rapidly increasing energy demands and yet ensure a clean environment and meet international commitments. Sustainable development of the energy sector should maximise efficiency of energy generation, emphasise the use of renewable resources and promote a culture of energy conservation by all users, whilst minimising environmental impacts.

Future development of the energy sector in Ireland will be heavily influenced by the Kyoto agreement on Climate Change. The Kyoto limit has already been exceeded (Chapter 4). Significant reductions in greenhouse gas emissions from relevant sectors, including the energy sector, must be achieved, in the context of the forthcoming National Greenhouse Gas Abatement Strategy.

A recent report on greenhouse gases stated that the largest single emissions reduction could be achieved by the energy sector, with large reductions obtained through switching fuels for electricity, especially from peat or coal to gas (ERM, 1998). It is important to note that the Kyoto Protocol represents one step towards combating climate change. Ireland will face an even greater challenge in positioning its economy to deal with stronger targets which will be agreed for the post Kyoto period (DPE, 1999). This will require further radical measures.

Ireland is also committed to reducing and limiting SO_2 emissions and NO_X emissions under other international agreements (the Oslo and Sofia Protocols respectively). Limits set for NO_X have not been achieved, and future emissions reductions (of for example SO_2 and NO_X) required under the proposed EU national emissions ceilings Directive and the multi-pollutant multi-effects Protocol

will have significant implications for the energy sector (Chapter 4).

All of these considerations raise questions in particular over the future of the large coal burning power station at Moneypoint and emphasise the general need for fuel switching to natural gas along with measures such as maximising the potential for combined heat and power (CHP). Much greater use of renewables must be achieved in the longer term.

An issue that has been researched for more than two decades is the possible health effects of electromagnetic fields (EMF), and yet there is still great uncertainty concerning whether certain EMF exposure is safe or unsafe. For this reason, further research has been recommended.

INDUSTRY

The National Development Plan notes that the manufacturing industry in Ireland has performed exceptionally well in recent years. Ireland's impressive manufacturing performance has been driven by its ability to attract large-scale high-tech, high value-added projects of foreign direct investment. Key challenges facing the indigenous sector include lack of scale and low productivity. The Plan includes provision for capital investment in the food sector including fish processing.

The services sector is now the dominant sector of economic activity in all developed economies, including Ireland, and four out of every five new jobs are generated in this sector. Services accounted for 63 per cent of national employment in 1996. The greater Dublin area has been a major beneficiary of the growth in internationally traded services.

There will be a strong emphasis on attracting high value-added projects to the Border Midland and Western (BMW) Region and the weaker areas in the Southern and Eastern (S&E) Region in line with a policy of balanced regional development. As noted earlier, the aim is towards delivering more than half of all new jobs from future green-field projects into the BMW Region. In this context, there will be a special focus on 'gateway towns' which will be catalysts for overall regional growth.

The report of the Health and Life Sciences Panel for Technology Foresight Ireland states that virtually all analysts predict that biotechnology is the basis for major economic growth. The report notes the need to consider ways of dealing with the pressures that are created between public demand for products/processes that enhance the quality of life and public concerns about the long term effects of genetically modified products/processes. Also, as pressure for higher EU standards increases, and as legislation is increasingly applied, the environmental industry looks set to grow steadily (ICSTI, 1999).

Challenges Ahead

In the future, sustainable industrial development will depend on optimised use of non-renewable resources and the development of substitutes. This will be largely facilitated through increased application and enforcement of IPC licensing and extension of cleaner production technology and environmental management systems to a wider variety of industry. Manufacturing industry faces the particular challenge of delivering

environmentally friendly products taking into account the full life cycle of a product.

Changes to the licensing provisions of the EPA Act, 1992 are expected shortly, to comply with the European Directive on integrated pollution prevention and control (IPPC). However, the general principles of the IPPC Directive are broadly in line with the IPC licensing system currently operated by the EPA.

The adherence to international agreements on hazardous substances and the development of tools nationally such as the Pollution Emissions Register to track these substances will help improve industrial environmental performance. Greater application of aspects of the Waste Management Act, 1996, in relation to areas such as producer responsibility obligations (which is limited to packaging waste and farm plastics at present) and the polluter pays principle will have future consequences for industry. In addition, as industry is the largest producer of hazardous wastes in Ireland, the National Hazardous Waste Management Plan, being prepared by the EPA, will have implications for the industrial sector.

Industry, like all relevant sectors, will need to play an increased role in achieving control of the emissions of greenhouse gases. The cement industry is a particularly significant source of these emissions among Irish industries.

TRANSPORT

Projections have been made (ERM *et al.*, 1998) of the numbers of cars and of goods vehicles up to the year 2010. These are shown in Figures 16.2 and 16.3. The projections are that by 2010 the number of cars will rise to almost 1.5 million and the number of goods vehicles will exceed 0.25 million. The recent pattern is of car numbers exceeding the projections.

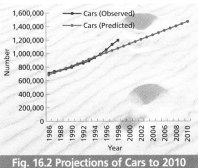

Fig. 16.2 Projections of Cars to 2010
(Sources: ERM *et al.*, 1998; DELG)

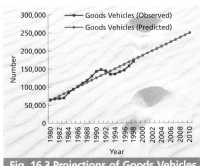

Fig. 16.3 Projections of Goods Vehicles
(Sources: ERM *et al.*, 1998; DELG)

For the Dublin Transportation Initiative (DTI), transport demand assessments were undertaken for the year 2011 for a number of land use scenarios. An overall growth in transport demand of over 40 per cent was envisaged for a number of scenarios of projected increases in population, employment and car ownership.

The technology for alternative fuel options such as liquid petroleum gas (LPG) and compressed natural gas (CNG) is already quite widely available. Bio-diesel, ethanol/methanol, and electric and fuel cell technologies, while developing towards commercial

Box 16.5 Sustainable Transport

The measures considered a priority (DPE, 1999) for sustainable transport include the following:

In the short term:
- vehicle efficiency and emissions standards;
- investigating alternative fuels and new technologies;
- taxation and other fiscal measures;
- higher quality public transport;
- telecommuting and implementation of Green Commuter Plans;
- traffic management initiatives;
- encouraging cycling and walking.

In the medium term:
- promoting new technologies and alternative fuels;
- further development of public transport;
- encouraging 'green fleets' in the public and private sectors and voluntary agreements on freight transport management;
- road charging.

In the long term:
- continuing development of transport infrastructure to ensure a more sustainable balance between road, rail, public and private transport;
- the promotion of appropriate land use options.

DPE, 1999

availability, are still at the research and development stage with a large emphasis on potential application in the commercial fleet (DPE, 1999). CNG and LPG fuelled buses are undergoing trial demonstration in Dublin. A Study Group has been formed to investigate the issue of alternative fuels in the public transport bus fleet.

The National Roads Authority has carried out a National Road Needs Study (1999). The Study identified deficiencies and devised a summary of national road development needs (2000 – 2019) that would provide essential road infrastructural support for economic development and sustainable

employment. Given the emphasis in national development policy on development of the regions, transport demand in ~~rural~~ areas is likely to increase into the future.

Challenges Ahead

The Green Paper on Sustainable Energy, notes that measures need to be identified that improve efficiency and reduce emissions in the transport sector without restricting access and mobility in real terms. Measures likely to be successful in meeting this objective fall into two main categories as follows:

- technological developments in vehicle production leading to better energy efficiency and lower emissions in the national fleet;
- increasing the availability of alternatives to current vehicle usage trends through the development of public transport networks and travel demand management policies.

A series of European Directives (CEC, 1994; CEC, 1996a, 1996b) has been aimed at motor vehicles, in terms of reducing emissions, and Ireland complies with all EU vehicle emission control standards. The EU Auto Oil Programme has set more stringent fuel specifications to come into effect in 2000 and 2005. Also, voluntary agreements have been

reached between the European Commission and the European, Korean and Japanese automobile manufacturers to limit CO_2 emissions for new cars by 2008/2009, which will represent a significant reduction on 1995 new car emissions (Chapter 14). However, these measures are not expected to compensate for the increase in traffic growth and fundamental changes in transport management will be required if Ireland is to meet its commitments under the Kyoto agreement on Climate Change and international air quality limits.

The rapid increase in road traffic volume is environmentally unsustainable. A greater effort is necessary to provide alternative modes of transport, that car trips are discouraged and that both measures are applied simultaneously, particularly in urban and suburban areas. Demand management and integrated land use and transportation planning are required to achieve this goal. Recent guidelines (BSM, 1999; DELG, 1999a) favour the minimisation of the potential growth in transport through the planning system and aim at bringing benefits in terms of the economic use of existing infrastructure, sustainable commuting patterns and reduced need for investments in new infrastructure. However, much work remains to be done to counteract previous policies

which led to the proliferation of unsustainable, sprawling low density housing estates (Gribben, 1999).

A more advanced information technology based logistics and transport sector is advocated by Forfas because of the contribution of the sector to a competitive industrial structure. Modern information technology must be promoted for traffic management and intermodal integration (Forfas, 1999). As noted previously, the Government has stated that it will eco-audit individual operational programmes within the National Development Plan.

TOURISM

The National Development Plan notes that over the past 10 years visitor numbers to Ireland have doubled and foreign exchange earnings have tripled. An important factor has been the emergence of Dublin as a popular city breaks destination. The current spatial spread of tourism is a major problem. There is a recognition within the industry of significant untapped potential in many counties that to date is largely ignored by tourists, while it is generally accepted that the infrastructure of those counties that have been successful in attracting tourists is in need of investment to protect their product. As international tourism expenditure is

forecast to grow by close to 6 per cent per annum in real terms over the next decade, further considerable growth in market share by Ireland is achievable. Helping the industry to achieve a wider seasonal and regional distribution of tourist business can contribute to sustainable development. The strategy to achieve these objectives includes the following:

- to market Ireland internationally on an all-Ireland basis as a tourism destination;

- international marketing of niche special interest products.

Such special interest products (including golf, cruising, angling, marine tourism, walking and gardens) are regarded as particularly important in developing a sustainable tourism industry.

Challenges Ahead

The main challenge for the tourism industry is to develop and promote a product that is environmentally sustainable within the context of a currently rapidly expanding sector. This will require ensuring that existing and new developments for tourist use incorporate adequate environmental protection measures. The maintenance of a clean environment will be one of the major

strengths of Ireland in a very competitive EU tourism market.

The Department of Arts, Heritage, Gaeltacht and the Islands is currently developing management plans for all the National Parks and managing tourism and recreation in these areas should form a fundamental part of the plans. Management plans are also being developed for conservation of designated sites (e.g., SACs and SPAs) and it is important that sustainable tourism management is incorporated into these plans where this is an issue. While tourism may adversely affect biodiversity and the environment in general, biodiversity and the environment are important assets for tourism. Eco-tourism (for example dolphin watching) is on the increase. Given the rapid increase in tourist numbers (Chapter 3) careful planning and management of tourism and recreation is required nationally so that environmental damage is prevented. In this context the publication and implementation of a National Coastal Zone Management Policy is particularly important.

TRADE

The Department of Enterprise Trade and Employment has noted that for Ireland, it is necessary to plan on the assumption that the trend towards global economic liberalisation will continue. In a scenario of global free movement of goods, services and investment and further limits on State intervention, competitiveness will become the vitally important ingredient to continued success in trade.

Even in a situation of global free trade, an expanded EU Single Market is likely to remain our main market. However, there could be changes in the composition of our trade with non-EU markets arising especially from the rapid economic development of major countries such as China and India. There is also likely to be a significant impact arising from the process of globalisation of production and distribution and the rapid development of electronic commerce.

The ESRI (Duffy *et al.*, 1999) has noted that world trade growth slowed substantially in recent years, reflecting the decline in activity as a result of various crises, particularly the Asian crisis. As these regions recover world trade growth is expected to pick up to an annual average of 6.8 per cent in the first five years of the decade, with a further improvement to 7.2 per cent in the following five years. Exports have played a major role in fuelling much of the recent growth, with Irish products being extremely competitive on international markets throughout much of the 1990s. The growth in exports is forecast to be far less rapid over the next decade as the growth in the volume of industrial output slows down. The ESRI expect that the growth rate in exports will slow to an annual average rate of 6.2 per cent between 2000 and 2005 and 5.3 per cent per annum thereafter to 2010.

Challenges Ahead

International co-operation is particularly important in addressing transboundary and global environmental challenges beyond the control of any individual nation. Increasing international economic integration and growth reinforce the need for sound environmental policies at the national and international level. Possible measures suggested to increase trade sustainability include the removal of trade barriers on environment-friendly goods and services, for example, goods that reduce the costs of investing in clean production technologies and environmental management systems. In addition, subsidies that harm the environment, for example in areas such as energy, agriculture or fishing, should be reduced or removed (WTO, 1999).

However, there are concerns that a general increase in trade liberalisation

may adversely impact on the environment and society, particularly of developing economies, as evidenced by protests at the controversial World Trade Organisation (WTO) negotiations in Seattle, in 1999. While liberalising trade may have certain economic benefits, it is important that Multilateral Environmental Agreements are recognised and respected and that sound national environmental protection measures - including, for example, restrictions on trade to protect endangered wildlife, and eco-labelling schemes that promote environmentally friendly products - are accepted by all.

THE MAJOR ENVIRONMENTAL CHALLENGES - OUTLOOK

The main issues relating to Ireland's environment at the turn of the millennium have been outlined in Chapter 13, and the present responses to them in economic terms and in respect of management and control have been set out respectively in Chapters 14 and 15. In this chapter, projections on the future prospects for the economy as a whole and for the individual strategic sectors have been presented. The environmental challenges facing each sector have been outlined. Finally, a brief overview is presented of the future prospects for the challenges that have been identified.

Eutrophication of Inland Waters

The full implementation of the urban waste water treatment Directive will result in secondary treatment serving around 89 per cent of the overall EU population, and nutrient removal serving around 45 per cent. (Differing figures will apply in individual countries). As a consequence, nitrogen and phosphorus loading of European rivers and lakes is expected to decrease by about 20 and 30 per cent respectively between 1995 and 2010.

If measures are not taken simultaneously to reduce the diffuse inputs of phosphorus from agriculture, it is likely that eutrophication of rivers and lakes located in intensively farmed regions will remain a problem (EEA, 1999a).

In Ireland, eutrophication is probably our most serious environmental pollution problem (Chapter 13). This threat to our widespread game fish populations has resulted mainly from economic growth giving rise to increased use of phosphorus in various sectors. Around three-quarters of all inputs of phosphorus to inland waters are from agriculture. While there are some mitigating factors in the nature and timing of agricultural phosphorus emissions, they are nevertheless the major cause of increasing eutrophication.

The recent reduction in the sales of phosphorus fertilisers (Chapter 3) is an encouraging signal. However, nutrient management planning is necessary on a broad scale, and in some catchments there is likely to be a need for restriction on certain forms of intensive farming. At a time when agriculture as a sector is facing many challenges, preventing eutrophication is one further challenge that the sector must be encouraged and supported in addressing as a matter of urgency.

While urban and industrial inputs of phosphorus are much smaller, the nature and timing of them tend to counterbalance this to some extent. There is a strong case for the incorporation of phosphorus removal on all significant treatment plants discharging to inland waters (Chapter 13).

The further development of catchment monitoring and management systems, undertaken to date in the L. Derg/L. Ree catchment and ongoing for the catchments of L. Leane and the Boyne, Liffey and Suir (The Three Rivers Project), can provide the necessary detailed information and methodologies to address the problem. It is evident that effective management across the many river catchments where eutrophication is an issue will require a significant co-operative effort by local authorities, the agriculture sector and all other players.

Much depends on how local authorities succeed in implementing the Phosphorus Regulations (Chapter 15). Local authorities have significant tools available to them to limit diffuse pollution including powers to adopt bye-laws controlling agricultural activity and powers to require nutrient management planning on farms. These powers will need to be applied more widely if the problem of eutrophication is to be tackled effectively.

The recent voluntary agreement between the Government and the Irish Detergents and Allied Products Association to effectively provide for the phasing-out of phosphate based domestic laundry detergent products is one further encouraging signal. However, the scale of the effort required, across all sectors, to overcome the challenge of eutrophication should not be underestimated.

Waste

Between 1990 and 1995, when economic growth was about 6.6 per cent at constant prices, reported waste generation within the EU increased by nearly 10 per cent. It has been concluded that most forms of waste will probably increase in Europe. It is predicted that by 2010 the generation of paper and cardboard, glass and plastic waste will increase by around 40 to 60 per cent compared with 1990 levels (EEA, 1999a).

Thus, the challenge of de-linking waste generation from economic growth is considerable. Waste prevention and minimisation are essential, with an emphasis on cleaner

production and reduced resource use in manufacturing (for example smaller, lighter products) and reduced waste. The materials used should be recycled or recyclable wherever possible. Improved information and labelling are needed to help bring about changes in attitudes and lifestyles that will ensure that such products will be favoured by consumers.

Projections for population growth, household sizes, sewage treatment and general economic growth in Ireland suggest a continued trend of increased volumes of waste. In recent local authority waste management plans, household waste has been projected to increase by between 1 and 3 per cent per annum in the short term, falling somewhat to between 0.5 and 2 per cent per annum from 2005 onwards. These plans and the proposed National Hazardous Waste Management Plan place strong emphasis on waste prevention and minimisation. They can only succeed if adequate staffing and resources are provided for their implementation. Waste prevention must be a priority in all control functions; for example, in the full use of all available planning controls on proposed developments (for example supermarkets) likely to give rise to large amounts of waste.

Currently Ireland has relatively low levels of materials recycling, no significant biological waste treatment capacity and no infrastructure for thermal treatment with energy recovery. Recovery rates for packaging waste in 1998 remained well short of the targets for 2001 and 2005, and much better progress is needed. Considerable development of centralised composting for organic waste is strongly recommended (Chapter 6). The recently established Task Force on recycling of construction and demolition waste (DELG, 1999a) is an important initiative for one of the largest waste categories.

Across Europe, landfilling is expected to decrease and recycling and incineration with energy recovery are likely to increase over the coming decade. These trends are likely to be repeated in Ireland. It is essential that the necessary investment is made in an appropriate waste management infrastructure, with the highest operating standards.

The ubiquitous problem of litter must be tackled through education, penalties and their enforcement. Its adverse impact on tourism is frequently quoted, but it must also come to be considered entirely socially unacceptable in a country at Ireland's present level of development.

Further and more radical measures will be needed to tackle the problems of waste and litter. Deficiencies in the waste management infrastructure need to be remedied in a co-ordinated manner. A heightened sense of civic responsibility must be developed in order to minimise both waste and litter.

The Urban Environment and Transport

In Europe as a whole urban air quality is expected to continue improving up to 2010. The number of city inhabitants exposed to concentrations above the recommended levels is expected to fall by 50 per cent between 1990 and 2010. In 2010 the most significant exceedances are expected to be fine particles (PM_{10}), ozone, NO_X and benzo(a)pyrene, while substantial improvements can be expected across Europe for benzene and SO_2 (EEA, 1999a).

Road traffic is the greatest threat to urban air quality in Ireland, with NO_X and particulate matter being the major problem pollutants. New standards adopted under the air framework Directive will be challenging with regard to these pollutants, particularly in heavily trafficked areas.

As noted earlier, increases of population in Dublin and other Irish cities are expected to continue. Projections of future vehicle ownership in Ireland (see above) are also for a continuing increase. There is a need to evaluate all aspects of how these increases may impact on the urban environment and to actively develop demand management strategies to restrict vehicle use and to encourage more sustainable commuting patterns. A comprehensive and environmentally friendly public transport system is the most urgent need. Infrastructure to divert heavy vehicles away from city and town centres is also essential. The Dublin Transportation Initiative

(DTI) strategy is currently considerably behind initial targets but this initiative and additional measures (Chapter 15) should eventually help to alleviate traffic congestion when completed. More sophisticated traffic management and control systems will need to be utilised fully in terms of their potential environmental benefits. Some encouraging signals towards easing pressures on the urban environment include suburban office parks and prospects for telework.

It is a matter of some concern that most Irish cities are significantly larger in surface area than European cities of similar population (Gribbin, 1999). Such 'suburbanisation' of our cities leads to increased reliance on the private car and results in associated problems with air quality, noise and congestion. The application of recent planning guidelines will be important in this regard (BSM, 1999; DELG, 1999b). Well-planned measures to increase the density of residential developments and encouraging the use of derelict sites can help to prevent further extensive urban sprawl and associated transport problems. Higher residential densities will increase the importance of preserving and enhancing the urban environment including existing

green space. As note above, education and enforcement must be redoubled to deal with the problem of urban litter.

Finally, it is clear that continuing failure to deal with this challenge has consequences that are as much socio-economic as environmental.

Climate Change and Greenhouse Gases

Despite concerted international efforts to stabilise greenhouse gas emissions at 1990 levels, such emissions are projected to increase in the EU by 6 per cent from 1990 to 2010. For the period 1990 to 2050, atmospheric concentrations of CO_2, CH_4 and N_2O could increase respectively by as much as 45, 80 and 20 per cent. Temperatures are forecast to rise by 1 to 2 degrees C for the Northern Hemisphere by 2050. The rate of sea level rise is predicted to accelerate, amounting to an increase of about 15 - 20 cm by 2050 and 40 - 50 cm by 2100 (EEA, 1999a).

While initial temperature increases could give rise to some benign effects, there is evidence that in a relatively brief period, no more than a few decades, a larger change can happen, which would have serious consequences in terms of extremes of temperature, flooding and storms - and the possibility that an alteration in the Gulf Stream would make Europe's climate much colder.

For Ireland, the projected increase in greenhouse gas emissions in a business as usual scenario of 30 per cent compared to our Kyoto target of 13 per cent (Chapter 4) underlines the scale of this challenge. If growth projections for the Irish economy are exceeded (as has happened in recent years) the magnitude of the challenge will further increase accordingly.

The Green Paper on Sustainable Energy outlines how the Government proposes to meet the State's future energy requirements in an environmentally and economically sustainable way (DPE, 1999). A draft National Greenhouse Gas Abatement Strategy has been prepared by the Department of the Environment and Local Government, and the strategy is due to be published shortly after the publication of the present report.

The key sectors in respect of carbon dioxide emissions are energy, transport, services, households and industry (Chapter 4). The greatest scope for abatement of emissions is likely to be in the energy sector. Reducing energy intensity and improving energy efficiency are clearly major issues.

Switching to less carbon-intensive fuels (peat being the most carbon intensive, followed by coal and oil) and particularly reducing Ireland's high level of dependence on fossil fuels will be important. In this regard, a concerted effort is likely to be needed to harness Ireland's renewable resources, such as wind energy and biomass. The largest projected percentage increase in greenhouse gas emissions, in a business as usual scenario, is for transport. Limiting future growth in transport demand (e.g., through integrated transport and land use planning) and reducing dependence on private road transport are major issues.

With emissions of the greenhouse gases methane and nitrous oxide making agriculture the largest single source of greenhouse gas emissions (Chapter 4), reducing stocking levels in the context of CAP reform and controlling the use of nitrogenous fertilisers are likely to be key considerations. The role of forestry, in its different forms, in the long-term as well as short-term sequestration of carbon will need to be established.

Overall, abating Ireland's greenhouse gas emissions will require a rapid and far-reaching mobilisation of effort and effective tracking of progress. It is likely to require restricting and discouraging (e.g., through greenhouse

gas emission taxes) certain forms of activity but this cannot succeed unless more acceptable alternatives are made available. In addition, consideration will need to be given to the role of mechanisms such as emissions trading. Innovative and well thought-out solutions will be needed, so that:

- there is an equitable sharing of the burden as far as possible;
- both long-term and short-term needs are taken into account;
- possibilities for synergies are fully explored and utilised, including benefits to the economy and opportunities for ameliorating other environmental problems;
- dealing with this environmental problem does not seriously affect the environment and natural resources in other ways.

The significance of this issue for Ireland's future is such that all major sectors of society and the economy are likely to have to play a significant role.

Protection of Natural Resources

Ireland's natural resources are coming under increasing pressure (Chapter 13). In some cases this is a direct result of technological developments that increase the capacity to exploit certain resources, while in other cases the issue is one of a steady rate of loss and damage owing to diverse factors.

Ireland's landscape has long been influenced by human activity, and is a blend of natural and cultural features (Chapter 11). Factors that can impact increasingly on the landscape in future years include increased housing in those areas convenient to towns and cities, and in areas generally attractive for tourism and recreation such as the coast (see below). With unprecedented levels of new housing proposed, landscapes in these areas are now at greater risk than ever from intrusive housing development. Accordingly, the conservation of landscapes must receive high priority. A pilot study of landscape character in Co. Clare,

initiated by the Heritage Council, is an example of the type of work needed to inform landscape conservation.

Other activities that pose a challenge in relation to maintaining landscape quality in Ireland include wind farms and the proposed expansion of forest cover from 9 to 17 per cent of the area of the country. These activities may have significant environmental benefits if undertaken appropriately. Careful planning is needed also on the future uses of cutaway bogs.

Over half the population of Ireland now lives within 10 km of the coast and this proportion looks set to rise. Satellite imagery shows that the proportion of the coastal zone covered by discontinuous urban fabric (including industrial and commercial units) has increased by over 25 per cent in 15 years. Coastal development can be an insidious problem, steadily eroding natural assets. Scenic coastal landscapes warrant particular attention to ensure the sensitive siting of buildings, roads, car parks, camping/caravan sites and commercial operations. Although much of Ireland's coastline is still relatively undisturbed, there is insufficient information on the

environmental implications of coastal development (Boelens *et al.*, 1999). The Government published a draft policy on coastal zone management in 1997 and details regarding its implementation are expected. Experience shows that rigorous planning and strict regulation are needed to ensure that the spatial scale of development is consistent with the ecological values to be protected.

The extent of Ireland's marine territory greatly exceeds the land area and the use of this resource must be sustainable. As elsewhere in the world's oceans, modern technology has hugely increased the pressure on fish stocks. By-catch must be minimised by using appropriate gear and practices. Developing the sea-fishing sector in a sustainable way is now a major challenge, aspects of which have been discussed earlier in this chapter. More effort needs to be directed towards the development of aquaculture in an environmentally friendly manner. New potential pressures may include the use of areas of the seabed as sources of aggregates for construction. Action in Ireland targeted specifically at the conservation of biodiversity in the marine environment is limited.

Overall, Ireland's natural heritage appears to be better resourced in some respects now than in the past (Chapter 12). Significant resources have been devoted to the protection of areas of importance in the national and European context and further resources will be needed. Little attention has been given, however, to sites of significance in a local context; these may be of small size and so at greater risk, and now require attention. While small individually, when taken together these sites constitute an important part of Ireland's natural heritage. The diverse threats to biodiversity deriving from the economic sectors and urban development are now giving rise to accelerating rates of loss. As noted in Chapter 12, it has been reported that coastal habitats have been damaged by a variety of causes (Fig. 16.4). The impact of overgrazing by sheep on upland areas has been discussed in earlier chapters. The increase in motorised recreational vehicles is an example of a new threat, increasing the potential for access and hence disturbance and damage to remote wilderness or semi-wilderness areas. Tourism now includes wilderness activities, which while raising awareness can also cause harm if not managed properly.

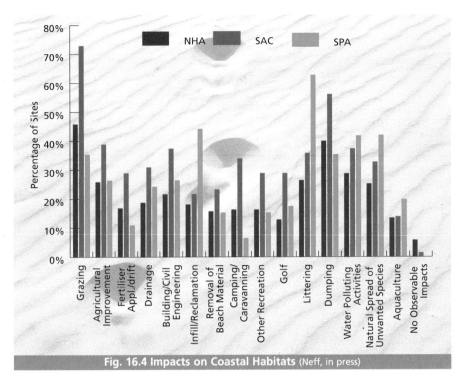

Fig. 16.4 Impacts on Coastal Habitats (Neff, in press)

Peatland soils in Ireland have been drastically affected by modern development including mechanised turf extraction schemes, commercial forestry, overgrazing, drainage and agricultural intensification. There is concern that many of these unique ecosystems may be lost in the near future unless such development is controlled effectively (Foss, 1998). Many important peatland areas in Ireland remain proposed NHAs, which currently affords them little protection against certain types of development. The Wildlife Amendment Bill currently before the Dail, aims at providing protection for

these areas. Given that Ireland's peatlands are of such international importance, it is imperative that remaining peatlands of ecological significance are conserved and managed appropriately.

Over the past five years the number of deliberate releases of genetically modified organisms (GMOs) into the environment within the European community has increased considerably, and much of this involves similar releases at different sites all across Europe. This underlines the need for improved information transfer and harmonised

inspection and enforcement among the European competent authorities dealing with this sensitive subject.

With increased economic resources deriving from economic growth, there is an opportunity now to take the necessary measures to halt the erosion of natural heritage and perhaps to regain some of what has been lost. For example, there is a plan to reintroduce golden eagles to Ireland at Glenveagh National Park in a five-year programme. Success will depend on a carefully managed introduction programme, especially consultations with farmers and effective control of poisons. The last eagles bred in north Mayo in 1912. If the re-introduction programme is a success, there is the prospect that after a century's absence, eagles will rear their young again on the remote cliffs and mountains of Ireland.

Overview of Sectors and Challenges

In Table 16.3 an attempt is made to summarise the way that the five key challenges outlined above apply to the strategic sectors discussed in this report. It is to be expected that all sectors will become more and more involved in integrating all aspects of the environment into their sectoral plans and decision-making. Nevertheless, it is clear that in some sectors, particular attention must be focused on certain issues.

Table 16.3 Key Environmental Challenges for Strategic Sectors

Sector	Control of Greenhouse Gases	Reducing Eutrophication	Preventing and Managing Waste	Protecting the Urban Environment	Protecting Natural Resources
Agriculture	■	■	■	-	■
Forestry	■	□	□	-	■
Marine Resources	-	□	▣	-	■
Energy	■	-	□	□	▣
Industry	■	■	■	□	▣
Transport	■	-	□	■	▣
Trade	□	-	□	□	▣
Tourism	-	□	▣	▣	■

■ highest priority needed
▣ high priority needed
□ priority needed
■ benefit to be realised

Table 16.4 Key Environmental Challenges for Public Authorities and Households					
Sector	Control of Greenhouse Gases	Reducing Eutrophication	Preventing and Managing Waste	Protecting the Urban Environment	Protecting Natural Resources
Public authorities	■	■	■	■	■
Households	■	■	■	■	□

■ highest priority needed
■ high priority needed
□ priority needed

For the most part, these challenges apply also to the public authorities (including in particular local authorities) and to households and individuals, as indicated in Table 16.4.

IN CONCLUSION

Overall, Ireland's environment has been subject to fewer pressures than the environment of most of Europe and consequently is of a relatively high standard in most respects. However, many pressures on the environment, such as those from transport and energy growth, changed agricultural practices, urbanisation and, in particular, the general acceleration of economic development, are increasing in Ireland at higher rates than in most European countries. This means that while Ireland's environmental quality is of a higher standard, at the same time that quality is at risk of being eroded at a faster rate than is happening in most other European countries. Furthermore, emissions, e.g., from agriculture and the growth in traffic, are occurring at levels that will make it extremely difficult to meet our international obligations. The magnitude of the environmental challenges that Ireland now faces should not be underestimated.

Improvements will be needed to meet existing and proposed more stringent standards set by the EU. The recent EU framework Directive on air quality and its 'daughter directives' are setting stricter requirements for air quality in future years. The proposed framework Directive on water will also set more demanding standards and will introduce a comprehensive approach to monitoring and managing our water resources. Achieving the full implementation of both directives will not be easy but can lead to significant benefits for Ireland's environment.

Towards the end of the twentieth century, international acceptance of the concept of sustainable development represented a major step forward. Making this concept a reality will require many further shifts in thinking, attitudes and behaviours. It has been argued, for example, that there remains an underlining assumption that nature and mankind are two separate systems, man versus nature where one side always has to lose. Bringing mankind and nature back into alignment will require more than just improved environmental management systems leading to increased eco-efficiency. Quantity, in terms of materials and energy used and products purchased, is not the only issue. Quality, in terms of the preferred use of renewable energy resources and safe and recyclable materials, has a particular role to play. People's natural need to consume can be quite compatible with the environment when it is used in this way (Datschefski, 2000).

Ireland's environmental challenges include, in particular, the five challenges discussed in this final part of the report. Meeting these challenges will require a broadly based approach including
- ensuring that the problems are fully understood through monitoring, research and assessment;
- ensuring that policies, incentives and actions across all sectors take environmental considerations fully into account; (businesses world-wide are becoming increasingly aware that a bad environmental record can be bad for business);
- developing infrastructure and services that meet development

needs and are consistent with environmental protection objectives; this will require better integration of physical planning and environmental protection.

Ireland's increased economic prosperity entails certain threats to the environment, as outlined above, but also opportunities. We now have a greater opportunity than ever to make the necessary public and private investment in all aspects of environmental protection.

The challenges will not be overcome, however, unless there is a sea change in attitudes to the environment in Ireland (see Chapter 2). Education on the environment is needed across a broad front and more co-operation is needed at different levels: national, sectoral, regional and local. Part of that investment, therefore, must be made towards obtaining and disseminating information on the environment.

Timely and relevant information is essential to understand environmental problems and to orient decision-making towards their solution. Such information must be widely disseminated and acted upon before it is too late to prevent processes becoming irreversible (EEA, 1999b).

Accordingly, this report and its proposed associated products (pocket book, posters, exhibition, website information and proposed video series) are intended not just to inform but also to inspire and guide action on protecting and conserving Ireland's environment and natural resources. The time has come for us all to take the environment into account and to act accordingly. It should be a factor in how we manage our homes, in how we travel, in our working lives and in our consumer choices. The difference between the new environmental challenges and many of those encountered previously is that the solution to overcoming them lies with many different key players and, for

most of the challenges, each person has a role to play.

REFERENCES

Auken, S., 1999. Global Renewable Energy. In *The Sustainable Development Agenda 2000*. Campden Publishing Limited, London.

Boelens, R.G.V., Maloney, D.M., Parsons, A.P. & Walsh, A.R., 1999. *Ireland's Marine and Coastal Areas and Adjacent Seas: An Environmental Assessment*. Prepared by the Marine Institute on behalf of the Department of the Environment and Local Government and the Department of the Marine and Natural Resources. Marine Institute, Dublin.

BSM (Brady Shipman Martin), 1999. *Strategic Planning Guidelines for the Greater Dublin Area*. Brady Shipman Martin, Dublin.

CEC (Council of the European Communities), 1994. Directive of 23 March 1994 relating to measures to be taken against air pollution by emissions from motor vehicles and amending Directive 70/220/EEC (94/12/EC). *O. J.* No. L 100/42.

CEC (Council of the European Communities), 1996a. Directive of 27 March 1996 adapting to technical progress Council Directive 70/157/EEC relating to the permissible sound level and the exhaust system of motor vehicles (96/20/EC). *O. J.* No. L 92/23.

CEC (Council of the European Communities), 1996b. Directive of 22 January 1996 amending Directive 88/77/EEC on the approximation of the laws of the Member States relating to the measures to be taken against the emission of gaseous and particulate pollutants from diesel engines for use in vehicles (96/1/EC). *O. J.* No. L 40/1.

CSO (Central Statistics Office), 1999. *Population and Labour Force Projections 2001-2031*. Stationery Office, Dublin.

DAF (Department of Agriculture and Food), 1999. *Evaluation of the Rural Environmental Protection Scheme. Operated under Council Regulation 2078/92*. Department of Agriculture and Food, Dublin.

DAFF (Department of Agriculture, Food and Forestry), 1996. *Growing for the future. A Strategic Plan for the Development of the Forestry Sector in Ireland*. Department of Agriculture, Food and Forestry, Dublin.

Datschefski, E., 2000. Sustainability: 100%. *Industrial Environment Management*. February 2000.

DELG (Department of the Environment and Local Government), 1999a. *Environment Bulletin*. Issue 44. Department of the Environment and Local Government, Dublin.

DELG (Department of Environment and Local Government), 1999b. *Residential Density. Guidelines for Planning Authorities*. Department of Environment and Local Government, Dublin.

DELG (Department of the Environment and Local Government), 2000. *The National Spatial Strategy. What are the Issues?* Consultation Paper No. 1. DELG, Dublin.

DMNR (Department of the Marine and Natural Resources), 1998. *Making the Most of Ireland's Marine and Natural Resources. Statement of Strategy*. Department of the Marine and Natural Resources, Dublin.

DPE (Department of Public Enterprise), 1999. *Green Paper on Sustainable Energy.* Stationery Office, Dublin.

Duffy, D., FitzGerald, J., Kearney, I. and Smyth, D., 1999. *Medium Term Review 1999-2005*. Economic and Social Research Institute, Dublin.

EEA (European Environment Agency), 1999a. *Environment in the European Union at the turn of the century*. EEA, Copenhagen.

EEA (European Environment Agency), 1999b. *A new model of environmental communication for Europe: from consumption to use of information. Executive Summary*. Environmental issues series No 13. EEA, Copenhagen.

ERM (Environmental Resource Management), Byrne O'Cleirigh and the Economic and Social Research Institute, 1998. *Limitation and Reduction of CO_2 and other Greenhouse Gases in Ireland*. Report prepared for the Department of Public Enterprise and the Department of the Environment.

Forfas, 1999. *1998 Review and 1999 Outlook Statement*. Forfas. Dublin.

Gribben, E., 1999. Dublin: Increasing Housing Densities – the Path to Sustainability. *Irish Planning and Environmental Law Journal*, 6(3), 87-98.

Hamell, M., 1999. *Environmental Protection Requirements for Agriculture - Perspective for the New Millennium.* Carton, O.T. (ed.), pp. 24-31. Teagasc, Johnstown Castle, Wexford.

Heritage Council, 1999. *Policy Paper on Forestry and the National Heritage.* Heritage Council, Kilkenny.

ICSTI (Irish Council for Science, Technology and Innovation), 1999. *Technology Foresight Ireland - an ICSTI Overview.* Irish Council for Science, Technology and Innovation, Dublin.

Lehane, M. (ed.), 1999. *Environment in Focus – A Discussion Document on Key National Environmental Indicators.* Environmental Protection Agency, Wexford.

Lipietz, A., 1999. *Working for World Ecological Sustainability: Towards a 'New Great Transformation'.* In OECD, 1999a.

Lipsey, R.G., 1999. *Sources of Continued Long-run Economic Dynamism in the 21st Century.* In OECD, 1999a.

Marine Institute, 1998. *A Marine Research, Technology, Development and Innovation Strategy for Ireland.* Marine Institute, Dublin.

Michalski, W., Miller, R. and Stevens, B. *Anatomy of a Long Boom.* In OECD, 1999a.

Moll, S. and Gee, D. 1999. *Making sustainability accountable: Eco-efficiency, resource productivity and innovation.* Topic Report No. 11/1999. European Environment Agency, Copenhagen.

Neff, J. in press. *Irish coastal habitats: a study of impacts on designated conservation areas.* Heritage Council, Kilkenny.

OECD (Organisation for Economic Co-operation and Development), 1998. *The Agricultural Outlook 1998-2003.* OECD, Paris.

OECD (Organisation for Economic Co-operation and Development), 1999a. *The Future of the Global Economy: Towards a Long Boom?* OECD, Paris.

OECD (Organisation for Economic Co-operation and Development), 1999b. *Energy: The next Fifty Years.* OECD, Paris.

WTO (World Trade Organisation), 1999. *Trade and Environment. Special Studies 4.* WTO, Geneva.

Acronyms & Abbreviations
and
Glossary

AER	Annual Environmental Report		DTO	Dublin Transportation Office
APE	Alkylphenol ethoxylate		DTSR	Department of Tourism, Sport and Recreation
BAT	Best Available Techniques		EA	Environment Agency, UK
BATNEEC	Best Available Technology not Entailing Excessive Costs		EAGS	Energy Audit Grant Support Scheme
BIM	Bord Iascaigh Mhara		EAGGF	European Agricultural Guidance and Guarantee Fund
BMW	Border, Midland and Western		EC	European Communities/Commission
BOD	Biochemical Oxygen Demand		ECU	European Currency Unit
Bq	Becquerel		EEA	European Environment Agency
CAP	Common Agricultural Policy		EEISS	Energy Efficiency Investment Support Scheme
CEC	Council/Commission of the European Communities		EIA	Environmental Impact Assessment
CFB	Central Fisheries Board		EIS	Environmental Impact Statement
CFC	Chlorofluorocarbon		EMAS	Eco-Management and Audit Scheme
CFP	1) Common Fisheries Policy 2) Control of Farmyard Pollution		EMEP	European Monitoring and Evaluation Programme
CH_4	Methane		EMS	Environmental Management System
CHP	Combined heat and power		ENFO	Environmental Information Service
CITES	Convention on International Trade in Endangered Species of Wild Fauna and Flora		EQO	Environmental Quality Objective
CLRTAP	Convention on Long-Range Transboundary Air Pollution		EQS	Environmental Quality Standard
			ERDF	European Regional Development Fund
CNG	Compressed Natural Gas		ERU	Environmental Research Unit
CO	Carbon Monoxide		ESB	Electricity Supply Board
CO_2	Carbon Dioxide		ESF	European Social Fund
COP	Conference of the Parties		ESRI	Economic and Social Research Institute
CSF	Community Support Framework		EU	European Union
CSO	Central Statistics Office		FCCC	Framework Convention on Climate Change
DAF	Department of Agriculture and Food		FIFG	Financial Instrument for Fisheries Guidance
DAFF	Department of Agriculture, Food and Forestry		FIPS	Forest Inventory and Planning System
DAFRD	Department of Agriculture, Food and Rural Development		FRC	Fisheries Research Centre
DAHGI	Department of Arts, Heritage, Gaeltacht and the Islands		GE	Genetic Engineering
			GIS	Geographic Information System
DART	Dublin Area Rapid Transit		GMM	Genetically Modified Micro-organism
DDT	Dichlorodiphenyltrichloroethane		GMO	Genetically Modified Organism
DELG	Department of the Environment and Local Government		GNP	Gross National Product
			GDP	Gross Domestic Product
DETE	Department of Enterprise, Trade and Employment		GWP	Global Warming Potential
			HCFC	Hydrochlorofluorocarbon
DMNR	Department of Marine and Natural Resources		HFC	Hydrofluorocarbon
DO	Dissolved Oxygen		IBEC	Irish Business and Employers Confederation
DoE	Department of Environment		ICES	International Council for the Exploration of the Seas
DPE	Department of Public Enterprise			
DTI	Dublin Transportation Initiative		ICSTI	Irish Council for Science, Technology and Innovation

ICT	Information and Communication Technologies		PFC	Perfluorocarbon
IDA	Industrial Development Authority		$PM_{2.5}$	Particulate Matter measuring less than 2.5 microns in diameter
IFFPG	Irish Farm Film Producers Group		PM_{10}	Particulate Matter measuring less than 10 microns in diameter
IMES	Irish Marine Emergency Service			
IMO	International Maritime Organisation		POP	Persistent Organic Pollutant
IPC	Integrated Pollution Control		ppb	parts per billion
IPCC	1) Intergovernmental Panel on Climate Change		R&D	Research and Development
	2) Irish Peatland Conservation Council		REPS	Rural Environment Protection Scheme
IPS	Informal Priority Setting		RPII	Radiological Protection Institute of Ireland
ISO	International Standards Organisation		RTDI	Research, Technological Development and Innovation
IUCC	Information Unit on Climate Change			
kW	kiloWatt		S&E	Southern and Eastern
LIFE	Community Financial Instrument for Environment		SAAO	Special Amenity Area Order
			SAC	Special Area of Conservation
LCP	Large Combustion Plant		SCI	Site of Community Importance
LPG	Liquid Petroleum Gas		SEA	Strategic Environmental Assessment
MARPOL	Marine Pollution Monitoring and Research Programme		SIL	International Society for Freshwater Research
mSv	milliSievert		SF_6	Sulphur Hexafluoride
MW	MegaWatt		SO_2	Sulphur Dioxide
N_2O	Nitrous Oxide		SPA	Special Protection Area
NAB	National Accreditation Board		TAC	Total Allowable Catch
NAPS	National Anti-Poverty Strategy		TAM	Tourism Angling Measure
NESC	National Economic and Social Council		TBT	Tributyltin
NGO	Non-governmental organisation		TDS	Tonnes Dried Solids
NH_3	Ammonia		TOE	Tonnes of Oil Equivalent
NH_4	Ammonium		TPER	Total Primary Energy Requirement
NHA	Natural Heritage Area		UN	United Nations
NO	Nitric Oxide		UNECE	United Nations Economic Commission for Europe
NO_2	Nitrogen Dioxide			
NO_3	Nitrate		UNEP	United Nations Environment Programme
NO_X	Nitrogen Oxides		UNESCO	United Nations Educational, Scientific and Cultural Organisation
O_3	Ozone			
OECD	Organisation for Economic Co-operation and Development		UV	Ultraviolet
			VOC	Volatile Organic Compound
OP	Operational Programme		VRT	Vehicle Registration Tax
OPW	Office of Public Works		WTO	World Trade Organisation
OSPAR	Oslo and Paris Convention		WWF	Worldwide Fund for Nature
p.e.	population equivalent			
PAH	Polyaromatic Hydrocarbon			
PCB	Polychlorinated Biphenyl			
PER	Pollution Emissions Register			

Acidification
Continuing loss of capacity to neutralise acid inputs indicated by declining alkalinity and increasing hydrogen ion concentration (i.e., the decrease in pH of water or soil resulting from increases in acidic anion inputs such as sulphate).

Acid Sensitive
Surface water and soils that, due chiefly to their low calcium concentration, have little or no resistance to acid inputs.

Algae
Simple aquatic plants that may be attached or free floating (planktonic) and occur as single cells, colonies, branched and unbranched filaments.

Algal Bloom
Dense growth of planktonic algae or most commonly Cyanobacteria (blue-green bacteria formerly classified as algae) in nutrient enriched lakes causing discoloration of the water.

Algal Cysts
Thick walled resting algal cells.

Ammonia (NH_3)
A simple form of nitrogen primarily originating in waste discharges. It can be toxic to fish under certain circumstances and is a source of nitrogen for plants and algae.

Anthropogenic
Produced as a result of human activities.

AOT_{40}
The sum of the differences between hourly ozone concentration and 40 ppb for each hour when the concentration exceeds 40 ppb during a relevant growing season, e.g., for forests or crops.

Aquaculture
The breeding and rearing of freshwater or marine fish in captivity.

Aquifer
A rock unit that will yield water in a usable quantity to a well or spring. A geological formation through which water can percolate, sometimes very slowly for long distances.

Becquerel (Bq)
A standard unit of radioactivity of a substance that is decaying spontaneously at the rate of one radioactive disintegration per second.

Beneficial Use
A use of the environment, or some part of it, (e.g., for recreation, agriculture and water storage) that benefits a human population and should be protected.

Biochemical Oxygen Demand (BOD)
A simple measure of the oxygen consuming capacity of a water sample resulting from the biochemical oxidation of organic matter in the water. BOD is normally measured by incubating a standard volume of water or waste water for five days at 20°C in the absence of sunlight and measuring the amount of oxygen consumed.

Biodegradation
The breakdown of substances by micro-organisms.

Biodiversity (Biological Diversity)
A word that describes all aspects of biological diversity but especially species richness, the complexity of ecosystems, and genetic variation.

Biogenetic Reserves
Network of protected areas with certain characteristic criteria, to guarantee the biological balance and to make the ecosystems available for biological research.

Biomass
The weight of biological matter. Standing crop is the amount of biomass (e.g., algae) in a waterbody.

Biosphere
That part of the land, sea, and atmosphere in which organisms live.

Biosphere Reserves
An area of land or coast that has been designated by IUCN and UNESCO as being of international importance for conservation and study.

Biota
The flora and fauna of an area.

Biotechnology (Bioengineering)
The employment of biochemical processes on an industrial scale, most notably recombinant DNA techniques, to reproduce drugs or (by means of fermentation) bulk foodstuffs for humans or livestock, sometimes by the recycling of wastes.

Biotope
A habitat which is uniform in its main climatic, soil and biotic (living or biological in origin) conditions.

Bivalve
Species consisting of two valves or shells, e.g., cockles and mussels.

Black Smoke
The fraction of total suspended particulates in air determined from the blackness measurement of the stain produced by passing the air through standard filter paper.

Blanket Bog
An area, often very extensive, of acid peatland, found in constantly wet climates, characteristic of broad flat upland areas, which develops where drainage is impeded and the soil is acid.

Brackish Water
Water which contains 0.5 - 30 parts per thousand of salinity.

Bryophyte
A non-woody plant of small size that reproduces by spores, e.g., mosses and liverworts.

Carbon Dioxide (CO$_2$)
A colourless, odourless, incombustible gas present in the atmosphere.

Catchment Area
The area from which a major river system or lake derives its water (i.e., the area drained by a river system).

CFCs (Chlorofluorocarbons)
A range of compounds of chlorine, fluorine and carbon implicated mainly in the destruction of stratospheric ozone but also in enhancing the greenhouse effect.

Chlorophyll
The green pigment found in algae and higher plants which is involved in photosynthesis.

Cutaway Bog
The peatland area left after peat extraction.

DDT (Dichlorodiphenyltrichloroethane)
A persistent organochlorine insecticide which was introduced in the 1940s.

Decibel (dB)
The unit of measurement of sound intensity.

Demersal
Describes organisms that inhabit the region of the bed of the sea.

Denitrification
The breakdown of nitrates by bacteria resulting in the release of free nitrogen.

Deoxygenation
The reduction of dissolved oxygen in water.

Desmids
Microscopic single-celled green algae, which occur in a wide variety of freshwater habitats typically in neutral or acid waters.

Dioxins
A collective name given to a group of 75 closely related chemical compounds known as polychlorinated dibenzodioxins (PCDDs). Dioxins can form during combustion of organic materials containing chlorine and as undesirable by-products during chemical manufacture and bleaching operations.

Dissolved Oxygen (DO)
A measure of the concentration of oxygen in a liquid, such as water or waste water, usually expressed in mg/l or per cent saturation.

DPSIR Framework
A conceptual system for the organisation of environmental information, including indicators, into Driving Forces, Pressures, State, Impact and Responses, for the purposes of integrated assessment.

Drumlin
A low hill of glacial boulder clay, considered to have been fashioned beneath an ice-sheet.

Ecology
The study of the relationships among organisms and between those organisms and their non-living environment.

Ecosystem
A community of interdependent organisms together with the environment they inhabit and with which they interact, and which is distinct from adjacent communities and environments.

Effluent
Liquid wastes.

Emission Limit Values (ELVs)
Legally enforceable limits on the physical, chemical or biological characteristics of a point source of emission to water or air, normally expressed as a maximum permissible concentration of a specified substance.

Endocrine Disrupters
Chemicals that disturb the endocrine system and the organs that respond to hormonal signals.

Environmental Medium
Major compartment of the environment, e.g., air, water and soil.

Environmental Quality Objectives (EQOs)
Descriptions of the intended use of an environmental medium; the use to which the medium is to be put defines the quality required to be maintained.

Environmental Quality Standards (EQSs)
The concentrations of specific parameters in an environmental medium required to achieve or sustain a particular EQO.

Esker
A long, sinuous ridge of sand and gravel, formed by a sub-glacial stream but which, after the melting of the ice-sheet, was left unrelated to the surrounding topography.

Eutrophic
Greek for well nourished. Applied to waterbodies with high nutrient concentrations leading to large algal standing crops.

Eutrophication
The changes associated with enrichment of a waterbody with inorganic plant nutrients particularly nitrogen and phosphorus.

Evapotranspiration
The loss of water from the earth's surface as a result of the combined effects of evaporation directly and transpiration, which is the loss of water from the pores in the leaves of plants.

Exotic Organism
A species found in a region to which it is not native.

Fauna
Animals

Fen
An area of waterlogged peat which, unlike bog, is alkaline or only slightly acid.

Fertiliser
Any substance that is applied to land as a source of nutrients for plant growth.

Flora
Plants

Furans
Derivatives of furan, a heterocyclic compound of chemical formula C_4H_4O comprising a ring of four carbon and one oxygen atom, with a hydrogen atom attached to each carbon atom.

Geographical Information System (GIS)
A set of integrated techniques for storing, retrieving, transforming and displaying spatially referenced thematic data in map form.

Geomorphology
The study of the form and development of the Earth, and especially of its surface and physical features, and of the relationship between these features and the geological structures beneath.

Genetically Modified Organisms (GMOs)
Bacteria, viruses, fungi, plant and animal cells, plants and animals capable of replication or of transferring genetic material in which the genetic material has been altered in a way that does not occur naturally by mating and/or by natural recombination.

Green Accounting
Accounting methods which take into consideration positive or negative impacts on the environment and natural resources.

Greenhouse Effect
Warming of the atmosphere due to the reduction in outgoing solar radiation; resulting from concentrations of gases such as CO_2.

Groundwater
Water that occupies pores and crevices in rock and soil, below the surface and above a layer of impermeable material (see aquifer).

Growth Limiting Nutrient
Essential element of a food chain, supplies of which are readily exhausted, thus a factor which controls the growth of organisms.

Habitat
The dwelling place of a species or community, providing a particular set of environmental conditions (e.g., forest floor, sea shore).

HCH (Hexachlorocyclohexane)
An organochlorine insecticide used to control insect soil pests, aphids, mites.

Heathland
Any tract of land which is typically the habitat of many of the ericaceous (woody) shrubs.

Heavy Metal
A metal with a high relative density.

Herbicide
A chemical which is used to kill weeds.

HCFCs (Hydrochlorofluorocarbons)
Compounds which have been substituted for CFCs as the latter become phased out by international agreement.

HFCs (Hydrofluorocarbons)
See HCFCs

Integrated Pollution Control (IPC)
A system of licensing which covers all emissions to air, water and land, including noise and is intended to minimise the impact on the environment by taking account of pollution that may be transferred from one environmental medium to another.

Invertebrates
Animals which do not possess a backbone.

Leaching
The removal of the soluble constituents of a rock, soil or ore (that which is leached being known as the leachate) by the action of percolating waters.

Lichen
A 'plant' without stem or leaves, usually greyish in colour, growing, for example, on rocks or tree bark, and formed by an association between a fungus and algae.

Littoral
The area between the low and high spring tide levels (marine) or the shoreline (lakes).

Machair
Herb-rich calcareous (i.e., containing calcium carbonate) grassland which grows on shell sand.

Maërl
Calcareous red algae.

Macrophytes
Rooted and floating aquatic plants.

Methane (CH$_4$)
The simplest hydrocarbon and an important greenhouse gas. It is a product of anaerobic decomposition.

Mollusc
A member of the Mollusca, a large division of the animal kingdom, including snails, oysters and octopuses.

Natura 2000
A coherent European ecological network of sites comprising SACs designated under the habitats Directive and SPAs designated under the birds Directive.

Natural Pollutant
A substance of natural origin that may be regarded as a pollutant when present in excess (e.g. volcanic dust, particles of sea salt, products of forest fires).

Nitrate (NO$_3$)
A salt of nitric acid (HNO$_3$).

Nitrogen Fixation
Any reaction as a result of which gaseous nitrogen forms a soluble compound that is available as a plant nutrient either directly or after it has engaged in further reactions.

Nitrogen Oxides (NO$_x$)
Usually includes the two pollutants nitric oxide (NO) and nitrogen dioxide (NO$_2$), produced by high temperature combustion and some natural processes. NO$_2$ is the most important form, which can contribute to adverse health effects, ozone formation and acid deposition.

Nutrient
Element or chemical essential for growth, e.g., phosphorus, nitrogen, silica, oxygen and carbon.

Organochlorine (Chlorinated Hydrocarbon)
An organic compound containing chlorine. Many organochlorines have biocidal properties and are used as the active ingredients for pesticides with a high persistence, which they derive from their chemical stability and low solubility in water.

Oxidation-Reduction
Chemical reaction involving the transfer of electrons from one chemical species to another. The species from which the electrons are lost is said to be 'oxidised' and the species to which the electrons are transferred is said to be 'reduced'. Compounds which undergo reduction readily, such as molecular oxygen, are called oxidising agents or oxidants.

Ozone (O$_3$)
A secondary pollutant in which the molecule of oxygen consists of three atoms rather than two.

Ozone Layer
A layer of the atmosphere, over 20 km above the Earth's surface, in which the concentration of ozone is higher than it is elsewhere in the atmosphere owing to its accumulation through vertical air movements from a higher altitude, where it forms by the dissociation and reformation of oxygen molecules exposed to high frequency ultraviolet radiation.

PCBs (Polychlorinated Biphenyls)
A group of closely-related organochlorines the principal use of which has been as liquid insulators in high-voltage transformers.

Pelagic
Describes organisms which inhabit the open water of a sea or lake in contrast to the sea or lake bed.

Pesticide
A general term for any chemical agent which is used in order to kill unwanted plants ('weeds'), animal pests, or disease causing fungi.

pH
The measure of the acidity or alkalinity of a substance.

Phosphate (PO$_4$)
The commonly occurring form of phosphorus taken up by plants in the aquatic environment and essential for their growth.

Photochemical Smog
A characteristic, mainly of urban atmospheres, associated with the build up of primary pollutants and photochemical oxidants usually under slow moving, warm, high pressure systems.

Phycotoxin
A compound, toxic to humans and animals, produced by some phytoplankton groups, particularly dinoflagellates, and by cyanobacteria.

Phytoplankton
Microscopically small plants which float or swim weakly in fresh or salt water bodies.

Plankton
Organisms suspended in water by currents, the presence of air sacks or by their own swimming movements. Phytoplankton refers to microscopic plants, and zooplankton refers to microscopic animals.

PM$_{10}$
Particulate matter measuring less than 10 microns in diameter.

Pollution
The direct or indirect alteration of the physical, chemical, thermal, biological, or radioactive properties of any part of the environment in such a way as to create a hazard or potential hazard to the health, safety, or welfare of living species.

PVC (Polyvinylchloride)
One of the most common plastics, used in the manufacture of clothing, furniture, and containers.

Population Equivalent

The organic biodegradable waste load having a five day biochemical oxygen demand (BOD_5) of 60 grams of oxygen per day is defined as one population equivalent (i.e., the amount produced by one person) in the urban waste water treatment Directive.

Precipitation

The manner by which water and other matter in the atmosphere reach the earth's surface. Wet precipitation includes rainfall, snow, hail, mist and fog. Dry precipitation describes the deposition of gases, aerosols and particles not dissolved in atmospheric borne water.

Primary Pollutant

A pollutant which is emitted directly into air or water.

Radon

An element occurring naturally as a colourless, odourless, noble gas, chemically almost inert, which is the immediate breakdown product of radium-226.

Raised Bog

An area of ombrogenous (i.e., originating as a result of wet climates) acid peatland with a convex profile.

Renewable Resource

A resource that can be exploited without depletion because it is constantly replenished, e.g., solar radiation and wind.

Salmonid Waters

High quality waters suitable for the maintenance of viable self-sustaining populations of wild salmon and trout.

Secondary Pollutant

A pollutant created through interactions between primary pollutants and various other components.

Sewage

Liquid wastes from communities, conveyed in sewers. Sewage may be a mixture of domestic sewage effluents from residential areas and industrial liquid waste.

Sewage Sludge

Semi-solid and solid waste matter removed from sewage at sewage treatment plants.

Sewerage

A network of pipes and associated equipment for the collection and transportation of sewage.

Silage

A farm livestock feed made from mown grass or other suitable herbage, which is compressed and partly fermented anaerobically.

Sludge

The suspended matter removed from industrial effluent or sewage.

Slurry

The animal waste generated in animal housing units that have slatted floors and in which there is no use made of bedding material.

Sulphate (SO₄)

A constituent of rain and acid aerosols produced by oxidation of SO_2, in the atmosphere.

Sulphur Dioxide (SO₂)

A colourless gas produced mainly by oxidising the sulphur in fossil fuels through combustion.

Sustainable Development

Defined by the Bruntland Commission (1987) as 'development that meets the needs of the present without compromising the ability of the future generations to meet their own needs'.

Tailings

Those portions of washed ore that are considered too poor to be treated further.

Trace Element

An element which is necessary in extremely small amounts for the proper functioning of metabolism in plants or animals.

Trophic State

The extent of enrichment of a waterbody as assessed by the nutrient concentrations, amount of planktonic algae and macrophytes, water transparency and oxygen levels. The trophic categories oligotrophic, mesotrophic, eutrophic and hypertrophic are used to describe waters varying from un-enriched to highly enriched.

Turlough

A temporary shallow lake in limestone country which fills and empties through cracks, in response to the local water table.

Volatile Organic Compounds (VOC)

Organic compounds which evaporate readily and contribute to air pollution mainly through the production of secondary pollutants such as ozone.

Waste Arisings

A measure of the amount of waste generated by a specified sector or activity.

Wetland

An area covered permanently, occasionally, or periodically by fresh or salt water (e.g., flooded pasture land, marshland, inland lakes, rivers and their estuaries); also includes bogs.

Wildfowl Sanctuaries

Areas of importance for bird life where the shooting of traditional game bird species is prohibited under the Wildlife Act 1976.

98-percentile Value

The value of a ranked distribution above (or below) which 98 per cent of values in the distribution lie, depending on application.

Reader Comment Form

Note: comments to be forwarded to: *Ireland's Environment - A Millennium Report,* Environmental Monitoring and Laboratory Services, Environmental Protection Agency, PO Box 3000, Johnstown Castle Estate, Co. Wexford, or by email to irenv2000@epa.ie

Document title: Ireland's Environment - A Millennium Report

NAME_____

ADDRESS_____

ORGANISATION_____

DATE_____ TELEPHONE_____FAX_____EMAIL_____

COMMENTS

Q-indices — ab European Env.
Up to data legislation